BARRON'S

LSAT®

LOGIC GAMES

Carolyn Nelson, Esq.
Founder of Nelson Test Prep

BARRON'S

®LSAT is a registered trademark of Law School Admissions Council, Inc., which does not endorse this product.

Dedications

To my students, your courage to *not* defer your dream inspires me to be a better teacher.

To my husband Patrick, thank you for your love and support and most especially for the airport. . . .

To my sons Morgan and Julian, I could have done this without your constant nagging and complaining but not without the love, humor and the light that you both are in my life.

To Matthew, your suggestions were great, but your friendship even greater.

To Mom, there simply are no words. I love you.

All inquiries should be addressed to:
Barron's Educational Series, Inc.
250 Wireless Boulevard
Hauppauge, New York 11788
www.barronseduc.com

ISBN: 978-1-4380-0205-7

Library of Congress Control Number: 2014931308

PRINTED IN THE UNITED STATES OF AMERICA
9 8 7 6 5 4 3 2 1

10%
POST-CONSUMER WASTE
Paper contains a minimum of 10% post-consumer waste (PCW). Paper used in this book was derived from certified, sustainable forestlands.

CONTENTS

Preface

Welcome to Barron's *LSAT Logic Games.* This study guide is designed to prepare you for the LSAT's Analytical Reasoning Section, commonly known as the Logic Games Section. Whether you are self-studying or enrolled in a course, this guide will ensure that you're ready for the challenge.

Twenty years of teaching LSAT prep courses has convinced me that an approach based on simplicity has universal practicality; it's suited to struggling students and to those competitive students who are aiming to maximize their scores. That's why all the solutions in this book are structured as simply as possible. No matter where your score falls in the range of LSAT scores, you will find my step-by-step dissections of each problem very helpful.

If you're new to logic games, you may find them daunting. Don't despair. The simple techniques outlined here have helped countless LSAT takers realize that they can successfully solve logic games and achieve dramatic improvements in their scores. You might notice that throughout *LSAT Logic Games,* I repeat a particular mantra—a very important one that I've used with students throughout my decades of teaching:

> You take the LSAT; the LSAT doesn't take you!

Keeping this in mind as you prepare for the exam will remind you that *you* are in total control of how you approach the test. When the time comes to take the actual LSAT, it is *you* who will determine your best strategy for tackling the questions. This guide will teach you to stay in control when the pressure is on.

About the Guide

Beginning with Chapter 2, you will learn strategies for tackling the five basic types of LSAT games. You will learn how to balance accuracy with speed and how to set up a study schedule. Chapter 3 provides an overview of the games sections and question types and breaks down a game into its different components. In Chapter 4, you will learn how to approach a game, and in Chapter 5 you will learn about conditional statements.

Chapters 6 through 9 each tackle a particular type of logic game. You will learn how to identify each type and the task you are being asked to complete. Practice drills are included to help strengthen each individual step. You will be provided with the means to diagnose the specific areas you may be struggling with and the steps to take to counter your struggles. Once you have determined the areas that are causing you difficulty, repeat the drills as often as necessary to increase your understanding of the games.

This book contains fifty logic games, each inspired by an actual LSAT game. Work through all the games. Repetition and practice will reinforce the concepts you need to master to enable you to reach your best possible score.

LSAT Strategy

OVERVIEW

Since the introduction of the current LSAT format in 1991, the LSAT has included five multiple-choice sections (four scored and one unscored), as well as one unscored writing section. The multiple-choice sections are thirty-five minutes each and are broken down as follows:

- one reading comprehension section,
- two logical reasoning sections,
- one analytical reasoning section,
- one unscored experimental section.

It's important to remember that each correct answer on the LSAT is worth one point, regardless of the difficulty level of the question. Unlike the SAT, penalties are not given for wrong answers, so you should answer every question. When it's necessary to guess on an answer, pick a letter between A and E and spend thirty seconds or so filling in all unanswered questions on your answer sheet.

Here's a sobering fact to consider. Fewer than two percent of LSAT takers ever achieve a score above 170. If you've had a chance to practice this test under timed conditions, you can probably guess why. There's simply not enough time! That said, this information shouldn't discourage you. It's extremely important to remember that law schools are full of people who scored less than 170 on the LSAT. Your journey to entering law school begins with a well-defined strategy—one that will enable you to achieve your best LSAT score, and one that you can develop right here with the help of this guide.

BEST SCORE AND EMOTIONAL MATURITY

A winning LSAT strategy requires emotional maturity, and that means accepting what your own best score is going to be.

LSAT scores generally range from 120 to 180, with a median score of about 151. So, what qualifies as a "good" score? A good score is simply *your best score*. Think about that for a moment. You can't obtain a score that is better than your own best potential score. True, law school admissions are highly competitive and the LSAT often counts for half of the admission decision, so you will want to present an impressive LSAT result. However, if you automatically presume that your score must be over 170, you're likely to attempt every single question. This could be a costly mistake because, most likely, you will end up wasting a great deal of your precious time. It's not your best strategy to tackle the test this way.

Many prospective law students have Type A personalities. If this describes you, it's likely that when presented with really difficult problems, you tend to tackle them head on.

However, where the LSAT is concerned, focusing too much on particularly difficult questions is often counterproductive to achieving your best score. You might successfully answer the tough question, but at what cost? Remember how precious your time is.

> Time is your currency on the LSAT. Do not spend it unless you can get something valuable in return: the correct answer!

On the test you will likely find some games more challenging than others. Your objective is to correctly answer as many questions as possible in thirty-five minutes. Think strategically and remember that you can work on the games in any order. Be sure to do the least challenging games first. When you arrive at a difficult question that is giving you trouble, skip it and quickly move on.

This is where emotional maturity becomes important. During the test, keep your ego in check and keep the three following tips in mind.

1. **YOU ARE NOT YOUR LSAT SCORE.** As explained earlier, the LSAT score is determined solely by the number of correct responses, which doesn't necessarily correlate to the number of questions answered. Based on this information, you should realize that you do not need to attempt each and every question on the LSAT. (That is, unless you fall into the less than two percent of all LSAT takers who are realistically targeting a score of 170 or more.) If you're like most LSAT test takers, you need to become comfortable with this fact and realize that the number of questions you attempt is not a reflection of your intelligence. Moreover, you must accept that your score in no way correlates to your ability to become a successful law student and ultimately a successful lawyer. Accepting this idea takes emotional maturity.

2. **KNOW THYSELF** You are given just thirty-five minutes in each section to answer twenty-three to twenty-eight questions. Some are moderately difficult, others extraordinarily difficult. You probably feel that given enough time you could ace them all… and you're not alone. What you need to understand is that the LSAT is not designed in such a way that the average test taker will be able to answer all the questions accurately within the given time frame. In fact, it's *deliberately* made up of questions that most test takers will be unable to complete with a high degree of accuracy in thirty-five minutes! This is why you must have a well-crafted LSAT strategy. For example, you should determine in advance how many questions in each section you are likely to answer correctly.

   Don't forget that every question on the LSAT, whether easy or difficult, has the same value: one point. This means your "best score strategy" should be to answer as many questions as possible correctly in the allotted time. Test takers generally want to answer as many questions correctly as possible, and many believe that answering *all the questions* increases their likelihood of a high score. Wrong! Maximizing the number of correct answers requires a clear and objective understanding of your own strengths and weaknesses. This self-awareness will help you determine how many questions, and which questions, you should spend your time on.

3. **SLOWER AND STEADY WINS THE RACE** LSAT questions are among the most difficult questions in all of standardized testing. If you don't take the time to completely understand the question and each answer choice, it is highly probable that you will choose a

wrong answer. If you spend one and a half minutes on a question and choose the wrong answer, you have wasted the entire one and a half minutes. A better strategy that will contribute to your best score is spending more time on the question to ensure the correct response. Perhaps you'd be better off spending two minutes on it instead of just one and a half. Remember, time is currency. Don't spend valuable time unless you are going to get something valuable in return.

ACCURACY VERSUS SPEED

Striking a perfect balance between accuracy and speed is difficult. Completing four games in thirty-five minutes translates into roughly eight and a half minutes per game. Most LSAT takers will struggle with this time constraint. Speed is a wonderful thing, but when it comes at the expense of accuracy, the price is much too high.

Completing all four games with less than fifty percent accuracy is diametrically opposed to your goal of achieving your best score. If you had sacrificed just one of the four games, it's likely that your accuracy would have improved substantially, resulting in more correct answers overall. Here is a useful rule of thumb when deciding how many questions you should personally aim for. The number of questions you attempt under timed conditions on any section of the LSAT should be just four more than the amount answered correctly on your last timed section. For example, if you completed four games and answered twelve questions correctly, you should attempt sixteen questions (12 + 4) on your next timed section. Suppose you attempt these sixteen questions and get fourteen correct; this would allow you to attempt eighteen questions (14 + 4) on your next timed section. Finally, let's imagine that you attempt eighteen questions and your number of correct responses is only twelve. At this point, you would know that you're close to the point of diminishing returns.

STUDY SCHEDULE

Success in solving logic games requires practice. Practice requires commitment and tenacity, and the best way to remain committed and tenacious is to establish a *realistic* study schedule. Do not create a schedule that you can't possibly keep. For example, don't plan on studying ten hours a day in addition to going to work and/or school full time. This would be impossible for anyone. A realistic study schedule is one that can be maintained over an extended period of time.

A good schedule is made up of daily study sessions at least six days a week. Although the number of study hours is important, frequency is equally crucial. The surest way to derail a study schedule is by setting up unrealistic expectations about how many hours you can devote to it. Be realistic about what you can accomplish.

If you don't have other demands on your time and can study four or five hours per day, that's great. However, if you're like most people and have other daily commitments, you will have to give your plan more thought. You may have to get creative. For example, rather than planning on studying for a three-hour session every evening, find ways to break up the task over the course of your day. Maybe plan on getting up thirty minutes earlier in the morning to study. Perhaps you can study on the bus or train while you commute to and from work or school. Could you study for thirty minutes during your lunch hour? Considering all the possible pockets of time in your day will help you come up with a personal study schedule that works for you.

LSAT Logic Games

2

If you read the preface, you are already familiar with my favorite mantra:

> **You take the LSAT; the LSAT doesn't take you!**

Memorize it and believe it. What does it mean exactly? It means that *you* should be in total control of the order and the manner in which you process the information on the LSAT. For example, with each game in the Analytical Reasoning Section, you must decide whether to tackle it immediately, later, or possibly not at all. Your only constraint is the time frame of thirty-five minutes.

LOGIC GAMES OVERVIEW

The LSAT's Logic Games Section is made up of four games and contains a total of twenty-two to twenty-four questions. Since the new 1991 version of the LSAT, the format and structure of the logic games has been quite consistent with the games generally falling into one of three very broad categories. (There are numerous subcategories within each of these broader ones; they are individually addressed in later chapters.) Basically, the three game types require you to either:

- put things into order one after another (sequencing),
- put things into groups (grouping),
- put things into order and into groups (sequencing/grouping combinations).

Besides the differing types of games, the degree of difficulty also varies from game to game. The level of difficulty depends on how challenging it is to make the necessary deductions. The harder to make a deduction, the higher the price of "LSAT currency"—time. You can expect the Logic Games Section to include:

- Two doable games. With the required amount of practice and good technique, "doable" games can be handled successfully by most test takers. Uncovering all, or even most, of the deductions will allow you to work through these games fairly quickly. The failure to uncover all, or even most of the deductions, usually will not prevent you from solving the game, but it might cost you precious time.
- One challenging game. "Challenging" means more difficult than doable. Here, the deductions will be more difficult to uncover, and the failure to uncover all or most of the deductions will often, but not always, derail the solution. It will, however, always cost you more time.

- One killer game. This, the hardest of all four games, requires you to make most, if not all, your deductions before you begin. Failure to do so will most definitely derail your solution and/or result in a catastrophic consumption of time.

Your first strategic move should be to preview each game and put them in order of difficulty. Even if your realistic strategy is to attempt all four games, you still want to rank the games into order of difficulty and move from least to most difficult. This will prevent you from spending too much time on the killer game at the expense of completing the doable games. It's important to note that the type of game does determine its level of difficulty. There are varying levels of difficulty within each and every type of game. So, if type isn't a factor, how can you identify the level of difficulty of each game?

Determining the Level of Difficulty

When determining the level of difficulty of a logic game, don't underestimate the value of good old-fashioned common sense. You will often have a very visceral response to the killer game. If you read through a game and think "huh?" and then reread it and still feel lost, trust your instincts! They might be more telling than a formal analysis.

That said, a more methodical approach to ascertaining the level of difficulty of a game does exist. It involves reading the scenario and then asking yourself these four questions:

1. **DOES A DIAGRAM COME TO MIND?** Hopefully the answer is yes. The more familiar you are with the type of diagram required, the better. Answering yes to this question usually means that you fundamentally understand what you are being asked to do. A good start! Answering no to this question means you will likely have trouble figuring out how to begin, since the first step to a solution is normally drawing a diagram.

2. **HOW SPECIFIC ARE THE CLUES?** Very specific clues will narrow down your possible arrangements more than less specific clues will. The more specific the clues, the easier the deductions. Consider this example: "There are exactly two cars after the red car and before the blue car." In this clue, there is only one possible slot for the red car once you have placed the blue car and vice versa. The red car will always be three spaces to the left of the blue car. Contrast that clue with this one: "There are at least two cars between the red car and the blue car." With this clue, the possible arrangements have increased. It is now possible for the blue car to appear before the red car. Likewise, it is now possible for there to be more than two spaces separating the red and the blue car. More possibilities usually require more currency—that is, more time spent on solving the game.

3. **HOW WELL DO I UNDERSTAND THE CLUES?** The ability to effectively and efficiently solve a logic game necessitates that you understand each and every clue. Often games contain one clue that is difficult to understand and easy to misinterpret. Consider this example: "At least as many red cars as blue cars are selected." This clue might cause you to pause as you sort out whether the solution requires equal or greater red cars as blue cars versus equal or greater blue cars as red cars. The former is the correct interpretation.

4. **WHAT IS THE RATIO OF RESTRICTED TO UNRESTRICTED QUESTIONS?** Note that with these logic games, you are always moving from less difficult questions to more difficult questions. Likewise, note that restricted questions are easier than unrestricted questions. Therefore, the doable games will usually include more restricted questions and fewer unrestricted questions.

Anatomy of an LSAT Logic Game

Each LSAT logic game is comprised of a setup that houses three important pieces of information:

1. the backdrop,
2. the components,
3. the clues/rules.

Five to seven questions then immediately follow the setup.

THE BACKDROP

To help understand the role of each piece of information, try to think of each game as if it were a play. The backdrop is like the stage. It reveals time, manner, and place. It allows you to visualize and draw your diagram. It also provides enough information for you to answer the question, "What are they asking me to do?" For example, are you being asked to put things in sequential order? Are you being asked to divide things into groups? Or are you required to place things into groups and then order those things within the group? The backdrop can sometimes also hide clues.

THE COMPONENTS

The components can be compared to the actors in a play. When thinking through the components, ask yourself questions that you might ask about real actors. How many are there? What are their roles in the ensemble cast? Do the actors' roles require them to work in groups or independently?

THE CLUES/RULES

Your clues/rules function much as the director of a play would. The clues tell the components how they are to interact with the backdrop, and they inform them how to interact with one another.

READING FOR UNDERSTANDING

The importance of reading the setup carefully cannot be stressed enough. Never ever put your pencil to paper before reading through the *entire* setup. It's common for students to read the first sentence of the setup, immediately begin to draw the diagram, and ultimately end up going down the wrong path. Here's a scenario that illustrates what can happen: a setup begins, "There are six stores numbered 1 through 6." Immediately the student begins to draw a sequential diagram with "1" through "6" marked on top; this is all done before finding out what is to be done with the stores. The numbers 1 through 6 have a natural order, so it's likely that they are supposed to be placed in sequence; however, it's also possible that despite the natural order of the store numbers, they are actually supposed to be divided into two groups: those that close at 6 P.M. and those that close at 7 P.M. Read all the information very carefully before beginning!

QUESTION TYPES

Every question that follows the setup must adhere to each and every clue, except for those questions that ask you to ignore a clue and/or substitute one clue for another. Logic game questions can be divided into four major categories:

- catch-a-clue questions,
- restricted questions,
- unrestricted questions,
- modifiers.

Remember that your best score strategy involves doing the least difficult questions before attempting the more difficult ones. With that in mind, study the graphic below.

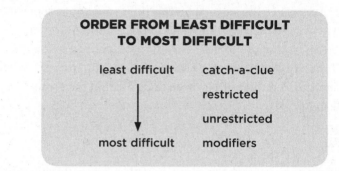

**ORDER FROM LEAST DIFFICULT
TO MOST DIFFICULT**

least difficult   catch-a-clue

restricted

unrestricted

most difficult   modifiers

CATCH-A-CLUE QUESTIONS

Catch-a-clue questions, also referred to by the Law School Admission Council (LSAC) as "orientation questions," almost always begin with the word *which*. All catch-a-clue questions will ask you for a possible arrangement of the components. In a sequence game, a catch-a-clue question will ask you for a possible order of your components. In a grouping game, a catch-a-clue question will ask you for a possible grouping of your components. With this type of question, you should "catch" or identify the first clue/rule, then review the possible answers to find one that violates the clue/rule, and then cross it out. Catch the next clue and repeat until you are left with only one answer.

Approximately eighty percent of logic games on past LSATs have had at least one catch-a-clue question. Because these questions do not require diagrams or deductions, you should do them first. Completing these questions first will also give you the opportunity to verify that you understand each of the clues/rules.

Sometimes a clue will not have an answer choice that violates it. Don't panic. This is typical of games involving more than four clues. Other times, two answer choices might violate the clue. This too is normal and often occurs if the game has fewer than four clues. One single clue, however, can never be violated by four answer choices. If you think a clue is violated by four possible answers, you have definitely misunderstood the clue. By uncovering this misinterpretation early, you will be able to avoid problems later.

RESTRICTED QUESTIONS

Restricted questions should be completed immediately after the catch-a-clue questions. Usually beginning with the word *if*, restricted questions add on a supplementary clue that further limits your possibilities. This additional restriction makes these questions next in line in terms of difficulty. Also, it is important to note that this additional restriction applies just to that question and does not carry forward or backwards to other questions.

UNRESTRICTED QUESTIONS

Unrestricted questions most often begin with the word *which*. They are global in nature, which means that they mainly ask for solutions that can be deduced just from the original clues. If you are able to readily come up with the deductions, that's great. However, if you are experiencing difficulty, attempting these questions at the outset will waste your time. By completing the catch-a-clue and restricted questions first, you will build a history of possible arrangements of your components. This information can often assist in eliminating answers to the unrestricted (deduction-seeking) questions. For this reason, these questions are positioned third in the question order.

MODIFIERS

These questions ask you to ignore an original clue and/or substitute a new clue in its place. Modifiers should always be done last. In your diagram and deduction plans, you will not want to change an element for the modifier question and then have to revert to the original version to answer something else. This can be confusing for you, and it wastes valuable time.

"COULD BE TRUE" VERSUS "MUST BE TRUE"

The questions in the Logic Games Section test your ability to determine, based on limited given information, what *must be* true or false versus what *could be* true or false. The difference between these definitions is generally quite clear to us, but under test conditions it can become elusive. LSAT designers almost always include things that could be true among the answer choices to a "must be true" question; therefore, it's vital that you develop a method to remain fully aware of which one of these types of questions you are being asked to answer.

To mentally reinforce which question type is being asked, try adding a few clarifying words to the question. For example, with a "must be" question, say to yourself "____ must be true/false *always*." For each "could be" question, say to yourself, "____could be true/false *just once*."

"EXCEPT" QUESTIONS

"EXCEPT" questions do ask you to identify answers that are true; however, instead of requiring you to select these answers directly, they demand that you select the one response that is untrue. This is in opposition to your habitual reflex, which is to select a *correct* answer. This direct assault on a student's normal thought process can often lead to errors. Many test takers simply forget that the question they are answering is an "EXCEPT" question, and instinctively select a true response.

Contrary to popular opinion, highlighting, underlining, or circling the word *except* in the question usually does little to aid the memory. This key word is always capitalized on the LSAT, so further emphasis is unwarranted. A much more effective retention tool is simply taking three seconds to rewrite the question so that you can follow your usual thought process. For example, "each of the following could be true EXCEPT" involves eliminating the four answer choices that could be true, leaving the one answer that cannot be true. So, rewrite the question in the margin as "which one of the following cannot be true" or "which one of the following must be false."

The Five-Step Approach

3

Your ability to effectively and efficiently decipher LSAT logic games requires that you organize your thoughts. The given information should be made readily accessible so that you can make quick deductions and ultimately answer the questions successfully. This five-step approach will help you develop key organizational skills.

STEP 1 Visualize and Draw a Diagram

The LSAT directions state that in solving the games "it may be useful to draw a rough diagram." This represents a tremendous understatement about the value of drawing a diagram! Many test takers become overwhelmed because they read the setup and then immediately attempt to answer the questions. Furthermore, they worry that they don't have enough time to answer all the questions in the allotted thirty-five minutes. Creating a diagram helps on both these counts—it facilitates the organization of information and actually enables faster response times.

Don't overthink your diagram. Just ask yourself, "What are they asking me to do? Are they asking me to put things in order? Or are they asking me to divide things into groups? Or are they asking me to do both—that is to determine which things are in each group and then put those things into some sort of order?"

STEP 2 Identify Components and Ascertain Ratio/Distribution

Once you've drawn your diagram, you're on your way to successfully solving the game. Next, think about the components. How many do you have and how often will they be placed into your diagram? The number of times your components need to be placed into your diagram should be equal to the number of slots in your diagram. Are there more slots than components, more components than slots, or is it balanced? How about the distribution of slots? Are there an appropriate number of slots under each diagram heading?

STEP 3 Symbolize the Clues

Your effectiveness and efficiency with logic games depends largely upon how well you symbolize your clues or rules. There are four guiding principles at work when you symbolize your clues:

C	Consistent
L	Logical
U	Understandable
E	Easy to follow

CONSISTENT: The symbol you assign to a particular concept must be used for that concept each and every time. You must rely on, know, and trust your symbols. Consistency leads to reliability.

LOGICAL: The symbols that you choose to represent each concept should make sense. Select a symbol that has a rational relationship to the meaning of the clue.

UNDERSTANDABLE: When drawn, your symbol should be clear and unambiguous so that its meaning is instantly recognizable.

EASY TO FOLLOW: The symbols for your clues should rely on graphics that are obvious and familiar. The more familiar the symbol, the more straightforward the application of it to a question will be.

By following these four principles, you'll avoid having to reinterpret symbols as you apply them, and you'll increase your speed and accuracy as you navigate the questions.

A SAMPLING OF SYMBOLS				
Symbol	**Meaning**	**Used When**	**Sample Clue**	**Represenation**
...	before/after earlier/later	exact spatial relationship between two components is unknown	Jackson arrives at some time before Franklin.	J ... F
☐	immediately before/after (adjacent)	spatial relationships of components are known to be next to each other	Jackson arrives immediately before Franklin.	J F
⧄	not immediately before/after (not adjacent)	a specific spatial relationship is forbidden	Jackson is not immediately before Franklin.	J̸F
_ _	slot holder	the number of slots betweeen two components is known	Franklin arrives exactly three days after Jackson.	J _ _ F
⌒	interchangeable either/or	relative order of components are interchangeable	Jackson and Franklin arrive on consecutive days.	J ⌒ F
_ _ ...	at least	the minimum number of slots separating two components is known	There are at least two songs performed after Jackson but before Franklin.	J _ _ ... F
≠	is not	an occurrence is universally forbidden	Jackson is not fourth.	J ≠ 4
=	is	an occurrence is universally accepted	Jackson is fourth.	J = 4
~	if not	an occurrence is forbidden in a particular instance	If Jackson is selected, then Franklin is not selected.	J → ~F
→	then	you introduce the necessary component	If Jackson is selected, then Franklin is selected.	J → F
↔	if and only if/ vice versa	each component is necessary and sufficient, or two components are always together	Jackson and Franklin must be in the same group.	J ↔ F

STEP 4 Make Deductions

The entire LSAT tests your ability to analyze information and determine which things must be true, cannot be true, and may or may not be true. The games are no exception. When making your deductions, you should focus on what you know; do not obsess about the things you don't know. Every single piece of information that you can deduce, no matter how small it may seem, should be written down. The LSAT rewards the process of elimination, so when you make your deductions, focus on determining where components *cannot* be placed. Don't focus on all the slots in which the components *can* be placed, that is, unless the element has been restricted to just one or two slots.

Concentrate on deducing where and how your components/slots are restricted. If you're restricted to certain bits of information, then those bits are all you need to know. Write down your most restricted element(s) and/or your most restricted slot(s) and look for commonality among your symbols.

> If it is all you know, then it is all that you need to know.

STEP 5 Tackle the Questions

Like everywhere else on the LSAT, each question here is worth one point. The order in which you tackle your questions can have a dramatic effect on the number of questions you're ultimately able to answer correctly. Reorder your questions from least difficult to most difficult. Remember, you should answer the question types in this order: 1. catch-a-clue; 2. restricted; 3. unrestricted; 4. modifiers.

Conditional Statements

4

Conditional statements most often appear in grouping games, but they do randomly pop up in all types of LSAT logic games. They're often difficult to understand, especially when you see the terms: *if/then, necessity versus sufficiency,* and *contrapositive.* Let's try to demystify these tricky logic clues.

IF/THEN

Conditional statements are either clues that actually possess the *if/then* format, or they are clues that can be converted by certain trigger words into an *if/then* format. These statements require that you decipher what occurrence (*if*) will compel another occurrence (*then*). Take the following statement as an example: *If you are admitted to law school,* **then** *you must take the LSAT.* This conditional clue can be symbolized as follows:

> admitted to law school → take the LSAT

The arrow (→) illustrates the "then" portion of the statement. It's useful to use the arrow to symbolize the clue because it reminds us to read the statement from left to right.

Like most things on the LSAT, conditional statements challenge you to deduce what *could be true* versus what *must be true* based on the information provided.

NECESSITY VERSUS SUFFICIENCY

In any conditional statement, there are two pieces of information that *could be* true but certainly do not *have to be* true. The first piece of information that *could be* true, but is not necessarily true, occurs when you simply reverse the original if/then statement and read it in the opposite direction of the arrow. Let's take a look at the previous example. If you take the LSAT, does it follow that you will certainly be admitted to law school?

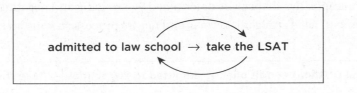

Now that the statement is reversed, it *could* be true, but it is not *necessarily* true. As you are well aware, simply taking the LSAT does not *necessarily* mean you will be admitted to law school.

Another piece of information that *could* be true, but is not *necessarily* true, reveals itself when the original statement is simply negated. Let's look at our example again. Is it certain that if you are *not* admitted to law school, you did not take the LSAT? Note that the *tilde* (~) below *represents not*.

> ~admitted to law school → ~take the LSAT

Again, although this could be true, it is not necessarily true. While it's certainly an uncomfortable thought, it is possible that you won't be admitted to law school, even though you do take the LSAT.

The "necessity versus sufficiency" concept distinguishes between that which is *necessary* for an occurrence and that which is *sufficient* to compel an occurrence. To understand the difference between the two, let's take the law school admissions process as an example. You already know the numerous conditions that must occur for your dream of law school admission to become a reality: in addition to taking the LSAT, you must earn a degree from an undergraduate institution, obtain letters of recommendation, and complete your application. All of these requirements must be satisfied in order for you to gain admission. In other words, each of these requirements is "necessary." Knowing this, we can safely say that *if*, in fact, you are admitted to law school, *then* each and every one of the conditions that needed to be satisfied has been satisfied.

That said, any one of these requirements alone is not *sufficient* to compel the occurrence. Because there are several requirements—in addition to taking the LSAT—that must be met, we cannot conclude with certainty that you have gained admission to law school by meeting one particular requirement.

In this scenario, *law school* is the *sufficient* element, and each of the other elements (*taking the LSAT, obtaining an undergraduate degree, submitting a completed application*) are the *necessary* elements. When formatting rules involving sufficient and necessary components, the sufficient element (*if*) is on the left, and the necessary element (*then*) is on the right.

> Sufficient → Necessary

THE CONTRAPOSITIVE

We've established that simply meeting one requirement (i.e., taking the LSAT) will not necessarily gain you admission to law school. So, based solely on the conditional statement, what else do you know that must be true? You know that it's absolutely true that the failure to meet *any one* of the requirements will result in the failure of that occurrence to happen (i.e., being admitted to law school). That bit of logic explains the *contrapositive*. Every conditional statement has a contrapositive that can be determined by reversing and negating the original conditional statement. Let's apply this reverse and negate process so you can see how it works.

Original (if/then) conditional:	admitted to law school → take the LSAT
Reversed:	take the LSAT → admitted to law school
Reversed and Negated:	~take the LSAT → ~admitted to law school

You know that if you do not take the LSAT, then you will not be admitted to law school. The contrapositive is the reverse and negative version of the original conditional statement, but their meanings are identical. It is simply another way to express it.

More Trigger Words for Conditional Statements

Like *if/then*, there are other common trigger words for *necessity/sufficiency* relationships that you should immediately recognize. The main ones are:

> *only if*
> *unless*
> *all* (including variations like *every* and *any*)
> *none* (including variations like *no* and *never*)

Let's look at how some of these trigger words work.

ONLY IF...

You will be admitted to law school *only if* you have taken the LSAT.

OR

Only if you have taken the LSAT, will you be admitted to law school.

> admitted to law school → taken the LSAT

UNLESS...

You will not be admitted to law school *unless* you have taken the LSAT.

OR

Unless you take the LSAT, you will not be admitted to law school.

> admitted to law school → taken the LSAT

This example is a little tricky. The word *unless* triggers the necessary condition; however, you must negate the sufficient condition to arrive at the correct conditional. Here the sufficient condition (i.e., *will not be admitted to law school*) is in a negative format; therefore, when we negate the negative, we end up with the positive (i.e., *admitted to law school*). Let's try another one...

You will be admitted to law school, *unless* you don't take the LSAT.

> ~admitted to law school → ~taken the LSAT

The meaning of this conditional is actually different than the meaning of the two previous statements. The contrapositive of the conditional (reverse and negate) is as follows: If you take the LSAT, you will be admitted to law school. And that is indeed how this conditional statement should be interpreted. This particular logic game format has tripped up many students because it's easy to mistakenly interpret the statement to mean "If you don't take the LSAT, then you will not be admitted to law school." In this particular scenario, not taking the LSAT is the only thing that could derail admission to law school, but it certainly does not have to derail admission to law school.

ALL...

All law school students have taken the LSAT.

> law student → taken the LSAT

NONE...

No law student is admitted to law school with only a GPA.

> law student → ~admitted with only a GPA

Practice is essential to achieving your best score. The drill exercises on the following pages provide the opportunity to practice everything you've learned so far about conditional statements. After you have completed the drill, check your answers on pages 21 and 22. Additional drills are located in Chapter 10. Completing all these drills should be part of your study schedule.

DRILL EXERCISES FOR CONDITIONAL STATEMENTS

Clue	Conditional	Contrapositive
P is selected if M is selected.	P → M	~M → ~P
N is selected only if P is selected.	N → P	~P → ~N
If N is selected, then J is also selected.	N → J	~J → ~N
M is not selected unless J is selected.	M → J	~J → ~M
If J is selected, then P is not selected.	J → ~P	P → ~J
If either J or N is selected, then the other must also be selected.	J ⟷ N	~J ⟷ ~N
H and L cannot both be selected.	H → ~L	L → ~H
All dogs are white.	d → W	~W → ~d
No birds live in the forest.	b → ~f	f → ~b
Every long sleeve shirt is ripped.	LSS → r	~r → ~LSS
None of the pencils have erasers.	P → ~E	E → ~P
If B is chosen, both F and G are chosen.	B → FG	~FG → ~B
G will be selected if, but only if, B is selected.	G ⟷ B	~B ⟷ ~G
A is selected, unless D is selected.	A → ~D	D → ~A
If W runs on day 2, X runs on day 6.	W2 → X6	~X6 → ~W2
If N is assigned, neither P nor S can be assigned.	N → ~PS	PS → ~N
If A is assigned to a team, then either B or C must be assigned to that team.	A → B or C	~B or C → ~A
If Q is not assigned, R and T are assigned.	~Q → RT	~RT → Q
G is not chosen unless either J or K is chosen.	G → J or K	~J or K → ~G

Clue	Conditional	Contrapositive
M and N cannot both join the class.	M → ~N	N → ~M
Neither S nor P can be on the same team as Q.	Q → ~S or P	S or P → ~Q
If M is selected, both J and K must be selected.	M → J and K	~J and K → ~M
G will go to the movies only if L goes to the movies.	G → L	~L → ~G
H will attend the opera if, and only if, J attends the opera.	H → J	~J → ~H
If A is not selected, then either B or C, but not both, will be selected.	~A → B or C	~B + C → A
If W is not selected, then X is selected.	~W → X	~X → W
P will dance only if S dances.	P → S	~S → ~P
None of the girls have gym.	G → ~Gym	Gym → ~G
Neither W nor X can be in the same boat as Y.	W or X → ~Y	Y → ~W or X
If F is selected, both Q and S must be selected.	F → QS	~QS → ~F
B will go to the concert only if H goes to the concert.	B → H	~H → ~B
A will go on vacation if, and only if, J goes on vacation.	A ⟷ J	~J ⟷ ~A
All professors have Ph.D.s.	Prof → PhD	~PhD → ~Prof
Jan will read the book if Paul reads the book.	P → J	~J → ~P
If Betty plays cards, Kenya will play cards.	B → K	~K → ~B
Rod will sing first only if Pam sings third.	R₁ → P₃	~P₃ → ~R₁
Lacy will attend church if, and only if, Jo attends church.	L ⟷ J	~J ⟷ ~L

ANSWER KEY

Clue	Conditional	Contrapositive
P is selected if M is selected.	$M \rightarrow P$	$\sim P \rightarrow \sim M$
N is selected only if P is selected.	$N \rightarrow P$	$\sim P \rightarrow \sim N$
If N is selected, then J is also selected.	$N \rightarrow J$	$\sim J \rightarrow \sim N$
M is not selected unless J is selected.	$M \rightarrow J$	$\sim J \rightarrow \sim M$
If J is selected, then P is not selected.	$J \rightarrow \sim P$	$P \rightarrow \sim J$
If either J or N is selected, then theother must also be selected.	$J \leftrightarrow N$	$\sim J \leftrightarrow \sim N$
H and L cannot both be selected.	$H \rightarrow \sim L$	$L \rightarrow \sim H$
All dogs are white.	dog $\rightarrow$ white	$\sim$white $\rightarrow$ $\sim$dog
No birds live in the forest.	bird $\rightarrow$ $\sim$live forest	live forest $\rightarrow$ $\sim$bird
Every long sleeve shirt is ripped.	LSS $\rightarrow$ ripped	$\sim$ripped $\rightarrow$ $\sim$LSS
None of the pencils have erasers.	pencil $\rightarrow$ $\sim$eraser	eraser $\rightarrow$ $\sim$pencil
If B is chosen, both F and G are chosen.	$B \rightarrow F$ and G	$\sim F$ or $\sim G \rightarrow \sim B$
G will be selected if, but only if, B isSelected.	$G \leftrightarrow B$	$\sim G \leftrightarrow \sim B$
A is selected, unless D is selected.	$\sim D \rightarrow A$	$\sim A \rightarrow D$
If W runs on day 2, X runs on day 6.	$W_2 \rightarrow X_6$	$\sim X_6 \rightarrow \sim W_2$
If N is assigned, neither P nor S can be assigned.	$N \rightarrow \sim P$ and $\sim S$	P or $S \rightarrow \sim N$
If A is assigned to a team, then either B or C must be assigned to that team.	$A \rightarrow B$ or C	$\sim B$ and $\sim C \rightarrow \sim A$
If Q is not assigned, R and T are assigned.	$\sim Q \rightarrow R$ and T	$\sim R$ or $\sim T \rightarrow Q$
G is not chosen unless either J or K is chosen.	$G \rightarrow J$ or K	$\sim J$ and $\sim K \rightarrow \sim G$
M and N cannot both join the class.	$M \rightarrow \sim N$	$N \rightarrow \sim M$
Neither S nor P can be on the same team as Q.	$Q \rightarrow \sim S$ and $\sim P$	S or $P \rightarrow \sim Q$
If M is selected, both J and K must be selected.	$M \rightarrow J$ and K	$\sim J$ or $\sim K \rightarrow \sim M$

Clue	Conditional	Contrapositive
G will go to the movies only if L goes to the movies.	G → L	~L → ~G
H will attend the opera if, and only if, J attends the opera.	H ↔ J	~H ↔ ~J
If A is not selected, then either B or C, but not both, will be selected.	~A → B or C ~A → ~(B and C)	~B and ~C → A B and C → A
If W is not selected, then X is selected.	~W → X	~X → W
P will dance only if S dances.	P → S	~S → ~P
None of the girls has gym.	girl → ~gym	gym → ~girl
Neither W nor X can be in the same boat as Y.	Y → ~W and ~X	W or X → ~Y
If F is selected, both Q and S must be selected.	F → Q and S	~Q or ~S → ~F
B will go to the concert only if H goes to the concert.	B → H	~H → ~B
A will go on vacation if, and only if, J goes on vacation.	A ↔ J	~A ↔ ~J
All professors have Ph.D.s.	prof → Ph.D.	~Ph.D. → ~prof
Jan will read the book if Paul reads the book.	P → J	~J → ~P
If Betty plays cards, Kenya will play cards.	B → K	~K → ~B
Rod will sing only if Pam sings.	$R_1 → P_3$	$~P_3 → ~R_1$
Lacy will attend church if, and only if, Jo attends church.	L ↔ J	~L ↔ ~J

Practicing Sequence Games

5

When doing sequencing games, you will encounter words and phrases, such as *sequential, consecutive, in order, one after another, ordered,* and *one at a time.* When you ask yourself, "What are they asking me to do?" you'll realize that you are being asked to place things in order. Most often there will be a natural order to the task, as when you are asked to set a schedule for Monday through Friday or the hours of the day from 1 P.M. to 7 P.M.

As with all games, determining the ratio of slots to components is very important. It is precisely this relationship that distinguishes the three subcategories of sequence games:

- one-to-one ratio,
- not-one-to-one ratio,
- chain game.

When the number of slots is equal to the number of components in a game, you have a *one-to-one ratio.* When the number of slots is not equal to the number of components, you have a *not-one-to-one ratio.* Finally, when the slots and components are equal but each of the clues also indicates the relative position of each element to at least one other element, you have a chain game.

Here you are provided with three practice games for each type of sequencing game. Remember the five-step approach outlined in Chapter 3 as you work through the games and questions. An answer key, with full explanations, is provided after each section.

ONE-TO-ONE RATIO

Let's look at the opening language in the first sample sequence game coming up:

> A microbiologist will test exactly eight drugs—F, G, H, J, K, L, M, and N—on a resistant bacterium. Each drug is tested one at a time and exactly once, consistent with the following conditions:

Here, the key words that will help ascertain the type and ratio of the game are: *exactly eight drugs; one at a time;* and *exactly once.* When you read *exactly eight drugs* and *one at a time,* you know that there are eight drugs being tested one after another. Right way you know this is a sequence game. Based on the words *exactly once,* you also know that this is a one-to-one ratio sequence game; the components (i.e., drugs) will be tested just once. This means they will not be repeated in your diagram.

Game 1

A microbiologist will test exactly eight drugs—F, G, H, J, K, L, M, and N—on a resistant bacterium. Each drug is tested one at a time and exactly once, consistent with the following conditions:

H is tested at some time before N but after G.
The fourth drug tested is either K or N.
There are exactly two drugs tested between F and L.
F is not tested fifth.
J is tested either immediately after G or immediately before M, but not both.

1. Which one of the following could be the order, from first to last, in which the drugs are tested?

    (A) G, F, H, K, N, L, J, M
    (B) M, J, G, K, L, H, N, F
    (C) G, F, H, N, L, J, M, K
    (D) F, G, J, L, K, H, N, M
    (E) G, J, F, N, H, L, K, M

2. If K is the first drug tested, then which one of the following must be true?

    (A) M is the eighth drug tested.
    (B) H is the fifth drug tested.
    (C) J is the sixth drug tested.
    (D) L is the third drug tested.
    (E) F is the second drug tested.

3. Which one of the following could be true?

    (A) N is the second drug tested.
    (B) L is the seventh drug tested.
    (C) L is the first drug tested.
    (D) G is the fifth drug tested.
    (E) H is the eighth drug tested.

4. If N is tested immediately before K, then each of the following must be false EXCEPT:

    (A) L is tested immediately before K.
    (B) F is tested immediately before H.
    (C) H is tested immediately before N.
    (D) G is tested immediately before F.
    (E) K is tested immediately before J.

5. If H is tested fifth, then which one of the following must be false?

    (A) J is the first drug tested.
    (B) M is the seventh drug tested.
    (C) F is the third drug tested.
    (D) M is tested before N.
    (E) K is tested before L.

6. Each of the following could be true EXCEPT:

    (A) L is the fifth drug tested.
    (B) L is the sixth drug tested.
    (C) G is the third drug tested.
    (D) G is the sixth drug tested.
    (E) J is the seventh drug tested.

STEP 1 Visualize and draw the diagram.

What are you being asked to figure out? This question is answerable from the language "*each drug is tested one at a time.*" The game requires you to determine the order in which the drugs are tested. Your diagram should look like the one below.

1	2	3	4	5	6	7	8

STEP 2 List the components and ascertain the ratio and/or distribution.

The components are F, G, H, J, K, L, M and N.
The ratio is one-to-one because you are told that each drug is tested "*exactly once.*"

STEP 3 Symbolize the clues.

Clue 1	H is tested at some time before N but after G.	G...H...N
Clue 2	The fourth drug tested is either K or N.	K/N = 4
Clue 3	There are exactly two drugs tested between F and L.	F _ _ L (with arc)
Clue 4	F is not tested fifth.	F ≠ 5
Clue 5	J is tested either immediately after G or immediately before M, but not both.	GJ JM ~~GJM~~

STEP 4 Make deductions.

Remember to determine which slots ban which components, and which slots focus on commonality. From Clue 1, you can deduce:

1. G cannot be placed in either slot 7 or 8 because at least two drugs (H and N) are tested after G.
2. H cannot be placed in slot 1 because at least one test (G) is tested before H, and likewise H cannot be placed in slot 8 because at least one test (N) is tested after H.
3. N cannot be placed in slot 1 nor in 2 because at least two drugs (G and H) are tested before N. Hence, your diagram will be updated as follows:

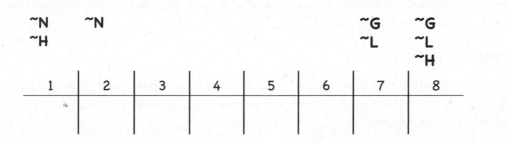

From Clue 2, you know that slot 4 is either K or N. Put this information directly into the diagram because you have narrowed the possibilities to no more than three.

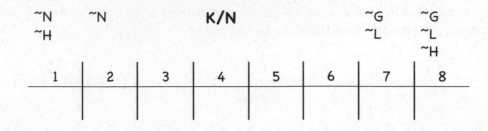

Clue 3, on its own, doesn't supply any additional deductions. However, in combination with Clue 2, it offers useful information:

1. Neither F nor L can be placed in slot 1. To do so with either one of them would force the other into slot 4, and that one is reserved for either K or N.
2. Similarly, F cannot be placed in slot 7. To do so would force L into slot 4. Again, you cannot put L in slot 4 because is reserved for either K or N. So now you have:

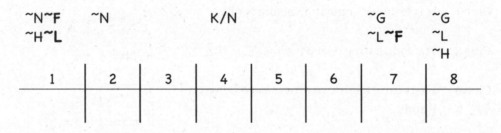

Clue 4 should be placed directly into the diagram. In addition, remember to look for commonality. Notice that F is a component common to Clues 3 and 4. Taken together, you can deduce that L cannot be placed in slot 2. To do so would force F into slot 5, which has been specifically prohibited by Clue 4.

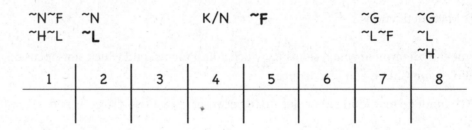

Clue 5 tells you that J must be part of a block, but it does not yield any deductions concerning the banning of components from any slots.

At this point, having ascertained which slots ban which components, you are able to determine that the most restricted slot is 4 and the most restricted components are L (with four restrictions) and F (with three restrictions). Armed with these deductions, you are well prepared to attack the questions.

STEP 5 Tackle the questions.

The order in which you answer the questions is important. Remember the optimal sequence: 1. catch-a-clue; 2. restricted; 3. unrestricted; 4. modifiers. For this particular game, that translates to the following order: 1, 2, 4, 5, 3, and then 6.

Answer Key

Answers

Question 1

This is a catch-a-clue question. Remember you only need to catch a rule, look for the answer choice that violates that rule, and then eliminate it.

> Which one of the following could be the order, from first to last, in which the drugs are tested?
>
> (A) G, F, H, K, N, L, J, M
> (B) M, J, G, K, L, H, N, F
> (C) G, F, H, N, L, J, M, K
> (D) F, G, J, L, K, H, N, M
> (E) G, J, F, N, H, L, K, M

The first clue (*H is tested at some time before N but after G*) eliminates answer choice E. The second clue (*the fourth drug tested is either K or N*) eliminates answer choice D. The third clue (*there are exactly two drugs tested between F and L*) eliminates answer choice A. The fourth clue (*F is not tested fifth*) does not eliminate any of the answer choices. The fifth clue (*J is tested either immediately after G or immediately before M, but not both*) eliminates answer choice B.

(C) is the correct answer.

Put the correct answer into the diagram.

~N~F ~H~L	~N ~L		K/N	~F		~G ~L~F	~G ~L ~H
1	2	3	4	5	6	7	8
G	F	H	N	L	J	M	N

Question 2

This one is a restricted, "must-be-true" question. Therefore, four answers are true sometimes but not always, or they are never true. The correct answer is always true.

> If K is the first drug tested, then which one of the following must be true?
>
> (A) M is the eighth drug tested.
> (B) H is the fifth drug tested.
> (C) J is the sixth drug tested.
> (D) L is the third drug tested.
> (E) F is the second drug tested.

Begin by placing the additional restriction into the diagram.

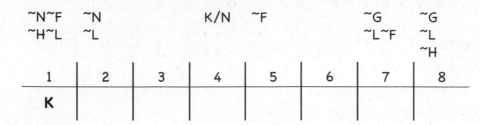

With component K in play, Clue 2 is triggered. With K in slot 1, N must be placed in slot 4.

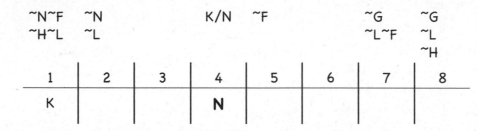

Clue 1 requires that both G and H be tested before N (to the left). There are only two unoccupied slots before N. Accordingly, G and H are placed in slots 2 and 3, respectively.

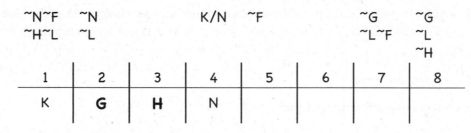

Let's look at the most restricted components. Prior deductions banned L from slots 7 and 8. Now L is also banned from slot 6. If L were in slot 6, F would necessarily be placed in slot 3, which is now impossible because H already occupies slot 3. Therefore, L must be placed in slot 5, and because of Clue 3, F must be placed in slot 8.

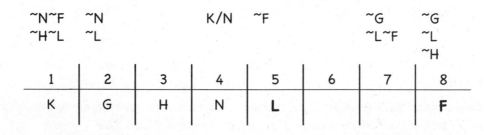

The only remaining components are J and M. Clue 5 requires either ⟨GJ⟩ or ⟨JM⟩. ⟨GJ⟩ is precluded because G is already immediately before H. Therefore, J and M must be placed in slots 6 and 7, respectively.

~N~F ~H~L	~N ~L		K/N	~F		~G ~L~F	~G ~L ~H
1	2	3	4	5	6	7	8
K	G	H	N	L	**J**	**M**	F

(C) is the correct answer.

Question 4

This is a restricted, "must-be-false-EXCEPT" question. Therefore, four answers with this restriction are never true. These are the wrong answers. One answer could be true at least once, but not always, or the answer is always true. This one is the correct answer.

  If N is tested immediately before K, then each of the following must be false EXCEPT:

  (A) L is tested immediately before K.
  (B) F is tested immediately before H.
  (C) H is tested immediately before N.
  (D) G is tested immediately before F.
  (E) K is tested immediately before J.

This restriction will appear as $\boxed{\text{NK}}$ or $\boxed{\text{KN}}$ in the diagram. With the inclusion of N and K in this question, Clue 2 is triggered. Since either K or N must be placed in slot 4, you have two options.

~N~F ~H~L	~N ~L		K/N	~F		~G ~L~F	~G ~L ~H
1	2	3	4	5	6	7	8
		 N	N K	K			

Let's work out the top option first. Look at the most restricted component: L. Prior deductions indicate that L cannot be placed in slots 1, 2, 7, or 8. In the top option, slots 4 and 5 are occupied by N and K, respectively. The only remaining slots for L are 3 and 6. By operation of Clue 3, if L is placed in slot 3, F must be placed in slot 6. Likewise, if L is placed in slot 6, F must be placed in slot 3.

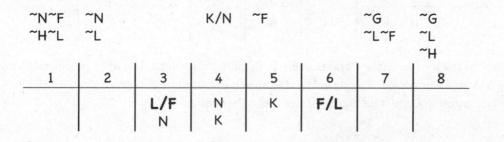

~N~F ~H~L	~N ~L		K/N	~F		~G ~L~F	~G ~L ~H
1	2	3	4	5	6	7	8
		L/F N	N K	K	**F/L**		

By operation of Clue 1, G and H must be placed in slots 1 and 2, respectively.

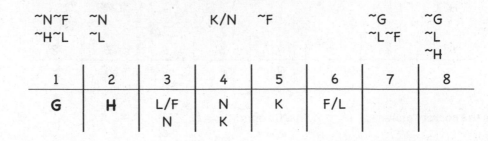

~N~F ~H~L	~N ~L		K/N	~F		~G ~L~F	~G ~L ~H
1	2	3	4	5	6	7	8
G	H	L/F N	N K	K	F/L		

The remaining two components are J and M. By operation of Clue 5, GJ is not possible. Therefore, JM must be placed in slots 7 and 8, respectively.

~N~F ~H~L	~N ~L		K/N	~F		~G ~L~F	~G ~L ~H
1	2	3	4	5	6	7	8
G	H	L/F N	N K	K	F/L	J	M

With the first option worked out, do a quick review of the answer choices to determine whether you have revealed that one of the answer choices could be true. You haven't, so you must continue to work out the second option. Let's do it.

~N~F ~H~L	~N ~L		K/N	~F		~G ~L~F	~G ~L ~H
1	2	3	4	5	6	7	8
		N	K				

By operation of Clue 1, G and H must be placed in slots 1 and 2, respectively.

~N~F ~H~L	~N ~L		K/N	~F		~G ~L~F	~G ~L ~H
1	2	3	4	5	6	7	8
G	H	N	K				

Pivot to the most restricted component: L. By prior deductions, L cannot be placed in slots 7 or 8. Also, L cannot be placed in slot 6 because it would force F in slot 3 by operation of Clue 3. Accordingly, L must be placed in slot 5 and F in slot 8.

	1	2	3	4	5	6	7	8
~N~F ~H~L	~N ~L			K/N	~F		~G ~L~F	~G ~L ~H
	G	H	N	K	**L**			**F**

J and M are the remaining components. By operation of Clue 5, they must be placed in slots 6 and 7, respectively.

	1	2	3	4	5	6	7	8
~N~F ~H~L	~N ~L			K/N	~F		~G ~L~F	~G ~L ~H
	G	H	N	K	L	**J**	**M**	F

With this option worked out, it is revealed that H can be immediately before N. Answer choices A, B, D, and E must be false. You are looking for the EXCEPTION; answer choice C can be true.

(C) is the correct answer.

Question 5

In this restricted, "must-be-false" question, four answers could be true. These are the wrong answers. One answer choice can never be true. This is the correct answer.

If H is tested fifth, then which one of the following must be false?

(A) J is the first drug tested.
(B) M is the seventh drug tested.
(C) F is the third drug tested.
(D) M is tested before N.
(E) K is tested before L.

As always, you begin by placing the additional restriction into the diagram.

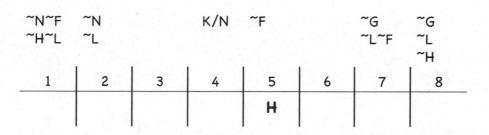

	1	2	3	4	5	6	7	8
~N~F ~H~L	~N ~L			K/N	~F		~G ~L~F	~G ~L ~H
					H			

Component H is referenced in Clue 1, and, thus Clue 1 is triggered. By operation of Clue 1, N must be placed after H. Therefore, Clue 2, which governs the most restricted slot, requires that K be placed in slot 4.

~N~F ~H~L	~N ~L		K/N	~F		~G ~L~F	~G ~L ~H
1	2	3	4	5	6	7	8
			K	H			

Pivot to our most restricted component: L. Prior deductions ban L from slots 1, 2, 7, and 8, so L must be placed in either slot 3 or 6. By operation of Clue 3, if L is placed in slot 3, F must be placed in slot 6. Likewise, if L is placed in slot 6, F must be placed in slot 3.

~N~F ~H~L	~N ~L		K/N	~F		~G ~L~F	~G ~L ~H
1	2	3	4	5	6	7	8
		L/F	K	H	F/L		

Clue 5 requires the placement of either GJ or JM . As previously mentioned, by operation of Clue 1, N must be placed after H. As such, N must be placed in either slots 7 or 8. Since N must occupy either slot 7 or 8, GJ or JM must be placed in slots 1 and 2, respectively. Also by operation of Clue 1, G must be before H, and, therefore, goes in either slot 1 or 2. Accordingly, JM cannot occupy slots 1 and 2. Therefore, GJ must be placed in slots 1 and 2.

~N~F ~H~L	~N ~L		K/N	~F		~G ~L~F	~G ~L ~H
1	2	3	4	5	6	7	8
G	J	L/F	K	H	F/L		

M and N are the only components remaining. Either can be placed in slot 7 or 8.

~N~F ~H~L	~N ~L		K/N	~F		~G ~L~F	~G ~L ~H
1	2	3	4	5	6	7	8
G	J	L/F	K	H	F/L	M/N	N/M

Answer choices B, C, D, and E can each be true at least once. Answer choice A is never true.

(A) is the correct answer.

Question 3

This one is an unrestricted, "could-be-true" question. Four answers are never true. These are the wrong answers. One answer choice can be true at least once. This is the correct answer.

Which one of the following could be true?

(A) N is the second drug tested.
(B) L is the seventh drug tested.
(C) L is the first drug tested.
(D) G is the fifth drug tested.
(E) H is the eighth drug tested.

You can answer this question by simply reviewing the deductions.

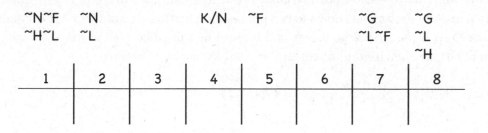

Answer choices A, B, C, and E are never true.

(D) is the correct answer.

Question 6

This unrestricted, "could-be-true-EXCEPT" question, is identical to a "must-be-false" question. Four answers could be true at least once. These are the wrong answers. One answer choice can never be true. This is the correct answer.

Each of the following could be true EXCEPT:

(A) L is the fifth drug tested.
(B) L is the sixth drug tested.
(C) G is the third drug tested.
(D) G is the sixth drug tested.
(E) J is the seventh drug tested.

This question is answerable, in part, by reviewing your previous work. Remember that each of the possibilities you worked out on the restricted questions is in compliance with all of the clues and can be relied upon to answer the unrestricted questions. Let's take a look at all of your work.

	1	2	3	4	5	6	7	8
	~N~F ~H~L	~N ~L		K/N	~F		~G ~L~F	~G ~L ~H
#1	G	F	H	N	L	J	M	N
#2	K	G	H	N	L	J	M	F
#4	G	H	L/F	N	K	F/L	J	M
	G	H	N	K	L	J	M	F
#5	G	J	L/F	K	H	F/L	N/M	M/N

Answer choice A (*L is the fifth drug tested*) can be true, as shown in the explanations of questions 1, 2, and 4. So this is not the correct answer. Answer choice B (*L is the sixth drug tested*) can be true as shown in our explanations of questions 4 and 5. So, neither is this the correct answer. The prior work doesn't prove that answer choices C or D can be true, so you cannot eliminate either of these yet. The explanation to question 4 showed that answer choice E (*J is the seventh drug tested*) can be true, so it can be safely eliminated.

Now we've narrowed our possible answers down to just two: either C or D. Whenever you have narrowed the answers down to two possibilities, test just one of them. Let's try answer choice D (*G is the sixth drug tested*), and if it can be true, then it's the wrong answer. If it cannot be true, then it's the correct answer. Start by placing G in slot 6.

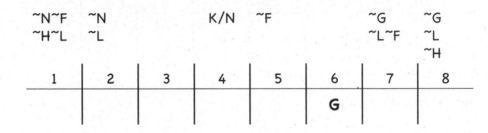

Because of Clue 1, H and N must be placed in slots 7 and 8, respectively.

	1	2	3	4	5	6	7	8
	~N~F ~H~L	~N ~L		K/N	~F		~G ~L~F	~G ~L ~H
						G	H	N

With N placed in slot 8, Clue 2 requires the placement of K in slot 4.

	1	2	3	4	5	6	7	8
	~N~F ~H~L	~N ~L		K/N	~F		~G ~L~F	~G ~L ~H
				K		G	H	N

Next look at the most restricted component: L. Prior deductions ban the placement of L in slots 1 or 2. In this scenario, by operation of Clue 3, L cannot be placed in slot 3 because to do so would require the placement of F in slot 6. Thus, the only remaining slot for L is slot 5, which forces component F into slot 2.

	~N~F ~H~L	~N ~L		K/N	~F		~G ~L~F	~G ~L ~H
1	**2**	**3**	**4**	**5**	**6**	**7**	**8**
	F		K	L	G	H	N

Clue 5 requires the placement of the JM block. As you can see, you do not have two adjacent available slots for the block. This answer choice does not work and therefore cannot be true.

(D) is the correct answer.

Game 2

During a period of six consecutive days—from day 1 through day 6—each of exactly six surgeons—Fisher, Hong, Klein, Lee, Moreno, and Nelson—will each perform operations exactly once. Each day, exactly one surgeon will perform an operation in accordance with the following conditions:

Lee operates on an earlier day than the day Klein operates.
Klein operates on the day either immediately before or immediately after the day Fisher operates.
If Moreno does not operate on day 1, then Moreno operates on day 6.
Hong operates on day 2, unless Klein operates on day 6.

1. Which one of the following could be the order in which the surgeons perform operations, from day 1 through day 6?

   (A) Hong, Nelson, Lee, Fisher, Klein, Moreno
   (B) Lee, Hong, Fisher, Nelson, Klein, Moreno
   (C) Moreno, Fisher, Klein, Nelson, Lee, Hong
   (D) Moreno, Nelson, Hong, Lee, Fisher, Klein
   (E) Hong, Lee, Fisher, Klein, Moreno, Nelson

2. Which one of the following is a pair of surgeons, neither of whom can operate on day 1?

   (A) Hong and Nelson
   (B) Lee and Nelson
   (C) Fisher and Hong
   (D) Klein and Nelson
   (E) Lee and Hong

3. Each of the following CANNOT be true EXCEPT:

   (A) Fisher operates on day 1.
   (B) Hong operates on day 6.
   (C) Lee operates on day 5.
   (D) Hong operates on day 4.
   (E) Klein operates on day 1.

4. If Lee operates on day 4, then which one of the following could be false?

   (A) Moreno operates on some day before Hong.
   (B) Nelson operates on some day before Lee.
   (C) Lee operates on some day before Klein.
   (D) Hong operates on some day before Fisher.
   (E) Nelson operates on some day before Hong.

5. If the operations of Hong and Klein are scheduled on consecutive days, then each one of the following must be true EXCEPT:

   (A) Lee operates on day 1.
   (B) Fisher operates on day 4.
   (C) Nelson operates on day 5.
   (D) Moreno operates on day 1.
   (E) Klein operates on day 3.

6. If Klein operates on day 4, then each of the following could be true EXCEPT:

   (A) Klein operates on the day immediately before Nelson.
   (B) Fisher operates on the day immediately before Nelson.
   (C) Nelson operates on the day immediately after Hong.
   (D) Lee operates on the day immediately after Nelson.
   (E) Fisher operates on the day immediately before Moreno.

Visualize and draw the diagram.

What are they asking you to figure out? This question is answerable from the language "during a period of six consecutive days." The game is asking you to determine the order in which the surgeons perform operations. The diagram is as follows:

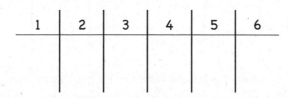

STEP 2 List the components and ascertain the ratio and/or distribution.

The components are F, H, K, L, M, and N. The ratio is one-to-one because each surgeon operates "exactly once."

STEP 3 Symbolize the clues.

Clue 1	Lee operates on an earlier day than the day Klein operates.	L...K
Clue 2	Klein operates on the day either immediately before or immediately after the day Fisher operates.	$\overset{\frown}{\boxed{F \quad K}}$
Clue 3	If Moreno does not operate on day 1, then Moreno operates on day 6.	M = 1, 6
Clue 4	Hong operates on day 2 unless Klein operates on day 6. (Remember to always perform the contrapositive.)	$\sim H_2 \rightarrow K_6$ $\sim K_6 \rightarrow H_2$

STEP 4 Make deductions.

Remember to determine what slots ban which components and to focus on commonality.

1. Combine Clue 1 (L...K) and Clue 2, since both clues have the component "K" in common. Hence L...$\overset{\frown}{\boxed{F \quad K}}$.

2. K cannot be placed in slot 1 because at least one surgeon (L) operates before K.
3. F cannot be placed in slot 1 because at least one surgeon (L) operates before F.
4. L cannot be placed in either slot 5 or 6 because at least two surgeons (F and K) operate after L. The diagram can be updated as follows:

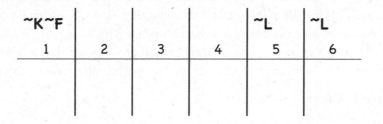

Clue 3 makes it clear that M is banned from slots 2, 3, 4, and 5.

~K~F	~M	~M	~M	~L~M	~L
1	2	3	4	5	6

Clue 4 is a conditional statement. Alone, it does not supply any additional deductions. Most deductions from conditional statements occur by linking the information in two or more of them.

Thanks to the above deductions, you have been able to determine that the most restricted components are M (four restrictions); L (2 restrictions); and F and K (one restriction each). Armed with these deductions, you are well prepared to attack the questions.

(STEP 5) Tackle the questions.

The order in which you answer the questions is important. Remember the optimal sequence: 1. catch-a-clue; 2. restricted; 3. unrestricted; 4. modifiers. For this particular game, that translates to the following order: 1, 4, 5, 6, 2, and then 3.

Answer Key

1. **D**   2. **C**   3. **D**   4. **E**   5. **D**   6. **D**

Answers

Question 1

This is a catch-a-clue question. Remember, you need only to catch a rule, look for the answer choice that violates that rule, and then eliminate it.

> Which one of the following could be the order in which the surgeons perform operations, from day 1 through day 6?
>
> (A) Hong, Nelson, Lee, Fisher, Klein, Moreno
> (B) Lee, Hong, Fisher, Nelson, Klein, Moreno
> (C) Moreno, Fisher, Klein, Nelson, Lee, Hong
> (D) Moreno, Nelson, Hong, Lee, Fisher, Klein
> (E) Hong, Lee, Fisher, Klein, Moreno, Nelson

The first clue (*Lee operates on an earlier day than the day Klein operates*) eliminates answer choice C. The second clue (*Klein operates on the day either immediately before or immediately after the day Fisher operates*) eliminates answer choice B. The third clue (*If Moreno does not operate on day 1, then Moreno operates on day 6*) eliminates answer choice E. The fourth clue (*Hong operates on day 2 unless Klein operates on day 6*) eliminates answer choice A.

(D) is the correct answer.

Put the correct answer into the diagram:

~K~F	~M	~M	~M	~L~M	~L
1	2	3	4	5	6
M	N	H	L	F	K

Question 4

This is a restricted, "could-be-false" question; therefore, four answers are always true. These are the wrong answers. The correct answer could be true.

If Lee operates on day 4, then which one of the following could be false?

(A) Moreno operates on some day before Hong.
(B) Nelson operates on some day before Lee.
(C) Lee operates on some day before Klein.
(D) Hong operates on some day before Fisher.
(E) Nelson operates on some day before Hong.

Begin by placing the additional restriction into the diagram.

~K~F	~M	~M	~M	~L~M	~L
1	2	3	4	5	6
			L		

By operation of Deduction 1, F and K must be placed in slots 5 and 6, interchangeably, thereby creating two options:

~K~F	~M	~M	~M	~L~M	~L
1	2	3	4	5	6
			L	F	K
			L	K	F

Let's work out the top option first. Pivot to the most restricted element: M. Clue 3 dictates that M is placed in either slot 1 or 6. Since slot 6 is filled, you must place M in slot 1.

~K~F	~M	~M	~M	~L~M	~L
1	2	3	4	5	6
M			L	F	K
			L	K	F

Placing K in slot 6 does not trigger the conditional in Clue 4 because it would be triggered if K were *not* placed in slot 6. Therefore, the remaining two components (H and N) are free to be placed in slots 2 and 3 interchangeably.

~K~F	~M	~M	~M	~L~M	~L
1	2	3	4	5	6
M	H/N	N/H	L	F	K
			L	K	F

Stop! Notice that you have enough information to answer the question. Answer choice E (*N operates on some day before Hong*) is not always true. It could be false.

(E) is the correct answer.

Question 5

This is a restricted, "must-be-true-EXCEPT" question. Therefore, four answers must be true at all times. These are the wrong answers. One answer could be false at least once. This is the correct answer.

> If the operations of Hong and Klein are scheduled on consecutive days, then each one of the following must be true EXCEPT:

(A) Lee operates on day 1.
(B) Fisher operates on day 4.
(C) Nelson operates on day 5.
(D) Moreno operates on day 1.
(E) Klein operates on day 3.

Begin by placing the additional restriction into the diagram. The question requires that you place H and K side by side. By operation of Clue 4, if H is not placed in slot 2, K must be placed in slot 6. By operation of Clue 2, F must, therefore, be placed in slot 5. As such, H and K would not be operating consecutively.

Since the additional restriction cannot be fulfilled without H being placed in slot 2, it must be placed there.

~K~F	~M	~M	~M	~L~M	~L
1	2	3	4	5	6
	H				

In order for K to be consecutive with H, K must be placed in either slot 1 or 3. By operation of Deduction 1, K is banned from slot 1. So it follows that K must be placed in slot 3.

~K~F	~M	~M	~M	~L~M	~L
1	2	3	4	5	6
	H	**K**			

By operation of Clue 2, F must be placed in slot 4.

~K~F	~M	~M	~M	~L~M	~L
1	2	3	4	5	6
	H	K	**F**		

By operation of Clue 1, L must be placed in slot 1.

~K~F	~M	~M	~M	~L~M	~L
1	2	3	4	5	6
L	H	K	F		

By operation of Clue 3, M must be placed in slot 6.

~K~F	~M	~M	~M	~L~M	~L
1	2	3	4	5	6
L	H	K	F		**M**

The only remaining component (N) must be placed in the only remaining available slot (5).

~K~F	~M	~M	~M	~L~M	~L
1	2	3	4	5	6
L	H	K	F	**N**	M

Answer choices A, B, C, and E must be true. Accordingly, those answer choices can be eliminated. Answer choice D is never true.

(D) is the correct answer.

Question 6

This is a restricted, "could-be-true-EXCEPT" question; therefore, four answers could be true at least once. These are the wrong answers. One answer is never true. This is the correct answer.

If Klein operates on day 4, then each of the following could be true EXCEPT:

(A) Klein operates on the day immediately before Nelson.
(B) Fisher operates on the day immediately before Nelson.
(C) Nelson operates on the day immediately after Hong.
(D) Lee operates on the day immediately after Nelson.
(E) Fisher operates on the day immediately before Moreno.

Place the additional restriction into the diagram.

~K~F	~M	~M	~M	~L~M	~L
1	2	3	4	5	6
			K		

By operation of Clue 2, F must be placed in either slot 3 or 5, thus creating two possible options.

~K~F	~M	~M	~M	~L~M	~L
1	2	3	4	5	6
		F	K		
			K	F	

Let's work out the top option first. The placement of K in slot 4 triggers the contrapositive of conditional Clue 4. Therefore, H must be placed in slot 2.

~K~F	~M	~M	~M	~L~M	~L
1	2	3	4	5	6
	H	F	K		
			K	F	

By operation of Clue 1, L must be placed in slot 1.

~K~F	~M	~M	~M	~L~M	~L
1	2	3	4	5	6
L	H	F	K		
			K	F	

Pivot to our most restricted component: M. It must be placed in slot 6.

~K~F	~M	~M	~M	~L~M	~L
1	2	3	4	5	6
L	H	F	K		**M**
			K	F	

The only remaining component (N) must be placed in the only remaining available slot (5).

~K~F	~M	~M	~M	~L~M	~L
1	2	3	4	5	6
L	H	F	K	**N**	M
			K	F	

Let's work out the second option.

The placement of K in slot 4 triggers the contrapositive of conditional Clue 4. Therefore, H must be placed in slot 2.

~K~F	~M	~M	~M	~L~M	~L
1	2	3	4	5	6
L	H	F	K	N	M
	H		K	F	

Pivot to the most restricted component: M. M must be placed in either slot 1 or 6, thus creating a third option.

~K~F	~M	~M	~M	~L~M	~L
1	2	3	4	5	6
L	H	F	K	N	M
M	H		K	F	
	H		K	F	**M**

Let's continue with the second option. By operation of Clue 1, L must be placed in slot 3. Therefore, the only remaining component (N) must be placed in the only remaining available slot (6).

~K~F	~M	~M	~M	~L~M	~L
1	2	3	4	5	6
L	H	F	K	N	M
M	H	L	K	F	N
	H		K	F	M

Now let's finish the third option. The two remaining components (L and N) should be placed in slots 1 and 3 interchangeably.

~K~F	~M	~M	~M	~L~M	~L
1	2	3	4	5	6
L	H	F	K	N	M
M	H	L	K	F	N
L/N	H	N/L	K	F	M

Answer choice A (*Klein operates on the day immediately before Nelson*) could be true in the first option. Eliminate answer choice A.

Answer choice B (*Fisher operates on the day immediately before Nelson*) could be true in the second option. Eliminate answer choice B.

Answer choice C (*Nelson operates on the day immediately after Hong*) could be true in the third option. Eliminate answer choice C.

Answer choice E (*Fisher operates on the day immediately before Moreno*) could be true in the third option. Eliminate answer choice E.

Answer choice D (*Lee operates on the day immediately after Nelson*) is never true.

(D) is the correct answer.

Question 2

In this unrestricted, "cannot-be-true" question, four answers could be true. These are the wrong answers. One answer choice is never true. This is the correct answer.

Which one of the following is a pair of surgeons, neither of whom can operate on day 1?

(A) Hong and Nelson
(B) Lee and Nelson
(C) Fisher and Hong
(D) Klein and Nelson
(E) Lee and Hong

Based on the deductions, you may be looking for the pair F and K, but none of the answer choices includes both F and K. Nonetheless, this question is completely answerable by reviewing the diagram history. A quick review of the diagram for question 6 (repeated below) indicates that L, M, and N can each operate on day 1. Therefore, any pair that includes any of that trio is incorrect.

~K~F	~M	~M	~M	~L~M	~L
1	2	3	4	5	6
L	H	F	K	N	M
M	H	L	K	F	N
L/N	H	**N/L**	K	F	**M**

Answer choices B and E include L, so eliminate them. Answer choices A and D include N as part of the pair so eliminate them. **(C) is the correct answer.** Note that H cannot operate on day 1, and even though the deduction wasn't done beforehand, we were still able to answer the question without any additional work.

(C) is the correct answer.

Question 3

This one is an unrestricted, "cannot-be-true-EXCEPT" question. Four answers are never true. These are the wrong answers. One answer is true at least once. This is the correct answer.

Each of the following CANNOT be true EXCEPT:

(A) Fisher operates on day 1.
(B) Hong operates on day 6.
(C) Lee operates on day 5.
(D) Hong operates on day 4.
(E) Klein operates on day 1.

This question is answerable, in part, by reviewing the prior deductions.

1. Deductions 2 and 3 indicate that neither K nor F can operate on day 1. Eliminate answer choices A and E.
2. Deduction 4 indicates that L cannot operate on day 5. Eliminate answer choice C.

We have narrowed down our answer choices to just two answers. When you are down to just two answer choices, just try one of them. Let's try answer choice B (*Hong operates on day 6.*)

When you attempt this answer choice, you may actually realize that this is not possible by operation of Clue 4. If H were placed in slot 6, then H would not be operating on day 2. As such, Clue 4 is triggered, and K would be relegated to operate on day 6. Since H and K cannot both operate on day 6, this cannot be true.

(D) is the correct answer.

Game 3

Seven coworkers—Lynda, Minoo, Natasha, Penelope, Quinn, Ritu, and Sherry—are to be scheduled to perform at a company talent show. Each coworker performs one at a time, consecutively, in accordance with the following conditions:

Minoo is scheduled to perform either immediately before or immediately after Penelope.
Natasha is scheduled to perform either immediately before or immediately after Ritu.
Sherry is scheduled to perform at some time after Minoo but at some time before Ritu.
Quinn is not scheduled to perform second.

1. Which one of the following is an acceptable schedule of performances, listed from first to seventh?

   (A) Lynda, Quinn, Minoo, Penelope, Sherry, Natasha, Ritu
   (B) Minoo, Penelope, Sherry, Lynda, Quinn, Ritu, Natasha
   (C) Minoo, Sherry, Penelope, Lynda, Natasha, Ritu, Quinn
   (D) Quinn, Penelope, Minoo, Sherry, Natasha, Lynda, Ritu
   (E) Penelope, Minoo, Lynda, Natasha, Ritu, Sherry, Quinn

2. Which one of the following must be true?

   (A) Penelope is scheduled to perform at some time before Natasha.
   (B) Quinn is scheduled to perform at some time before Ritu.
   (C) Lynda is scheduled to perform at some time before Natasha.
   (D) Minoo is scheduled to perform at some time before Quinn.
   (E) Ritu is scheduled to perform at some time before Lynda.

3. If Ritu is scheduled to perform fourth, which one of the following must be true?

   (A) Minoo is scheduled to perform first.
   (B) Quinn is scheduled to perform sixth.
   (C) Sherry is scheduled to perform third.
   (D) Lynda is scheduled to perform sixth.
   (E) Penelope is scheduled to perform second.

4. If Lynda is scheduled to perform second, any of the following could be true EXCEPT: Which is false.

   (A) Penelope is scheduled to perform fourth.
   (B) Natasha is scheduled to perform sixth.
   (C) Ritu is scheduled to perform sixth.
   (D) Sherry is scheduled to perform fifth.
   (E) Quinn is scheduled to perform fifth.

5. Which one of the following CANNOT be the performances scheduled fifth, sixth, and seventh, respectively?

(A) Lynda, Natasha, Ritu
(B) Ritu, Natasha, Quinn
(C) Natasha, Lynda, Quinn
(D) Sherry, Quinn, Lynda
(E) Quinn, Ritu, Natasha

6. Which one of the following, if substituted for the condition that Quinn cannot be scheduled to perform second, would have the same effect in determining the order of the performances?

(A) If Minoo's performance is scheduled third, then Quinn's performance is scheduled first.
(B) Quinn's performance is scheduled either immediately before or immediately after Sherry's performance.
(C) Either Penelope or Minoo's performance is scheduled second.
(D) Penelope's performance is scheduled at some time before Quinn's performance.
(E) There must be at least two performances scheduled before Quinn's performance, unless Quinn's performance is scheduled first.

STEP 1 Visualize and draw the diagram.

What are you being asked to figure out? The key language "one at a time, consecutively" can help you answer this question. The game asks you to determine the schedule in which the coworkers perform at the talent show. The diagram is as follows:

1	2	3	4	5	6	7

STEP 2 List the components and ascertain the ratio and/or distribution.

Our components are L, M, N, P, Q, R, and S.

The ratio is one-to-one because each surgeon operates *"one at a time."*

STEP 3 Symbolize the clues.

Clue 1 Minoo is scheduled to perform either immediately before or immediately after Penelope.

Clue 2 Natasha is scheduled to perform either immediately before or immediately after Ritu.

Clue 3 Sherry is scheduled to perform at some time after Minoo but at some time before Ritu. M...S...R

Clue 4 Quinn is not scheduled to perform second. Q≠2

STEP 4 Make deductions.

Remember to determine what slots ban which components and focus on commonality.

1. Combine Clue 1 and Clue 3, since both clues have the component M in common.

$$\boxed{\overset{\frown}{M\quad P}}...S...R$$

2. Combine Clue 2 with Deduction 1 (above) because both have the component R in common.

3. S cannot be placed in slot 1 or 2 because at least two performances (M and P) are scheduled before S. Likewise, S cannot be placed in slots 6 and 7 because at least two performances (N and R) are scheduled after S.

4. Both M and P cannot be placed in any of slots 5, 6, or 7 because at least three performances (S, N, and R) are performed after M or P (regardless of whether P is immediately before or immediately after M). Likewise, both N and R cannot be placed in either slot 1, 2, or 3 because at least three performances (M, P, and S) are performed before N and R (regardless of whether N is immediately before or immediately after R).

~R ~S~N	~R ~S~N	~R ~N		~M ~P	~M ~S~P	~M ~S~P
1	2	3	4	5	6	7

From Clue 4:

~R ~S~N	~R~Q ~S~N	~R ~N		~M ~P	~M ~S~P	~M ~S~P
1	2	3	4	5	6	7

With these deductions, you are able to determine that the most restricted components are S (four restrictions) and M, N, P, and R (three restrictions each). Armed with these deductions, you are well prepared to attack the questions.

STEP 5 Tackle the questions

The order in which you answer the questions is important. Remember the optimal sequence: 1. catch-a-clue; 2. restricted; 3. unrestricted; 4. modifiers. For this particular game, that translates to the following order: 1, 3, 4, 2, 5, and then 6.

Answer Key

1. **B**   2. **A**   3. **C**   4. **E**   5. **D**   6. **E**

Answers

Question 1

This is a catch-a-clue question. Remember you only need to catch a rule, look for the answer choice that violates that rule, and then eliminate it.

> Which one of the following is an acceptable schedule of performances, listed from first to seventh?
>
> (A) Lynda, Quinn, Minoo, Penelope, Sherry, Natasha, Ritu
> (B) Minoo, Penelope, Sherry, Lynda, Quinn, Ritu, Natasha
> (C) Minoo, Sherry, Penelope, Lynda, Natasha, Ritu, Quinn
> (D) Quinn, Penelope, Minoo, Sherry, Natasha, Lynda, Ritu
> (E) Penelope, Minoo, Lynda, Natasha, Ritu, Sherry, Quinn

The first clue (*Minoo is scheduled to perform either immediately before or immediately after Penelope*) eliminates answer choice C. The second clue (*Natasha is scheduled to perform either immediately before or immediately after Ritu*) eliminates answer choice D. The third clue (*Sherry is scheduled to perform at some time after Minoo but at some time before Ritu*) eliminates answer choice E. The fourth clue (*Q is not scheduled to perform second*) eliminates answer choice A.

(B) is the correct answer.

Put the correct answer into the diagram.

~R ~S~N	~R~Q ~S~N	~R ~N		~M ~P	~M ~S~P	~M ~S~P
1	2	3	4	5	6	7
M	P	S	L	Q	R	N

Question 3

This is a restricted, "must-be-true" question in which four answers are true sometimes but not always, or are never true. The correct answer is always true.

If Ritu is scheduled to perform fourth, which one of the following must be true?

(A) Minoo is scheduled to perform first.
(B) Quinn is scheduled to perform sixth.
(C) Sherry is scheduled to perform third.
(D) Lynda is scheduled to perform sixth.
(E) Penelope is scheduled to perform second.

Begin by placing the additional restriction into the diagram.

~R ~S~N	~R~Q ~S~N	~R ~N		~M ~P	~M ~S~P	~M ~S~P
1	2	3	4	5	6	7
			R			

With component R in slot 4, Clue 3 is triggered. Clue 3 requires that N be placed in either slot 3 or 5. However, there are only three unoccupied slots before R, and, at minimum, M, P, and S must be scheduled before R. As such, N cannot be placed in slot 3 and must be placed in slot 5.

~R ~S~N	~R~Q ~S~N	~R ~N		~M ~P	~M ~S~P	~M ~S~P
1	2	3	4	5	6	7
			R	N		

Pivot to the most restricted element: S. By operation of Deduction 3, S is banned from slots 1, 2, 6, and 7. As such, the only slot available for S is slot 3. Also, by operation of Deduction 2, M and P must be placed in slots 1 and 2 interchangeably.

~R ~S~N	~R~Q ~S~N	~R ~N		~M ~P	~M ~S~P	~M ~S~P
1	2	3	4	5	6	7
M/P	P/M	S	R	N		

The remaining two components are L and Q. Look to the clues and deductions for guidance. Only Clue 4 governs, and this requirement has been met. Therefore, L and Q can each be placed in either slot 6 or 7 interchangeably.

~R ~S~N	~R~Q ~S~N	~R ~N		~M ~P	~M ~S~P	~M ~S~P
1	2	3	4	5	6	7
M/P	P/M	S	R	N	L/Q	Q/L

Answer choices A, B, D, and E, each can be true, but are not necessarily true. Answer choice C is always true.

(C) is the correct answer.

Question 4

This is a restricted, "could-be-true-EXCEPT" question. Four answers could be true at least once. These are the wrong answers. One of the answer choices is never true—this is the correct answer.

If Lynda is scheduled to perform second, any of the following could be true EXCEPT:

(A) Penelope is scheduled to perform fourth.
(B) Natasha is scheduled to perform sixth.
(C) Ritu is scheduled to perform sixth.
(D) Sherry is scheduled to perform fifth.
(E) Quinn is scheduled to perform fifth.

Begin by placing the additional restriction into the diagram.

~R ~S~N	~R~Q ~S~N	~R ~N		~M ~P	~M ~S~P	~M ~S~P
1	2	3	4	5	6	7
	L					

By operation of Clue 1, M and P require two consecutive slots, so they must be placed after L. Look to the clues and the deduction for guidance. Deduction 2 requires that S and the NR block be placed after the MP block. Therefore, a total of five components must be placed after L as follows: M and P are placed in slots 3 and 4 interchangeably; S is placed in slot 5; and N and R are placed in slots 6 and 7 interchangeably.

~R ~S~N	~R~Q ~S~N	~R ~N		~M ~P	~M ~S~P	~M ~S~P
1	2	3	4	5	6	7
	L	M/P	P/M	S	N/R	R/N

The only remaining component is Q, and the only available slot is slot 1. Place Q in slot 1.

~R ~S~N	~R~Q ~S~N	~R ~N		~M ~P	~M ~S~P	~M ~S~P
1	2	3	4	5	6	7
Q	L	M/P	P/M	S	N/R	R/N

Answer choices A, B, and C each can be true at least once. Answer choice D is always true. Answer choice E is never true.

(E) is the correct answer.

Question 2

This is an unrestricted, "must-be-true" question which means the correct answer here is always true. Wrong answers will either be true sometimes but not always, *or* they will be false.

> Which one of the following must be true?
>
> (A) Penelope is scheduled to perform at some time before Natasha.
> (B) Quinn is scheduled to perform at some time before Ritu.
> (C) Lynda is scheduled to perform at some time before Natasha.
> (D) Minoo is scheduled to perform at some time before Quinn.
> (E) Ritu is scheduled to perform at some time before Lynda.

You can answer this question by simply reviewing the deductions, specifically Deduction 2 (*Penelope must be scheduled to perform before Natasha*).

(A) is the correct answer.

Question 5

This unrestricted, "cannot-be-true" question is identical to a "must-be-false" question. Four answers could be true. These are the wrong answers. One answer choice can never be true. This is the correct answer.

> Which one of the following CANNOT be the performances scheduled fifth, sixth, and seventh, respectively?
>
> (A) Lynda, Natasha, Ritu
> (B) Ritu, Natasha, Quinn
> (C) Natasha, Lynda, Quinn
> (D) Sherry, Quinn, Lynda
> (E) Quinn, Ritu, Natasha

This question is answerable, in part, by reviewing your previous work. Remember, each of the possibilities you worked out on the restricted questions is in compliance with all of the clues and can be relied upon to answer the unrestricted questions. Let's take a look at all of your prior work.

	~R ~S~N	~R~Q ~S~N	~R ~N		~M ~P	~M ~S~P	~M ~S~P
	1	2	3	4	5	6	7
#1	M	P	S	L	Q	R	N
#3	M/P	P/M	S	R	N	L/Q	Q/L
#4	Q	L	M/P	P/M	S	N/R	R/N

Answer choice C (*Natasha, Lynda, Quinn*) can be true as shown in the explanation to question 3, so this is not the correct answer. Answer choice E (*Quinn, Ritu, Natasha*) can be true as shown in the explanation of question 1, so neither is this the correct answer. Your prior work does not show that any of the remaining answer choices (A, B, D) can be true, so none of these can be eliminated just yet.

The answers are now narrowed down to three choices: either A, B, or D. You can certainly begin to test the remaining answer choices, but before you do, let's see if anything can be gleaned from prior deductions and/or from the most restricted components. From Deduction 2, it's clear that the most restricted component (S) must be followed by N and R (but not necessarily immediately). Now look at your remaining answer choices. Answer choice D indicates S for slot 5. In this case, N and R would have to occupy slots 6 and 7 interchangeably. Since N and R do not both follow S, answer choice D cannot represent the fifth, sixth, and seventh performances.

(D) is the correct answer.

Question 6

This is clearly a modifier question because it requires the substitution of one rule for another that has the same effect. The correct response is the substituting clue that is not any more limiting nor any less limiting than the original clue.

Which one of the following, if substituted for the condition that Quinn cannot be scheduled to perform second, would have the same effect in determining the order of the performances?

(A) If Minoo's performance is scheduled third, then Quinn's performance is scheduled first.
(B) Quinn's performance is scheduled either immediately before or immediately after Sherry's performance.
(C) Either Penelope or Minoo's performance is scheduled second.
(D) Penelope's performance is scheduled at some time before Quinn's performance.
(E) There must be at least two performances scheduled before Quinn's performance, unless Quinn's performance is scheduled first.

Use your previous work to test each individual answer choice. If you discover the proposed clue is violated in any of the previous work, that would indicate that the clue is more limiting than the original clue, and you should get rid of that answer choice. Let's look at the previous work and then test each individual answer choice.

	~R ~S~N	~R~Q ~S~N	~R ~N		~M ~P	~M ~S~P	~M ~S~P
	1	2	3	4	5	6	7
#1	M	P	S	L	Q	R	N
#3	M/P	P/M	S	R	N	L/Q	Q/L
#4	Q	L	M/P	P/M	S	N/R	R/N

Answer choice A—This clue is not violated by any of the workouts. Indeed, in the fourth workout if M is placed in slot 3, Q will be relegated to slot 1. However, in that same workout, you could have just as easily placed M in slot 4, and Q would have again been relegated to slot 1. This condition does not include all of the possibilities that would ban Q from slot 2; therefore, it is less limiting than the original clue. Cross it out.

Answer choice B—This clue is not satisfied in any of the three prior workouts and, therefore, is more limiting than the original clue. Cross it out.

Answer choice C— At first glance, this condition might seem to be a suitable replacement for the original clue. After all, if either Penelope or Minoo must be second, it would stand to reason that that Quinn is not second. However, it is not a suitable replacement. While this condition holds true in the workouts for questions 1 and 3, it is violated in the explanation of question 4 and, therefore, is more limiting than the original clue. Cross it out.

Answer choice D—This condition holds true for the workouts of questions 1 and 3; however, it is violated in the workout of question 4 and, therefore, is more limiting than the original rule. Cross it out.

Answer choice E—This substituted rule indicates that if Q is not first, then there must be at least two slots ahead of Q. In other words, Q must be third, fourth, fifth, sixth, or seventh—definitely *not* second. This clue is neither more nor less limiting.

(E) is the correct answer.

NOT ONE-TO-ONE RATIO/DISTRIBUTION

The sample games in the previous section each involved an equal number of components and slots. Although it's possible to encounter a one-to-one ratio logic game that also qualifies as a killer game, one-to-one ratio games are typically quite straightforward. Now let's move on to not-one-to-one ratio games. These might give the impression of offering a higher degree of difficulty, but that's not necessarily so. What is true, however, is that an additional layer of complexity is involved.

Take a look at the setup from Game 1 in the upcoming not-one-to-one ratio game:

> On each of six consecutive days—day 1 through day 6—a restaurant owner will choose exactly one dish for her daily specials menu. She must choose from among exactly four dishes—Fusilli, Gnocchi, Linguine, and Penne.

The key language is *on each of six consecutive days; exactly one dish is chosen;* and *from among exactly four dishes.* The game contains six days (one dish each day) but only four dishes from which to choose. Moreover, there is no requirement that each dish be chosen at least once, thereby creating a further complication to the solution of the game. No need to worry though. In the following pages you'll learn how the rules of this game do a good job of reducing the possibilities. You'll see why not-one-to-one ratio games can often (though not always) be classified as doable rather than killer.

Let's compare Game 1 and Game 2. Take a close look at the backdrop and the first clue for Game 2.

> During the course of five consecutive days—Monday through Friday—Rose receives exactly one text message from each of seven friends: J, K, M, N, P, Q, and R. The messages are received in accordance with the following conditions:
>
> Two of the text messages were received on Monday, two were received on Wednesday, and no other text message was received on the same day as any other text message.

The key language here is "*over the course of five consecutive days*" and "*exactly one text message from each of seven friends is received.*" Seven text messages are received from seven people—one text message per person. As such, the number of slots is equal to the number of components. This is a one-to-one ratio. However, the first clue alerts you to a not-one-to-one distribution. The clue assigns two messages to Monday and two to Wednesday. The number of slots is not equal to the number of diagram headings—the headings being *Monday* through *Friday*. Notice the distribution isn't one-to-one.

Let's try both these games.

Game 1

On each of six consecutive days—day 1 through day 6—a restaurant owner will choose exactly one dish for her daily specials menu. She must choose from among exactly four dishes—Fusilli, Gnocchi, Linguine, and Penne. Her choices must be in accordance with the following conditions:

No dish is chosen on two consecutive days.

She chooses the same dish on day 2 as she chooses on day 4.

Fusilli is chosen on exactly two days but not on day 1.

Gnocchi cannot be chosen immediately after Linguine.

She chooses Linguine on either day 1 or day 2.

1. Which one of the following could be the order in which the dishes are chosen, from day 1 through day 6?

   (A) Gnocchi, Fusilli, Gnocchi, Fusilli, Penne, Linguine
   (B) Fusilli, Linguine, Gnocchi, Linguine, Penne, Fusilli
   (C) Linguine, Fusilli, Penne, Linguine, Penne, Fusilli
   (D) Penne, Linguine, Fusilli, Linguine, Fusilli, Penne
   (E) Linguine, Fusilli, Gnocchi, Fusilli, Penne, Penne

2. If the restaurant owner chooses Gnocchi on day 1, which one of the following must be true?

   (A) Fusilli is chosen on day 6.
   (B) Penne is chosen on day 5.
   (C) Fusilli is chosen on day 3.
   (D) Gnocchi is not chosen on day 6.
   (E) Linguine is not chosen on day 6.

3. If the restaurant owner chooses Penne on day 3, then which one of the following could be true?

   (A) Gnocchi is chosen on day 1.
   (B) Gnocchi is chosen on day 6.
   (C) Penne is chosen on day 2.
   (D) Fusilli is chosen on day 5.
   (E) Penne is chosen on day 1.

4. If the restaurant owner chooses Linguine on day 5, which one of the following CANNOT be true?

   (A) Gnocchi and Penne are chosen on consecutive days.
   (B) Linguine and Penne are chosen on consecutive days.
   (C) Fusilli and Penne are chosen on consecutive days.
   (D) Linguine and Fusilli are chosen on consecutive days.
   (E) Fusilli and Gnocchi are chosen on consecutive days.

5. Each of the following could be a pair of dishes that are chosen on day 1 and day 5, respectively, EXCEPT:

   (A) Penne and Gnocchi
   (B) Linguine and Gnocchi
   (C) Penne and Fusilli
   (D) Gnocchi and Fusilli
   (E) Linguine and Penne

STEP 1 Visualize and draw the diagram.

What are you being asked to figure out? The key language (*each of six consecutive days—day 1 through day 6*) can help you answer this question. The game asks that you determine the order in which the dishes are chosen as daily specials. The diagram is as follows:

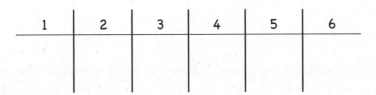

STEP 2 List the components and ascertain the ratio and/or distribution.

The components are F, G, L, and P.

You have *six* days and *four* choices; the ratio is *not-one-to-one*. The components must be utilized more than once. Also, notice the absence of any language indicating that each dish be chosen at least once. It's possible that some dishes will not be chosen at all.

STEP 3 Symbolize the clues.

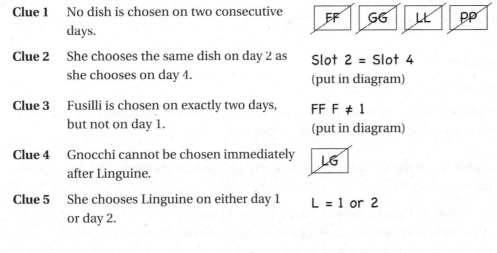

Clue 1	No dish is chosen on two consecutive days.	FF GG LL PP (all crossed out)
Clue 2	She chooses the same dish on day 2 as she chooses on day 4.	Slot 2 = Slot 4 (put in diagram)
Clue 3	Fusilli is chosen on exactly two days, but not on day 1.	FF F ≠ 1 (put in diagram)
Clue 4	Gnocchi cannot be chosen immediately after Linguine.	LG (crossed out)
Clue 5	She chooses Linguine on either day 1 or day 2.	L = 1 or 2

STEP 4 Make deductions.

Remember to determine what slots ban which components and focus on commonality.

Since the actual frequency of each dish is unknown, little can be deduced from the clues. However, you can deduce that G cannot be in placed onto either day 2 or day 4. How? If G were placed in day 2, then by operation of Clue 5, L must be placed in day 1 which would amount to a violation of Clue 4.

Sometimes clues can be placed directly into the diagram—here you can insert clues 2 and 4.

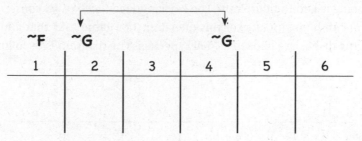

Note that the most restricted component is F. Although G may appear to be more restricted because it's banned from two slots, it's actually less restricted because there is some doubt as to whether G needs to be included at all. F, on the other hand, must be placed into exactly two slots. Slots 1, 2, and 4 are each important to the solution of game.

STEP 5 Tackle the question.

The order in which you answer the questions is important. Remember the optimal sequence: 1. catch-a-clue; 2. restricted; 3. unrestricted; 4. modifiers. For this particular game, that translates to the following order: 1, 2, 3, 4, and then 5.

Answer Key

1. **D**   2. **C**   3. **B**   4. **A**   5. **A**

Answers

Question 1

This is a catch-a-clue question. Remember you need only to catch a clue, look for the answer choice that violates that clue, and then eliminate it.

> Which one of the following could be the order in which the dishes are chosen, from day 1 through day 6?
>
> (A) Gnocchi, Fusilli, Gnocchi, Fusilli, Penne, Linguine
> (B) Fusilli, Linguine, Gnocchi, Linguine, Penne, Fusilli
> (C) Linguine, Fusilli, Penne, Linguine, Penne, Fusilli
> (D) Penne, Linguine, Fusilli, Linguine, Fusilli, Penne
> (E) Linguine, Fusilli, Gnocchi, Fusilli, Penne, Penne

The first clue (*No dish is chosen on two consecutive days*) eliminates answer choice E. The second clue (*She chooses the same dish on the day 2 as she does on day 4*) eliminates answer choice C. The third clue (*Fusilli is chosen on exactly two days, but not on day 1*) eliminates answer choice B. The fourth clue (*Gnocchi cannot be chosen immediately after Linguine*) eliminates answer choice B again, but it doesn't eliminate any additional answer choices. The fifth clue (*She chooses Linguine on either day 1 or day 2*) eliminates answer choice A.

(D) is the correct answer.

Put the correct answer into the diagram.

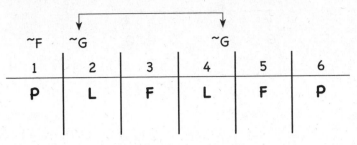

	~F	~G		~G		
	1	2	3	4	5	6
	P	L	F	L	F	P

Question 2

In this type of restricted, "must-be-true" question, four answers are true sometimes but not always, or they are never true. These four are the wrong answers. The correct answer is always true.

If the restaurant owner chooses Gnocchi on day 1, which one of the following must be true?

(A) Fusilli is chosen on day 6.
(B) Penne is chosen on day 5.
(C) Fusilli is chosen on day 3.
(D) Gnocchi is not chosen on day 6.
(E) Linguine is not chosen on day 6.

Begin by placing the additional restriction into the diagram.

	~F	~G		~G		
	1	2	3	4	5	6
	G					

By operation of Clue 5, L must be placed in slot 2.

	~F	~G		~G		
	1	2	3	4	5	6
	G	L				

With component L in slot 2, Clue 2 is triggered. Accordingly, L is placed in slot 4.

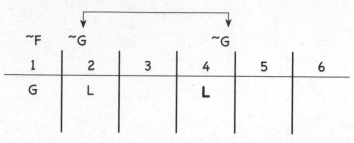

By operation of Clues 3 and 1, the two Fs cannot occupy both slots 5 and 6. Therefore, one of the Fs must occupy slot 3 and the remaining F will go in either slot 5 or 6.

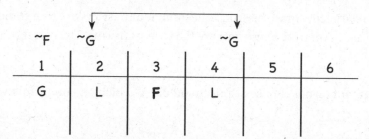

Answer choices A, B, D, and E can each be true at least once, but they are not always true.

(C) is the correct answer.

Question 3

This is a restricted, "could-be-true" question. Therefore, four answers are never true. These are the wrong answers. The correct answer is true at least once.

> If the restaurant owner chooses Penne on day 3, then which one of the following could be true?
>
> (A) Gnocchi is chosen on day 1.
> (B) Gnocchi is chosen on day 6.
> (C) Penne is chosen on day 2.
> (D) Fusilli is chosen on day 5.
> (E) Penne is chosen on day 1.

Place the additional restriction into the diagram.

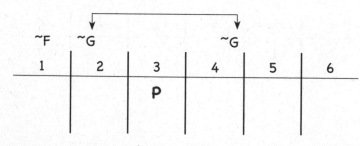

Pivot to the most restricted component: F. By operation of Clue 3, F must occupy exactly two slots. The remaining available slots are 2, 4, 5, and 6. By operation of Clue 2, F is in either slots

2 and 4 *or* in slots 5 and 6. Clue 1 makes it clear that F cannot occupy slots 5 and 6. Therefore, F occupies slots 2 and 4.

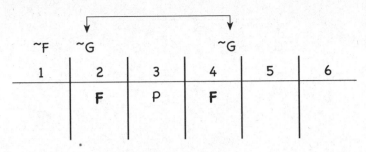

By operation of Clue 5, L must be placed in slot 1.

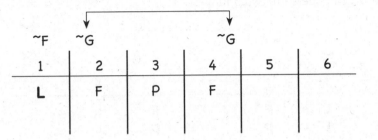

Stop! You now have enough information to answer the question. Answer choices A, C, D, and E are never true. Remember to check your answers after each big deduction.

(B) is the correct answer.

Question 4

This restricted, "cannot-be-true" question is identical to a "must-be-false" question. Four answers could be true. These are the wrong answers. One answer choice can never be true. This is the correct answer.

> If the restaurant owner chooses Linguine on day 5, which one of the following CANNOT be true?
>
> (A) Gnocchi and Penne are chosen on consecutive days.
> (B) Linguine and Penne are chosen on consecutive days.
> (C) Fusilli and Penne are chosen on consecutive days.
> (D) Linguine and Fusilli are chosen on consecutive days.
> (E) Fusilli and Gnocchi are chosen on consecutive days.

Place the additional restriction into the diagram.

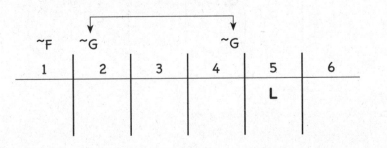

By operation of Clue 1, L cannot be placed in slot 4. By operation of Clue 2, L cannot be placed in slot 2. By operation of Clue 5, L must be placed in slot 1.

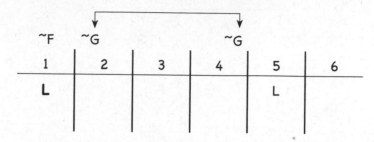

Deduction 1 proved that G can't be placed in slots 2 or 4; therefore, those slots must be occupied by either F or P. There are two options:

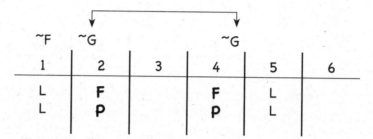

Let's think through the top option first. By operation of Clue 4, G cannot be placed in slot 6. By operation of Clue 1, L cannot be placed in slot 6. By operation of Clue 3, F cannot be placed in slot 6 because both Fs have been placed. Therefore, P is the only remaining component available. P must be placed in slot 6.

	~F	~G		~G		
	1	2	3	4	5	6
	L	F		F	L	P
	L	P		P	L	

The remaining slot (3) can be occupied by any of the remaining components except F.

	~F	~G		~G		
	1	2	3	4	5	6
	L	F	G/L/P	F	L	P
	L	P		P	L	

Now, let's work out the bottom option. By operation of Clue 3 (FF), the remaining two slots (3 and 5) must be occupied by two Fs.

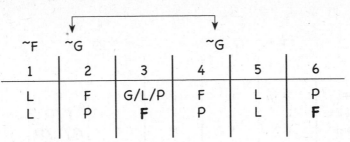

	~F	~G		~G		
	1	2	3	4	5	6
	L	F	G/L/P	F	L	P
	L	P	**F**	P	L	**F**

The dishes in answer choices B, C, D, and E can each be chosen on consecutive days.

(A) is the correct answer.

Question 5

This unrestricted, "could-be-true," EXCEPT question, is identical to a "must-be-false" question. Four answers could be true at least once. These are the wrong answers. One answer choice can never be true. This is the correct answer.

> Each of the following could be a pair of dishes that are chosen on day 1 and day 5, respectively, EXCEPT:
>
> (A) Penne and Gnocchi
> (B) Linguine and Gnocchi
> (C) Penne and Fusilli
> (D) Gnocchi and Fusilli
> (E) Linguine and Penne

Review the clues, deductions, and diagram history when answering unrestricted questions. There is very little in the way of clues and deductions to help you with this one. Take a look at all your work so far:

	~F	~G		~G		
	1	2	3	4	5	6
#1	P	L	F	L	F	P
#2	G	L	F	L		
#3	L	F	P	F		
#4a	L	F	G/L/P	F	L	P
#4b	L	P	F	P	L	F

Answer choice C (Penne and Fusilli) is the only one that can be eliminated with certainty because for questions 2 and 3, the possible day 5 dishes were not identified. Rather than test all three answer choices, let's take a moment to complete day 5 for questions 2 and 3.

Let's start with question 2. By operation of Clue 1, L cannot occupy slot 5. Likewise, by operation of Clue 5, G cannot occupy slot 5. Therefore, F and P are the only available components that can occupy slot 5.

On to question 3. By operation of Clue 1, F cannot occupy slot 5. Neither the clues nor the deductions place any additional restrictions on slot 5. Therefore, G, L, or P can occupy slot 5.

	~F	~G			~G	
	1	2	3	4	5	6
#1	P	L	F	L	F	P
#2	G	L	F	L	F/P	
#3	L	F	P	F	G/L/P	
#4a	L	F	G/L/P	F	L	P
#4b	L	P	F	P	L	F

According to the deductions for question 2, the dishes in answer choice D can each be seen on days 1 and 5, respectively. According to your work on question 3, the dishes in answer choices B and E can each be seen on days 1 and 5, respectively.

(A) is the correct answer.

Game 2

Directions: During the course of five consecutive days—Monday through Friday—Rose receives exactly one text message from each of seven friends: J, K, M, N, P, Q, and R. The messages are received in accordance with the following conditions:

Two of the text messages were received on Monday, two were received on Wednesday, and no other text message was received on the same day as any other text message.

M's text message was received on an earlier day than P's text message, but on a later day than K's text message.

At least three text messages were received before N's text message.

Q's text message was received on neither Monday nor Friday.

1. Which one of the following could be an accurate list of the text messages received on Tuesday, Wednesday, and Thursday, respectively?

   (A) Tues: P; Wed: J, R; Thurs: N
   (B) Tues: N; Wed: M, R; Thurs: Q
   (C) Tues: J; Wed: M, N; Thurs: P
   (D) Tues: M; Wed: Q; Thurs: N, P
   (E) Tues: K; Wed: M, Q; Thurs: N

2. Which one of the following is a pair of people whose text messages CANNOT both be received on Wednesday?

   (A) K and R
   (B) P and R
   (C) M and Q
   (D) K and N
   (E) M and N

3. If Q's text message was received on an earlier day than K's text message, then each of the following must be true EXCEPT:

   (A) J's text message was received on an earlier day than P's text message.
   (B) N's text message was received on an earlier day than M's text message.
   (C) R's text message was received on an earlier day than N's text message.
   (D) N's text message was received on an earlier day than Q's text message.
   (E) J's text message was received on an earlier day than N's text message.

4. If K's text message was the only text message received on that day, then which one of the following must be true?

   (A) Q's text message was received on Wednesday.
   (B) P's text message was received on Thursday.
   (C) N's text message was received on Friday.
   (D) M's text message was received on Wednesday.
   (E) J's text message was received on Monday.

5. If J's text message and M's text message were received on the same day, then each of the following must be true EXCEPT:

   (A) R's text message was received on Monday.
   (B) K's text message was received on Monday.
   (C) N's text message was received on Friday.
   (D) Q's text message was received on Tuesday.
   (E) M's text message was received on Wednesday.

STEP 1 Visualize and draw the diagram.

What are you being asked to figure out? The key language in this question (*during a course of five consecutive days*) reveals your answer. The game is asking you to determine the order in which the text messages are received. The diagram is as follows:

Mon	Tue	Wed	Thurs	Fri

STEP 2 List the components and ascertain the ratio and/or distribution.

The components are J, K, M, N, P, Q, and R.

The ratio is one-to-one because "*exactly one*" text message is received from each friend. The distribution, however, is not one-to-one because two of the text messages are received on Monday and two are received on Wednesday. Update the diagram as follows:

Mon	Tue	Wed	Thurs	Fri
_ _	_	_ _	_	_

STEP 3 Symbolize the clues.

Clue 1	Two of the text messages were received on Monday, two were received on Wednesday. No other text message was received on the same day as any other text message.	(put in diagram)
Clue 2	M's text message was received on an earlier day than P's text message, but on a later day than K's text message.	K...M...P
Clue 3	At least three text messages were received before N's text message.	_ _ _ ...N
Clue 4	Q's text message was received on neither Monday nor Friday.	Q ≠ Mon or Fri

STEP 4 Make deductions.

Remember to determine what slots ban which components and focus on commonality.

1. Much can be deduced from Clue 1.

   - K is banned from Thursday and Friday because at least two text messages (M and P) are received after K.

- The text message from M cannot be received on Monday because at least the text message from K is received on an earlier day than M. Likewise, M cannot be received on Friday because at least the text message from P is received the day after M.
- The text message from P cannot be received on either Monday or Tuesday because at least two text messages (received on different days) were received before the text message from P. Update the diagram as follows:

~M~P	~P		~K	~K~M
Mon	Tue	Wed	Thurs	Fri
— —	—	— —	—	—

2. From Clue 2, you can deduce that the text message from N cannot be received on either Monday or Tuesday. At minimum, the two text messages received on Monday and the one text message on Tuesday must be received before N.

~N	~N			
~M~P	~P		~K	~K~M
Mon	Tue	Wed	Thurs	Fri
— —	—	— —	—	—

Clue 4 can be placed directly into the diagram.

~N~Q	~N			~Q
~M~P	~P		~K	~K~M
Mon	Tue	Wed	Thurs	Fri
— —	—	— —	—	—

3. Take note of the most restricted components: K, M, N, P, and Q. Each has two restrictions. More importantly, note that the most restricted day is Monday: only J, K, and R can be received on Monday.

(STEP 5) Tackle the Questions

The order in which you answer the questions is important. Remember the optimal sequence: 1. catch-a-clue; 2. restricted; 3. unrestricted; 4. modifiers. For this particular game, that translates to the following order: 1, 3, 4, 5, 2.

Answer Key

Answers

Question 1

This is a catch-a-clue question. Remember you need only to catch a rule, look for the answer choice that violates that rule, and then eliminate it.

> Which one of the following could be an accurate list of the text messages received on Tuesday, Wednesday, and Thursday, respectively?
>
> (A) Tues: P; Wed: J, R; Thurs: N
> (B) Tues: N; Wed: M, R; Thurs: Q
> (C) Tues: J; Wed: M, N; Thurs: P
> (D) Tues: M; Wed: Q; Thurs: N, P
> (E) Tues: K; Wed: M, Q; Thurs: N

Notice that these are only partial lists of the text messages received. In situations like this, it's sometimes necessary to determine (by using the clues) the remainder of the list. For example, here you may need to figure out what components would be relegated to Monday and Friday (the missing part of the list).

The first clue (*Two of the text messages were received on Monday, two were received on Wednesday, and no other text message was received on the same day as any other text message*) eliminates answer choice D. The second clue (*M's text message was received on an earlier day than P's text message, but on a later day than K's text message*) eliminates answer choice A because with P's text message received on Tuesday, K and M's text messages are both received on Monday. The third clue (*At least three text messages were received before N's text message*) eliminates answer choice B because with N's text message received on Tuesday, there are only two text messages (received on Monday) before N. The fourth clue (*Q's text message was received on neither Monday nor Friday*) eliminates answer choice C because Q's text is not seen on Tuesday, Wednesday, or Thursday. Therefore, it must be placed in either Monday or Friday. Notice that the elimination of answer choices via the second, third, and fourth clues required determining the remainder of the list.

(E) is the correct answer.

Put the correct answer into the diagram.

~N~Q	~N			~Q
~M~P	~P		~K	~K~M
Mon	Tue	Wed	Thurs	Fri
J R	K	M Q	N	P

Note that the remaining slots have been filled in as directed by the clues.

Question 3

This is a restricted, "must-be-true," EXCEPT question. Here, four answers are always true, and these are the wrong choices. One answer is sometimes but not always true, or it is never true. This one is the correct choice.

> If Q's text message was received on an earlier day than K's text message, then each of the following must be true EXCEPT:
>
> (A) J's text message was received on an earlier day than P's text message.
> (B) N's text message was received on an earlier day than M's text message.
> (C) R's text message was received on an earlier day than N's text message.
> (D) N's text message was received on an earlier day than Q's text message.
> (E) J's text message was received on an earlier day than N's text message.

This question places the additional restriction that Q's text message was received on an earlier day than K's text message. As you look for commonality, Clue 1 is triggered. Let's link this clue with the new restriction:

$$Q...K...M...P$$

Since Q now has at least three text messages received after it (on separate days), Q's text message cannot be received on Wednesday, Thursday, or Friday.

By operation of Clue 4, Q's text message cannot be received on Monday. Therefore, Q's text message must be received on Tuesday; and K, M, and P's messages must be received on Wednesday, Thursday, and Friday, respectively.

~N~Q ~M~P	~N ~P		~K	~Q ~K~M
Mon	Tue	Wed	Thurs	Fri
_ _	Q	K _	M	P

Now turn your attention to the most restricted slot: Monday. Deduction 3 proves that because K's text message is received on Wednesday, the only remaining text messages possible for Monday are J and R's.

~N~Q ~M~P	~N ~P		~K	~Q ~K~M
Mon	Tue	Wed	Thurs	Fri
J R	Q	K _	M	P

The last text message (N) is placed in the final slot on Wednesday.

	~N~Q ~M~P	~N ~P			~K	~Q ~K~M
	Mon	Tue	Wed	Thurs	Fri
	J R	Q	K **N**	M	P

Answer choices A, B, C, and E are always true; these answer choices can be eliminated. Answer choice D is never true.

(D) is the correct answer.

Question 4

This is a restricted, "must-be-true" question, meaning four answers are true sometimes but not always, or they are never true. The correct answer is always true.

> If K's text message was the only text message received on that day, then which one of the following must be true?

(A) Q's text message was received on Wednesday.
(B) P's text message was received on Thursday.
(C) N's text message was received on Friday.
(D) M's text message was received on Wednesday.
(E) J's text message was received on Monday.

Deduction 1 shows that K's text message cannot be received on either Thursday or Friday. Therefore, Tuesday is the only remaining day where there is just one text message received. You must place K on Tuesday.

~N~Q ~M~P	~N ~P			~K	~Q ~K~M
Mon	Tue	Wed	Thurs	Fri
_ _	**K**	_ _	_	_

Pivot to the most restricted slot: Monday. By operation of Deduction 3, since K's text message is received on Tuesday, the only remaining text messages that can be received on Monday are J and R.

~N~Q ~M~P	~N ~P			~Q ~K~M
Mon	Tue	Wed	Thurs	Fri
J R	K	– –	–	–

Stop! You now know enough to answer the question.

(E) is the correct answer.

Question 5

This restricted, "must-be-true," EXCEPT question is identical to a "could-be-false" question. Four answers must be true always. These are the wrong answers. One answer choice is not always true. This is the correct answer.

If J's text message and M's text message were received on the same day, then each of the following must be true EXCEPT:

(A) R's text message was received on Monday.
(B) K's text message was received on Monday.
(C) N's text message was received on Friday.
(D) Q's text message was received on Tuesday.
(E) M's text message was received on Wednesday.

There are only two days that allow two text messages to be received on the same day: Monday and Wednesday. By operation of Deduction 1, M's text message cannot be received on Monday. As such, J and M's text messages must be received on Wednesday.

~N~Q ~M~P	~N ~P			~Q ~K~M
Mon	Tue	Wed	Thurs	Fri
– –	–	J M	–	–

Deduction 3 shows that with J's text message received on Wednesday, the only two text messages available to be received on Monday are K and R's. Place both K and R in Monday's slot.

~N~Q ~M~P	~N ~P			~Q ~K~M
Mon	Tue	Wed	Thurs	Fri
K R	–	J M	–	–

By operation of Deduction 2, N's text message cannot be received on Tuesday. Likewise, by operation of Deduction 1, P's text message cannot be received on Tuesday. Therefore, Q's text message must be received on Tuesday.

~N~Q ~M~P	~N ~P		~K	~Q ~K~M
Mon	Tue	Wed	Thurs	Fri
K R	**Q**	J M	_	_

Having no additional restrictions, the remaining text messages (P and N) can be received on Thursday or Friday, interchangeably.

~N~Q ~M~P	~N ~P		~K	~Q ~K~M
Mon	Tue	Wed	Thurs	Fri
K R	Q	J M	**P/N**	**N/P**

Answer choices A, B, D, and E are always true, so they can be eliminated. Answer choice C is true sometimes, but not always.

(C) is the correct answer.

Question 2

This is an unrestricted, "cannot-be-true" question. As such, four answers are sometimes or always true. These are the wrong choices. The correct answer is never true.

> Which one of the following is a pair of people whose text messages CANNOT both be received on Wednesday?
>
> (A) K and R
> (B) P and R
> (C) M and Q
> (D) K and N
> (E) M and N

This problem can be partially solved by reviewing the diagram history, and can be solved completely by reviewing the prior deductions. Remember, the primary reason for delaying answering unrestricted questions until after you've completed the restricted questions is to allow you to readily eliminate answer choices and/or to discover the answer outright by simply referring to the completed diagram.

In this case, two answers can be eliminated by reviewing the diagram history. Consider the diagram below:

	Mon	Tue	Wed	Thurs	Fri
#1	J R	K	M Q	N	P
#3	J R	Q	K N	M	P
#5	K R	Q	J M	P/N	N/P

Question 1 proved that M/Q is a possible pair, so answer choice C can be eliminated. Question 3 proved that K/N is a possible pair, so answer choice D is out. Without Deduction 3, you would have needed to test the remaining answer choices. However, Deduction 3 makes it clear that only J, K, and R can be received on Monday and this information is enormously helpful. K and R cannot both be placed on Wednesday, since to do so would render just one text message (J) available for Monday.

(A) is the correct answer.

CHAIN GAME

The chain game is another common sequential game. Although it can be solved using the five-step approach, it is one of the few games that can be solved without it. An alternate shortcut approach can be used instead. While difficult to understand at first, it's important to master the shortcut; chain games are a favorite of LSAT designers and having this approach in your arsenal will ultimately translate to major time savings for you.

The chain game can be distinguished from an ordinary sequence game by its specific rules. Chain game rules provide the relative position of each component to at least one other component. Common wording embedded in the chain game conditions are *before/after, low/high,* and *more than/less than.* For example, the upcoming sample chain game includes the following language:

> Both R and P are planted **before** Q.
> R is planted **before** Z but **after** S.
> W is planted **before** R.
> T is planted **after** Z.
> U is planted **before** Z.

Notice *before* and *after* in all of the conditions. All components have a relationship to another component. Compare this to a traditional sequence game setup:

> J is exactly two days before K.
> H is neither first nor seventh.
> L is either fourth or fifth.

Note that in a traditional sequence game, there are rules that don't disclose the relationship of one component to another but rather the relationship of the component to the diagram. A traditional sequence game may include rules where some components relate to other components, but they will also feature other relationships. Chain games *only* have rules that contain components related to one another.

Once you have identified a game as a chain game, you still need to represent the rules visually. Each rule is represented as a "chain."

Game 1

A landscaper is planting exactly eight different flowers—P, Q, R, S, T, U, W, and Z. Each flower is planted exactly once, and no two flowers are planted at the same time. The flowers are planted in accordance with the following conditions:

Both R and P are planted before Q.

R is planted before Z but after S.

W is planted before R.

T is planted after Z.

U is planted before Z.

1. Which one of the following could be the order, from first to last, in which the flowers were planted?

   (A) S, W, P, R, T, U, Z, Q
   (B) U, P, W, S, R, Z, Q, T
   (C) W, P, S, R, Z, Q, U, T
   (D) S, U, P, R, Q, W, Z, T
   (E) U, W, P, S, Q, R, Z, T

2. Which one of the following must be true?

   (A) No more than two flowers are planted before R.
   (B) No more than four flowers are planted before Q.
   (C) At least one flower is planted before U.
   (D) At least two flowers are planted after Z.
   (E) At least four flowers are planted after S.

3. If R is the fifth flower planted, then each of the following could be true EXCEPT:

   (A) Z is planted sixth.
   (B) T is planted eighth.
   (C) S is planted third.
   (D) Q is planted fourth.
   (E) W is planted third.

4. If P is planted later than Z, then which one of the following must be false?

   (A) Q is planted eighth.
   (B) Z is planted seventh.
   (C) T is planted sixth.
   (D) R is planted earlier than P.
   (E) T is planted later than Q.

5. Each of the following could be the third flower planted EXCEPT:

   (A) Q
   (B) U
   (C) R
   (D) W
   (E) S

6. If Q is the fifth flower planted, then which one of the following must be true?

   (A) U is planted later than R.
   (B) S is planted earlier than P.
   (C) W is planted later than U.
   (D) P is planted later than R.
   (E) Z is planted earlier than Q.

STEP 1 Symbolize the clues.

When symbolizing the game clues or conditions, be sure to place the *before* components on the left.

Both R and P are planted **before** Q.	R....Q and P....Q
R is planted **before** Z but **after** S.	S....R....Z
W is planted **before** R.	W....R
T is planted **after** Z.	Z....T
U is planted **before** Z.	U....Z

STEP 2 Connect the chains.

Connect the individual chains to create the longest possible chain of components on a horizontal line. In this game, this would involve connecting S....R....Z and Z....T. The resulting diagram is your baseline.

$$S \text{ ----------- } R \text{ ----------- } Z \text{ ----------- } T$$

STEP 3 Attach the remaining clues.

Now each of the remaining clues must be incorporated into the baseline. In this example, when you attach W....R to the chain, the result is:

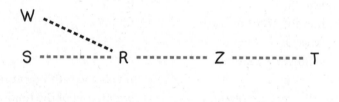

Attaching U....Z to the diagram results in this additional chain:

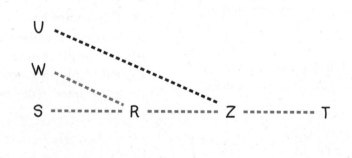

Attach R....Q to the diagram, and the result is:

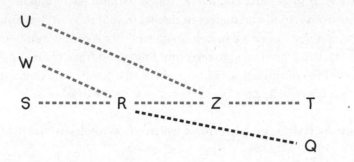

Attach P....Q to the diagram, and the result is:

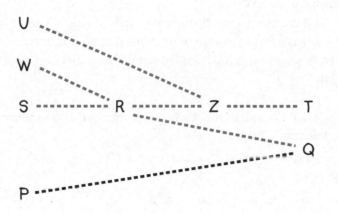

Now that all the chains have been joined together, the key to answering the chain game questions successfully lies in your ability to read this diagram accurately and make all the necessary inferences quickly. In interpreting the chain, you need to remember two rules:

RULE 1 The relative position of two components can only be ascertained when those two components are connected *horizontally* by a pathway, without a zigzag or a switch in direction.

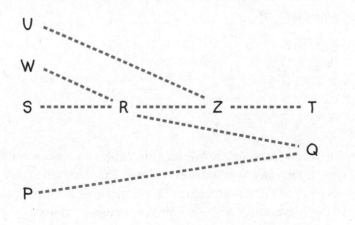

For example, applying this rule here would enable you to deduce that W must come before Z. You can take your finger and connect Z with W without switching directions. You would take your finger from Z to R, and then continue on from R to W in the same direction. Rule 1 also tells you that it's not possible to determine whether Z comes before or after Q. In order to connect Z to Q, you would need to take your finger and trace from Z to R, and then *switch directions* in order to continue onward to Q. Since a switch in direction happens, you immediately know that it's equally possible for Q to come *before* **or** *after* Z.

RULE 2 Identify the floaters and determine which components can be first and which can be last.

"Floaters" are simply any components not on the original baseline. Those components not preceded by a chain to another element can be first, and those not followed by a chain to another component can be last.

Application of Rule 2 enables you to deduce that U, W, S, and P can all be the first flowers planted because there are no preceding components that are connected to them. Also, T and Q are the only two flowers that can be planted last because there are no succeeding components connected to T or Q.

(STEP 4) Now let's tackle the questions. Refer to the chain diagram above while answering each question in the order given.

Answer Key

1. **B**   2. **E**   3. **D**   4. **B**   5. **A**   6. **A**

Answers

Question 1

This is a catch-a-clue question. Remember you need only to catch a clue, look for the answer choice that violates that rule, and then eliminate it. Catch the clue and repeat until you are left with just one answer choice.

Which one of the following could be the order, from first to last, in which the flowers were planted?

(A) S, W, P, R, T, U, Z, Q
(B) U, P, W, S, R, Z, Q, T
(C) W, P, S, R, Z, Q, U, T
(D) S, U, P, R, Q, W, Z, T
(E) U, W, P, S, Q, R, Z, T

The first clue (*Both R and P are planted before Q*) eliminates answer choice E. The second clue (*R is planted before Z but after S*) eliminates nothing. The third clue (*W is planted before R*) eliminates answer choice D. The fourth clue (*T is planted after Z*) eliminates answer choice A. Finally, the last clue (*U is planted before Z*) eliminates answer choice C.

(B) is the correct answer.

Question 2

In this type of unrestricted, "must-be-true" question, the correct answer is always true. Wrong answers will either be true sometimes but not always, or they will be false.

Which one of the following must be true?

(A) No more than two flowers are planted before R.
(B) No more than four flowers are planted before Q.
(C) At least one flower is planted before U.
(D) At least two flowers are planted after Z.
(E) At least four flowers are planted after S.

Answer choice A: W and S must be before R, but P and U could be before R as well. Therefore, there could be as many as four flowers before R. This choice can be eliminated.

Answer choice B: Q can be last, so all of the remaining flowers could be before Q. This choice can be eliminated.

Answer choice C: U can be first. Therefore, you do not need at least one flower before U. This choice can be eliminated.

Answer choice D: Only T must be after Z. Q and P could be after Z, but this is not a requirement. This choice can be eliminated.

Answer choice E: This is the correct answer. S must have R, Z, T, and Q after it. U and P could also go after S, but this is not a requirement. As such, there are at least four flowers after S.

(E) is the correct answer.

Question 3

This is a restricted, "could-be-true-EXCEPT" question. Therefore, four answers could be true at least once. These are the wrong choices. One answer is never true; this one is the correct choice.

If R is the fifth flower planted, then each of the following could be true EXCEPT:

(A) Z is planted sixth.
(B) T is planted eighth.
(C) S is planted third.
(D) Q is planted fourth.
(E) W is planted third.

If R is fifth, then you know that there are four flowers before it: U, W, S, and P. Q cannot be the fourth flower planted because one of the rules dictates that Q must come after R, and R is fifth.

The correct answer is (D).

Question 4

In this restricted, "must-be-false" question, four answers could be true. These are the wrong choices. Only one answer choice can never be true; this is the correct answer.

If P is planted later than Z, then which one of the following must be false?

(A) Q is planted eighth.
(B) Z is planted seventh.
(C) T is planted sixth.
(D) R is planted earlier than P.
(E) T is planted later than Q.

Answer choice A: Q can always be eighth (last). There is a very real advantage in knowing which components can be first and which components can be last. This choice can be eliminated.

Answer choice B: If Z is seventh and P comes after Z, that would make P eighth. Q must come after P and now there aren't any spaces for Q. This must be false. **This is the correct answer.**

Answer choice C: T could be sixth and P and Q would be seventh and eighth, respectively. This choice can be eliminated.

Answer choice D: R must be planted earlier than P because R is before Z and P is after Z. This choice can be eliminated.

Answer choice E: T can be later than Q because T can always be last. This choice can be eliminated.

(B) is the correct answer.

Question 5

This is an unrestricted, "could-be-true-EXCEPT" question. Therefore, four answers could be true at least once. These are the wrong choices. One answer is never true; this is the correct choice.

Each of the following could be the third flower planted EXCEPT:

(A) Q
(B) U
(C) R
(D) W
(E) S

According to the chain diagram, U, R, W, and S can all be third. Q must have W, S, R, and P before it. Therefore, the earliest Q can be is fifth.

(A) is the correct answer.

Question 6

This is a restricted, "must-be-true" question, so the correct answer is always true. Wrong answers will either be true sometimes but not always, or they will be false.

If Q is the fifth flower planted, then which one of the following must be true?

(A) U is planted later than R.
(B) S is planted earlier than P.
(C) W is planted later than U.
(D) P is planted later than R.
(E) Z is planted earlier than Q.

If Q is the fifth flower planted, W, S, R, and P (the four flowers that must be before Q) are now the only flowers that can be before Q. Their order relative to each other is without restriction except that R (needing W and S before it) can only be third or fourth. The remaining three flowers (W, S, and P) can be any of the first four flowers planted. Therefore, answer choices B and D could be true, but they do not always have to be true. In addition, U, Z, and T must follow Q and must do so in that order making U sixth, Z seventh, and T eighth. Therefore, answer choices C and E must be false. The correct choice is A because R will be third or fourth and U must be sixth.

(A) is the correct answer.

Game 2

Six famous painters—Cezanne, DaVinci, Kandinsky, Monet, Picasso, and Rembrandt are ranked from most famous (first) to least famous (sixth) by an art critic. There are no ties. The ranking must meet the following conditions:

DaVinci is more famous than Cezanne.
Monet is more famous than both DaVinci and Kandinsky.
Kandinsky and Picasso are each more famous than Cezanne.

1. Which one of the following could be an accurate ranking of the painters, from most famous to least famous?

   (A) Picasso, Kandinsky, Monet, DaVinci, Cezanne, Rembrandt
   (B) Monet, Picasso, Kandinsky, Cezanne, DaVinci, Rembrandt
   (C) Rembrandt, Kandinsky, Monet, Picasso, DaVinci, Cezanne
   (D) Monet, Picasso, Rembrandt, Kandinsky, DaVinci, Cezanne
   (E) Monet, Rembrandt, Kandinsky, DaVinci, Cezanne, Picasso

2. Which one of the following CANNOT be true?

   (A) Picasso is ranked first.
   (B) DaVinci is ranked third.
   (C) Rembrandt is ranked first.
   (D) Kandinsky is ranked fifth.
   (E) Cezanne is ranked fourth.

3. If Cezanne is ranked fifth, then which one of the following must be true?

   (A) Monet is ranked first.
   (B) DaVinci is ranked fourth.
   (C) Rembrandt is ranked sixth.
   (D) Picasso is ranked second.
   (E) Rembrandt is ranked third.

4. If Picasso is ranked higher than Monet, then which one of the following must be false?

   (A) Kandinsky is ranked higher than DaVinci.
   (B) Rembrandt is ranked higher than Monet.
   (C) DaVinci is ranked higher than Picasso.
   (D) DaVinci is ranked higher than Kandinsky.
   (E) Monet is ranked higher than Cezanne.

5. Of the six painters, what is the maximum number of painters that could be more famous than Monet?

   (A) None
   (B) One
   (C) Two
   (D) Three
   (E) Four

6. Which one of the following is a complete and accurate list of the painters that CANNOT be ranked first?

   (A) DaVinci, Kandinsky, Picasso
   (B) Cezanne, Monet, Picasso, Rembrandt
   (C) Cezanne, DaVinci, Kandinsky
   (D) Cezanne, DaVinci, Kandinsky, Monet
   (E) Cezanne, DaVinci, Picasso

STEP 1 Symbolize your clues.

Symbolize the game clues, making sure to place the *before* components on the left. Use just the first initial of each artist's name for your clues.

DaVinci is *more* famous than Cezanne.	D....C
Monet is *more* famous than *both* DaVinci and Kandinsky.	M....D and M....K
Kandinsky and Picasso are *each more* famous than Cezanne.	K....C and P....C

STEP 2 Connect the chains.

Bring the individual chains together to create the longest possible chain of components on a horizontal line. In this game, there are actually two options that will give you the same length in the baseline. One option involves connecting M....D with D....C; so you end up with M....D....C. The second option involves connecting M....K with K....C. In this case, the baseline would look like M....K....C. Both options are equally acceptable, but the first one is used in the example below:

STEP 3 Attach the remaining clues.

When you attach M....K and K....C, the result is:

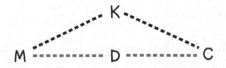

Next, attach P....C to the diagram:

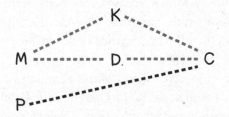

In interpreting the chain, remember the two rules you learned in the last game. Also, note that Rembrandt is not attached to the chain. There are no conditions that indicate Rembrandt's relationship to any of the other painters. Accordingly, Rembrandt can be ranked anywhere from first to last. To assist in remembering Rembrandt's lack of restriction, symbolize it as follows:

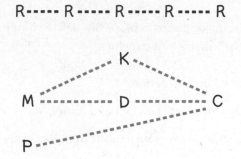

Placing Rembrandt along the entire chain provides a visual reminder that he can be ranked in any of the six positions.

(STEP 4) Now let's tackle the game. Refer to the above chain diagram while you answer the questions in the order given.

Answer Key

1. **D**   2. **E**   3. **C**   4. **C**   5. **C**   6. **C**

Answers

Question 1

This is a catch-a-clue question. Remember you need only to catch a clue, look for the answer choice that violates that clue, and then eliminate it. Catch the next clue and repeat until you are left with just one answer choice.

Which one of the following could be an accurate ranking of the painters, from most famous to least famous?

(A) Picasso, Kandinsky, Monet, DaVinci, Cezanne, Rembrandt
(B) Monet, Picasso, Kandinsky, Cezanne, DaVinci, Rembrandt
(C) Rembrandt, Kandinsky, Monet, Picasso, DaVinci, Cezanne
(D) Monet, Picasso, Rembrandt, Kandinsky, DaVinci, Cezanne
(E) Monet, Rembrandt, Kandinsky, DaVinci, Cezanne, Picasso

The first clue (*DaVinci is more famous than Cezanne*) eliminates answer choice B. The second clue (*Monet is more famous than both DaVinci and Kandinsky*) eliminates answer choices A and C. The third clue (*Kandinsky and Picasso are each more famous than Cezanne*) eliminates answer choice E.

(D) is the correct answer.

Question 2

This unrestricted, "cannot-be-true" question is identical to a "must-be-false" question. Four answers could be true. These are the wrong answers. One answer choice can never be true. This is the correct answer.

Which one of the following CANNOT be true?

(A) Picasso is ranked first.
(B) DaVinci is ranked third.
(C) Rembrandt is ranked first.
(D) Kandinsky is ranked fifth.
(E) Cezanne is ranked fourth.

Answer choice A: Picasso could be ranked first. Even though all the painters, except Cezanne, could be ranked higher than Picasso, there is no painter that must be ranked higher than Picasso. This choice can be eliminated.

Answer choice B: DaVinci could be ranked third. If DaVinci is to be ranked third, exactly two painters will be ranked higher than DaVinci. Monet must be ranked higher than DaVinci and either Picasso or Kandinsky or Rembrandt each could be ranked higher than DaVinci. This choice can be eliminated.

Answer choice C: Rembrandt can be ranked first. Remember, Rembrandt can be ranked anywhere from first through sixth. This choice can be eliminated.

Answer choice D: Kandinsky can be ranked fifth. If Kandinsky is ranked fifth, exactly four painters will be ranked higher than Kandinsky. Monet must be ranked higher than Kandinsky and DaVinci, and Picasso and Rembrandt can each be ranked higher than Kandinsky, bringing the total to four. This choice can be eliminated.

Answer choice A: This is the correct answer. Cezanne cannot be ranked fourth. DaVinci, Monet, Kandinsky, and Picasso must each be ranked higher than Cezanne. The highest ranking Cezanne could have is fifth.

(E) is the correct answer.

Question 3

In this restricted, "must-be-true" question the correct answer is always true. Wrong answers will either be true sometimes but not always, *or* they will be false.

If Cezanne is ranked fifth, then which one of the following must be true?

(A) Monet is ranked first.
(B) DaVinci is ranked fourth.
(C) Rembrandt is ranked sixth.
(D) Picasso is ranked second.
(E) Rembrandt is ranked third.

If Cezanne is ranked fifth, then you know that there are exactly four painters ranked higher than Cezanne. There are four painters that must be ranked higher than Cezanne. They are Monet, DaVinci, Kandinsky, and Picasso. Accordingly, all of those painters must be before Cezanne and no other painters. Therefore, the remaining painter, Rembrandt, must be ranked sixth after Cezanne. Answer choices A, B, and D each could be true but are not necessarily true. Answer choice E must be false because Rembrandt must be ranked sixth.

(C) is the correct answer.

Question 4

This is a restricted, "must-be-false" question. Four answers could be true. These are the wrong answers. One answer choice can never be true. This is the correct answer.

If Picasso is ranked higher than Monet, then which one of the following must be false?

(A) Kandinsky is ranked higher than DaVinci.
(B) Rembrandt is ranked higher than Monet.
(C) DaVinci is ranked higher than Picasso.
(D) DaVinci is ranked higher than Kandinsky.
(E) Monet is ranked higher than Cezanne.

Monet is ranked higher than DaVinci, Kandinsky, and Cezanne. If Picasso is ranked higher than Monet, then Picasso is likewise ranked higher than DaVinci, Kandinsky, and Cezanne. Therefore, DaVinci cannot be ranked higher than Picasso—this must be false.

(C) is the correct answer.

Question 5

This is an unrestricted, "could-be-true" question. Four answers are never true. These are the wrong answers. One answer is true at least once. This is the correct answer.

Of the six painters, what is the maximum number of painters that could be more famous than Monet?

(A) None
(B) One
(C) Two
(D) Three
(E) Four

According to the chain, Picasso and Rembrandt are the only two painters that can be ranked higher than Monet. Kandinsky, Cezanne, and DaVinci are each less famous than Monet.

(C) is the correct answer.

Question 6

This unrestricted, "cannot-be-true" question is identical to a "must-be-false" question. Four answers could be true. These are the wrong choices. One answer choice can never be true. This is the correct answer.

> Which one of the following is a complete and accurate list of the painters that CANNOT be ranked first?
>
> (A) DaVinci, Kandinsky, Picasso
> (B) Cezanne, Monet, Picasso, Rembrandt
> (C) Cezanne, DaVinci, Kandinsky
> (D) Cezanne, DaVinci, Kandinsky, Monet
> (E) Cezanne, DaVinci, Picasso

According to the chain, Cezanne, DaVinci, and Kandinsky each have at least one painter connected by a chain to the left (more famous) of them. Accordingly, Cezanne, DaVinci, and Kandinsky cannot be ranked first. Both Monet and Picasso do not have anyone that must be ranked higher. They can be ranked first. Rembrandt has no restrictions whatsoever, so he too can be ranked first.

(C) is the correct answer.

Game 3

A competition is being held at a university to select the best student film. Each of six students—Berger, Davis, Franklin, Hughes, Jimenez, and Kim—has submitted exactly one film. There are exactly six films, and they are presented one at a time to the panel of judges, each film presented exactly once. The following conditions must apply:

Berger's film is presented at some time before Hughes' and after Kim's.

Franklin's film is presented at some time before Berger's.

If Kim's film is presented at some time before Davis', then Jimenez's film is presented at some time before Franklin's.

Either Davis' film is presented at some time before Franklin's or at some time after Hughes', but not both.

1. Which one of the following could be the order in which the films are presented from first to last?

   (A) Davis, Kim, Hughes, Franklin, Berger, Jimenez
   (B) Davis, Kim, Berger, Hughes, Franklin, Jimenez
   (C) Jimenez, Franklin, Kim, Berger, Davis, Hughes
   (D) Franklin, Kim, Jimenez, Berger, Hughes, Davis
   (E) Davis, Kim, Franklin, Berger, Jimenez, Hughes

2. Exactly how many films are there, any one of which could be first?

   (A) One
   (B) Two
   (C) Three
   (D) Four
   (E) Five

3. If Jimenez's film is presented sixth, then each of the following must be true EXCEPT:

   (A) Franklin's film is presented at some time before Kim's film is presented.
   (B) Berger's film is presented at some time before Hughes' film is presented.
   (C) Davis' film is presented at some time before Kim's film is presented.
   (D) Kim's film is presented at some time before Hughes' film is presented.
   (E) Davis' film is presented at some time before Franklin's film is presented.

4. If Berger's film is presented before Jimenez's, then which one of the following could be true?

   (A) Jimenez's film is presented first.
   (B) Kim's film is presented first.
   (C) Franklin's film is presented third.
   (D) Berger's film is presented third.
   (E) Davis' film is presented second.

5. Which one of the following must be true?

   (A) Jimenez's film is presented at some time before Berger's film is presented.
   (B) Davis' film is presented at some time before Berger's film is presented.
   (C) Berger's film is presented at some time before Jimenez's film is presented.
   (D) Franklin's film is presented at some time before Hughes' film is presented.
   (E) Kim's film is presented at some time before Jimenez's film is presented.

6. Which one of the following could be an accurate partial list of the students, each matched with his or her film's place in the order in which the films are presented?

   (A) fourth: Kim; fifth: Franklin; sixth: Hughes
   (B) third: Hughes; fifth: Davis; sixth: Jimenez
   (C) first: Berger; fourth: Hughes: fifth: Davis
   (D) first: Franklin; third: Kim; sixth: Hughes
   (E) second: Jimenez; third: Davis; fourth: Franklin

STEP 1 Symbolize the clues.

Symbolize the clues in the game, making sure to place the *before* components to the left.

Berger's film is presented at some time before Hughes' and after Kim's.

K....B....H

Franklin's film is presented at some time before Berger's.

F....B

If Kim's film is presented earlier than Davis', then Jimenez's film is presented before Franklin's.

K....D → J....F and the contrapositive F....J → D....K

Either Davis' film is presented at some time before Franklin's or at some time after Hughes', but not both.

D....F or H....D, and not H....D....F nor F....D....H

STEP 2 Connect the chains.

Bring the individual chains together to create the longest possible chain of components on a horizontal line. In this game, the longest chain possible is already given in the first clue. Your baseline is K....B....H.

K ----------- B ----------- H

STEP 3 Attach the remaining clues.

When you attach F....B to the baseline, the result is:

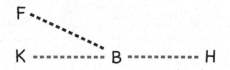

Now that all the chains are joined together, note that Davis and Jimenez are not represented on the diagram. While Franklin can be readily identified as a floater (i.e., not on the original baseline), Davis and Jimenez are not even attached to the baseline. Their relationship to the baseline is controlled by the remaining clues, namely: "*if Kim's film is presented at some time before Davis', then Jimenez's film is presented at some time before Franklin's*" and "*either Davis' film is presented at some time before Franklin's or at some time after Hughes', but not both.*" Therefore, let's simply refer to D and J as superfloaters.

The original clues for reading the chain remain intact. However, you need to also consider how the last two clues affect the chain. The last clue requires you to choose either D....F *or* H....D, but not both. This fact, therefore, limits the effect that the clue has on the baseline to two distinct possibilities. You should ascertain both of these.

CHAIN POSSIBILITY 1: Here, D....F is connected to the baseline:

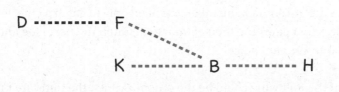

In this possibility, you no longer need to concern yourself with H....D because D is already before H. However, since it cannot be ascertained whether D is before K or if K is before D, you still need to refer to the third condition (K...D → J...F and its contrapositive F...J → D...K) when answering questions that relate to this chain possibility.

CHAIN POSSIBILITY 2: Here, you begin by connecting H....D to the baseline:

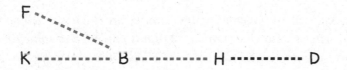

In this scenario, you no longer need to concern yourself with D....F because F is already before D. However, unlike Chain Possibility 1, this scenario activates the conditional sequence rule of K...D → J...F because K is before D. Therefore, J....F must be attached to the baseline to complete Chain Possibility 2:

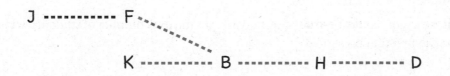

Notice how all six of the components (student films) are represented in this diagram. Refer to the diagrams of Chain Possibility 1 and Chain Possibility 2 to answer each question.

STEP 4 Now let's tackle the questions. Refer to the appropriate chain(s) above to answer each question in the order given.

Answer Key

Answers

Question 1

This is a catch-a-clue question. Remember you need only to catch a clue, look for the answer choice that violates that clue, and then eliminate it. Catch the next clue and repeat until you are left with just one answer choice.

Which one of the following could be the order in which the films are presented from first to last?

(A) Davis, Kim, Hughes, Franklin, Berger, Jimenez
(B) Davis, Kim, Berger, Hughes, Franklin, Jimenez
(C) Jimenez, Franklin, Kim, Berger, Davis, Hughes
(D) Franklin, Kim, Jimenez, Berger, Hughes, Davis
(E) Davis, Kim, Franklin, Berger, Jimenez, Hughes

The first clue (*Berger's film is presented at some time before Hughes' and after Kim's*) eliminates answer choice A. The second clue (*Franklin's film is presented at some time before Berger's*) eliminates answer choice B. The third clue (*If Kim's film is presented at some time before Davis', then Jimenez's film is presented at some time before Franklin's*) eliminates answer choice D. Finally, the last clue (*Either Davis' film is presented at some time before Franklin's or at some time after Hughes' but not both*) eliminates answer choice C.

(E) is the correct answer.

Question 2

This unrestricted, "could-be-true" question asks for the total number of students whose films could be the first film presented.

Exactly how many films are there, any one of which could be first?

(A) One
(B) Two
(C) Three
(D) Four
(E) Five

Chain Possibility 1 shows that Davis and Kim can be the first films presented. Chain Possibility 2 shows that Jimenez and Kim can be the first films presented. As such, the total number of student films that can be presented first is three (D, K, J).

(C) is correct answer.

Question 3

This is a restricted, "must-be-true-EXCEPT" question. Therefore, four answers must be true at all times. These are the wrong choices. One answer could be false at least once. This is the correct answer.

   If Jimenez's film is presented sixth, then each of the following must be true EXCEPT:

   (A) Franklin's film is presented at some time before Kim's film is presented.
   (B) Berger's film is presented at some time before Hughes' film is presented.
   (C) Davis' film is presented at some time before Kim's film is presented.
   (D) Kim's film is presented at some time before Hughes' film is presented.
   (E) Davis' film is presented at some time before Franklin's film is presented.

Chain Possibility 2 is inapplicable because Jimenez can only be sixth in Chain Possibility 1.

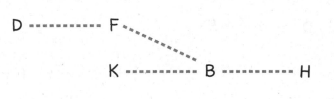

The only way for Jimenez to be sixth is if he or she comes after H.

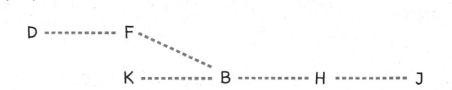

Accordingly, B, D, and E must be true and are the wrong answers because the correct answer may be false. Now consider the conditional sequence rule (*If Kim's film is presented at some time before Davis', then Jimenez's film is presented before Franklin's*) and its contrapositive (*If Franklin is presented at some time before Jimenez, then Davis' is presented at some time before Kim*). This can be represented as: K....D → J....F and F....J → D....K.

   In this scenario, Franklin is before Jimenez. Therefore, Davis must present his or her film before Kim.

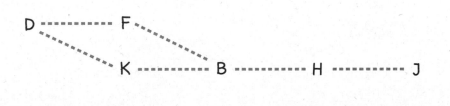

This shows that answer choice C also must be true. Franklin's film is presented before Kim's film could be false because Franklin's film could also be presented after Kim's film is presented.

(A) is the correct answer.

Question 4

This is a restricted, "could-be-true" question, so four answers are never true. These are the wrong answers. One answer choice can be true at least once—this one is correct.

If Berger's film is presented before Jimenez's, then which one of the following could be true?

(A) Jimenez's film is presented first.
(B) Kim's film is presented first.
(C) Franklin's film is presented third.
(D) Berger's film is presented third.
(E) Davis' film is presented second.

Berger can only be before Jimenez in the first possibility, so let's start with Chain Possibility 1:

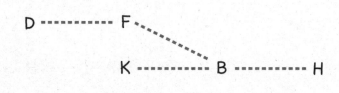

Next, attach Jimenez after Berger (B...J):

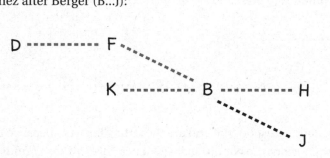

Now consider the third conditional sequence rule (*If Kim's film is presented at some time before Davis', then Jimenez's film is presented before Franklin's*) and its contrapositive (*If Franklin is presented at some time before Jimenez, then Davis' is presented at some time before Kim*). In this scenario, Franklin is before Jimenez. Therefore, Davis must present before Kim.

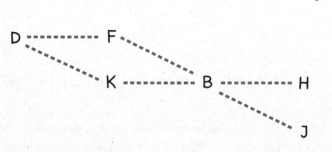

Answer choice A: Jimenez's film is presented first is the wrong answer. Jimenez can only be fifth or sixth.

Answer choice B: Kim's film is presented first is the wrong answer. Davis must be before Kim.

Answer choice C: Franklin's film is presented third is the **correct answer**. Franklin can be either second or third.

Answer choice D: Berger's film is presented third is the wrong answer. Berger has Davis, Franklin, and Kim before him/her and Hughes and Jimenez must be after Berger. Thus, Berger is fourth.

Answer choice E: Davis' film is presented second is the wrong answer. Davis must be first.

(C) is the correct answer.

Question 5

In this unrestricted, "must-be-true" question, the correct answer is always true. Wrong answers will either be true sometimes but not always, *or* they will be false.

Which one of the following must be true?

(A) Jimenez's film is presented at some time before Berger's film is presented.
(B) Davis' film is presented at some time before Berger's film is presented.
(C) Berger's film is presented at some time before Jimenez's film is presented.
(D) Franklin's film is presented at some time before Hughes' film is presented.
(E) Kim's film is presented at some time before Jimenez's film is presented.

According to the chain diagram, Franklin must come before Hughes.

(D) is the correct answer.

Question 6

This is an unrestricted, "could-be-true" question. The correct answer is true at least once. Wrong answers will never be true.

Which one of the following could be an accurate partial list of the students, each matched with his or her film's place in the order in which the films are presented?

(A) fourth: Kim; fifth: Franklin; sixth: Hughes
(B) third: Hughes; fifth: Davis; sixth: Jimenez
(C) first: Berger; fourth: Hughes: fifth: Davis
(D) first: Franklin; third: Kim; sixth: Hughes
(E) second: Jimenez; third: Davis; fourth: Franklin

Answer choice A: Clue 1 tells you that Berger must be between Kim and Hughes. This is the wrong answer.

Answer choice B: Clue 3 (specifically the contrapositive, F....J → D....K) indicates that Jimenez is sixth; therefore, Franklin goes before Jimenez. That means that Davis must go before Kim. With Davis fifth and Jimenez sixth, there is no place for Kim after Davis. This is the wrong answer.

Answer choice C: The first clue tells you that Berger cannot be first, so this is the wrong answer.

Answer choice D: The last clue makes it clear that with Franklin first, D....F is not possible. Also, with Hughes sixth, H....D is not possible. This is the wrong answer.

Answer choice E: This is the correct answer.

(E) is the correct answer.

Grouping Games

6

The focus of this guide so far has been on games that have asked you to put things into order, one after another: in other words, sequential games. Within the sequencing context, you have delved into subcategories based primarily on mathematical ratios—that is, a comparison of the number of components versus the number of slots. The games in this chapter, however, will have you divide the components into groups rather than put them in order. Our exploration of subcategories will largely depend on mathematical ratios *and distributions*. So in addition to ascertaining the number of slots versus the number of the components, you will also be considering the distribution of the components across the groups.

The upcoming games involve grouping and challenge you to ascertain how many components are assigned to each group. There are three subtypes within these grouping or distribution games: fixed, maximum/minimum, and unknown distribution grouping games.

Let's start by previewing the first sample grouping game. Consider this setup:

> During four days—Tuesday through Friday—a farmer will harvest exactly eight varieties of apples: Cortland, Empire, Fuji, Gala, Honeycrisp, Jonagold, McIntosh, and Red Delicious. *Each variety will be harvested once,* and *exactly two varieties will be harvested per day.* Harvesting must occur according to the following conditions:

Notice the highlighted language "*each variety will be harvested once.*" From this, you can determine that the ratio is one-to-one. The language "*exactly two varieties will be harvested per day,*" indicates exactly how many components are assigned to each day. The days will be our diagram headings. When the distribution is completely determined, as in this example, the distribution is *fixed*.

Let's preview the third game in this chapter. Consider this setup and the first clue:

> Each of seven Freshmen Senators—Johnson, Katz, Lewis, Morris, Ng, Patel, and Rao—will be assigned to exactly one of three committees: Finance, Homeland Security, and Judiciary. The assignment of Senators must conform to following conditions:
>
> Each committee is assigned at least two, but no more than three, of the seven Senators.

From the language "*each of seven Freshman Senators … will be assigned to exactly one of three committees,*" you know that you are dealing with a one-to-one ratio (an equal number of components to slots). Unlike in the first game, the language in the first clue (*Each committee is assigned at least two, but no more than three*) does not completely determine the number of components in each group, but it does give some parameters. In this example, the distribution is partially, but not completely, determined; this is called *minimum/maximum* distribution.

Let's consider the one remaining distributional option—one in which very little or no concrete information is given about how many components are in each group. Consider the setup and the second clue of yet another game in this chapter:

> **Each of the three coffee shops sells at least one of five types of coffee drinks: cappuccino, espresso, frappe, latte, or macchiato. None of the coffee shops sells any other type of coffee drinks.** *Among the three coffee shops at least one of each type of coffee drink is sold.* **The following conditions must hold:**
>
> *Beantown sells exactly one type of coffee drink.*

Right now, you might be thinking to yourself, "That's impossible! I need more information than that!" Take a deep breath, and focus on the highlighted language again. The only distributional information given is that each group is assigned at least one type of coffee, and that Beantown is assigned exactly one coffee drink. No clue speaks directly to the distribution of the other two groups. As you begin to unravel this game, however, you will very likely uncover clues that enable you to at least narrow the possible distribution of components to just two or three options. In this guide, games like this one in which the distribution is unknown are called unknown distribution grouping games.

To summarize, the mathematical distribution (number of slots assigned to each of the grouping headings) will fall into three categories:

1. **FIXED.** The number of components to be placed in each group is completely determined and fixed.
2. **MINIMUM/MAXIMUM.** The number of components to be placed in each group is somewhat, but not completely, determined. In this case, a minimum and a maximum number of components to be included are given.
3. **UNKNOWN DISTRIBUTION GROUPING GAMES.** There are very little or no restrictions on the number of components to be placed each group(s).

In addition to the distributional aspect of grouping, many of the clues will focus on which components must be in the same group with each other and which components cannot be in the same group as each other. In the latter case, it often happens that between two or more components that cannot be in the same group together, there are no clues that mandate that one or another be placed into a specific group. In these instances, do not waste time and space creating separate and distinct groupings. Instead, split the slots and place the components into your diagram *"interchangeably."*

GROUPING

(Fixed)

Game 1

During four days—Tuesday through Friday—a farmer will harvest exactly eight varieties of apples: Cortland, Empire, Fuji, Gala, Honeycrisp, Jonagold, McIntosh, and Red Delicious. Each variety will be harvested once, and exactly two varieties will be harvested per day. Harvesting must occur according to the following conditions:

Gala and Jonagold are not harvested on the same day.

Cortland and Fuji are harvested on the same day.

If Gala is harvested on Wednesday, then Empire is harvested on Friday.

If McIntosh is harvested on Friday, then Honeycrisp is harvested on Tuesday.

Neither Jonagold nor Honeycrisp is harvested on Wednesday.

Red Delicious is harvested on Thursday.

1. Which one of the following could be a complete and accurate matching of apple varieties to the days on which they are harvested?

   (A) Tuesday: Empire, Honeycrisp
       Wednesday: Gala, McIntosh
       Thursday: Jonagold, Red Delicious
       Friday: Cortland, Fuji
   (B) Tuesday: Cortland, Fuji
       Wednesday: Gala, Honeycrisp
       Thursday: McIntosh, Red Delicious
       Friday: Empire, Jonagold
   (C) Tuesday: Cortland, Fuji
       Wednesday: Gala, McIntosh
       Thursday: Honeycrisp, Red Delicious
       Friday: Empire, Jonagold
   (D) Tuesday: Gala, Jonagold
       Wednesday: Empire, McIntosh
       Thursday: Honeycrisp, Red Delicious
       Friday: Cortland, Fuji
   (E) Tuesday: Empire, Gala
       Wednesday: Cortland, Fuji
       Thursday: Honeycrisp, Red Delicious
       Friday: Jonagold, McIntosh

2. If McIntosh and Honeycrisp are harvested on the same day, then which one of the following must be true?

   (A) Gala is harvested on Friday.
   (B) Empire is harvested on Friday.
   (C) Jonagold is not harvested on Thursday.
   (D) Red Delicious is harvested on the same day as Empire.
   (E) Gala is harvested on the same day as Empire.

3. If Cortland is harvested on Friday, then which one of the following must be true?

   (A) Gala is harvested on Thursday.
   (B) McIntosh is harvested on Tuesday.
   (C) Jonagold is harvested on Tuesday.
   (D) Honeycrisp is harvested on Thursday.
   (E) Empire is harvested on Thursday.

Continued on next page ⮕

4. If Gala is harvested on Wednesday, then each of the following could be a pair of apple varieties harvested on the same day EXCEPT:

(A) Empire and Honeycrisp
(B) Honeycrisp and Jonagold
(C) Empire and Jonagold
(D) Gala and McIntosh
(E) Jonagold and Red Delicious

5. If Empire is harvested on Thursday, then exactly how many apple varieties are there any one of which could be harvested on Tuesday?

(A) Two
(B) Three
(C) Four
(D) Five
(E) Six

STEP 1 Visualize and draw the diagram.

What are you being asked to figure out? The game asks you to ascertain which varieties of apple are harvested on Tuesday, on Wednesday, on Thursday, and on Friday. The diagram is as follows:

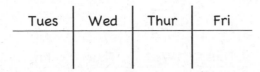

STEP 2 List the components and ascertain the ratio and/or distribution.

There are eight components: C, E, F, G, H, J, M, and R (the first letter of each variety of apple). Since you have eight components and eight slots, the ratio is one-to-one. However, the distribution is fixed and is ascertained from this language in the setup: *exactly two varieties will be harvested per day*. The diagram is now modified as follows:

Tues	Wed	Thur	Fri
_ _	_ _	_ _	_ _

STEP 3 Symbolize the clues.

Remember to always write down the contrapositive as well.

Clue 1	Gala and Jonagold are not harvested on the same day.	$G \to \sim J$; $J \to \sim G$
Clue 2	Cortland and Fuji are harvested on the same day.	$C \leftrightarrow F$; $\sim C \leftrightarrow \sim F$
Clue 3	If Gala is harvested on Wednesday, then Empire is harvested on Friday.	$G_{wed} \to E_{fri}$; $\sim E_{fri} \to \sim G_{wed}$
Clue 4	If McIntosh is harvested on Friday, then Honeycrisp is harvested on Tuesday.	$M_{fri} \to H_{tue}$; $\sim H_{tue} \to \sim M_{fri}$
Clue 5	Neither Jonagold nor Honeycrisp is harvested on Wednesday.	$J \neq Wed$; $H \neq Wed$ (put in diagram)
Clue 6	Red Delicious is harvested on Thursday.	$R = Thur$ (put in diagram)

STEP 4 Make deductions.

Remember that linking the conditional statements is often crucial.

Clue 5 and Clue 6 should be placed directly into the diagram.

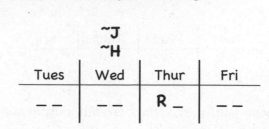

Deduction 1: In this instance, the conditionals are not linkable. However, Clue 1 and Clue 3 together do provide an additional deduction: *neither C nor F can be harvested on Thursday.* How do you know this? With the placement of R on Thursday, there is just one additional slot available, and C and F are always harvested on the same day.

	~J	~C	
	~H	~F	
Tues	Wed	Thur	Fri
_ _	_ _	R _	_ _

STEP 5 Tackle the questions.

The order in which you answer the questions is important. Remember the optimal sequence: 1. catch-a-clue; 2. restricted; 3. unrestricted; 4. modifiers. For this particular game, that translates to the following order: 1, 2, 3, 4, and then 5.

Answer Key

1. **C**   2. **B**   3. **D**   4. **B**   5. **C**

Answers

Question 1

This is a catch-a-clue question. Here are the answer choices again:

(A) Tuesday: Empire, Honeycrisp
Wednesday: Gala, McIntosh
Thursday: Jonagold, Red Delicious
Friday: Cortland, Fuji

(B) Tuesday: Cortland, Fuji
Wednesday: Gala, Honeycrisp
Thursday: McIntosh, Red Delicious
Friday: Empire, Jonagold

(C) Tuesday: Cortland, Fuji
Wednesday: Gala, McIntosh
Thursday: Honeycrisp, Red Delicious
Friday: Empire, Jonagold

(D) Tuesday: Gala, Jonagold
Wednesday: Empire, McIntosh
Thursday: Honeycrisp, Red Delicious
Friday: Cortland, Fuji

(E) Tuesday: Empire, Gala
Wednesday: Cortland, Fuji
Thursday: Honeycrisp, Red Delicious
Friday: Jonagold, McIntosh

The first rule (*Gala and Jonagold are not harvested on the same day*) eliminates answer choice D. The second clue (*Cortland and Fuji are harvested on the same day*) does not eliminate any answer choices. The third clue (*If Gala is harvested on Wednesday, then Empire is harvested on Friday*) eliminates answer choice A. The fourth clue (*If McIntosh is harvested on Friday, then Honeycrisp is harvested on Tuesday*) eliminates answer choice E. The fifth clue (*Neither Jonagold nor Honeycrisp is harvested on Wednesday*) eliminates answer choice B.

(C) is the correct answer.

Question 2

This one is a restricted, "must-be-true" question. Therefore, four answers are never true or they are true at least once but not always. These are the wrong answers. One answer is always true. This is the correct answer.

> If McIntosh and Honeycrisp are harvested on the same day, then which one of the following must be true?
>
> (A) Gala is harvested on Friday.
> (B) Empire is harvested on Friday.
> (C) Jonagold is not harvested on Thursday.
> (D) Red Delicious is harvested on the same day as Empire.
> (E) Gala is harvested on the same day as Empire.

This question places M and H on the same day. Clue 4 tells you that M and H cannot be together on Friday. By operation of Clue 6, M and H cannot be together on Thursday. Clue 5 determines that M and H cannot be together on Wednesday. Therefore, M and H must be harvested on Tuesday.

		~J ~H		~C ~F		
	Tues	Wed		Thur		Fri
	M H	_	_	R	_	_ _

Pivot to one of the most restricted slot: Wednesday. The only remaining components available for harvesting on Wednesday are C, E, F, and G. Since by operation of Clue 2, Cortland and Fuji are always harvested on the same day, your only options for Wednesday are either (C and F) or (E and G).

By operation of Clue 3, E and G cannot both be placed together on Wednesday. Therefore, C and F must be placed on Wednesday.

		~J ~H	~C ~F	
	Tues	Wed	Thur	Fri
	M H	C F	R _	_ _

By operation of Clue 1, G and J must be placed in slots for Thursday and Friday interchangeably, thereby relegating the last component (E) to the last slot on Friday.

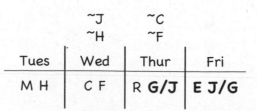

Answer choices A, C, and E are each true sometimes but not always. Answer choice D is never true. Answer choice B is always true.

(B) is the correct answer.

Question 3

This is a restricted, "must-be-true" question. Therefore, four answers are never true, or they are true at least once but not always. These are the wrong answers. One answer is always true. This is the correct answer.

> If Cortland is harvested on Friday, then which one of the following must be true?

(A) Gala is harvested on Thursday.
(B) McIntosh is harvested on Tuesday.
(C) Jonagold is harvested on Tuesday.
(D) Honeycrisp is harvested on Thursday.
(E) Empire is harvested on Thursday.

The question itself places C on Friday:

| | | ~J | ~C |
| | | ~H | ~F |
Tues	Wed	Thur	Fri
_ _	_ _	R _	C _

By operation of Clue 2, F must be placed on Friday:

| | | ~J | ~C |
| | | ~H | ~F |
Tues	Wed	Thur	Fri
_ _	_ _	R _	C **F**

By operation of the contrapositive of Clue 3, G cannot be placed on Wednesday.

Pivot to one of our most restricted slots: Wednesday. Neither J, H, R, C, F, nor G can be placed onto Wednesday. The only remaining components available for harvesting on Wednesday are E and M.

| | | ~J | ~C |
| | | ~H | ~F |
Tues	Wed	Thur	Fri
_ _	**E M**	R _	C F

By operation of Clue 1, G and J must be placed in slots Tuesday and Thursday interchangeably, relegating the last component (H) to the last slot on Tuesday.

	~J ~H	~C ~F	
Tues	Wed	Thur	Fri
H G/J	E M	R J/G	C F

Answer choices A and C are true sometimes but not always. Answer choices B and E are never true. Answer choice D is always true.

(D) is the correct answer.

Question 4

This restricted, "could-be-true," EXCEPT question is identical to a "must-be-false" question. Four answers could be true. These are the wrong answers. One answer choice is never true. This is the correct answer.

> If Gala is harvested on Wednesday, then each of the following could be a pair of apple varieties harvested on the same day EXCEPT:
>
> (A) Empire and Honeycrisp
> (B) Honeycrisp and Jonagold
> (C) Empire and Jonagold
> (D) Gala and McIntosh
> (E) Jonagold and Red Delicious

The question itself restricts the placement of Gala to Wednesday.

	~J ~H	~C ~F	
Tues	Wed	Thur	Fri
_ _	G _	R _	_ _

By operation of Clue 3, E must be placed on Friday.

	~J ~H	~C ~F	
Tues	Wed	Thur	Fri
_ _	G _	R _	E _

By operation of Clue 2, which requires that C and F be harvested together, C and F must be placed on Tuesday.

| | | ~J
~H | ~C
~F | |
Tues	Wed	Thur	Fri
C F	G _	R _	E _

Pivot to one of the most restricted slots: Wednesday. By operation of Clue 5, the only remaining component available for placement on Wednesday is M.

| | | ~J
~H | ~C
~F | |
Tues	Wed	Thur	Fri
C F	G M	R _	E _

The remaining components (J and H) must be placed in the remaining slots on Thursday and Friday interchangeably.

| | | ~J
~H | ~C
~F | |
Tues	Wed	Thur	Fri
C F	G M	R H/J	E J/H

Answer choices A, C, and E are each true at least once. Answer choice D is always true. Answer choice B is never true.

(B) is the correct answer.

Question 5

This is a restricted, "could-be-true" question. The correct answer is true at least once. Wrong answers will never be true.

If Empire is harvested on Thursday, then exactly how many apple varieties are there any one of which could be harvested on Tuesday?

(A) Two
(B) Three
(C) Four
(D) Five
(E) Six

This question places E in Thursday:

		~J ~H		~C ~F		
Tues		Wed		Thur		Fri
— —		— —		R **E**		— —

By operation of Clue 3, G cannot be placed in Wednesday, which is one of the most restricted slots. J, H, R, and E cannot be placed in Wednesday either. The only remaining components available for harvesting on Wednesday are C, F, and M. By operation of Clue 2, neither C nor F can be placed with M. Therefore, C and F must be placed in Wednesday.

		~J ~H		~C ~F		
Tues		Wed		Thur		Fri
— —		**C F**		R E		— —

By operation of Clue 1, G and J must be placed in slots Tuesday and Friday interchangeably.

		~J ~H		~C ~F		
Tues		Wed		Thur		Fri
_ **G/J**		C F		R E		_ **G/J**

Likewise, by operation of Clue 4, M and H must be placed into slots in Tuesday and Friday interchangeably. How do you know? If M were to be placed on Friday, H would be placed on Tuesday in compliance with Clue 4. Conversely, if M were to be placed on Tuesday, Clue 4 would be inapplicable; there would be no constraints attached to the placement of H. As such, H could be placed on Friday.

		~J ~H				
Tues		Wed		Thur		Fri
H/M G/J		C F		R E		**M/H** J/G

Accordingly, a total of four apple varieties (G, H, J, and M) can each be harvested on Tuesday.

(C) is the correct answer.

Game 2

Seven college basketball players—Morgan, Ned, Ross, Saul, Tyrone, Wesley, and Yung—are drafted by three professional basketball teams: the Comets, the Lightning, and the Sharks. One player is drafted by the Comets, three players by the Lightning, and three players by the Sharks. The following conditions must apply:

Ross and Tyrone are drafted by the same team.

Saul and Wesley are not drafted by the same team.

If Morgan is drafted by the Sharks, Yung is drafted by the Sharks.

Saul is drafted by the Lightning only if Ned is drafted by the Lightning.

1. Which one of the following could be a complete and accurate list of the players who are drafted by each basketball team?

   (A) Comets: Yung
       Lightning: Morgan, Ned, Saul
       Sharks: Ross, Tyrone, Wesley
   (B) Comets: Ross
       Lightning: Morgan, Ned, Saul
       Sharks: Tyrone, Wesley, Yung
   (C) Comets: Yung
       Lightning: Ross, Tyrone, Wesley
       Sharks: Morgan, Ned, Saul
   (D) Comets: Morgan
       Lightning: Ned, Saul, Wesley
       Sharks: Ross, Tyrone, Yung
   (E) Comets: Morgan
       Lightning: Ross, Saul, Tyrone
       Sharks: Ned, Wesley, Yung

2. If neither Ned nor Ross is drafted by the Lightning, then each of the following could be true EXCEPT:

   (A) Ned is drafted by the Comets.
   (B) Saul is drafted by the Comets.
   (C) Morgan is drafted by the Sharks.
   (D) Yung is drafted by the Lightning.
   (E) Saul is drafted by the Sharks.

3. If Yung is drafted by the Comets, then which of the following must be true?

   (A) Saul is drafted by the Sharks.
   (B) Wesley is drafted by the Sharks.
   (C) Ned is drafted by the Lightning.
   (D) Ross is drafted by the Lightning.
   (E) Saul is drafted by the Lightning.

4. If Morgan and Tyrone are drafted by the same team, then each of the following must be true EXCEPT:

   (A) Ross is drafted by the Lightning.
   (B) Ned is drafted by the Sharks.
   (C) Yung is drafted by the Sharks.
   (D) Saul and Ross are not drafted by the same team as each other.
   (E) None of the other players are drafted to the same team as Wesley.

5. Which one of the following CANNOT be true?

   (A) Saul and Tyrone are both drafted by the Lightning.
   (B) Morgan and Ross are both drafted by the Lightning.
   (C) Ned and Saul are both drafted by the Lightning.
   (D) Wesley and Yung are both drafted by the Sharks.
   (E) Ross and Wesley are both drafted by the Sharks.

STEP 1 Visualize and draw the diagram.

What are you being asked to figure out? The game is asking you to ascertain which basketball players are drafted by which teams. The diagram is as follows:

Comets	Lightning	Sharks

STEP 2 List the components and ascertain the ratio and distribution.

There are seven components: M, N, R, S, T, W, and Y (the first letter of each basketball player's name). Each player is drafted by just one team, so the ratio is one-to-one. You can ascertain that the distribution is fixed from the language "*one player is drafted by the Comets; three, by the Lightning; and three, by the Sharks.*" The diagram is now modified as follows:

Comets	Lightning	Sharks
—	— — —	— — —

STEP 3 Symbolize the clues.

Remember to always write down the contrapositive as well.

Clue 1   Ross and Tyrone are drafted by the same team. $R \leftrightarrow T$; $\sim\!R \leftrightarrow \sim\!T$

Clue 2   Saul and Wesley are not drafted by the same team. $S \rightarrow \sim\!W$; $W \rightarrow \sim\!S$

Clue 3   If Morgan is drafted by the Sharks, Yung is drafted $M_{sharks} \rightarrow Y_{sharks}$;
by the Sharks. $\sim\!Y_{sharks} \rightarrow \sim\!M_{sharks}$

Clue 4   Saul is drafted by the Lightning only if Ned $S_{light} \rightarrow N_{light}$;
is drafted by the Lightning. $\sim\!N_{light} \rightarrow \sim\!S_{light}$

STEP 4 Make deductions.

Remember that linking the conditional statements is crucial. Here you will want to link Clue 1 and the relevant distributional clue (*the Comets draft one player*) to make your deduction.

Deduction 1: Neither R nor T is drafted by the Comets.

How do you know? Since R and T are always drafted by the same team, they cannot be drafted by a team that drafts just one player.

Tackle the questions.

Remember the optimal sequence for answering questions: 1. catch-a-clue; 2. restricted; 3. unrestricted; 4. modifiers. For this particular game, that translates to the following order: 1, 2, 3, 4, and then 5.

Answer Key

1. **A**   2. **C**   3. **C**   4. **E**   5. **A**

Answers

Question 1

This is a catch-a-clue question. Remember you need only catch a rule, look for the answer choice that violates that rule, and then eliminate it.

> Which one of the following could be a complete and accurate list of the players who are drafted by each basketball team?
>
> (A) Comets: Yung
> Lightning: Morgan, Ned, Saul
> Sharks: Ross, Tyrone, Wesley
>
> (B) Comets: Ross
> Lightning: Morgan, Ned, Saul
> Sharks: Tyrone, Wesley, Yung
>
> (C) Comets: Yung
> Lightning: Ross, Tyrone, Wesley
> Sharks: Morgan, Ned, Saul
>
> (D) Comets: Morgan
> Lightning: Ned, Saul, Wesley
> Sharks: Ross, Tyrone, Yung
>
> (E) Comets: Morgan
> Lightning: Ross, Saul, Tyrone
> Sharks: Ned, Wesley, Yung

The first clue (*Ross and Tyrone are drafted by the same team*) eliminates answer choice B. The second clue (*Saul and Wesley are not drafted by the same team*) eliminates answer choice D. The third clue (*If Morgan is drafted by the Sharks, Yung is drafted by the Sharks*) eliminates answer choice C. The fourth clue (*Saul is drafted by the Lightning only if Ned is drafted by the Lightning*) eliminates answer choice E.

(A) is the correct answer.

Place the correct answer into the diagram.

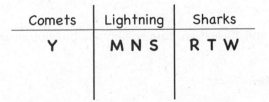

Comets	Lightning	Sharks
Y	M N S	R T W

Question 2

This a restricted, "could-be-true-EXCEPT" question, which is identical to a "must-be-false" question. Four answers could be true. These are the wrong answers. One answer choice is never true. This is the correct answer.

If neither Ned nor Ross is drafted by the Lightning, then each of the following could be true EXCEPT:

(A) Ned is drafted by the Comets.
(B) Saul is drafted by the Comets.
(C) Morgan is drafted by the Sharks.
(D) Yung is drafted by the Lightning.
(E) Saul is drafted by the Sharks.

By operation of the contrapositive of Clue 1, you know that if R is not drafted by the Lightning, then T is not drafted by the Lightning. Also, with the additional restriction that bans N from being drafted by the Lightning, the contrapositive of Clue 4 is triggered. Therefore, S is not drafted by the Lightning. Accordingly, the Lightning cannot draft R, T, N, or S, so the three remaining players (M, W, and Y) must be drafted by the Lightning.

Comets	Lightning	Sharks
—	M W Y	_ _ _

No other player can be drafted by the Lightning. Accordingly, by operation of Deduction 1 (*Neither R nor T are drafted by the Comets*), R and T must be drafted by the Sharks.

Comets	Lightning	Sharks
—	M W Y	R T _

There are no clues that govern the placement of the remaining players (N and S), so they can be assigned to either the Comets or the Sharks interchangeably.

Comets	Lightning	Sharks
N/S	M W Y	R T N/S

Answer choices A, B, and E each are true sometimes but not always. Answer choice D is always true.

(C) is the correct answer.

Question 3

This is a restricted, "must-be-true" question. Therefore, four answers are never true or they are true at least once but not always. These are the wrong answers. One answer is always true. This is the correct answer.

> If Yung is drafted by the Comets, then which of the following must be true?
>
> (A) Saul is drafted by the Sharks.
> (B) Wesley is drafted by the Sharks.
> (C) Ned is drafted by the Lightning.
> (D) Ross is drafted by the Lightning.
> (E) Saul is drafted by the Lightning.

The question itself restricts the placement of Y to the Comets. Place this additional restriction into the diagram is as follows:

Comets	Lightning	Sharks
Y	_ _ _	_ _ _

By operation of the contrapositive of Clue 3, M cannot be drafted by the Sharks. Therefore, M must be drafted by the Lightning.

Comets	Lightning	Sharks
Y	M _ _	_ _ _

By operation of Clue 2, S and W cannot be drafted by the same team, so they must be assigned interchangeably to the Lightning and the Sharks.

Comets	Lightning	Sharks
Y	M S/W _	S/W _ _

With just one slot remaining on the Lightning team, the R/T duo are forced onto the Sharks.

Comets	Lightning	Sharks
Y	M S/W _	S/W R T

The remaining player (N) must be assigned to the only remaining slot on the Lightning team.

Comets	Lightning	Sharks
Y	M S/W **N**	S/W R T

Answer choices A, B, and E are true sometimes, but not always. Answer choice D is never true.

(C) is the correct answer.

Question 4

This is a restricted, "must-be-true-EXCEPT" question. Therefore, four answers must be always true. These are the wrong answers. One answer is either sometimes true but not always true, or it is never true. This is the correct answer.

> If Morgan and Tyrone are drafted by the same team, then each of the following must be true EXCEPT:
>
> (A) Ross is drafted by the Lightning.
> (B) Ned is drafted by the Sharks.
> (C) Yung is drafted by the Sharks.
> (D) Saul and Ross are not drafted by the same team as each other.
> (E) None of the other players are drafted to the same team as Wesley.

The question itself tells you that M and T are drafted by the same team. By operation of Clue 1, R must also be included in that same team, so now that team includes M, R, and T. This threesome will be drafted either by the Lightning or the Sharks.

The inclusion of M onto the team triggers Clue 3. Therefore, if the threesome were drafted onto the Sharks, it would necessarily include Y and become a foursome. Accordingly, the threesome must be drafted by the Lightning.

Comets	Lightning	Sharks
—	**M R T**	— — —

By operation of Clue 2, S and W must be drafted by different teams. One of the pair will be drafted by the Comets, and the other by the Sharks interchangeably.

Comets	Lightning	Sharks
S/W	M R T	**S/W** _ _

The remaining two players (N and Y) are drafted by the only team available—the Sharks.

Comets	Lightning	Sharks
S/W	M R T	S/W **N Y**

Answer choices A, B, C, and D are always true. Answer choice E could be true if, in fact, W were drafted by the Comets. However, this is not necessarily true because W can also be drafted by the Sharks.

(E) is the correct answer.

Question 5

This unrestricted, "cannot-be-true" question is identical to a "must-be-false" question. Four answers could be true. These are the wrong answers. One answer choice can never be true. This is the correct answer.

Which one of the following CANNOT be true?

(A) Saul and Tyrone are both drafted by the Lightning.
(B) Morgan and Ross are both drafted by the Lightning.
(C) Ned and Saul are both drafted by the Lightning.
(D) Wesley and Yung are both drafted by the Sharks.
(E) Ross and Wesley are both drafted by the Sharks.

As you attempt to eliminate answer choices with unrestricted questions, the first step is to review the diagram history.

	Comets	Lightning	Sharks
1	Y	M N S	R T W
2	N/S	M W Y	R T N/S
3	Y	M S/W N	S/W R T
4	S/W	M R T	S/W N Y

The pair in answer choice B can be drafted by the Lightning as shown in your workout to question 4. The pair in answer choice C can be drafted by the Lightning as shown in your workouts to questions 1 and 3. The pair in answer choice E can be drafted by the Sharks as shown in your workouts to questions 1 and 3. The pair in answer choice D can be drafted by the Sharks as shown in your workout to question 4. Saul and Tyrone cannot both be drafted by the Lightning.

(A) is the correct answer.

You may have been able to deduce this earlier. Ross must be drafted with Tyrone (Clue 1). Also, if Saul is drafted by the Lightning, Ned must also be drafted by the Lightning (Clue 4). So, if Saul and Tyrone are both drafted by the Lightning, you will end up with four players. Therefore, both Saul and Tyrone cannot be drafted by the Lightning.

GROUPING

(Minimum/Maximum)

Each of seven Freshmen Senators—Johnson, Katz, Lewis, Morris, Ng, Patel, and Rao—will be assigned to exactly one of three committees: Finance, Homeland Security, and Judiciary. The assignment of Senators must conform to following conditions:

Each committee is assigned at least two but no more than three of the seven Senators.

Lopez is assigned to either the Finance or Judiciary Committee.

Johnson is not assigned to the same committee as either Katz or Rao.

Patel is assigned to the same committee as either Katz or Lopez, but not both.

Morris is not assigned to the Judiciary Committee if Johnson is not assigned to the Judiciary Committee.

1. Which one of the following is an acceptable assignment of Senators to the committees?

   (A) Finance: Ng, Rao
       Homeland Security: Katz, Lopez, Patel
       Judiciary: Morris, Johnson
   (B) Finance: Patel, Rao
       Homeland Security: Johnson, Morris
       Judiciary: Katz, Lopez, Ng
   (C) Finance: Katz, Johnson
       Homeland Security: Morris, Ng, Rao
       Judiciary: Lopez, Patel
   (D) Finance: Lopez, Patel
       Homeland Security: Katz, Morris, Rao
       Judiciary: Johnson, Ng
   (E) Finance: Johnson, Ng
       Homeland Security: Katz, Rao
       Judiciary: Morris, Lopez, Patel

2. Which one of the following pairs of Senators CANNOT be assigned to the Homeland Security Committee together?

   (A) Morris and Rao
   (B) Katz and Rao
   (C) Johnson and Patel
   (D) Katz and Morris
   (E) Ng and Patel

3. If Patel is assigned to the Homeland Security Committee along with two other Senators, which one of the following could be true?

   (A) Katz and Ng are assigned to the Finance Committee.
   (B) Johnson and Rao are assigned to the Finance Committee.
   (C) Lopez and Ng are assigned to the Finance Committee.
   (D) Morris and Rao are assigned to the Judiciary Committee.
   (E) Morris and Ng are assigned to the Homeland Security Committee.

4. If Morris and Ng are assigned to the Judiciary Committee, any of the following could be false EXCEPT:

   (A) Patel is assigned to the Finance Committee.
   (B) Rao is assigned to the Finance Committee.
   (C) Rao is assigned to the Homeland Security Committee.
   (D) Katz is assigned to the Finance Committee.
   (E) Katz is assigned to the Homeland Security Committee.

Continued on next page ⮕

5. If Johnson and Patel are assigned to the
    Finance Committee, which one of the
    following must be false?

    (A) Morris is assigned to the Judiciary
        Committee.
    (B) Morris is assigned to the Homeland
        Security Committee.
    (C) Rao is assigned to the Judiciary
        Committee.
    (D) Rao is assigned to the Homeland
        Security Committee.
    (E) Katz is assigned to the Homeland
        Security Committee.

6. Each of the following pairs of Senators
    could be assigned to the Judiciary
    Committee together EXCEPT:

    (A) Ng and Rao
    (B) Johnson and Ng
    (C) Katz and Rao
    (D) Morris and Patel
    (E) Johnson and Morris

STEP 1 Visualize and draw the diagram.

What are you being asked to figure out? The game is asking you to assign Freshman Senators to exactly one of three committees. The diagram is as follows:

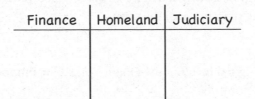

Note that the committee names have not been abbreviated—this is to avoid confusing the diagram labels with the components.

STEP 2 List the components and ascertain the ratio and distribution.

There are seven components—J, K, L, M, N, P, and R (the first letter of each Senator's surname). The ratio is ascertained from the language "*each of seven… will be assigned to exactly one of three committees.*" Every Senator is placed on one only committee. There are seven Senators and seven slots, so the ratio is one-to-one.

The distribution is ascertained from the first clue: "*Each committee is assigned at least two but no more than three of the seven Senators.*" This is minimum/maximum distribution. You have seven Senators and three committees. Each committee must be assigned a minimum of two Senators. If each committee were assigned exactly two Senators, it would total six Senators. But there are seven Senators. Therefore, that extra Senator must be assigned to one committee creating a 3-2-2 distribution (not necessarily corresponding with the committee names as they appear in the diagram). The diagram is now modified as follows:

Finance	Homeland	Judiciary
_ _ ···	_ _ ···	_ _ ···

The solid lines represent slots that *must* be occupied, whereas, the dotted lines represent slots that *could* be occupied.

STEP 3 Symbolize the clues.

Remember to always write down the contrapositive as well.

Clue 1	Each committee is assigned at least two, but no more than three, of the seven Senators.	Incorporated into the diagram

Clue 2 Lopez is assigned to either the Finance or Judiciary Committee.

L = Finance or Judiciary

Clue 3 Johnson is not assigned to the same committee as either Katz or Rao.

$J \rightarrow \sim K$ and $\sim R$; K or R $\rightarrow \sim J$

or [J̶K̶] [J̶R̶]

Clue 4 Patel is assigned to the same committee as either Katz or Lopez, but not both.

[PK] or [PL] [P̶L̶K̶]

Clue 5 Morris is not assigned to the Judiciary Committee if Johnson is not assigned to the Judiciary Committee.

$\sim J_{jud} \rightarrow \sim M_{jud}$; $M_{jud} \rightarrow J_{jud}$

STEP 4 Make deductions.

Remember that linking the conditional statements is crucial.

Deduction 1: From Clue 2, you can deduce that L is not assigned to the Homeland Security Committee.

	~L	
Finance	Homeland	Judiciary
_ _ ...	_ _ ...	_ _ ...

Deduction 2: By linking Conditions 3 and 5, you will begin to arrive at the next deduction. Here's the link:

$$M_{jud} \rightarrow J_{jud} \text{ and } J \rightarrow \sim K \text{ and } \sim R.$$

What next? If M is on the Judiciary Committee, then J is on the Judiciary Committee. Since J cannot be on the same committee as K or R, it follows that K and R cannot be on the Judiciary Committee when M is on it too.

$$M_{jud} \rightarrow \sim K_{jud \text{ and }} \sim R_{jud}$$

Tackle the questions.

Remember the optimal sequence for answering questions: 1. catch-a-clue; 2. restricted; 3. unrestricted; 4. modifiers. For this particular game, that translates to the following order: 1, 3, 4, 5, 2, and then 6.

Answer Key

1. **D**   2. **C**   3. **C**   4. **E**   5. **A**   6. **D**

Answers

Question 1

This is a catch-a-clue question.

> Which one of the following is an acceptable assignment of Senators to the committees?
>
> (A) Finance: Ng, Rao
>   Homeland Security: Katz, Lopez, Patel
>   Judiciary: Morris, Johnson
> (B) Finance: Patel, Rao
>   Homeland Security: Johnson, Morris
>   Judiciary: Katz, Lopez, Ng
> (C) Finance: Katz, Johnson
>   Homeland Security: Morris, Ng, Rao
>   Judiciary: Lopcz, Patel
> (D) Finance: Lopez, Patel
>   Homeland Security: Katz, Morris, Rao
>   Judiciary: Johnson, Ng
> (E) Finance: Johnson, Ng
>   Homeland Security: Katz, Rao
>   Judiciary: Morris, Lopez, Patel

The first clue (*Each committee is assigned at least two, but no more than three, of the seven Senators*) does not eliminate any answer choices. The second clue (*Lopez is assigned to either the Finance or Judiciary Committee*) eliminates answer choice A. The third clue (*Johnson is not assigned to the same committee as either Katz or Rao*) eliminates answer choice C. The fourth clue (*Patel is assigned to the same committee as either Katz or Lopez but not both*) eliminates answer choice B. The fifth clue (*Morris is not assigned to the Judiciary Committee if Johnson is not assigned to the Judiciary Committee*) eliminates answer choice E.

(D) is the correct answer.

Question 3

This one is a restricted, "could-be-true" question. Therefore, four answers are never true. These are the wrong answers. One answer is true at least once. This is the correct answer.

If Patel is assigned to the Homeland Security Committee along with two other Senators, which one of the following could be true?

(A) Katz and Ng are assigned to the Finance Committee.
(B) Johnson and Rao are assigned to the Finance Committee.
(C) Lopez and Ng are assigned to the Finance Committee.
(D) Morris and Rao are assigned to the Judiciary Committee.
(E) Morris and Ng are assigned to the Homeland Security Committee.

The question itself places Patel and two other Senators on the Homeland Committee. This means that the distribution is now known—both the Finance Committee and the Judiciary Committee will be assigned two Senators, and the Homeland Security Committee will be assigned three Senators. Let's place P on the Homeland Security Committee and adjust the distribution accordingly.

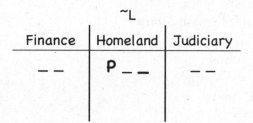

P must be assigned to the same committee as either Katz or Lopez (PK or PL), and L cannot be assigned to the Homeland Security Committee (Deduction 1). Therefore, K must be placed on the Homeland Security Committee with P. Update the diagram as follows:

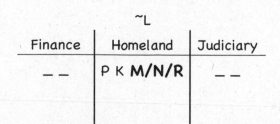

By operation of Clue 3, J is now banned from the Homeland Security Committee. The only available Senators for the last slot on the Homeland Security Committee are M, N, and R.

~L

Finance	Homeland	Judiciary
_ _	P K M/N/R	_ _

Answer choice A cannot be true because K is on the Homeland Security Committee and, therefore, cannot be on the Finance Committee. Answer choice B cannot be true because it violates Clue 3. Similarly, answer choice D cannot be true because it places M on the Judiciary Committee with R instead of J—this violates Clue 5. Lastly, answer choice E cannot be true because there are insufficient slots remaining on the Homeland Security Committee to place M and N. Answer choice C could be true.

(C) is the correct answer.

Question 4

This restricted, "could-be-false-EXCEPT" question is identical to a "must-be-true" question. Four answers could be false. These are the wrong answers. One answer choice is always true. This is the correct answer.

If Morris and Ng are assigned to the Judiciary Committee, any of the following could be false EXCEPT:

(A) Patel is assigned to the Finance Committee.
(B) Rao is assigned to the Finance Committee.
(C) Rao is assigned to the Homeland Security Committee.
(D) Katz is assigned to the Finance Committee.
(E) Katz is assigned to the Homeland Security Committee.

This question places M and N onto the Judiciary Committee. Update the diagram as follows:

Finance	Homeland	Judiciary
_ _ ...	_ _ ...	M N ...

By operation of Clue 5, you are now required to place J onto the Judiciary Committee. You can now deduce that the Finance Committee and the Homeland Security Committee are assigned two Senators each.

	~L	
Finance	Homeland	Judiciary
_ _	_ _	M N J

Pivot to L, the most restricted component. Deduction 1 shows that L is banned from the Homeland Security Committee. With the addition of J to the Judiciary Committee, it's now at its maximum of three and, therefore, there is no more room for L. Accordingly, L must be placed onto the Finance Committee, which is the only remaining spot.

| | ~L | |
Finance	Homeland	Judiciary
L _	_ _	M N J

By operation of Clue 4, P must be placed onto a committee with either K or L. Therefore, P will either join L on the Finance Committee, or it will couple with K and be assigned to the Homeland Security Committee. You now have the following two options:

| | ~L | |
Finance	Homeland	Judiciary
L P	_ _	M N J
_ _	P K	M N J

Finally, in the top option the only remaining components are R and K; both must be placed onto the Homeland Security Committee in order to fulfill the distributional requirements. Likewise, in the bottom option L and R are the last two remaining components; they must be placed onto the Finance Committee.

| | ~L | |
Finance	Homeland	Judiciary
L P	R K	M N J
L R	P K	M N J

Answer choices A, B, and C are each true once but not always. Answer choice D is never true. Answer choice E is true in both options.

(E) is the correct answer.

Question 5

This is a restricted, "must-be-false" question. Four answers could be true at least once. These are the wrong answers. One answer choice is never true. This is the correct answer.

> If Johnson and Patel are assigned to the Finance Committee, which one of the following must be false?
>
> (A) Morris is assigned to the Judiciary Committee.
> (B) Morris is assigned to the Homeland Security Committee.
> (C) Rao is assigned to the Judiciary Committee.
> (D) Rao is assigned to the Homeland Security Committee.
> (E) Katz is assigned to the Homeland Security Committee.

The question itself places J and P onto the Finance Committee. Update the diagram as follows:

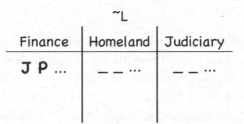

By operation of Clue 4, P must be placed onto a committee with either K or L. Therefore, either K or L must be placed onto the Finance Committee. However, by operation of Clue 3, J's placement onto the Finance Committee eliminates K as a possibility. As such, L must be placed onto the Finance Committee. This also solidifies the distribution as having three Senators on the Finance Committee and two Senators on the remaining committees.

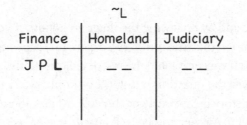

By operation of Clue 5, J's placement onto the Finance Committee disallows M's placement onto the Judiciary Committee. Since the Finance Committee has reached its maximum, M is likewise banned from the Finance Committee, so M must be placed onto the only remaining committee (Homeland Security).

The remaining components K, N, and R are each free to occupy the remaining three slots (one on the Homeland Security Committee and two on the Judiciary Committee) interchangeably.

| | ~L | |
Finance	Homeland	Judiciary
J P L	M **K/N/R**	**K/N/R** **K/N/R**

Answer choices C, D, and E are each true at least once. Answer choice B is always true. Answer choice A is never true.

(A) is the correct answer.

Question 2

This unrestricted, "cannot-be-true" question is identical to a "must-be-false" question. Four answers could be true at least once. These are the wrong answers. One answer choice can never be true. This is the correct answer.

> Which one of the following pairs of Senators CANNOT be assigned to the Homeland Security Committee together?
>
> (A) Morris and Rao
> (B) Katz and Rao
> (C) Johnson and Patel
> (D) Katz and Morris
> (E) Ng and Patel

This question is answerable by reviewing the diagram history if you have not already made this deduction. Remember that the primary reason for delaying answering unrestricted questions until after you have completed the restricted questions is to allow you to eliminate answer choices or answer the question outright by simply referring to the diagram history. Consider the diagram history below. Answer choice A (M and R) is seen as a possibility in the work for questions 1 and 5. Answer choice B (K and R) is seen as a possibility in the work for questions 1 and 3. Answer choice D (K and M) is seen as a possibility in the work for questions 1 and 5. Answer choice E (N and P) is seen as a possibility in the work for question 3. Therefore, answer choices A, B, D, and E can be eliminated.

(C) is the correct answer.

	Finance	Homeland	Judiciary
		~L	
#1	L P	K M R	J N
#3		P K M/N/R	
#4	L P	R K	M N J
	L R	P K	M N J
#5	J P L	M K/N/R	K/N/R K/N/R

Like most unrestricted questions, this question was also answerable be making a deduction. Specifically, by operation of Clue 4, Patel must be assigned to a committee with either K or L. By operation of Deduction 1, L cannot be assigned to the Homeland Security Committee. Therefore, if P is to be placed onto the Homeland Security Committee, P must be placed with K. However, by operation of Clue 3, J and K cannot be assigned to the same committee, thus creating a violation of one of the clues. As such, J and P cannot be placed onto the Homeland Security Committee together.

Question 6

This unrestricted, "could-be-true-EXCEPT" question is identical to a "must-be-false" question. Four answers could be true at least once. These are the wrong answers. One answer choice can never be true. This is the correct answer.

> Each of the following pairs of Senators could be assigned to the Judiciary
> Committee together EXCEPT:
>
> (A) Ng and Rao
> (B) Johnson and Ng
> (C) Katz and Rao
> (D) Morris and Patel
> (E) Johnson and Morris

Again, this unrestricted question is answerable by reviewing the diagram history. Answer choice A (N and R) is seen as a possibility in the work for question 5. Answer choice B (J and N) is seen as a possibility in the work for questions 1 and 4. Answer choice C (K and R) is seen as a possibility in the work for question 5. Answer choice E (J and M) is seen as a possibility in the work for question 4. Therefore, you can eliminate choices A, B, C, and E.

(D) is the correct answer.

Like question 2, this question could have been answered by making a deduction. By operation of contrapositive of Clue 5, if M is placed onto the Judiciary Committee, J must also be placed there. Also by operation of Clue 4, P must be placed on any committee with either K or L. The committee would now consist of M, P, J, and either K or L. This is a total of four Senators when a maximum of only three is allowed.

GROUPING

(Unknown Distribution)

Game 1

To prepare for study abroad, exactly five students—M, N, P, R, and T—will learn at least one of four languages: French, Hindi, Italian, and Spanish. No student learns any other language. The following conditions must apply:

No student learns all four languages.

At least two of the students learn French.

Any language that is learned by R is not learned by N.

If French is learned by any student, then that student learns Italian.

If Hindi is learned by any student, then that student learns Spanish.

P learns French.

1. If N learns Italian, then which one of the following must be true?

   (A) M learns French.
   (B) M learns Spanish.
   (C) N learns French.
   (D) R learns Hindi.
   (E) R learns Spanish.

2. Which one of the following could be true?

   (A) At least one student learns neither Italian nor Spanish.
   (B) All five students learn Spanish.
   (C) At least one student learns French and Spanish.
   (D) Exactly one of the students learns Italian.
   (E) At least one student learns French and Hindi.

3. If any one student learns three of the languages, then which one of the following must be true about that student?

   (A) The student does not learn French.
   (B) The student does not learn Italian.
   (C) The student learns French and Italian.
   (D) The student learns Italian and Spanish.
   (E) The student learns Hindi and Spanish.

4. Each of the following can be true EXCEPT:

   (A) M learns Italian.
   (B) N learns Italian.
   (C) N learns Spanish.
   (D) P learns Hindi.
   (E) R learns Italian.

5. Which one of the following is a pair of languages that CANNOT both be learned by student R?

   (A) French and Italian
   (B) French and Spanish
   (C) Hindi and Italian
   (D) Italian and Spanish
   (E) Hindi and Spanish

6. If three of the students learn Hindi, then each of the following could be true EXCEPT:

   (A) Exactly two students learn Italian.
   (B) Exactly three students learn Italian.
   (C) Exactly four students learn Spanish.
   (D) Exactly two students learn French.
   (E) Exactly three students learn French.

STEP 1 Visualize and draw the diagram.

What are you being asked to figure out? The game is asking you to ascertain which languages are learned by each of five students—M, N, P, R, and T. The diagram is as follows:

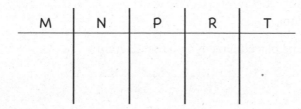

This diagram may have been a little tricky since you're accustomed so far to initials representing the components. Indeed, this game is solvable (albeit with a little more difficulty) if the languages head the diagram. However, the first clue (*no student learns all four languages*) is the reason that the above diagram is preferable. This clue is symbolized as FHIS. If the languages headed the diagram, the symbolization of this clue would be more complicated (i.e., M_{french} and M_{hindi} and $M_{italian} \rightarrow \sim M_{spanish}$, and so on).

STEP 2 List the components and ascertain the ratio and distribution.

There are four components—F, H, I, and S (the first letter of each language). There are five students and four languages. There is no language to suggest how often each language will be learned, except the fact that French is learned by at least two students. Therefore, the total number of slots is unknown.

The distribution is ascertained from the language "*exactly five students….will learn at least one of four languages.*" Therefore, the minimum number of languages learned by any student is one. Additionally, the first clue (*no student learns all four languages*) fixes your maximum. This clue sets the maximum number of languages learned by each student to three. This is minimum/maximum distribution.

STEP 3 Symbolize the clues.

Remember to always write down the contrapositive as well.

Clue 1	No student learns all four languages.	FHIS
Clue 2	At least two of the students learn French.	FF $^+$
Clue 3	Any language that is learned by R is not learned by N.	Slot R $\rightarrow$ ~Slot N Slot N $\rightarrow$ ~Slot R (put into diagram)
Clue 4	If French is learned by any student, then that student learns Italian.	F $\rightarrow$ I; ~I $\rightarrow$ ~F

	Clue 5	If Hindi is learned by any student, then that student learns Spanish.	H → S; ~S → ~H
	Clue 6	P learns French.	F = P
			(put into diagram)

STEP 4 Make deductions.

Clues 3 and 6 should be placed directly into the diagram:

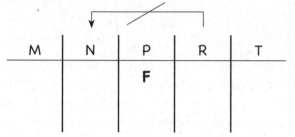

Deduction 1: From Clue 4, you can deduce that I must be placed in P.

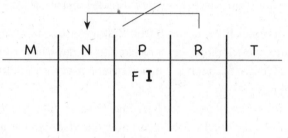

Also, by combining Clues 2 and 4, you can deduce that there are at least two students that will learn Italian (I I $^+$).

Deduction 2: From Clue 5 and Clue 1, you can deduce that H is banned from P. How do you know this? If P were to learn H, then he/she would also learn S, bringing the total number of languages learned by P to four. This is in violation of Clue 1. Additionally, it can be deduced that because all four languages cannot be learned by the same student that F → ~H.

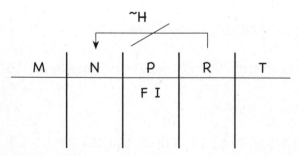

Noticeably absent is any indication that each language is learned by a least one student. This leaves your distribution wide open.

STEP 5 Tackle the questions.

Remember the optimal sequence for answering questions: 1. catch-a-clue; 2. restricted; 3. unrestricted; 4. modifiers. For this particular game, that translates to the following order: 1, 3, 6, 2, 4, and then 5.

Answer Key

1. **E**   2. **C**   3. **D**   4. **D**   5. **D**   6. **E**

Answers

Question 1

This is a restricted, "must-be-true" question. Therefore, four answers are never true, or they are true at least once but not always. These are the wrong answers. One answer is always true. This is the correct answer.

If N learns Italian, then which one of the following must be true?

(A) M learns French.
(B) M learns Spanish.
(C) N learns French.
(D) R learns Hindi.
(E) R learns Spanish.

By operation of the contrapositive of Clue 3, if a language is learned by N, then that language is likewise not learned by R; therefore, banning Italian from student R. By operation of the contrapositive of Clue 4, French is also banned from student R.

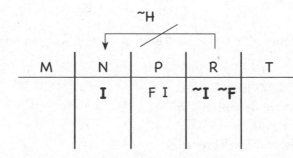

The only available languages available for student R are both Hindi and Spanish or Spanish alone. In either option, student R must learn Spanish.

Answer choices A, B, C, and D can each be true, but they are not always true.

(E) is the correct answer.

Question 3

This is a restricted, "must-be-true" question. Therefore, four answers are never true, or they are true at least once but not always. These are the wrong answers. One answer is always true. This is the correct answer.

> If any one student learns three of the languages, then which one of the following must be true about that student?
>
> (A) The student does not learn French.
> (B) The student does not learn Italian.
> (C) The student learns French and Italian.
> (D) The student learns Italian and Spanish.
> (E) The student learns Hindi and Spanish.

This question adds an additional condition, which is actually very restraining given that the only options are one, two, or three languages. There is little to be gained by randomly plugging the components into the diagram. This is rarely the best course of action. In fact, this question's mystery student calls for a deduction.

Let's look at Deduction 2 (F → ~H). If a student learns exactly three languages and that student cannot learn French and Hindi, then the only options are Italian and Spanish with either French or Hindi.

(D) is the correct answer.

Question 6

This restricted, "could-be-true-EXCEPT" question is identical to a "must-be-false" question. Four answers could be true. These are the wrong answers. One answer choice must be false. This is the correct answer.

> If three of the students learn Hindi, then each of the following could be true EXCEPT:
>
> (A) Exactly two students learn Italian.
> (B) Exactly three students learn Italian.
> (C) Exactly four students learn Spanish.
> (D) Exactly two students learn French.
> (E) Exactly three students learn French.

You can answer this question by simply referring to Deduction 2. Specifically, if three students learn H and the students cannot learn both H and F, then the number of students learning F is relegated to exactly two. Answer choice E is the correct answer. Nonetheless, let's work it out the long way.

Pivot to the most restricted component: Hindi. By operation of Deduction 2, Hindi is banned from student R. Since Hindi must be assigned to three students, and students N and R cannot learn the same languages, Hindi must be assigned to both students M and T and either N (top option) or R (bottom option). Option 1 is as follows:

~H

M	N	P	R	T
H	H	F I		H
H		F I	H	H

By operation of Clue 5, Spanish must be assigned to every student learning H. Therefore, Spanish must be assigned to students M, N, and T in the top option and students M, R, and T in the bottom option.

~H

M	N	P	R	T
H S	H S	F I		H S
H S		F I	H S	H S

By operation of Clue 4 and Deduction 1, French and Italian must be assigned to student R in the top option and to student N in the bottom option.

~H

M	N	P	R	T
H S	H S	F I	F I	H S
H S	F I	F I	H S	H S

Answer choices A and D could be true. Italian (alone and without French) can certainly be assigned to either student M, N, or T in the top option, or to student M, R, or T in the bottom option. This would bring the total number of students learning Italian to three. Therefore, answer choice B can be true. Likewise, you can assign Spanish (alone and without Hindi) to student P in both the top and the bottom options, bringing the total number of students learning Spanish to four. This means answer choice C can be true.

(E) is the correct answer.

Question 2

This is an unrestricted, "could-be-true" question. Therefore, four answers are never true. These are the wrong answers. The correct answer is true either sometimes or always true.

Which one of the following could be true?

(A) At least one student learns neither Italian nor Spanish.
(B) All five students learn Spanish.
(C) At least one student learns French and Spanish.
(D) Exactly one of the students learns Italian.
(E) At least one student learns French and Hindi.

This game has generated very little diagram history; nonetheless, if you were to review the diagram and explanations from question 6, you could ascertain that student P is learning French and Italian and could also learn Spanish.

(C) is the correct answer.

Take a look at why the other four answer choices are wrong, and see how you could have deduced your way to the correct answer even if you hadn't realized the diagram history provided it.

Answer choice A: If a student learns neither Italian nor Spanish, then that means he/she doesn't learn French (~I → ~F) nor Hindi (~S → ~H). This is in violation of the condition that each student learns at least one language. This answer can be eliminated.

Answer choice B: Clue 3 does not allow students N and R to learn the same languages. This answer can be eliminated.

Answer choice D: Deduction 1 indicates that there must be at least two students learning Italian. This answer can be eliminated.

Answer choice E: By operation of Deduction 2, French and Hindi cannot be learned by the same student. This answer can be eliminated.

Question 4

This unrestricted, "could-be-true-EXCEPT" question is identical to a "must-be-false" question. Four answers could be true. These are the wrong answers. One answer choice is never true. This is the correct answer.

Each of the following can be true EXCEPT:

(A) M learns Italian.
(B) N learns Italian.
(C) N learns Spanish.
(D) P learns Hindi.
(E) R learns Italian.

This question is answerable by reviewing the prior deductions. Review Deduction 2 where it was proven that student P, who must learn French (Clue 6) and also Italian (Clue 4), cannot also learn Hindi.

(D) is the correct answer.

Question 5

This is an unrestricted, "cannot-be-true" question. Therefore, four answers are always true, or they are true at least once but not always. These are the wrong answers. One answer is never true. This is the correct answer.

> Which one of the following is a pair of languages that CANNOT both be learned
> by student R?
>
> (A) French and Italian
> (B) French and Spanish
> (C) Hindi and Italian
> (D) Italian and Spanish
> (E) Hindi and Spanish

This question is completely answerable. If you were to review the diagram and explanations from question 6, you would ascertain that answer choices A, B, C, and E can be true. R cannot learn both Italian and Spanish. How would you know? If student R were to learn both Italian and Spanish, then by operation of Clue 3, student N could learn neither Italian nor Spanish. By operation of the contrapositive Clue 4, student N could not learn French and by operation of Clue 5, student N could not learn Hindi—thus violating the condition that each student must learn at least one language.

(D) is the correct answer.

Game 2

In Springfield there are exactly three coffee shops—Beantown, Grinders, and Perk-Up. Each of the three coffee shops sells at least one of five types of coffee drinks: cappuccino, espresso, frappe, latte, or macchiato. None of the coffee shops sells any other type of coffee drinks. Among the three coffee shops, at least one of each type of coffee drink is sold. The following conditions must hold:

Exactly two of the three coffee shops sell macchiato.

Beantown sells exactly one type of coffee drink.

Perk-Up sells espresso but not latte.

Any coffee shop that sells frappe does not also sell cappuccino.

Any coffee shop that sells latte must also sell macchiato.

Any coffee shop that sells espresso must also sell frappe.

1. Which one of the following could be a complete and accurate matching of each coffee shop to its coffee drinks?

   (A) Beantown: cappuccino; Grinders: latte, macchiato; Perk-Up: espresso, frappe, macchiato
   (B) Beantown: latte; Grinders: espresso, cappuccino, macchiato; Perk-Up: espresso, frappe, macchiato
   (C) Beantown: cappuccino, macchiato; Grinders: latte, macchiato; Perk-Up: espresso, frappe
   (D) Beantown: frappe; Grinders: latte, macchiato; Perk-Up: espresso, macchiato
   (E) Beantown: macchiato; Grinders: cappuccino, frappe, latte, macchiato; Perk-Up: espresso, frappe

2. Which one of the following could be true?

   (A) Both Beantown and Perk-Up sell macchiato.
   (B) Both Beantown and Perk-Up sell cappuccino.
   (C) Both Beantown and Grinders sell frappe.
   (D) Both Beantown and Grinders sell latte.
   (E) Both Beantown and Grinders sell cappuccino.

3. If Grinders sells exactly three coffee drinks, then each of the following could be true EXCEPT:

   (A) Beantown does not sell cappuccino.
   (B) Beantown sells macchiato.
   (C) Grinders sells espresso.
   (D) Grinders sells frappe.
   (E) Perk-Up sells macchiato.

4. If each of exactly two of the coffee shops sells cappuccino, then which one of the following could be true?

   (A) Beantown does not sell cappuccino.
   (B) Grinders sells exactly three types of coffee drinks.
   (C) Grinders sells exactly four types of coffee drinks.
   (D) Perk-Up does not sell macchiato.
   (E) Perk-Up sells exactly two types of coffee drinks.

5. If a type of coffee drink sold at Beantown is the same type of coffee drink sold at Perk-Up, then which one of the following must be true?

(A) Beantown sells cappuccino.
(B) Beantown sells espresso.
(C) Beantown sells macchiato.
(D) Grinders sell frappe.
(E) Perk-Up sells macchiato.

6. Each of the following could be true EXCEPT:

(A) Neither Perk-Up nor Beantown sell latte.
(B) Neither Perk-Up nor Beantown sell macchiato.
(C) Neither Perk-Up nor Grinders sell cappuccino.
(D) Neither Beantown nor Grinders sell espresso.
(E) Neither Beantown nor Grinders sell frappe.

STEP 1 Visualize and draw the diagram.

What are you being asked to figure out? The game is asking you to ascertain which types of coffee drinks are sold at three different coffee shops—Beantown, Grinders, and Perk-Up. The diagram is as follows:

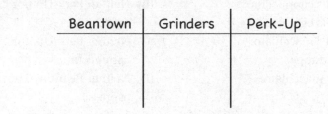

STEP 2 List the components and ascertain the ratio and distribution.

There are five components—C, E, F, L, and M (the first letter of each type of coffee drink). You have three coffee shops and five types of coffee drinks, but the exact ratio is unknown because the scenario reads "among the three coffee shops *at least one of each type of coffee drink is sold.*" Note that one of the clues is quite helpful in determining how many types of coffee drinks are sold at *one* of the coffee shops. Specifically, the second clue reads "*Beantown sells exactly one type of coffee drink.*" The diagram is modified as follows:

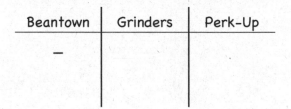

STEP 3 Symbolize the clues.

Remember to always write down the contrapositive as well.

Clue 1   Exactly two of the three coffee shops sell macchiato.   M M

Clue 2   Beantown sells exactly one type of coffee drink.   (This has already been represented in the diagram.)

Clue 3   Perk-Up sells espresso but not latte. This is best represented directly in the diagram. The diagram is modified as follows:

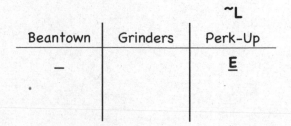

Clue 4 Any coffee shop that sells frappe does not also sell cappuccino.

$F \rightarrow \sim C; \ C \rightarrow \sim F$

Clue 5 Any coffee shop that sells latte must also sell macchiato.

$L \rightarrow M; \ \sim M \rightarrow \sim L$

Clue 6 Any coffee shop that sells espresso must also sell frappe.

$E \rightarrow F; \ \sim F \rightarrow \sim E$

STEP 4 Make deductions.

Remember that linking the conditional statements is crucial. Here Clues 6 and 1 can be linked:

$$E \rightarrow F \text{ and } F \rightarrow \sim C$$

1. The following clue can be deduced from the link above: $E \rightarrow \sim C$ and $C \rightarrow \sim E$
2. From Clue 3 and linkage of Clues 6 and 1 ($E \rightarrow F$ and $F \rightarrow \sim C$), you can deduce that Perk-Up carries F and does not carry C. Place this information directly into your diagram:

		~L ~C
Beantown	Grinders	Perk-Up
—		<u>E</u> <u>F</u>

3. From Clue 2 (*Beantown sells exactly one type of coffee*), Clue 5, and Clue 6, you can deduce that Beantown does not carry L nor E. How? Each and every time L is included among the coffee drinks sold at a coffee shop, M must also be sold by that same coffee shop. Therefore, the inclusion of L at any coffee shop requires the coffee shop to sell a minimum of two types of coffee drinks. Since, Beantown *sells just one type of coffee drink, it cannot sell L*. Similarly, Clue 6 dictates that each and every time a coffee shop sells E, it must also sell F. Accordingly, Beantown cannot carry E as well. Update the diagram as follows:

~E ~L		~L ~C
Beantown	Grinders	Perk-Up
—		<u>E</u> <u>F</u>

4. Pivot to L which has emerged as the most restricted component. Notice that L cannot be sold by either Beantown or Perk-Up. Since the scenario indicates that from among the three coffee shops *at least one of **each** type of coffee drink is sold,* you know that each and every component must be placed into the diagram a minimum of one time. Therefore, L must be sold by Grinders. Likewise, by operation of Clue 5, M is also sold at Grinders. Update the diagram as follows:

~E ~L		~L ~C
Beantown	Grinders	Perk-Up
—	<u>L</u> <u>M</u>	<u>E</u> <u>F</u>

(STEP 5) Tackle the questions.

Remember the optimal sequence for answering questions: 1. catch-a-clue; 2. restricted; 3. unrestricted; 4. modifiers. For this particular game, that translates to the following order: 1, 3, 4, 5, 2, and then 6.

Answer Key

1. **A**   2. **E**   3. **C**   4. **B**   5. **E**   6. **B**

Answers

Question 1

This is a catch-a-clue question. Here are the answer choices again:

(A) Beantown: cappuccino; Grinders: latte, macchiato; Perk-Up: espresso, frappe, macchiato
(B) Beantown: latte; Grinders: espresso, cappuccino, macchiato; Perk-Up: espresso, frappe, macchiato
(C) Beantown: cappuccino, macchiato; Grinders: latte, macchiato; Perk-Up: espresso, frappe
(D) Beantown: frappe; Grinders: latte, macchiato; Perk-Up: espresso, macchiato
(E) Beantown: macchiato; Grinders: cappuccino, frappe, latte, macchiato; Perk-Up: espresso, frappe

The first rule (*Exactly two of the three coffee shops sell macchiato*) does not eliminate any of the answer choices. The second clue (*Beantown sells exactly one type of coffee drink*) eliminates answer choice C. The third clue (*Perk-Up sells espresso but not latte*) does not eliminate any of the answer choices. The fourth clue (*Any coffee shop that sells frappe does not sell cappuccino*) eliminates answer choice E. The fifth clue (*Any coffee shop that sells latte must also sell macchiato*) eliminates answer choice B. The sixth clue (*Any coffee shop that sells espresso must also sell frappe*) eliminates answer choice D.

(A) is the correct answer.

Question 3

This restricted, "could-be-true-EXCEPT" question is identical to a "must-be-false" question. Four answers could be true. These are the wrong answers. One answer choice is never be true. This is the correct answer.

> If Grinders sells exactly three coffee drinks, then each of the following could be true EXCEPT:
>
> (A) Beantown does not sell cappuccino.
> (B) Beantown sells macchiato.
> (C) Grinders sells espresso.
> (D) Grinders sells frappe.
> (E) Perk-Up sells macchiato.

This question requires that Grinders sell exactly three coffee drinks. It has already been deduced that two of the five coffee drinks (L and M) must be sold by Grinders. From Clue 6, you can deduce that E cannot be assigned to Grinders; this is because every time a coffee shop sells E, it must also sell F, thereby bringing the total number of coffee drinks sold to four. Therefore, your options for the third drink sold by Grinders are limited to either C or F. Update the diagram as follows:

~E ~L		~L ~C
Beantown	Grinders	Perk-Up
—	L M **C/F**	E F

The remaining M could be sold by either Beantown or Perk-Up. Additionally, Beantown could sell either F or C.

Answer choices A, B, D, and E are each true sometimes but not always. Answer choice C is never true.

(C) is the correct answer.

Question 4

This is a restricted, "could-be-true" question. The correct answer is true at least once. Wrong answers will never be true.

> If each of exactly two of the coffee shops sells cappuccino, then which one of the following could be true?
>
> (A) Beantown does not sell cappuccino.
> (B) Grinders sells exactly three types of coffee drinks.
> (C) Grinders sells exactly four types of coffee drinks.
> (D) Perk-Up does not sell macchiato.
> (E) Perk-Up sells exactly two types of coffee drinks.

This question stipulates that there will be exactly two coffee shops that sell C. Prior deductions ban C from Perk-Up, so C must be sold by both Beantown and Grinders.

	~E ~L			~L ~C
	Beantown	Grinders		Perk-Up
	C	L M C		E F

With the assignment of C to Grinders, the prior deduction linking the contrapositive of Clue 4 and Clue 6 is triggered (C → ~F → ~E). This bans F and E from Grinders.

   With the sole Beantown slot filled, the remaining M must be assigned to Perk-Up.

	~E ~L			~L ~C
	Beantown	Grinders		Perk-Up
	C	L M C		E F M

Answer choices A, C, D, and E are never true. Answer choice B is always true. You may be saying to yourself that answer choice B actually "must be" true, and you are correct. But remember everything that must be true could be true. This is one of those rare instances where your understanding of that concept is being put to the test.

(B) is the correct answer.

Question 5

This is a restricted, "must-be-true" question. Therefore, four answers are true sometimes but not always, or they are never true. The correct answer is always true.

   If a type of coffee drink sold at Beantown is the same type of coffee drink sold at Perk-Up, then which one of the following must be true?

   (A) Beantown sells cappuccino.
   (B) Beantown sells espresso.
   (C) Beantown sells macchiato.
   (D) Grinders sell frappe.
   (E) Perk-Up sells macchiato.

This question requires that the sole coffee drink sold at Beantown be one of the coffee drinks sold at Perk-Up. Prior deductions have banned E and L from Beantown. Likewise, prior deductions have banned C and L from Perk-Up. Accordingly, Beantown and Perk-Up shops cannot both sell C, E, or L.

Also, since M is sold by exactly two coffee shops, and you have deduced that one of those coffee shops is Grinders, it follows that M cannot be a coffee drink sold by both Beantown and Perk-Up since that would bring the total number of coffee shops selling M to three. The only component remaining that could be sold by both Beantown and Perk-Up is F.

	~E ~L		~L ~C
	Beantown	Grinders	Perk-Up
	<u>F</u>	<u>L</u> <u>M</u>	<u>E</u> <u>F</u>

Finally, as the sole slot in Beantown is filled, the remaining M must be assigned to Perk-Up.

	~E ~L		~L ~C
	Beantown	Grinders	Perk-Up
	<u>F</u>	<u>L</u> M	<u>E</u> <u>F</u> <u>M</u>

Answer choices A, B, and C are never true. Answer choice D could be true sometimes but is not always true. Answer choice E is always true.

(E) is the correct answer.

Question 2

In this unrestricted, "could-be-true" question, four answers are never true. These are the wrong answers. One answer choice can be true at least once. This is the correct answer.

Which one of the following could be true?

(A) Both Beantown and Perk-Up sell macchiato.
(B) Both Beantown and Perk-Up sell cappuccino.
(C) Both Beantown and Grinders sell frappe.
(D) Both Beantown and Grinders sell latte.
(E) Both Beantown and Grinders sell cappuccino.

If you review the diagram and explanations from question 4, you will ascertain that answer choice E can be true.

(E) is the correct response.

Although the question has been answered, let's take a look at why the other four choices are wrong, and review how you could have deduced your way to the correct answer.

Answer choice A: Clue 1 tells you that there are exactly two coffee shops that sell macchiato. Deduction 4 indicates that Grinders must sell macchiato. Therefore, if both Beantown and Perk-up were to sell macchiato, that would bring the total number of shops selling macchiato to three; this violates Clue 1. This answer choice can be eliminated.

Answer choice B: Deduction 2 indicates that Perk-up does not sell cappuccino. This answer choice can be eliminated.

Answer choice C: Deduction 2 proved that Perk-up sells frappes. Therefore, if both Beantown and Perk-up were to sell frappes, then each and every coffee shop would be selling frappes. By operation of Clue 4, none of the coffee shops could sell cappuccino since it contradicts the condition that "*at least one of each type of coffee drink is sold.*" This answer choice can be eliminated.

Answer choice D: By operation of Deduction 3, Beantown does not sell lattes. This answer choice can be eliminated.

Question 6

This unrestricted "could-be-true-EXCEPT" question is identical to a "must-be-false" question. Four answers could be true. These are the wrong answers. One answer choice is never true. This is the correct answer.

Each of the following could be true EXCEPT:

(A) Neither Perk-Up nor Beantown sell latte.
(B) Neither Perk-Up nor Beantown sell macchiato.
(C) Neither Perk-Up nor Grinders sell cappuccino.
(D) Neither Beantown nor Grinders sell espresso.
(E) Neither Beantown nor Grinders sell frappe.

In your review of the diagram and explanation from question 4, you will ascertain that answer choices A, D, and E can be true. With just two answers remaining, you could try out one of the answers or you hopefully realize that answer choice B (*neither Perk-Up nor Beantown sell macchiato*), violates Clue 1 which requires that macchiato be sold to exactly two of the three coffee shops. Answer choice B cannot be true.

(B) is the correct answer.

IN/OUT GROUPING GAMES

Previously in this chapter, you were charged with placing the game components into slots within designated groups. First, each of the components was placed into one group and only one group. There were an equal number of components and available slots and the distribution was mostly fixed. Later, you were exposed to games where each component was placed into a group, and some of the components were placed into more than one group. In these instances, the number of slots exceeded the number of components and the distribution was less definitive.

The games in this section are somewhat different. These ones will involve placing some of the components into a group(s), while simultaneously leaving other components out of any group(s). Now the number of slots is less than the number of components. These logic games are referred to here simply as *in/out grouping games.* As always, start these logic games by asking yourself, "What am I being asked to figure out?" In doing so, you will almost always arrive at a point where you can visualize and draw your diagram (Step 1).

Let's explore the entire five-step process as it relates specifically to in/out grouping games. Consider the setup below:

> *From among a group of seven teachers*—King, London, Mendez, Newsome, Oliver, Pittman, and Reed—*exactly four will be selected* to serve on the Education Committee. The following conditions must be met:
>
> If Mendez is selected, then Oliver is not selected.
>
> If King is selected, then Newsome is selected.
>
> If Mendez is not selected, then London is selected.

Notice the highlighted language: *"from among a group of seven teachers … exactly four will be selected."* This is very traditional in/out grouping language, and it's precisely this language that will help you answer "What am I being asked to figure out?" It indicates that you have a larger set of components (*seven teachers*), and from that larger set, you will choose exactly four to serve on the Education Committee. Three components will be left out of the group of participants. How will you draw your diagram? Perhaps you think that a four-slot diagram, like the one below, would be appropriate.

— — — —

If you were to choose this diagram, you would still need to find a way to keep track of the three unselected components. You might try to keep track of this information in your head, but this tactic almost always leads to errors. Perhaps you could scribble down notes about the components that are forced out of the group. Scribbling, however, often leads to disorganized information, which can increase the amount of time required to complete the questions.

Take a moment and think back to the one-to-one ratio sequence game that you encountered earlier in this book. Compare the level of difficulty of that logic game to the not-one-to-one ratio sequence game that you also solved. Remember how much simpler it felt to have an equal number of slots and components? With that in mind, consider the following diagram:

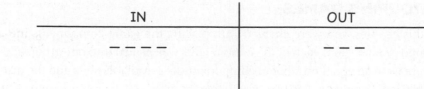

IN	OUT
– – – –	– – –

The use of both an in-column (for the four teachers selected to serve on the committee) and an out-column (for the three teachers forced off the committee) allows you to transform a game that is not technically a one-to-one ratio game into one that is. With the addition of the out-column, every component now has a slot. Often in these types of games, you'll be able to fill in the fixed number of slots in the out-column first, and then simply by deduction all the leftovers would be placed in the in-column.

Next let's consider Step 2 of the five-step approach: listing the components and ascertaining the ratio and distribution. In/out games, even with the inclusion of an out-column, are not quite as simple and straightforward as regular one-to-one ratio games. Consider the following setup:

> **The bride-to-be must select *at least five and at most six* dishes from a group of nine dishes offered at the catering hall. The dishes are lasagna, meatballs, noodles, oysters, pork chops, quail, roast beef, salmon, and tacos. Selection must conform to the following regulations:**
>
> **Meatballs and Lasagna may not both be selected.**
>
> **Noodles are selected, if and only if, quail is selected.**
>
> **Oysters are selected if quail is selected.**

Note the minimum/maximum language: *at least five and at most six*. In this case, since the number of components *in* the group and the number of components *out* of the group are not completely determined or fixed, you may be tempted to abandon the whole idea of an out-column. However, its inclusion would still be quite useful. Consider the following diagram:

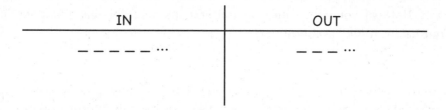

IN	OUT
– – – – – ⋯	– – – ⋯

The solid lines represent slots that *must* be occupied, whereas the dotted lines represent slots that *could* be occupied. The diagram becomes a constant visual reminder of the number of components that must be in the group as well as how many that could be in the group.

Probably the most challenging ratio to navigate within the in/out grouping games is the unknown distribution grouping games type. With these, no restrictions are placed on the number of components in the group(s) nor on the number of components to be left out of the group(s), although typically, there must be at least one component in each group(s). The conditions are your only guide in determining the final number of ins and outs. Consider the following setup:

A professor will choose at least one student to give a speech at the university's commencement from among six students—Garcia, Han, Johnson, Khanna, Lai, and Murray. The selection of students is consistent with the following conditions:

If Han is selected, then Garcia is not selected.

If Johnson is not selected, then Han is selected.

If Murray is selected, then Garcia is also selected.

If Khanna is selected, then both Garcia and Lai are selected.

While you have a clear set of six students from which to make your selection, noticeably absent is any language indicating how many will be selected. Your only parameters are controlled by the conditions. Consider the following diagram:

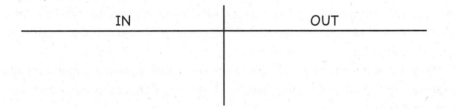

Without any real parameters, the slots that were present in the first two setups have disappeared. The out-column remains, as it continues to provide the organizational benefit of supplying one area of your page designated for components that are forced *out* of your group when a condition requires it.

To summarize, the mathematical distributions (whether the number of components in your in-column is known) will fall into three categories:

1. **FIXED.** The number of components to be placed *in* the group and the number to be left *out* of the group are determined and fixed.

2. **MINIMUM/MAXIMUM.** The number of components to be placed *in* the group and the number of components to be left *out* of the group are somewhat, but not completely, determined. In this case, a minimum and a maximum number of components to be included are given.

3. **UNKNOWN DISTRIBUTION GROUPING GAMES.** There are no restrictions on the number of components to be placed *in* the group(s) nor on the number of components to be left *out* of the group(s), although typically, there must be at least one component *in*.

Before proceeding with the solution to each of the sample setups, let's take a look at how conditional statements can be affected by the addition of an out-column to your diagram. In fact, you might find it useful at this point to review Chapter 4 on Conditional Statements.

Step 3 directs the symbolization of the clues. Let's consider two very typical conditions often presented with in/out grouping. While doing so, think about what each condition means to the in/out diagram and, more importantly, what it doesn't mean.

Condition 1: If A is selected, then B is not selected.

This may appear relatively straightforward, especially after you review the material on conditional statements. If A is placed in the in-column, then you must necessarily place B in the out-column. Simply put, A and B cannot both be placed in the in-column simultaneously. It is sometimes erroneously concluded that A and B cannot likewise be placed in the out-column simultaneously. This is not true. It is possible (based solely on this condition) that A and B are both assigned to the out-column.

Condition 2: If A is not selected, then B is selected.

Conditions like this one are often stumbling blocks to completing in/out games successfully. Essentially, it translates to this: if A is placed in the out-column, then B must necessarily be placed in the in-column. More simply put, A and B cannot be placed in the out-column simultaneously. From there it's often erroneously concluded that, likewise, A and B cannot be placed in the in-column simultaneously. Not true. It is possible that both A and B are assigned to the in-column at the same time.

As for Step 4 where you will be making deductions, the approach for in/out games is the same as it was for the other grouping games. Most of the deductions are ascertained via the linking of conditional statements.

Finally, do not forget to attack these questions in the order you have determined is the most advantageous—specifically catch-a-clue, restrictive, unrestrictive, and then modifiers.

Game 1

A debate coach will select exactly five students to serve on the debate team, from among nine students: three freshmen—G, H, J; three juniors—M, N, P; and three seniors—S, T, V. The selection of team members will meet the following conditions:

The team must include at least one freshman, at least one junior, and at least one senior.

M and N cannot both be selected.

G and T cannot both be selected.

If either S or T is selected, both must be selected.

H cannot be selected unless P is selected.

V cannot be selected unless M is selected.

1. Which one of the following could be a complete and accurate list of the students selected for the debate team?

   (A) H, J, P, S, T
   (B) G, H, M, N, V
   (C) G, J, M, S, V
   (D) G, M, P, S, T
   (E) H, P, S, T, V

2. Which one of the following could be true?

   (A) N and V are both selected.
   (B) G and S are both selected.
   (C) All three freshmen are selected.
   (D) All three juniors are selected.
   (E) All three seniors are selected.

3. If N and T are selected, which one of the following is a pair of students who could also be selected?

   (A) G and H
   (B) H and J
   (C) J and S
   (D) P and V
   (E) M and S

4. Each of the following is a pair of students that could be selected together EXCEPT:

   (A) J and V
   (B) P and T
   (C) M and H
   (D) N and G
   (E) G and V

5. Which one of the following is a pair of students of which the debate coach must select at least one?

   (A) M and V
   (B) N and J
   (C) M and T
   (D) G and V
   (E) G and J

6. If only one senior is selected, then each of the following must be true EXCEPT:

   (A) M is selected.
   (B) T is not selected.
   (C) H is selected.
   (D) P is selected.
   (E) N is not selected.

Visualize and draw the diagram.

What are you being asked to figure out? The game is asking you to ascertain which students are selected for the debate team. Since some students will be left out of the debate team, the diagram is as follows:

IN	OUT

(STEP 2) List the components and ascertain the ratio and/or distribution.

The components are:

Freshmen: G, H, J
Juniors: M, N, P
Seniors: S, T, V

There are exactly five students chosen from a total group of nine students. The distribution is fixed. Update the diagram as follows:

IN	OUT
_ _ _ _ _	_ _ _ _

(STEP 3) Symbolize the clues.

Remember to always write down the contrapositive as well.

Clue 1   The team must include at least one freshman,
at least one junior, and at least one senior.

Freshmen: G, H, J—choose 1 or more
Juniors: M, N, P—choose 1 or more
Seniors: S, T, V—choose 1 or more

Clue 2   M and N cannot both be selected.   M → ~N; N → ~M

Clue 3   G and T cannot both be selected.   G → ~T; T → ~G

Clue 4   If either S or T is selected, both must be selected.   S ↔ T; ~S ↔ ~T

Clue 5   H cannot be selected unless P is selected.   H → P; ~P → ~H

Clue 6   V cannot be selected unless M is selected.   V → M; ~M → ~V

STEP 4 Make deductions.

Remember that linking the conditional statements is crucial.

Link: V → M and M → ~N

Deduction 1: V → ~N and, likewise, N → ~V

Link: G → ~T and ~T ↔ ~S

Deduction 2: G → ~S and, likewise, S → ~G

If you're able to ascertain these deductions prior to attacking the questions, you'll be off to a great start resulting in major time savings. As you will see, the ability to quickly link these conditional statements enables you to later answer all the questions with ease. As you attempt to get better at this skill, please remember to do the practice drills on pages 271–275. For now, let's proceed with the solution as if you were unable to make these deductions up front.

STEP 5 Tackle the questions.

Remember the optimal sequence for answering questions: 1. catch-a-clue; 2. restricted; 3. unrestricted; 4. modifiers. For this particular game, that translates to the following order: 1, 3, 6, 2, 4, and then 5.

Answer Key

1. **A**   2. **E**   3. **C**   4. **D**   5. **C**   6. **C**

Answers

Question 1

This is a catch-a-clue question. Remember you need only catch-a-clue, look for the answer choice that violates that clue, and then eliminate it. Catch the next clue and repeat until you are left with just one answer choice. Remember that if you get stuck on an in/out, catch-a-clue question, and you are not able to eliminate four answer choices, the rule violation is likely in the group that is not visually displayed. In this case, you should jot down the components in the other group (in this case, the out group) immediately adjacent to the answer choices to ascertain the violation in the other group.

IN	OUT
(A) H, J, P, S, T	
(B) G, J, M, N, V	
(C) G, J, M, S, V	
(D) G, M, P, S, T	
(E) H, P, S, T, V	

Catch the first clue (*The team must include at least one freshman, at least one junior, and at least one senior*). There is no violation of this rule in any of the answer choices. The second clue (*M and N cannot both be selected*) eliminates answer choice B. The third clue (*G and T cannot both be selected*) eliminates answer choice D. The fourth clue (*If either S or T is selected, both must be selected*) eliminates answer choice C. The fifth clue (*H cannot be selected unless P is selected*) is not violated in any of the remaining answer choices. The sixth clue (*V cannot be selected unless M is selected*) eliminates answer choice E.

(A) is the correct answer.

Remember that correct answers to the catch-a-clue questions should be placed into the diagram for future reference.

IN	OUT
H J P S T	_ _ _ _

Question 3

This is a restricted, "could-be-true" question. The correct answer is true at least once. Wrong answers will never be true.

If N and T are selected, which one of the following is a pair of students who could also be selected?

(A) G and H
(B) H and J
(C) J and S
(D) P and V
(E) M and S

This question places N and T in the in-column.

IN	OUT
N T _ _ _	_ _ _ _

Look at the rule symbols for guidance on what you know you must do.

1. The contrapositive of Clue 2 pushes M to the out-column.
2. The contrapositive of Clue 3 pushes G to the out-column.
3. Since T is in, S must also be in, pursuant to Clue 4.

IN	OUT
N T S _ _	M G _ _

Continue to refer to the rule symbols for further deductions. Placement of M in the out-column activates Condition 6.

If M is in the out-column, then V is in the out-column (the contrapositive of Condition 6—~M → ~V).

IN	OUT
N T S _ _	M G V _

With M, G, and V in the out-column, you are able to eliminate answer choices A, D, and E. Answer choices B and C remain. Focus on what you know. You know that three students have not been placed either in the in-column or in the out-column; they are H, J, and P.

Is there a clue that governs the obligations with respect to the remaining components? Clue 5 governs H and P. If P is in the out-column, then H must also be placed in the out-column. Since you only have one slot left in the out-column, you cannot place P in the out-column; P must be in the in-column.

IN	OUT
N T S P _	M G V _

With the inclusion of P in the in-column, you might be tempted to also place H in the in-column because of Condition 5. However, remember to read the condition in the direction of the arrow. If H is placed in the in-column, then P is placed in the out-column. But it's not necessarily true that if P is placed in the in-column, then H must be placed in the in-column. This *could be* true, but it's not necessarily true. This is why the remaining two components, H and J, are interchangeable.

IN	OUT
N T S P H/J	M G V J/H

In this restricted question, H and J cannot be chosen simultaneously. Answer choice B is eliminated.

(C) is the correct answer.

Question 6

In this restricted, "must-be-true-EXCEPT" question, four answers must always be true. These are the wrong answers. One answer is either sometimes true but not always true, or it is never true. This is the correct answer.

If only one senior is selected, then each of the following must be true EXCEPT:

(A) M is selected.
(B) T is not selected.
(C) H is selected.
(D) P is selected.
(E) N is not selected.

This question places exactly one senior in the in-column. By deduction, two seniors are placed in the out-column. Clue 4 requires that S and T are either both in together or both out together. Since the question calls for just one senior, that senior must be V. S and T are likewise placed in the out-column.

IN	OUT
V _ _ _ _	S T _ _

With V placed in the in-column, Clue 6 is activated. M must be placed in the in-column.

IN	OUT
V M _ _ _	S T _ _

With M placed in the in-column, Clue 2 is activated. N must be placed in the out-column.

IN	OUT
V M _ _ _	S T N _

So far, you can ascertain that answer choice A (*M is selected*) must be true. Answer choice B (*T is not selected*) must also be true. Answer choice E (*N is not selected*) must be true. Answer choices C and D remain. There is still more work to do. Repeat the strategy used in answering question 3. Focus on what you know: you know that four students (G, H, J, and P) have not been placed anywhere—neither in the in-column nor the out-column.

As in question 3, Clue 5 governs H and P. If P is in the out-column, then H must also be placed there. Since you only have one slot left in the out-column, you cannot place P in the out-column—so, P must be in the in-column.

IN	OUT
V M P _ _	S T N _

Answer choice D (*P is selected*) must be true and can be eliminated. For the reasons outlined in the explanation of question 3, H *could be*, but need not be, placed in the in-column. Therefore, G, H, and J are all interchangeable.

IN	OUT
V M P G/H/J H/J/G	S T N J/G/H

(C) is the correct answer.

Question 2

This is an unrestricted, "could-be-true" question. Four answers must be false. These are the wrong answers. One answer choice can be true at least once. This is the correct answer. Which one of the following could be true?

    (A) N and V are both selected.
    (B) G and S are both selected.
    (C) All three freshmen are selected.
    (D) All three juniors are selected.
    (E) All three seniors are selected.

Answer choice A: Deduction 1 illustrates that N and V cannot be selected simultaneously. This answer can be eliminated.

Answer choice B: Deduction 2 illustrates that G and S cannot be selected simultaneously. This answer can be eliminated.

Answer choice C: There is neither a deduction nor a condition that allows you to eliminate this answer choice outright. Let's leave this answer as an option for now.

Answer choice D: The juniors are M, N, and P. Condition 2 is activated. Since M and N cannot be selected simultaneously, this answer can be eliminated.

Answer choice E: There is neither a deduction nor a condition that allows you to eliminate this answer choice outright. Let's leave this answer as an option for now.

Now the answer choices are narrowed down to just two. Looking back at your previous work is not helpful in this case. There's no instance where all three freshmen are simultaneously selected, nor is there an instance where all three seniors are simultaneously selected. In cases like this where you've been able to use process of elimination to narrow the choices but your history does not definitively answer the question, just try one of the remaining choices. Let's try choice C (*all three freshmen are selected*).

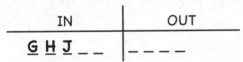

Clue 5 tells you that when H is placed in the in-column, P must be placed in the in-column.

IN	OUT
G H J P _	_ _ _ _

Again, Clue 4 requires that S and T are either both in together or out together. Since there is only one slot remaining in the in-column, you know that S and T must both be out together.

	IN	OUT
	G H J P _	S T _ _

With seniors S and T both placed in the out-column, Condition 1 makes it clear that the remaining senior must be placed in the in-column. You cannot place V in the in-column because to do so would require the inclusion of M as well, pursuant to Clue 6. There are not enough remaining slots. Therefore the selection of all three freshmen cannot be true.

(E) is the correct answer.

Question 4

This unrestricted, "could-be-true-EXCEPT" question is identical to a "must-be-false" question. Four answers could be true. These are the wrong answers. One answer choice can never be true. This is the correct answer.

> Each of the following is a pair of students that could be selected together EXCEPT:
>
> (A) J and V
> (B) P and T
> (C) M and H
> (D) N and G
> (E) G and V

As you attempt to eliminate answer choices, the first step is to review the diagram history.

	IN	OUT
1	H, J, P, S, T	G, M, N, V
3	N, T, S, P, H/J	G, M, V, J/H
6	V, M, P, G/H/J, H/J/G	N, S, T, J/G/H

The pairs in answer choices A, C, and E can be selected together as indicated in the possible selections in question 6. Likewise, the pair in answer choice B can be selected together as indicated in the catch-a-clue answer in question 1 and the answer in question 3. Answer choice D remains.

(D) is the correct answer.

Question 5

This is an unrestricted, "must-be-true" question. Therefore, four answers are never true, or they are true at least once but not always. These are the wrong answers. One answer is always true. This is the correct answer.

> Which one of the following is a pair of students of which the debate coach must select at least one?
>
> (A) M and V
> (B) N and J
> (C) M and T
> (D) G and V
> (E) G and J

This question is purposely convoluted in its phraseology. Deciphering the meaning of the question is the most difficult task. Essentially, the pair cannot be simultaneously out together. If you're required to select one from the pair (place it in the in-column), then that pair cannot be out together. Since, this is an unrestricted question, review the diagram history.

	IN	OUT
1	H, J, P, S, T	G, M, N, V
3	N, T, S, P, H/J	G, M, V, J/H
6	V, M, P, G/H/J H/J/G	N, S, T, J/G/H

The pairs in answer choices B and E can be out together as indicated in the out-column in question 6 and question 3, respectively. Likewise, the pairs in answer choices A and D can be out together as indicated in the catch-a-clue out-column in question 1 and question 3. Answer choice C remains.

(C) is the correct answer.

Game 2

Exactly eight swimmers—Carter, Daniel, Floyd, Gary, Henry, Ivan, Julian, and Karl—will be assigned to teams. The eight will be divided into exactly two 4-person teams—the *Butterfly Team* and the *Freestyle Team*. Each swimmer will be assigned to exactly one of the teams. The teams' composition must conform to the following conditions:

Daniel and Floyd are not assigned to the same team.

If Henry is assigned to the Freestyle Team, then Julian is assigned to the Freestyle Team.

If Karl is assigned to the Butterfly Team, then Gary is assigned to the Freestyle team.

If Karl is assigned to the Freestyle Team, then Ivan is assigned to the Freestyle Team.

1. Which one of the following could be a complete and accurate list of the students selected for the Freestyle Team?

   (A) Henry, Julian, Karl, and Ivan
   (B) Daniel, Floyd, Henry, and Karl
   (C) Floyd, Henry, Ivan, and Julian
   (D) Carter, Floyd, Julian, and Karl
   (E) Carter, Floyd, Gary, and Ivan

2. If Ivan is assigned to the Butterfly Team, then a pair of swimmers that could be, but need not be, assigned to the Freestyle Team is:

   (A) Carter and Henry
   (B) Henry and Karl
   (C) Carter and Floyd
   (D) Gary and Julian
   (E) Daniel and Karl

3. If Gary and Karl are assigned to the same team, then each of the following must be true EXCEPT:

   (A) Julian is assigned to the Butterfly Team.
   (B) Ivan is assigned to the Freestyle Team.
   (C) Henry is assigned to the Butterfly Team.
   (D) Carter is assigned to the Freestyle Team.
   (E) Gary is assigned to the Freestyle Team.

4. Which one of the following is a pair of swimmers who CANNOT both be on the Freestyle Team together?

   (A) Henry and Karl
   (B) Julian and Karl
   (C) Carter and Daniel
   (D) Gary and Karl
   (E) Ivan and Julian

5. If Ivan and Karl are not assigned to the same team, then each of the following is a swimmer who could be assigned to either the Butterfly Team or, alternatively, to the Freestyle Team EXCEPT:

   (A) Daniel
   (B) Henry
   (C) Julian
   (D) Carter
   (E) Floyd

6. If Gary is assigned to the Butterfly Team, then which one of the following must be true?

   (A) Henry is assigned to the Butterfly Team.
   (B) Carter is assigned to the Butterfly Team.
   (C) Julian is assigned to the Freestyle Team.
   (D) Ivan is assigned to the Butterfly Team.
   (E) Floyd is assigned to the Freestyle Team.

Visualize and draw the diagram.

What are you being asked to figure out? The game is asking you to ascertain which students are selected for the Butterfly Team and which students are selected for the Freestyle Team. Since every student is on exactly one team, and since if a student is not on one team then he must be on the other, this has the exact parameters of an in/out game. Specifically, if a student is not in the group, he's out. Similarly, if he's not on one team, then he's definitely on the other. The diagram is as follows:

Butterfly	Freestyle

STEP 2 List the components and ascertain the ratio and/or distribution.

The components are C, D, F, G, H, I, J, and K (the first initial of each swimmer's name). Since the number of slots (eight) is equal to the number of components (eight), you have a one-to-one ratio. There are exactly four students chosen for each team; therefore, the distribution is fixed. Update the diagram as follows:

Butterfly	Freestyle
_ _ _ _	_ _ _ _

STEP 3 Symbolize the clues.

Remember to always write down the contrapositive as well.

Clue 1	Daniel and Floyd are not assigned to the same team.	$D \rightarrow \sim F; F \rightarrow \sim D$
Clue 2	If Henry is assigned to the Freestyle Team, then Julian is assigned to the Freestyle Team.	$H_{free} \rightarrow J_{free};$ $J_{butter} \rightarrow H_{butter}$
Clue 3	If Karl is assigned to the Butterfly Team, then Gary is assigned to the Freestyle Team.	$K_{butter} \rightarrow G_{free};$ $G_{butter} \rightarrow K_{free}$
Clue 4	If Karl is assigned to the Freestyle Team, then Ivan is assigned to the Freestyle Team.	$K_{free} \rightarrow I_{free};$ $I_{butter} \rightarrow K_{butter}$

If the contrapositives looks odd to you, just remember what you read in Step 1: *Since every student is on exactly one team, and since if a student is not on one team then he must be on the other...* In other words, if a student is not on the Freestyle Team, then he is on the Butterfly Team and vice versa. For example, let's look at the first conditional in Clue 2: the contrapositive is technically $\sim J_{free} \rightarrow \sim H_{free}$. Because saying that a student is not on the Freestyle Team is the same as saying that he is on the Butterfly Team, the contrapositive can be rewritten as $J_{butter} \rightarrow H_{butter}$.

STEP 4 Make deductions.

Remember that linking the conditional statements is crucial.

Link: Contrapositive of Clue 4 ($I_{butter} \rightarrow K_{butter}$) and Clue 3 ($K_{butter} \rightarrow G_{free.}$)

Deduction 1: $I_{butter} \rightarrow G_{free}$

There are not a lot of possible links here, but don't panic. Remember what you learned in Chapter 3: *If it's all you know, then it's all you need to know.* Simply put, if you find little to no links, that means you won't need more links to unravel the game.

That said, this game will really test your ability to understand conditional statements. Specifically, you might erroneously interpret Clue 2 to mean that H and J are always placed onto the same team. This is not true. It's true that if H is placed on the Freestyle Team, then J must be placed on the same team; but it is possible for H and J to be placed on separate teams if H is placed on the Butterfly Team and J is placed on the Freestyle Team. This holds true for Clue 4 as well.

Also, it's easy to erroneously interpret Clue 3 as forbidding K and G from being placed on the same team. This is not true. While K and G cannot be placed simultaneously on the Butterfly Team, they can be placed simultaneously on the Freestyle Team.

STEP 5 Tackle the questions.

Remember the optimal sequence for answering questions: 1. catch-a-clue; 2. restricted; 3. unrestricted; 4. modifiers. For this particular game, that translates to the following order: 1, 2, 3, 5, 6, and then 4.

Answer Key

1. **E**   2. **C**   3. **D**   4. **A**   5. **B**   6. **A**

Answers

Question 1

This is a catch-a-clue question. Remember you need only catch a clue, look for the answer choice that violates that clue, and then eliminate it. Catch the next clue, and repeat until you are left with just one answer choice. Note that if you get stuck on an in/out grouping catch-a-clue question, meaning you're not able to eliminate four answer choices, there's a helpful trick to bear in mind: the rule violation is likely in the group that is not visually displayed. In this case, you should jot down the components in the other group (Butterfly Team) right beside the answer choices to ascertain the violation in the other group.

Which one of the following could be a complete and accurate list of the students selected for the Freestyle Team?

(A) Henry, Julian, Karl, and Ivan
(B) Daniel, Floyd, Henry, and Karl
(C) Floyd, Henry, Ivan, and Julian
(D) Carter, Floyd, Julian, and Karl
(E) Carter, Floyd, Gary, and Ivan

The first clue (*Daniel and Floyd are not assigned to the same team*) eliminates answer choices A and B. Remember that the violation of clues can be in the group that's not visually displayed. For example, look at answer choice A: the list given does not name Daniel or Floyd; in other words, both Daniel and Floyd are *not* on the list. Therefore, both Daniel and Floyd are assigned to the Butterfly Team (the group you don't see). This violates Clue 1. The second clue (*If Henry is assigned to the Freestyle Team, then Julian is assigned to the Freestyle Team*) does not eliminate any additional answer choices. The third clue (*If Karl is assigned to the Butterfly Team, then Gary is assigned to the Freestyle team*) eliminates answer choice C. The fourth clue (*If Karl is assigned to the Freestyle Team, then Ivan is assigned to the Freestyle Team*) eliminates answer choice D.

(E) is the correct answer.

Note that correct answers to the catch-a-clue should be placed into the diagram for future reference.

Butterfly	Freestyle
D H J K	C F G I

Question 2

In this restricted, "could-be-true" question, the correct answer is true at least once. Wrong answers will never be true. Normally, an answer choice that must be true could be the correct response to a "could-be-true" question. However, this particular question specifically excludes an answer choice that must be true.

If Ivan is assigned to the Butterfly Team, then a pair of swimmers that could be, but need not be, assigned to the Freestyle Team is:

(A) Carter and Henry
(B) Henry and Karl
(C) Carter and Floyd
(D) Gary and Julian
(E) Daniel and Karl

This question places Ivan on the Butterfly Team.

Butterfly	Freestyle
I _ _ _	_ _ _ _

Look at the rule symbols for guidance on what you know you must do.

With the inclusion of Ivan on the Butterfly Team, the contrapositive Clue 4 is triggered. Accordingly, Karl must be placed onto the Butterfly Team.

Butterfly	Freestyle
I K _ _	_ _ _ _

Also with the inclusion Karl onto the Butterfly Team, Clue 3 is triggered. Accordingly, Gary must be placed onto the Freestyle Team.

Butterfly	Freestyle
I K _ _	**G** _ _ _

By operation of Clue 1, Daniel and Floyd cannot be assigned to the same team. Therefore, they are split between the Butterfly Team and the Freestyle Team. They are placed onto each of the teams interchangeably.

Butterfly	Freestyle
I K **D/F** _	G **F/D** _ _

By operation of the contrapositive of Clue 2, if you were to assign Julian to the Butterfly Team, you would have to assign Henry to the Butterfly Team. Because the Butterfly Team has just one available slot, assigning Julian to that team is not possible. Therefore, Julian must be assigned to the Freestyle Team.

Butterfly	Freestyle
I K D/F _	G F/D **J** _

The remaining components are Carter and Henry. Remember Clue 2 does not require that Henry and Julian always be assigned to the same team. As such, Carter and Henry can be placed on both teams interchangeably.

Butterfly	Freestyle
I K D/F **C/H**	G F/D J **H/C**

Because Karl cannot be placed on the Freestyle Team, eliminate answer choices B and E. Gary and Julian must both be placed onto the Freestyle Team, and you are looking for a pair that could be, but need not be, placed onto the Butterfly Team. So you can eliminate answer choice D. Either Carter or Henry is placed onto the Freestyle Team. Carter and Henry cannot both be placed onto the Freestyle Team, so you can eliminate answer choice A. Carter and Floyd could both be placed onto the Butterfly Team, but neither need to be placed on the Freestyle Team.

(C) is the correct answer.

Question 3

This is a restricted, "must-be-true-EXCEPT" question. Therefore, four answers are always true. These are the wrong answers. One answer is never true, or they are true at least once but not always. This is the correct answer.

> If Gary and Karl are assigned to the same team, then each of the following must be true EXCEPT:
>
> (A) Julian is assigned to the Butterfly Team.
> (B) Ivan is assigned to the Freestyle Team.
> (C) Henry is assigned to the Butterfly Team.
> (D) Carter is assigned to the Freestyle Team.
> (E) Gary is assigned to the Freestyle Team.

This question puts Gary and Karl on the same team. By operation of Clue 3, they cannot be placed on the Butterfly Team together, so they must be placed on the Freestyle Team.

Butterfly	Freestyle
_ _ _ _	G K _ _

By operation of Clue 4, Ivan must be placed onto the Freestyle Team.

Butterfly	Freestyle
_ _ _ _	G K **I** _

By operation of Clue 1, Daniel and Floyd cannot be assigned to the same team. They must be split between the Butterfly Team and the Freestyle Team. Place them on both teams interchangeably.

Butterfly	Freestyle
D/F _ _ _	G K I **F/D**

Since the Freestyle Team is filled, your three remaining components (C, H, J) must be placed on the Butterfly Team.

Butterfly	Freestyle
D/F **C H J**	G K I F/D

Answer choices A, B, C, and E are always true. Answer choice D is never true.

(D) is the correct answer.

Question 5

This restricted, "could-be-true-EXCEPT" question is identical to a "must-be-false" question. Four answers could be true at least once. These are the wrong answers. One answer choice can never be true. This is the correct answer.

> If Ivan and Karl are not assigned to the same team, then each of the following is a swimmer who could be assigned to either the Butterfly Team or, alternatively, to the Freestyle Team EXCEPT:

(A) Daniel
(B) Henry
(C) Julian
(D) Carter
(E) Floyd

This question places Ivan and Karl on different teams. By operation of Clue 4, if Karl is on the Freestyle Team, then Ivan must be placed on the Freestyle Team. Therefore, to allow for them being placed on different teams, you must place Karl on the Butterfly Team and Ivan on the Freestyle Team.

Butterfly	Freestyle
K _ _ _	I _ _ _

By operation of Clue 3, Gary must be placed on the Freestyle Team.

Butterfly	Freestyle
K _ _ _	I G _ _

By operation of Clue 1, Daniel and Floyd cannot be assigned to the same team. They must be split between the Butterfly Team and the Freestyle Team. Therefore, they are placed onto both teams interchangeably.

Butterfly	Freestyle
K D/F _ _	I G F/D _

By operation of Clue 2, if you were to assign Henry to the Freestyle Team, you would also be required to assign Julian to that team. Because the Freestyle Team has just one available slot, putting Henry there is not possible. Therefore, Henry must be assigned to the Butterfly Team.

Butterfly	Freestyle
K D/F H _	I G F/D _

The remaining components are Carter and Julian. Remember Clue 2 does not require that Henry and Julian always be assigned to the same team. Therefore, Carter and Julian can be placed on the Butterfly Team and Freestyle Team interchangeably.

Butterfly	Freestyle
K D/F H C/J	I G F/D J/C

Answer choices A, C, D, and E can each be placed onto either the Butterfly Team or the Freestyle Team. Answer choice B must be placed onto the Butterfly Team.

(B) is the correct answer.

Question 6

This is a restricted, "must-be-true" question. Four answers could be true at least once but not always, or they are never true. These are the wrong answers. One answer choice is always true. This is the correct answer.

If Gary is assigned to the Butterfly Team, then which one of the following must be true?

(A) Henry is assigned to the Butterfly Team.
(B) Carter is assigned to the Butterfly Team.
(C) Julian is assigned to the Freestyle Team.
(D) Ivan is assigned to the Butterfly Team.
(E) Floyd is assigned to the Freestyle Team.

This question places Gary onto the Butterfly Team.

Butterfly	Freestyle
G _ _ _	_ _ _ _

Look at the rule symbols for guidance on what you know you must do. With the inclusion of Gary on the Butterfly Team, the contrapositive of Clue 3 is triggered. Accordingly, Karl must be placed onto the Freestyle Team.

Butterfly	Freestyle
G _ _ _	K _ _ _

By operation of Clue 4, Ivan must be placed on the Freestyle Team.

Butterfly	Freestyle
G _ _ _	K I _ _

By operation of Clue 1, Daniel and Floyd cannot be assigned to the same team. They must be split between the Butterfly Team and the Freestyle Team. Therefore, they are placed onto both teams interchangeably.

Butterfly	Freestyle
G **D/F** _ _	K I **F/D** _

By operation of Clue 2, if you were to assign Henry to the Freestyle Team, you would also be required to put Julian there. So, because the Freestyle Team has just one available slot, placing Henry there is not possible. Therefore, Henry must be assigned to the Butterfly Team.

Butterfly	Freestyle
G D/F **H** _	K I F/D _

The remaining components are Carter and Julian. Remember Clue 2 does not require that Henry and Julian always be assigned to the same team, so Carter and Julian can be placed onto the Butterfly Team and the Freestyle Team interchangeably.

Butterfly	Freestyle
G D/F H **C/J**	K I F/D **J/C**

Answer choices B, C, and E are true sometimes, but not always. Answer choice D is never true.

(A) is the correct answer.

Question 4

This unrestricted, "cannot-be-true" question is identical to a "must-be-false" question. Four answers could be true. These are the wrong answers. One answer choice can never be true. This is the correct answer.

> Which one of the following is a pair of swimmers who CANNOT both be on
> the Freestyle Team together?
>
> (A) Henry and Karl
> (B) Julian and Karl
> (C) Carter and Daniel
> (D) Gary and Karl
> (E) Ivan and Julian

Reviewing the diagram history is your first step to eliminating answer choices for unrestricted questions.

	Butterfly	Freestyle
1	D, H, J, K	C, F, G, I
2	I, K, D/F, C/H	G, F/D, J, H/C
3	D/F, C, H, J	G, K, I, F/D
5	K, D/F, H, C/J	I, G, F/D, J/C
6	G, D/F, H, C/J	K, I, F/D, J/C

The pair in answer choice B can be selected together, as was shown in the work for question 6. Likewise, the pair in answer choice C can be selected together as shown in the work for questions 1, 5, and 6. The work for question 3 shows that the pair in answer choice D can be selected together. The pair in answer choice E can be selected together as shown in the work for questions 5 and 6. The pair in answer choice A (Henry and Karl) cannot be selected together.

You could have also answered this question using a new deduction—one that isn't shown in your previous work. Specifically, if Henry is on the Freestyle Team, then by operation of Clue 2, Julian is on the Freestyle Team. Likewise, if Karl is on the Freestyle Team, then by operation of Clue 4, Ivan is on the Freestyle team. This brings the total to four on the Freestyle Team and forces D and F together on the Butterfly team in violation of Clue 1.

(A) is the correct answer.

Game 3

The coordinator of a film festival must select at least three films from among a group of seven films—F, G, H, J, K, L, and M—to showcase during the upcoming festival. The coordinator's selection of films must conform to the following requirements:

If G is selected, then J is not selected.

If either J or M is selected, then L is not selected.

When the coordinator selects F, she cannot at the same time select any of the following: G, H, or M.

1. Which one of the following could be a complete and accurate list of the films that are NOT selected for the festival?

   (A) H, J, K, L
   (B) F, H, L, M
   (C) F, J, K, L
   (D) F, G, J
   (E) G, J, K, M

2. What is the maximum number of films that could be selected for showcasing during the upcoming festival?

   (A) Three
   (B) Four
   (C) Five
   (D) Six
   (E) Seven

3. If the coordinator selects F, then which one of the following films must the coordinator also select?

   (A) H
   (B) J
   (C) K
   (D) L
   (E) M

4. If M and J are both selected, then each of the following could be true EXCEPT:

   (A) Exactly three films are selected.
   (B) Exactly four films are selected.
   (C) Neither H nor K is selected.
   (D) Neither H nor F is selected
   (E) Neither K nor L is selected.

5. Which one of the following is a pair of films of which the coordinator must select at least one?

   (A) K and L
   (B) H and L
   (C) G and J
   (D) F and M
   (E) H and K

6. If the condition that if either J or M is selected, then L is not selected is suspended and all other conditions remain in effect, then which one of the following CANNOT be a complete and accurate list of the films selected?

   (A) F, J, K
   (B) G, J, H, M
   (C) F, J, K, L
   (D) G, H, J, K
   (E) G, H, L, M

STEP 1 Visualize and draw the diagram.

What are you being asked to figure out? The game is asking you to ascertain which films are selected for showcasing at a film festival. Since some will not be selected, the diagram is as follows:

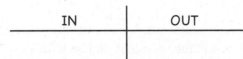

STEP 2 List the components and ascertain the ratio and distribution.

The components are F, G, H, J, K, L, and M. There are "*at least three*" films chosen from "*among a group of seven films*." The distribution is minimum/maximum. Update the diagram as follows:

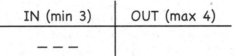

STEP 3 Symbolize the clues.

Remember to always write down the contrapositive as well.

Clue 1	If G is selected, then J is not selected.	G → ~J; J → ~G
Clue 2	If either J or M is selected, then L is not selected.	J → ~L; L → ~J; M → ~L; L → ~M
Clue 3	When the coordinator selects F, she cannot at the same time select any of the following: G, H, or M.	F → ~G; G → ~F; F → ~H; H → ~F; F → ~M; M → ~F

STEP 4 Make deductions.

Normally your first step is to link the conditional statements, but here there are no links. There are just the clues. Don't hit the panic button. Remember the mantra: *If it's all you know, then it's all you need to know.* Simply put, if there are no links, then you do not need them to unravel the game.

STEP 5 Tackle the questions.

Remember the optimal sequence for answering questions: 1. catch-a-clue; 2. restricted; 3. unrestricted; 4. modifiers. For this particular game, that translates to the following order: 1, 6, 3, 4, 2, and then 5.

Answer Key

1. **C**   2. **B**   3. **C**   4. **C**   5. **D**   6. **D**

Answers

Question 1

This is a catch-a-clue question. Remember you need to catch a clue, look for the answer choice that violates that clue, and then eliminate it. Catch the next rule and repeat until you are left with just one answer choice.

> Which one of the following could be a complete and accurate list of the films that are NOT selected for the festival?
>
> (A) H, J, K, L
> (B) F, H, L, M
> (C) F, J, K, L
> (D) F, G, J
> (E) G, J, K, M

Notice that the question is not asking you for a possible list of films selected. Rather it is asking for a valid list of the films *not* selected. The answers choices are the out-column in the diagram, not the in-column. In this scenario, it's highly likely that the clue is in the group that is not visually displayed: the in-column. You should jot down the components in the other group (in this case, the in group) right next to the answer choices to ascertain the violation in the other group.

	IN	OUT
(A)	F, G, M	H, J, K, L
(B)	G, J, K	F, H, L, M
(C)	G, H, M	F, J, K, L
(D)	H, K, L, M	F, G, J
(E)	F, H, L	G, J, K, M

The first clue (*If G is selected, then J is not selected*) eliminates answer choice B. The second clue (*If either J or M is selected, then L is not selected*) eliminates answer choice D. The third clue (*When the coordinator selects F, she cannot at the same time select any of the following: G, H, or M*) eliminates answer choices A and E.

(C) is the correct answer.

Remember that correct answers to the catch-a-clue should be placed into the diagram for future reference.

IN (min 3)	OUT (max 4)
G H M	F J K L

Question 6

This catch-a-clue question has two minor wrinkles. The first one is that the question is asking which list of films is *not* a complete and accurate list of films. In other words, the answer will violate a clue. So instead of catching the clue, looking for the violation, and then eliminating it, you are catching a clue, looking for the violation, and choosing that as the correct answer. The second wrinkle is that the question asks you to suspend the application of Clue 2. So just ignore Clue 2 and proceed: catch-a-clue, look for the answer choice that violates that clue, and then choose it.

If the condition that "*if either J or M is selected, then L is not selected*" is suspended and all other conditions remain in effect, then which one of the following CANNOT be a complete and accurate list of the films selected?

(A) F, J, K
(B) G, J, H, M
(C) F, J, K, L
(D) G, J, H, K
(E) G, H, L, M

	IN	OUT
(A)	G, H, L, M	F, J, K
(B)	F, K, L	G, J, H, M
(C)	G, H, M	F, J, K, L
(D)	F, L, M	G, H, J, K
(E)	F, J, K	G, H, L, M

Catch the first clue "*If G is selected, the J is not selected.*" This clue is not violated. Remember to ignore Clue 2. Catch Clue 3 "*When the coordinator selects F, she cannot at the same time select any of the following: G, H, or M.*" This clue is violated in answer choice D.

(D) is the correct answer.

Do not put the answer in the chart because it does not comply with every clue.

Question 3

This is a restricted, "must-be-true" question. Therefore, four answers are true sometimes but not always, or they are never true. The correct answer is always true.

If the coordinator selects F, then which one of the following films must the coordinator also select?

(A) H
(B) J
(C) K
(D) L
(E) M

This question places F in the in-column:

IN (min 3)	OUT (max 4)
F _ _	

With the inclusion of F in the in-column, Clue 3 is triggered. Accordingly, G, H, and M are forced into the out-column.

IN (min 3)	OUT (max 4)
F _ _	G H M

Identify the remaining components: J, K, and L. Continue to refer to the clue illustrations to determine what clues may be triggered by any of those components. Notice that Clue 2 is triggered. What alerts you to this is *if J is selected then L is not selected* (J → ~L). J and L cannot both be in together. At least one of the J/L pair must be out. The out-column has a maximum capacity of four. Therefore, either J or L must be placed in the in-column, and the other must be placed in the out-column.

IN (min 3)	OUT (max 4)
F J/L _	G H M L/J

The only remaining component (K) must, therefore, be placed in the in-column to meet the minimum three film requirement.

IN (min 3)	OUT (max 4)
F J/L K	G H M L/J

H and M cannot be selected. Accordingly, answer choices A and E are false. J and L could be selected, but neither is mandatory. Eliminate answer choices B and D. Component K must be selected.

(C) is the correct answer.

Question 4

This is a restricted, "could-be-true-EXCEPT" question; therefore, four answers could be true at least once. These are the wrong answers. One answer is never true. This is the correct answer.

If M and J are both selected, then each of the following could be true EXCEPT:

(A) Exactly three films are selected.
(B) Exactly four films are selected.
(C) Neither H nor K is selected.
(D) Neither H nor F is selected
(E) Neither K nor L is selected.

This question places components M and J in the in-column. Place the additional restriction into the diagram.

IN (min 3)	OUT (max 4)
M̲ J̲ _	

With J placed in the in-column, the contrapositive of Clue 1 is activated. G must be placed in the out-column.

IN (min 3)	OUT (max 4)
M̲ J̲ _	G

With M placed in the in-column, Clue 2 and the contrapositive of Clue 3 are activated. Accordingly, F and L must be placed in the out-column.

IN (min 3)	OUT (max 4)
M̲ J̲ _	G **F** L

H and K are the remaining components. H and/or K must be placed in the in-column.

IN (min 3)	OUT (max 4)
M̲ J̲ **H/K**	G F L **K/H**
or	or
M J **H K**	G F L

Answer choice A: There could be exactly three films selected if H *or* K is selected and *not both* H and K. This answer can be eliminated.

Answer choice B: There could be exactly four films selected if *both* H and K are selected. This answer can be eliminated.

Answer choice C: *Neither H nor K is selected* cannot be true. At least one of either H or K must be chosen to meet the minimum three-film selection requirement. This is the correct answer.

Answer choice D: *Neither H nor F is selected* can be true if K is placed in the in-column and H is placed in the out-column. This answer can be eliminated.

Answer choice E: Neither K nor L is selected can be true if H is placed in the in-column and K is placed in the out-column. This answer can be eliminated.

(C) is the correct answer.

Question 2

This is an unrestricted, "could-be-true" question. Four answers must be false. These are the wrong answers. One answer choice can be true at least once. This is the correct answer.

What is the maximum number of films that could be selected for showcasing during the upcoming festival?

(A) Three
(B) Four
(C) Five
(D) Six
(E) Seven

A review of diagram history shows you that there can be at least four films selected. Accordingly, answer choice A can be eliminated. Now ask yourself, "Can there ever be more than four films selected?" To determine if it's possible, consider pairs that cannot be *in* together. If at least one film in one of the pairs must be *out*, the maximum is reduced. In your search for pairs, look for ones that do not share a component in common.

Therefore, Clue 1 tells you that between G and J, one film in the pair must be placed in the out-column. Answer choice E (*Seven*) can be eliminated. Next, search for another pair that cannot be in together that does not include either G or J. There are five remaining components (F, H, K, L, M). The question now becomes whether there are any other clues involving the remaining five components that involve a pair that cannot both be in together.

Part of Clue 2 tells you that between M and L, one film in the pair must be placed in the out-column. There are at least two films in the out-column. Answer choice D (*Six*) can be eliminated. There are three remaining components (F, H, K). The question now becomes whether or not there are any other clues involving the remaining five components that involve a pair that cannot both be in together.

Part of Clue 3 tells you that between F and H, one film in the pair must be placed in the out-column. There are least three films in the out-column. Answer choice C (*Five*) can be eliminated. Four is the maximum number of films that can be selected.

(B) is the correct answer.

Question 5

This is an unrestricted, "must-be-true" question. Therefore, four answers are true sometimes but not always, or they are never true. These are the wrong answers. One answer choice is always true. This is the correct answer.

Which one of the following is a pair of films of which the coordinator must select at least one?

(A) K and L
(B) H and L
(C) G and J
(D) F and M
(E) H and K

This phraseology is one of the most convoluted in the logic games. Before you look at the diagram history in an attempt to answer the question, let's make sure you understand the question and how the diagram history will help you. The question is asking from which pair of films must the coordinator choose at least one. In other words, which pair cannot be placed in *out* simultaneously. Therefore, as you review the diagram history, try to ascertain whether you ever observe the pair of films in each choice placed in the out-column simultaneously. Here is the diagram history.

	IN	OUT
1	G, H, M	F, J, K, L
3	F, J/L, K	G, H, L/J, M
4a	M, J, H/K,	G, F, L, K/H
4b	M, J, H, K	G, F, L

Answer choice A: K and L are out simultaneously in answer 4a. This choice can be eliminated.

Answer choice B: H and L are out simultaneously in answers 3 and 4a. This choice can be eliminated.

Answer choice C: G and J are out simultaneously in answer 3. This choice can be eliminated.

Answer choice D: None of the answers have F and M out simultaneously. Keep this answer choice as an option.

Answer choice E: Similarly, none of the answers have H and K out simultaneously. Keep this answer choice as an option.

You have narrowed down the answers to just two choices (D or E). Let's try choice E (H and K).

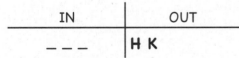

With H and K placed in the out-column simultaneously, the remaining components are F, G, J, L, and M. F cannot be placed in the in-column because it would force both G and M into the out-column (Clue 3), thereby forcing the remaining three components (F, J, L) into the in-column. F, J, and L cannot simultaneously be placed in the in-column; this would violate Clue 2. So, F must be placed in the out-column.

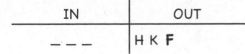

The remaining components are G, J, L, and M. Clue 2 prohibits the placement of L in the in-column with either J or M. Therefore, L would force two of the remaining components into the out-column, thereby violating the three-film minimum requirement. Accordingly, L must be placed in the out-column.

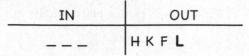

The remaining three components (G, J, M) cannot be placed in the in-column simultaneously because Clue 1 states that G and J cannot be in together. Therefore, it's not possible to have both H and K in the out-column at the same time. You must select at least one of the H/K pair.

(D) is the correct answer.

Game 4

From among nine professors, at least five and at most six will be selected to serve on a university's board of directors. Five of the professors—M, N, P, R, and S—are tenured and four—J, K, L, and T—are untenured. Five professors—J, K, M, N, and S—are English professors and L, P, R, and T are Math professors. The selection of professors must conform to following conditions:

At most two untenured professors are selected.

At least three but no more than four English professors are selected.

If M is selected, then either J or K, but not both, are selected.

If P is selected, then S is selected.

1. Which one of the following is an acceptable selection of professors for the board of directors?

   (A) J, L, M, S, T
   (B) M, N, P, S, T
   (C) L, K, N, P, S
   (D) K, M, N, P, T
   (E) J, L, P, R, S

2. Which one of the following could be true?

   (A) Exactly two tenured professors are selected.
   (B) No Math professors are selected.
   (C) All five tenured professors are selected.
   (D) All four Math professors are selected.
   (E) No untenured professors are selected.

3. If the professors selected include three tenured English professors, which one of the following could be a complete and accurate list of the remaining professors selected?

   (A) P and R
   (B) J, K, and R
   (C) K, P, and T
   (D) J, L, P, and T
   (E) J, L, and T

4. If S is not selected, which one of the following professors must be selected?

   (A) J
   (B) N
   (C) K
   (D) L
   (E) T

5. If neither P nor R is selected, any of the following could be true EXCEPT:

   (A) Neither J nor L is selected.
   (B) Neither L nor T is selected.
   (C) Neither K nor T is selected.
   (D) Neither J nor L is selected.
   (E) Neither K nor L is selected.

6. Which one of the following is a pair of professors of which at least one must be selected to serve on the board of directors?

   (A) M and K
   (B) N and S
   (C) P and S
   (D) K and S
   (E) L and T

STEP 1 Visualize and draw the diagram.

What are you being asked to figure out? The game is asking you to ascertain which professors are selected for a university's board of directors. Since some will not be selected, the diagram is as follows:

IN	OUT

STEP 2 List the components and ascertain the ratio and/or distribution.

The components are J, K, L, M, N, P, R, S, and T. Note that the components have two of following four characteristics—Tenured, Untenured, English, and Math. Specifically, the components are divided as follows:

Tenured: M, N, P, R, S

Untenured: J, K, L, T

English: J, K, M, N, S

Math: L, P, R, T

To quickly and readily ascertain which two out of the four characteristics each component has, organize the components in a T-chart as follows:

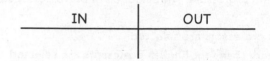

Tenured	Untenured	
MNS	JK	English
PR	LT	Math

Let's determine the distribution. There are "*at least five and at most six*" professors chosen from "*among nine professors.*" The distribution is minimum/maximum. Update the diagram as follows:

IN	OUT
_ _ _ _ _	_ _ _ _ ....

STEP 3 Symbolize the clues.

Remember to always write down the contrapositive as well.

Clue 1   At most two untenured professors are selected.   Update onto the T-chart (See below.)

Clue 2   At least three but no more than four English professors are selected. Update the T-chart as follows:

2 or less
↓

Tenured	Untenured		
MNS	JK	English	← **3 or 4**
PR	LT	Math	

Clue 3   If M is selected, then either J or K, but not both, are selected.

$M \rightarrow J$ or K;
$\sim$J and $\sim$K $\rightarrow \sim$M;
M and K $\rightarrow \sim$J;
M and J $\rightarrow \sim$K

Clue 4   If P is selected, then S is selected.

$P \rightarrow S$; $\sim$S $\rightarrow \sim$P

STEP 4 Make deductions.

Normally you would begin by linking the conditional statements, but here there are no links. There are just the clues and a lot of math.

Deduction 1: If there are at most two untenured professors selected, and a minimum of five and a maximum of six professors selected, you can deduce that you must select a minimum of three tenured professors.

Deduction 2: Likewise, since you must select "*at least three but no more than four*" English professors, and since again you must select a minimum of five and a maximum of six professors, you can deduce that at least one but no more than three Math professors must be selected.

Place these deductions into the T-chart as follows:

3 or more   2 or less
↓   ↓

Tenured	Untenured		
MNS	JK	English	← 3 or 4
PR	LT	Math	← **1-3**

STEP 5 Tackle the questions.

Remember the optimal sequence for answering questions: 1. catch-a-clue; 2. restricted; 3. unrestricted; 4. modifiers. For this particular game, that translates to the following order: 1, 3, 4, 5, 2, and then 6.

Answer Key

1. **C**   2. **C**   3. **C**   4. **B**   5. **B**   6. **B**

Answers

Question 1

This is a catch-a-clue question. Remember you need to catch a clue, look for the answer choice that violates that clue, and then eliminate it. Catch the next rule and repeat until you are left with just one answer choice.

> Which one of the following is an acceptable selection of professors for the board of directors?
>
> (A) J, L, M, S, T
> (B) M, N, P, S, T
> (C) L, K, N, P, S
> (D) K, M, N, P, T
> (E) J, L, P, R, S

The first clue (*At most two untenured professors are selected*) eliminates answer choice A. The second clue (*At least three but no more than four English professors are selected*) eliminates answer choice E. The third clue (*If M is selected, then either J or K, but not both, are selected*) eliminates answer choice B. The fourth clue (*If P is selected, then S is selected*) eliminates answer choice D.

(C) is the correct answer.

Remember that correct answers to the catch-a-clue should be placed into the diagram for future reference.

IN	OUT
L K N P S	J M R T

Question 3

This is a restricted, "could-be-true" question; therefore, four answers are always false. These are the wrong choices. The correct answer is true at least once.

If the professors selected include three tenured English professors, which one of the following could be a complete and accurate list of the remaining professors selected?

(A) P and R

(B) J, K, and R

(C) K, P, and T

(D) J, L, P, and T

(E) J, L, and T

If you look at the T-chart, you'll see that this question places M, N, and S (as the only three tenured English professors) in the in-column.

IN	OUT
M N S _ _	_ _ _ ....

With the inclusion of M in the in-column, Clue 3 is triggered. Accordingly, either J or K must be placed in the in-column; the other will be forced into the out-column.

IN	OUT
M N S **J/K** _	**J/K** _ _ ....

You should rule out any options that do not include either J or K, so answer choice A can be eliminated. Similarly, you should rule out any options that contain both J and K, so answer choice B can be eliminated.

Identify the remaining components: L, P, R, and T. Continue to refer to the T-chart for deductions and other clues. Clue 1 is triggered; specifically, more than two untenured professors cannot be selected. With the inclusion of either J or K (both of which are untenured professors), there is room for just one more untenured professor. Therefore, of the remaining untenured professors (L and T), just one can be selected. You can rule out any answer choices that include both L and T, so D and E can be eliminated. Note that answer choice D can also be eliminated because with its inclusion of four professors, it violates the "maximum of six" restriction.

(C) is the correct answer.

Question 4

This is a restricted, "must-be-true" question; therefore, four answers are either sometimes true but not always true, or they are never true. These are the wrong answers. One answer is always true. This is the correct answer.

If S is not selected, which one of the following professors must be selected?

(A) J
(B) N
(C) K
(D) L
(E) T

This question places component S in the out-column. Place the additional restriction into the diagram.

IN	OUT
_ _ _ _ _	S _ _ ....

With S placed in the out-column, the contrapositive of Clue 4 is activated. P must be placed in the out-column.

IN	OUT
_ _ _ _ _	S **P** _ ....

Pivot to the mathematical condition that requires the selection of either three or four English professors. The remaining English professors are M, N, J, and K. With the placement of S in the out-column, you must select a least three out of the four remaining English professors. From Clue 3, you can deduce that if M is included in the in-column, then you must necessarily include either J or K with N in order to meet the minimum requirement of three English professors.

IN	OUT
M J/K N _ _	S P **J/K** ....

Of the three remaining professors (L, R, T) two of them (L ,T) are untenured. Since you've already selected one untenured professor (either J or K), by operation of Clue 1, you can only select one more untenured professor. Therefore, L and T must be placed in the in-column and out-column interchangeably.

IN	OUT
M J/K N **L/T** _	S P J/K **T/L**

Now that the out-column is filled, the remaining component (R) must be placed in the in-column.

Likewise, if M is not selected, the remaining three professors (N, J, K) must necessarily be selected in order to meet the minimum requirement of three English professors. However, this selection is not acceptable. With the inclusion of J and K, you have reached the maximum number of untenured professors, so the remaining two untenured professors (L and T) must be placed in the out-column. This would bring the total number in the out-column to five (S, P, M, L, T). A maximum of four professors is allowed in the out-column, so this would be wrong.

(B) is the correct answer.

Question 5

This restricted, "could-be-true-EXCEPT" question is identical to a "must-be-false" question. Four answers could be true. These are the wrong answers. One answer choice is never true: this one is the correct answer.

If neither P nor R is selected, any of the following could be true EXCEPT:

(A) Neither J nor L is selected.
(B) Neither L nor T is selected.
(C) Neither K nor T is selected.
(D) Neither J nor L is selected.
(E) Neither K nor L is selected.

This question places components P and R in the out-column. Place the additional restriction into the diagram.

IN	OUT
_ _ _ _ _	P R _ ....

Both P and R are tenured professors. With their placement in the out-column, you're left with just three tenured professors available for selection. Deduction 1 (*you must select three or more tenured professors*) is triggered. Therefore, all three of the three remaining tenured professors (M, N, and S) must be placed in the in-column.

IN	OUT
M N S _ _	P R _ ....

From Clue 3, you can deduce that if M is included in the in-column, then you must necessarily include exactly one of either J or K with the one not selected necessarily being placed in the out-column.

IN	OUT
M N S **J/K** _	P R **J/K** ....

It's possible to simultaneously place both J and L in the out-column. You are looking for the exception, so answer choice A is eliminated. Similarly, it's possible to simultaneously place both K and T (answer choice C), both L and J (answer choice D), and both K and L (answer choice E) in the out-column. As such, answer choices C, D, and E are eliminated. You cannot simultaneously place both L and T in the out-column because only a maximum of four is allowed.

(B) is the correct answer.

Question 2

This is an unrestricted, "could-be-true" question. Therefore, four answers are never true. These are the wrong answers. One answer choice is true at least once. This is the correct answer.

Which one of the following could be true?

(A) Exactly two tenured professors are selected.
(B) No Math professors are selected.
(C) All five tenured professors are selected.
(D) All four Math professors are selected.
(E) No untenured professors are selected.

A review of the diagram history is not helpful for answering this question since none of the possible answer choices can be found there. However, your clues and your deductions will prove very helpful. Deduction 1 (*you must select at least three tenured professors*) allows you to eliminate answer choice A. Deduction 2 (*you must select a minimum of one and a maximum of three Math professors*) allows you to eliminate answer choices B and D.

So, now you have narrowed down your possible answers to just two. Let's attempt just one of these: answer choice E (*no untenured professors are selected*).

IN	OUT
_ _ _ _ _	J K L T

By deduction, the remaining five professors (all tenured) must be placed in the in-column to meet the minimum selection of five professors.

IN	OUT
M N P R S	J K L T

By operation of the contrapositive of Clue 3, this configuration is not possible. Answer choice E is eliminated.

(C) is the correct answer.

Question 6

This is an unrestricted, "must-be-true" question. Therefore, four answers are never true, or they are true at least once but not always. These are the wrong answers. One answer is always true. This is the correct answer.

> Which one of the following is a pair of professors of which at least one must be selected to serve on the board of directors?
>
> (A) M and K
> (B) N and S
> (C) P and S
> (D) K and S
> (E) L and T

This question is purposely convoluted in its phraseology. The hardest part is deciphering the meaning of the question. Essentially you are being asked to determine which pair cannot be simultaneously out. Again, your prior work offers little help in answering this question. The only pair that you see out together is P/S in your work for question 4. So, you can eliminate answer choice C. Since you haven't ascertained the possibility of any of the other pairs appearing simultaneously in the out-column, place each remaining pair in the out-column and let your clues guide you.

	IN	OUT
(A)		M, K
(B)		N, S
(C)		P̶ S̶
(D)		K, S
(E)		L, T

Answer choice A: With M and K (both English professors) placed in the out-column, J, N, and S must necessarily be placed in the in-column to satisfy Clue 2. There is no violation here. This answer choice can be eliminated.

Answer choice B: With both N and S placed in the out-column, M, J, and K must necessarily be placed in the in-column to satisfy Clue 2. However, the placement of M with both J and K in the in-column violates Clue 3. Therefore, N and S cannot both be placed in the out-column simultaneously.

(B) is the correct answer.

Let's check the remaining answer choices.

> Answer choice B: With K and S (both English professors) placed in the out-column, J, M, and N must necessarily be placed in the in-column to satisfy Clue 2. There is no violation here. This answer choice can be eliminated.

> Answer choice C: With L and T (both untenured professors) placed in the out-column, there are no requirements dictating which professors must be selected. The possibilities are numerous and many involve no violations of any of the clues. This answer choice can be eliminated.

Game 5

A professor will choose at least one student to give a speech at the university's commencement from among six students—Garcia, Han, Johnson, Khanna, Lai, and Murray. The selection of students is consistent with the following conditions:

If Han is selected, then Garcia is not selected.

If Johnson is not selected, then Han is selected.

If Murray is selected, then Garcia is also selected.

If Khanna is selected, then both Garcia and Lai are selected.

1. Which one of the following could be a complete and accurate list of the students selected to give a speech?

    (A) Han, Murray
    (B) Garcia, Han, Murray
    (C) Han, Johnson, Khanna, Lai
    (D) Han, Lai
    (E) Garcia, Khanna, Lai, Murray

2. Which one of the following could be the only student selected to give a speech?

    (A) Garcia
    (B) Han
    (C) Murray
    (D) Khanna
    (E) Lai

3. If Garcia is selected, then each of the following could be true EXCEPT:

    (A) Khanna is not selected.
    (B) Johnson is not selected.
    (C) Murray is not selected.
    (D) Lai is selected.
    (E) Lai is not selected.

4. Which one of the following pairs of students CANNOT be among the students selected to give a speech?

    (A) Han, Johnson
    (B) Garcia, Lai
    (C) Han, Murray
    (D) Khanna, Johnson
    (E) Han, Lai

5. If Johnson is not selected, then which one of the following must be false?

    (A) Lai is selected.
    (B) Kai is not selected.
    (C) Neither Khanna nor Han are selected.
    (D) Neither Khanna nor Lai are selected.
    (E) Han is selected, but Lai is not selected.

STEP 1 Visualize and draw the diagram.

This was already done for you earlier in this chapter:

STEP 2 List the components and ascertain the ratio and distribution.

The components are G, H, J, K, L, and M (just use the first letter of each name). The distribution was also determined earlier when the diagram was created; as you can see, there are no parameters. The game is a unknown distribution grouping game.

STEP 3 Symbolize the clues.

Remember to always write down the contrapositive as well.

Clue 1	If Han is selected, then Garcia is not selected.	H → ~G; G → ~H
Clue 2	If Johnson is not selected, then Han is selected.	~J → H; ~H → J
Clue 3	If Murray is selected, then Garcia is also selected.	M → G; ~G → ~M
Clue 4	If Khanna is selected, then both Garcia and Lai are selected.	K → G; ~G → ~K K → L; ~L → ~K

STEP 4 Make deductions.

Remember that linking the conditional statements is crucial.

Link: G → ~H and ~H → J
Deduction 1: G → J and, likewise, ~J → ~G

Link: M → G and G → ~H
Deduction 2: M → ~H and, likewise, H → ~M

Link: K → G and G → ~H
Deduction 3: K → ~H and, likewise, H → ~K

If you are able to make these deductions before attacking the questions, you are off to a great start—one that will result in major time savings. As you'll see, having the ability to quickly link these conditional statements enables you to answer all of the questions with ease. To improve your mastery of this skill, please remember to do the practice drills on pages 271–275. For now, let's proceed with the solution as if you were unable to make these deductions up front.

STEP 5 Tackle the questions.

Answer Key

1. **D**   2. **B**   3. **B**   4. **C**   5. **C**

Answers

Question 1

This is a catch-a-clue question. Remember you need only catch a clue, look for the answer choice that violates that clue, and then eliminate it. Catch the next clue and repeat until you are left with just one answer choice. Also, remember that with grouping catch-a-clue questions, it is often a good idea to jot down the components in the other group (in this case, the out group) right next to the answer choices because the violation is sometimes in the group that is not visually displayed.

	IN	OUT
(A)	Han, Murray	G, J, K, L
(B)	Garcia, Han, Murray	J, K, L
(C)	Han, Johnson, Khanna, Lai	G, M
(D)	Han, Lai	G, J, K, M
(E)	Garcia, Khanna, Lai, Murray	H, J

The first clue (*If Han is selected, then Garcia is not selected*) eliminates answer choice B. The second clue (*If Johnson is not selected, then Han is selected*) eliminates answer choice E. The third clue (*If Murray is selected, then Garcia is also selected*) eliminates answer choice A. The fourth clue (*If Khanna is selected, then both Garcia and Lai are selected*) eliminates answer choice C.

(D) is the correct answer.

Question 2

This is also a catch-a-clue question because by asking, "*Which one of the following could be the only student selected to give a speech?,*" it is also asking for a possible grouping of the components with one component placed in the in-column and the remaining five components placed in the out-column. Repeat the steps followed in question 1.

	IN	OUT
(A)	Garcia	H, J, K, L, M
(B)	Han	G, J, K, L, M
(C)	Murray	G, H, J, K, L
(D)	Khanna	G, H, J, M, L
(E)	Lai	G, H, J, K, M

The first clue (*If Han is selected, then Garcia is not selected*) eliminates nothing. The second clue (*If Johnson is not selected, then Han is selected*) eliminates answer choices A, C, D, and E.

(B) is the correct answer.

Question 3

This is a restricted, "could-be-true-EXCEPT" question; therefore, four answers could be true at least once. These are the wrong answers. One answer is never true. This is the correct answer.

> If Garcia is selected, then each of the following could be true EXCEPT:
>
> (A) Khanna is not selected.
> (B) Johnson is not selected.
> (C) Murray is not selected.
> (D) Lai is selected.
> (E) Lai is not selected.

Placing Garcia in the in-column activates the clue "*If Garcia is selected, then Han is not selected.*"

IN	OUT
G	H

With Han placed in the out-column, the contrapositive of Clue 2 is activated.

IN	OUT
G, J	H

Johnson must be selected, so B is false.

(B) is the correct answer.

Question 4

This restricted, "cannot-be-true" question is identical to a "must-be-false" question. Four answers could be true. These are the wrong answers. One answer choice can never be true. This is the correct answer.

> Which one of the following pairs of students CANNOT be among the students selected to give a speech?

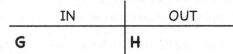

	IN	OUT
(A)	Han, Johnson	G, M
(B)	Garcia, Lai—J	H
(C)	Han, Murray	G, **M**
(D)	Khanna, Johnson—G, L	H
(E)	Han, Lai	G, K, M

Answer choice A: The inclusion of Han as part of the pair activates Rule 1 (*If Han is selected, then Garcia is not selected*). Thus, Garcia is placed in the out-column. Garcia's placement then activates the contrapositive of Rule 3 (*If Garcia is not selected, then Murray is not selected*); thus, Murray is placed in the out-column. No other rules are activated, and none of the conditions have been violated. This is a possible pair. This answer can be eliminated.

Answer choice B: The inclusion of Garcia as part of the pair activates the contrapositive of Clue 1 (*If Garcia is selected, then Han is not selected*). Han is placed in the out-column. The placement of Han in the out-column activates the contrapositive of Clue 2 (*If Han is not selected, then Johnson is selected*). Johnson is placed in the in-column. No other rules are activated, and none of the conditions have been violated. This is a possible pair. This answer can be eliminated.

Answer choice C: The inclusion of Han as part of the pair activates Clue 1 (*If Han is selected, then Garcia is not selected*); thus, Garcia is placed in the out-column. Garcia's placement activates the contrapositive of Clue 3 (*If Garcia is not selected, then Murray is not selected*), and, thus, Murray is placed in the out-column. However, Murray is the other part of the pair. This is not possible. **This is the correct answer.**

Answer choice D: The inclusion of Khanna in the in-column activates Clue 4 (*If Khanna is selected, then both Garcia and Lai are selected*). Garcia and Lai are added to the in-column. The placement of Garcia in the in-column activates the contrapositive of Clue 1 (*If Garcia is selected, then Han is not selected*). Han is placed in the out-column. The placement of Han in the out-column activates the contrapositive of Clue 2 (*If Han is not selected, then Johnson is selected*). Johnson is already part of the pair. No other clues are activated, and none of the conditions have been violated. This is a possible pair. This answer can be eliminated.

Answer choice E: The inclusion of Han as part of the pair activates Clue 1 (*If Han is selected, then Garcia is not selected*). Thus, Garcia is placed in the out-column. Garcia's placement activates the contrapositive of Clue 3 (*If Garcia is not selected, then Murray is not selected*), and, thus, Murray is placed in the out-column. The placement of Garcia in the out-column also activates the contrapositive to Clue 4 (*If Garcia is not selected, then Khanna is not selected*), and, thus, Khanna is placed in the out-column. No other clues are activated, and none of the clues have been violated. This is a possible pair. This answer can be eliminated.

(C) is the correct answer.

Question 5

This is a restricted, "must-be-false" question. Four answers could be true. These are the wrong answers. One answer choice can never be true. This is the correct answer.

If Johnson is not selected, then which one of the following must be false?

(A) Lai is selected.
(B) Kai is not selected.
(C) Neither Khanna nor Han are selected.
(D) Neither Khanna nor Lai are selected.
(E) Han is selected, but Lai is not selected.

Placing J in the out-column activates the condition "*If Johnson is not selected, then Han is selected.*"

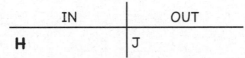

IN	OUT
H	J

You could continue linking conditional statements, but you already have your answer. Answer choice C indicates that H is not selected. Since you know that H is selected, this answer choice is false. Each of the other answer choices could be true. **(C) is the correct answer.** This is a perfect illustration of why it's important to periodically check your answer choices before wasting time making further unnecessary deductions.

(C) is the correct answer.

Sequence/Grouping Combo

7

In Chapters 5 and 6, you learned how to tackle sequencing and grouping games. This chapter focuses on games that have characteristics of both sequencing and grouping: these are known as *multi-tier* and *hybrid games*. You will start out by looking at multi-tier games, and then later you will be tackling the hybrid games.

MULTI-TIER GAMES

Multi-tier games are predominantly sequencing games. However, they are sequencing games with a grouping twist. In traditional sequencing games, you have *one* set of components that must be ordered. For example:

> On each of exactly seven consecutive days (day 1 through day 7), exactly seven flowers—Carnation, Daisy, Gardenia, Iris, Lily, Marigold, and Rose—are planted in a garden. No flower is planted on the same day as any other flower, and no flower is planted more than once. The flowers must be planted in accordance with the following conditions:

The answer to the question "What am I being asked to figure out?" is this: you must determine the order in which the one set of components (flowers) is planted. The diagram is as follows:

1	2	3	4	5	6	7
—	—	—	—	—	—	—

Multi-tier games involve at least two sets of components. So with another set of components added, the exact same scenario outlined above would be transformed into a multi-tier game. It could look as follows:

> On each of exactly seven consecutive days (day 1 through day 7), exactly seven flowers—Carnation, Daisy, Gardenia, Iris, Lily, Marigold, and Rose—are planted in a garden. No flower is planted on the same day as any other flower, and no flower is planted more than once. *Each flower is either white or yellow (but not both).* The flowers must be planted in accordance with the following conditions:

The highlighted sentence is the only difference between the two scenarios, and it is that sentence that creates a second tier.

STEP 1 Let's help you answer the question "What am I being asked to figure out?" You are being asked to (1) determine the *order* in which the first set of components (flowers) are planted *and* (2) determine which of the two members in the second set of components (white or yellow) is *grouped* with the first set of components (flowers). Notice the grouping twist referred to earlier. This additional set of components creates two tiers in the diagram. Specifically, one tier is created for the first set of components (the flowers), and a second tier for the second set of components (the colors). The diagram would need to be modified to include a second tier as follows:

1	2	3	4	5	6	7
Flower/Color	Flower/Color	Flower/Color	Flower/Color	Flower/Color	Flower/Color	Flower/Color
— —	— —	— —	— —	— —	— —	— —

Notice that in this example, whole words rather than first letters are used to identify the component categories on the diagram (that is, Flower/Color instead of F/C). While taking a few seconds to write a name instead of just a letter may seem like waste of time, it actually ends up saving you time. Firstly, it lessens the likelihood of confusing the actual components with the component category. For example, one of the flowers is a carnation and will be represented by the letter C in your diagram—you wouldn't want to have another C in the diagram that means something else. Secondly, the simple act of spending fifteen seconds to write *Flower/Color* five times across the top of the diagram reiterates and solidifies your ability to view your symbols more quickly and accurately. This will increase your capacity to make accurate deductions about where components (by category) cannot fit.

STEP 2 Ascertaining the ratio is a little more complex in multi-tier games because sometimes the different sets of components have the same ratio and sometimes they have varying ratios (as in the above scenario). In this example, there are seven days, seven flowers, and two colors—a 7:7:2 ratio. This is not a one-to-one-to-one ratio. Uncovering the varying ratio at the outset will help you clear numerous hurdles later in the process of solving the game.

STEP 3 Symbolizing the clues is always an important step for an efficient and successful approach to a logic game. However, it becomes even more important with multi-tier games because of the introduction of multiple sets of components. Remember the "CLUE" principles as they relate to symbolizing clues. Especially important are: L (logical) requires that the symbol have a rational relationship to the meaning of the clue; U (understandable) requires that the symbol should look as close as possible to the way it's going to look in the final diagram. Therefore, your symbols need to reflect all the tiers exactly as they are illustrated in the diagram.

For example, consider the following clue:

The Gardenia is planted on the day immediately before a white flower.

You might initially symbolize the clue as follows: | **G** | **W** |

In doing so, you increase the likelihood that you will confuse the two sets of components and overlook valuable deductions. Consider, however, a symbol that reflects the parameters of the diagram, so that within each day (day 1 through day 7) two slots are illustrated—one slot for the flower and one slot for color. A **C**onsistent, **L**ogical, **U**nderstandable, and **E**asy-to-follow symbol would look like this: | G _ | _ W |

Imagine that the above symbol is a transparent sticker that you are able to peel off the page and overlay onto the diagram. Being consistent with the placement of the components (always having the flower immediately to the left of the color) will greatly assist in your ability to make deductions about where the components will not fit.

STEP 4 Now let's look at making deductions. As with other sequencing games, most of the deductions focus on where and how the components and slots are restricted, which slots and components are the most restricted, and which symbols provide the greatest understanding.

STEP 5 Finally, you should tackle the questions in the following order: catch-a-clue, restricted, unrestricted, and modifiers.

Game 1

On a particular Saturday evening, a total of exactly seven entrees—Noodles, Pot Roast, Quiche, Ravioli, Salmon, Turkey, and Veal—will be tasted by a local food critic. Each entrée will be tasted exactly once, and no two entrees will be tasted concurrently. Each of the entrees is prepared by either Chef Garcia or Chef Haley (but not both). The following conditions must hold:

The Ravioli and the Turkey are both tasted at some time after the Pot Roast.

The Quiche is the sixth entrée tasted.

The Pot Roast is the second entrée prepared by Chef Garcia.

The chef who prepares the first entrée must be different from the chef who prepares the last entrée.

Each entrée prepared by Chef Garcia is immediately followed in the tasting by an entrée prepared by Chef Haley.

1. Which one of the following could be of the order, from first to last, in which the entrees are tasted?

    (A) Salmon, Noodles, Ravioli, Pot Roast, Turkey, Quiche, Veal
    (B) Noodles, Salmon, Veal, Pot Roast, Ravioli, Turkey, Quiche
    (C) Veal, Noodles, Pot Roast, Turkey, Salmon, Quiche, Ravioli
    (D) Pot Roast, Noodles, Ravioli, Veal, Turkey, Quiche, Salmon
    (E) Noodles, Turkey, Pot Roast, Veal, Ravioli, Quiche, Salmon

2. If Veal is the third entrée tasted, then which one of the following is a complete and accurate list of the entrées that must be prepared by Chef Haley?

    (A) Roast Beef, Quiche, Turkey, and Veal
    (B) Roast Beef, Turkey, and Veal
    (C) Noodles, Roast Beef, and Veal
    (D) Noodles, Salmon, Turkey, and Veal
    (E) Salmon, Turkey, and Veal

3. Which one of the following pairs of entrees CANNOT be tasted consecutively by the food critic?

    (A) Noodles and Salmon
    (B) Noodles and Veal
    (C) Pot Roast and Veal
    (D) Ravioli and Turkey
    (E) Pot Roast and Quiche

4. If Chef Garcia prepares the fourth entrée, then each of the following could be true EXCEPT:

    (A) The Salmon is prepared by Chef Garcia.
    (B) The Veal is prepared by Chef Haley.
    (C) The Quiche is prepared by Chef Garcia.
    (D) The Ravioli is prepared by Chef Garcia.
    (E) The Turkey is prepared by Chef Haley.

5. If the Noodles and the Veal are both prepared by Chef Haley, then which one of the following must be true?

   (A) Salmon is the first entrée tasted.
   (B) Veal is the second entrée tasted.
   (C) Pot Roast is the fourth entrée tasted.
   (D) Ravioli is the fifth entrée tasted.
   (E) Noodles is the third entrée tasted.

6. Which one of the following must be true?

   (A) Chef Haley prepares the third entrée.
   (B) Chef Haley prepares the second entrée.
   (C) Chef Garcia prepares the sixth entrée.
   (D) Chef Garcia prepares the third entrée.
   (E) Chef Garcia prepares the second entrée.

STEP 1 Visualize and draw the diagram.

What are you being asked to figure out? There are two tasks being asked of you: (1) to identify the order in which the entrées are tasted and, (2) to identify the chef that prepares the entrée. This is a multi-tier game, and the diagram is as follows:

1	2	3	4	5	6	7
Entrée/Chef	Entrée/Chef	Entrée/Chef	Entrée/Chef	Entrée/Chef	Entrée/Chef	Entrée/Chef
_ _	_ _	_ _	_ _	_ _	_ _	_ _

STEP 2 List the components and ascertain the ratio and/or distribution.

The components are:

Entrées: N, P, Q, R, S, T, and V
Chefs: G and H

There are tastings with seven entrées but only two chefs. The ratio of the entrées is 1:1, since the number of entrées is equal to the number of slots. However, the ratio of chefs is not 1:1, since there are only two chefs for seven slots.

STEP 3 Symbolize the clues.

Remember to symbolize clues in the two-tier format.

Clue 1   The Ravioli and the Turkey are both tasted at some time after the Pot Roast.

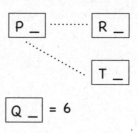

Clue 2   The Quiche is the sixth entrée tasted. (Put in diagram)

 = 6

Clue 3   The Pot Roast is the second entrée prepared by Chef Garcia.

PG_2

Clue 4   The chef who prepares the first entrée must be different from the chef who prepares the last entrée.

Chef 1 ≠ Chef 7
(Put in diagram)

Clue 5   Each entrée prepared by Chef Garcia is immediately followed in the tasting by an entrée prepared by Chef Haley.

STEP 4 Make deductions.

Remember to determine what slots ban which components and focus on commonality.

Deduction 1: Put Clue 2 directly into the diagram.

Deduction 2: From Clue 1 you can deduce:

- P cannot be placed in either slot 5 or 7 because at least two entrées (R and T) are tasted after P, and entrée Q already occupies slot 6.
- R and T cannot be placed in slot 1 because at least one entrée (P) is tasted before them.

The diagram is updated as follows:

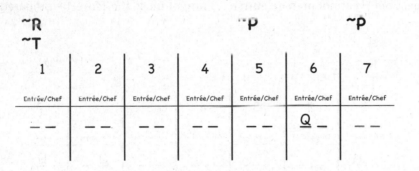

Deduction 3: From Clue 3, you can deduce that since P is the second entrée prepared by G, there is at least one entrée before P, so P cannot be in slot 1.

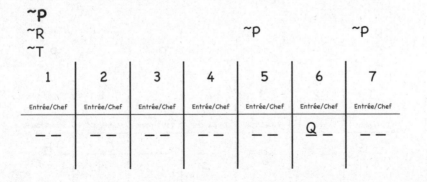

Deduction 4: From Clue 5, you can deduce that Chef H prepares entrée 7. How? Clue 5 requires that any entrée prepared by Chef G be immediately followed by an entrée prepared by Chef H. Since entrée 7 is not followed by any entrée, it cannot be prepared by Chef G, and, therefore, must be prepared by Chef H.

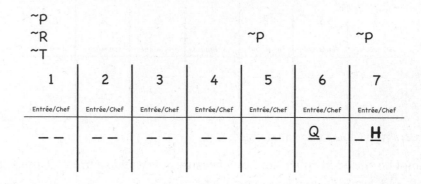

Deduction 5: From Clue 4, you can deduce that Chef G prepares entrée 1. How? From Deduction 4, you can ascertain that Chef H prepares entrée 7—the last entree. Since Clue 4 states that the chef who prepares the first entrée must be different from the chef who prepares the last entrée, Chef H cannot prepare entrée 1. Entrée 1 must, therefore, be prepared by Chef G.

~P ~R ~T				~P		~P
1	2	3	4	5	6	7
Entrée/Chef	Entrée/Chef	Entrée/Chef	Entrée/Chef	Entrée/Chef	Entrée/Chef	Entrée/Chef
_ G	_ _	_ _	_ _	_ _	Q _	_ H

Deduction 6: From Clue 5 and Deduction 4, you can deduce that Chef H prepares entrée 2.

~P ~R ~T				~P		~P
1	2	3	4	5	6	7
Entrée/Chef	Entrée/Chef	Entrée/Chef	Entrée/Chef	Entrée/Chef	Entrée/Chef	Entrée/Chef
_ G	_ H	_ _	_ _	_ _	Q _	_ H

Deduction 7: Now that you have deduced that Chef H prepares entrée 2, you can deduce from Clue 2 that P cannot be the second entrée prepared, and, thus, the earliest that entrée P can be tasted is third.

~P ~R ~T	~P			~P		~P
1	2	3	4	5	6	7
Entrée/Chef	Entrée/Chef	Entrée/Chef	Entrée/Chef	Entrée/Chef	Entrée/Chef	Entrée/Chef
_ G	_ H	_ _	_ _	_ _	Q _	_ H

Deduction 8: Finally, if you reapply Clue 1 to Deduction 7, you can deduce that R and T (because they must be tasted after P) cannot be tasted either second or third.

~P ~R ~T	~P ~R ~T	~R ~T		~P		~P
1	2	3	4	5	6	7
Entrée/Chef	Entrée/Chef	Entrée/Chef	Entrée/Chef	Entrée/Chef	Entrée/Chef	Entrée/Chef
_ G	_ H	_ _	_ _	_ _	Q _	_ H

There were a host of deductions here! Arming yourself with these before attacking the questions will allow you to manage them with greater ease.

STEP 5 Tackle the questions.

The order in which you answer the questions is important. Remember the optimal sequence: 1. catch-a-clue; 2. restricted; 3. unrestricted; 4. modifiers. For this particular game, that translates to the following order: 1, 2, 4, 5, 3, and then 6.

Answer Key

1. **C**   2. **B**   3. **E**   4. **D**   5. **A**   6. **B**

Answers

Question 1

This is a catch-a-clue question. Remember you need only catch a rule, look for the answer choice that violates that rule, and then eliminate it.

> Which one of the following could be of the order, from first to last, in which the entrees are tasted?
>
> (A) Salmon, Noodles, Ravioli, Pot Roast, Turkey, Quiche, Veal
> (B) Noodles, Salmon, Veal, Pot Roast, Ravioli, Turkey, Quiche
> (C) Veal, Noodles, Pot Roast, Turkey, Salmon, Quiche, Ravioli
> (D) Pot Roast, Noodles, Ravioli, Veal, Turkey, Quiche, Salmon
> (E) Noodles, Turkey, Pot Roast, Veal, Ravioli, Quiche, Salmon

The first clue (*The Ravioli and the Turkey are both tasted at some time after the Pot Roast*) eliminates answer choices A and E. The second clue (*The Quiche is the sixth entrée tasted*) eliminates answer choice B. The third clue (*The Pot Roast is the second entrée prepared by Chef Garcia*) eliminates answer choice D.

(C) is the correct answer.

Put the correct answer into the diagram.

~P ~R ~T	~P ~R ~T	~R ~T	~P	~P		~P
1	2	3	4	5	6	7
Entrée/Chef	Entrée/Chef	Entrée/Chef	Entrée/Chef	Entrée/Chef	Entrée/Chef	Entrée/Chef
<u>V</u> G	<u>N</u> H	<u>P</u> _	<u>T</u> _	<u>S</u> _	<u>Q</u> _	<u>R</u> H

Question 2

This is a restricted, "must-be-true" question. Therefore, four answers are true sometimes but not always, or they are never true. The correct answer is always true.

> If Veal is the third entrée tasted, then which one of the following is a complete and accurate list of the entrées that must be prepared by Chef Haley?
>
> (A) Roast Beef, Quiche, Turkey, and Veal
> (B) Roast Beef, Turkey, and Veal
> (C) Noodles, Roast Beef, and Veal
> (D) Noodles, Salmon, Turkey, and Veal
> (E) Salmon, Turkey, and Veal

Begin by placing the additional restriction into the diagram.

	~P ~R ~T	~P ~R ~T	~R ~T		~P		~P
	1	2	3	4	5	6	7
	Entrée/Chef	Entrée/Chef	Entrée/Chef	Entrée/Chef	Entrée/Chef	Entrée/Chef	Entrée/Chef
	_ G	_ H	V _	_ _	_ _	Q _	_ H

Pivot to the most restricted component: P. Prior deductions ban P from entrée slots 1, 2, 5, 6, and 7. With the placement of V in entrée slot 3, P is also banned from entrée slot 3. Therefore, P must be placed in entrée slot 4.

By operation of Clue 2, Chef G is likewise placed in chef slot 3. Additionally, because you know that P is the second entrée prepared by Chef G, you can deduce that V must be prepared by Chef H.

	~P ~R ~T	~P ~R ~T	~R ~T	~P			~P
	1	2	3	4	5	6	7
	Entrée/Chef	Entrée/Chef	Entrée/Chef	Entrée/Chef	Entrée/Chef	Entrée/Chef	Entrée/Chef
	_ G	_ H	V H	P G	_ _	Q _	_ H

By operation of Clue 1, R and T are relegated to entrée slots 5 and 7 interchangeably.

	~P ~R ~T	~P ~R ~T	~R ~T		~P		~P
	1	2	3	4	5	6	7
	Entrée/Chef	Entrée/Chef	Entrée/Chef	Entrée/Chef	Entrée/Chef	Entrée/Chef	Entrée/Chef
	_ G	_ H	V H	P G	R/T _	Q _	R/T H

Also, by operation of Clue 5, H must be placed in slot 5.

~P ~R ~T	~P ~R ~T	~R ~T		~P		~P
1	2	3	4	5	6	7
Entrée/Chef	Entrée/Chef	Entrée/Chef	Entrée/Chef	Entrée/Chef	Entrée/Chef	Entrée/Chef
_ G	_ H	V H	P G	R/T **H**	Q _	R/T **H**

The only remaining components are N and S. There are no clues or deductions that limit the placement of these components, so both N and R can be placed in entrée slots 1 and 2 interchangeably.

~P ~R ~T	~P ~R ~T	~R ~T		~P		~P
1	2	3	4	5	6	7
Entrée/Chef	Entrée/Chef	Entrée/Chef	Entrée/Chef	Entrée/Chef	Entrée/Chef	Entrée/Chef
N/S G	**N/S** H	V H	P G	R/T H	Q _	R/T **H**

Noodles, Quiche, and Salmon could each be prepared by Chef Haley but are not always prepared by Chef Haley. Any answer choices with Noodles, Quiche, or Salmon can be eliminated, so eliminate answer choices A, C, D, and E.

(B) is the correct answer.

Question 4

This restricted, "could-be-true-EXCEPT" question is identical to a "must-be-false" question. Therefore, four answers can be true at least once. These are the wrong answers. One answer is never true. This is the correct answer.

4. If Chef Garcia prepares the fourth entrée, then each of the following could be true EXCEPT:

   (A) The Salmon is prepared by Chef Garcia.
   (B) The Veal is prepared by Chef Haley.
   (C) The Quiche is prepared by Chef Garcia.
   (D) The Ravioli is prepared by Chef Garcia.
   (E) The Turkey is prepared by Chef Haley.

Place the additional restriction into the diagram.

~P ~R ~T	~P ~R ~T	~R ~T			~P	~P
1	**2**	**3**	**4**	**5**	**6**	**7**
Entrée/Chef	Entrée/Chef	Entrée/Chef	Entrée/Chef	Entrée/Chef	Entrée/Chef	Entrée/Chef
_ <u>G</u>	_ <u>H</u>	_ _	_ <u>G</u>	_ _	<u>Q</u> _	_ <u>H</u>

Pivot to the most restricted component: P. Prior deductions indicate that P must be placed in either entrée slot 3 or entrée slot 4.

By operation of Clue 2, P must be placed with Chef G. Therefore, Chef G must be placed in either chef slot 3 or chef slot 4. However, because of Clue 5, you cannot place Chef G in chef slot 3 because Chef H has not been placed in chef slot 4. As such, $\boxed{PG_2}$ must be placed in slot 4. In addition, Clue 5 requires that Chef H is placed in chef slot 5.

~P ~R ~T	~P ~R ~T	~R		~P		~P
1	**2**	**3**	**4**	**5**	**6**	**7**
Entrée/Chef	Entrée/Chef	Entrée/Chef	Entrée/Chef	Entrée/Chef	Entrée/Chef	Entrée/Chef
_ <u>G</u>	_ <u>H</u>	_ _	<u>P</u> <u>G</u>	_ <u>H</u>	<u>Q</u> _	_ <u>H</u>

By operation of Clue 1, R and T must occupy entrée slots 5 and 7 interchangeably.

~P ~R ~T	~P ~R ~T	~R ~T			~P		~P
1	**2**	**3**	**4**	**5**	**6**	**7**
Entrée/Chef	Entrée/Chef	Entrée/Chef	Entrée/Chef	Entrée/Chef	Entrée/Chef	Entrée/Chef
_ <u>G</u>	_ <u>H</u>	_ _	<u>P</u> <u>G</u>	**R/T** H	<u>Q</u> _	**R/T** H

Answer choices A, B, and C can be true, and answer choice E must be true. You are looking for the *exception*. Answer choice D cannot be true.

(D) is the correct answer.

Question 5

This is a restricted, "must-be-true" question. Therefore, four answers are true sometimes but not always, or they are never true. The correct answer is always true.

> If the Noodles and the Veal are both prepared by Chef Haley, then which one of the following must be true?
>
> (A) Salmon is the first entrée tasted.
> (B) Veal is the second entrée tasted.
> (C) Pot Roast is the fourth entrée tasted.
> (D) Ravioli is the fifth entrée tasted.
> (E) Noodles is the third entrée tasted.

Begin by placing the additional restriction into the diagram. But how to best incorporate this additional restriction? Let's take a look at the diagram with all of its deductions.

~P ~R ~T	~P ~R ~T	~R ~T		~P		~P
1	2	3	4	5	6	7
Entrée/Chef	Entrée/Chef	Entrée/Chef	Entrée/Chef	Entrée/Chef	Entrée/Chef	Entrée/Chef
_ G	_ H	_ _	_ _	_ _	Q _	_ H

So far you have ascertained that Chef G prepares entrée 1. Since the restriction requires that both the Noodles and the Veal be prepared by Chef H, you can deduce that neither the Noodles nor the Veal is prepared first. Entrees P, R, T and Q (Clue 2 places Q in entrée slot 6) have been banned from entrée slot 1, so the only remaining entrée available for entrée slot 1 is S. **(A) is the correct answer.**

Question 3

This unrestricted "cannot-be-true" question is identical to a "must-be-false" question. Four answers could be true at least once. These are the wrong answers. One answer choice can never be true. This is the correct answer.

> Which one of the following pairs of entrees CANNOT be tasted consecutively by the food critic?
>
> (A) Noodles and Salmon
> (B) Noodles and Veal
> (C) Pot Roast and Veal
> (D) Ravioli and Turkey
> (E) Pot Roast and Quiche

You can answer this question by simply reviewing the deductions or by reviewing your previous work. Remember, each of the possibilities you worked out on the restricted questions is in compliance with all of the clues and can be relied upon to answer the unrestricted questions. Let's take a look at all of your prior work.

	~P ~R ~T **1** Entrée/Chef	~P ~R ~T **2** Entrée/Chef	~R ~T **3** Entrée/Chef	**4** Entrée/Chef	~P **5** Entrée/Chef	**6** Entrée/Chef	~P **7** Entrée/Chef
1	V G	N H	P _	T _	S _	Q _	R H
2	N/S G	N/S H	V H	P G	R/T _	Q _	R/T H
4	_ G	_ H	_ _	P G	R/T H	Q _	R/T H

Answer choice A is not the correct answer because Noodles and Salmon can be tasted consecutively as shown in your work for question 2. Answer choice B is not correct because Noodles and Veal can be tasted consecutively as shown in your work for questions 1 and 2. Eliminate answer choice C because Pot Roast and Veal can be tasted consecutively as shown in the work for question 2.

Your prior work does not show whether or not answer choices C or D can be true, so you cannot eliminate either of those answer choices yet. The answers have been narrowed down to just two choices: either D or E. Whenever the answers are reduced to only two possibilities, just test one of them.

Remember, however, a point made earlier: this question is also answerable by deduction. The Pot Roast and the Quiche (answer choice E) cannot be tasted consecutively. The Quiche is tasted sixth (Clue 2), and it has been determined that that the Pot Roast must be tasted either third or fourth.

(E) is the correct answer.

Question 6

This is an unrestricted, "must-be-true" question. Therefore, four answers are true sometimes but not always, or they are never true. The correct answer is always true.

Which one of the following must be true?

(A) Chef Haley prepares the third entrée.
(B) Chef Haley prepares the second entrée.
(C) Chef Garcia prepares the sixth entrée.
(D) Chef Garcia prepares the third entrée.
(E) Chef Garcia prepares the second entrée.

You can answer this question by simply reviewing the deductions. Chef Haley prepares the second entrée.

(B) is the correct answer.

Game 2

Exactly five thoroughbred horses—Filly, Gem, Hawk, Jazz, and Kix—were born in the years 2002 through 2006. No horse was born in the same year as any other horse. At birth, each of the thoroughbred horses was assigned one of five trainers—Paige, Qiao, Roz, Sam, and Toni. The following conditions must apply:

Paige was assigned to train Hawk.

Toni was assigned to train the horse that was born in 2005.

The horses assigned to trainers Qiao and Roz were born in consecutive years.

Kix was born in the year immediately after the horse that was assigned to Toni.

1. Which one of the following must be true?

   (A) The horse born in 2003 was assigned to trainer Roz.
   (B) The horse born in 2006 was assigned to trainer Qiao.
   (C) The horse born in 2002 was assigned to trainer Roz.
   (D) The horse born in 2006 was assigned to trainer Sam.
   (E) The horse born in 2004 was assigned to trainer Sam.

2. If the horses trained by R and T were born in consecutive years, then any of the following could be true EXCEPT:

   (A) Filly was born in 2004.
   (B) Gem was born in 2005.
   (C) Hawk was born in 2004.
   (D) Jazz was born in 2003.
   (E) Jazz was born in 2004.

3. If there is exactly one year between the year that Filly was born and the year that Hawk was born, which one of the following must be false?

   (A) Qiao was assigned to train Filly.
   (B) Toni was assigned to train Filly.
   (C) Toni was assigned to train Jazz.
   (D) Qiao was assigned to train Jazz.
   (E) Roz was assigned to train Gem.

4. Which one of the following is a complete and accurate list of the horses each of whom could have been born in 2003?

   (A) Filly, Jazz
   (B) Filly, Gem, Jazz
   (C) Gem, Jazz, Kix
   (D) Filly, Gem, Jazz, Kix
   (E) Filly, Gem, Jazz, Hawk

5. If Gem was born in 2002, which one of the following must be true?

   (A) Qiao was assigned to train Filly.
   (B) Toni was assigned to train Jazz.
   (C) Roz was assigned to train Filly.
   (D) The horses trained by Paige and Qiao were born in consecutive years.
   (E) The horses trained by Paige and Toni were born in consecutive years.

6. Which one of the following CANNOT be the list of horses born in 2002, 2003, and 2004, respectively?

   (A) Hawk, Filly, Gem
   (B) Jazz, Gem, Hawk
   (C) Jazz, Filly, Gem
   (D) Gem, Filly, Hawk
   (E) Filly, Gem, Hawk

Visualize and draw the diagram.

What are you being asked to figure out? There are two tasks being asked of you: (1) identify the year in which the horses were born and (2) identify the trainer that was assigned to each horse. This is a multi-tier game, and the diagram is as follows:

STEP 2 List the components and ascertain the ratio and/or distribution.

The components are (first initial of the names):

> Horses: F, G, H, J, and K
> Trainers: P, Q, R, S, and T

There are five years, five horses, and five trainers. The ratio of horses is 1:1 because the number of horses is equal to the number of years. Similarly, the ratio of trainers is 1:1 because there are five trainer slots and exactly five trainers. Likewise, the distribution is 1:1 because exactly one horse and one trainer must be selected for each year.

STEP 3 Symbolize the clues.

Remember to symbolize clues in the two-tier format.

$\boxed{\text{HP}}$

Clue 1	Paige was assigned to train Hawk.

Clue 2	Toni was assigned to train the horse that was born in 2005.

$\boxed{\_\ \text{T}} = 2005$

(Put in diagram)

Clue 3	The horses assigned to trainers Qiao and Roz were born in consecutive years.

$\boxed{\_\ \text{Q}\ |\ \_\ \text{R}}$

Clue 4	Kix was born in the year immediately after the horse that was assigned to Toni.

$\boxed{\_\ \text{T}\ |\ \text{K}\ \_}$

STEP 4 Make deductions.

Remember to determine which slots ban which components and to focus on commonality.

Deduction 1: Put Clue 2 directly into the diagram.

2002	2003	2004	2005	2006
Horse/Trainer	Horse/Trainer	Horse/Trainer	Horse/Trainer	Horse/Trainer
_ _	_ _	_ _	_ T	_ _

Deduction 2: From Clue 4 (notice the commonality of T in both clues), you can deduce that Horse K was born in 2006.

2002	2003	2004	2005	2006
Horse/Trainer	Horse/Trainer	Horse/Trainer	Horse/Trainer	Horse/Trainer
_ _	_ _	_ _	_ T	K _

Deduction 3: From Clue 3, you can deduce that neither trainer Q nor trainer R is assigned to the horse that was born in 2006. How? Clue 3 requires that Q and R be assigned to train horses born in consecutive years. Since 2006 is the last year any of the horses could have been born, if either Q or R trained the horse born in 2006, the other would necessarily be assigned to train the horse born in 2005. However, this is not possible because T has already been assigned to train the horse born in 2005.

~R
~Q

2002	2003	2004	2005	2006
Horse/Trainer	Horse/Trainer	Horse/Trainer	Horse/Trainer	Horse/Trainer
_ _	_ _	_ _	_ T	K _

Deduction 4: From Clue 1, you can deduce that H was not the horse born in 2005 because T is the trainer assigned to the horse born that year—not P. Also, trainer P cannot be the trainer assigned to the horse born in 2006 because K was the horse born in that year. Remember to imagine the HP block as a transparency that you can peel off of the page and overlay onto the diagram. Provided you maintain the horse/trainer format with each clue, this can help you make difficult deductions.

~P
~R
~H   ~Q

2002	2003	2004	2005	2006
Horse/Trainer	Horse/Trainer	Horse/Trainer	Horse/Trainer	Horse/Trainer
_ _	_ _	_ _	_ T	K _

Furthermore, since T is assigned to train the horse born in 2005, and each trainer is assigned just one horse, you can also deduce that T does not train any of the other horses born in any of the other years, particularly the horse born in 2006.

Deduction 5: Therefore, it is clear that the horse born in 2006 cannot be trained by P, R, Q, or T. Accordingly, S, as the only remaining trainer, must be assigned to train the horse born in 2006.

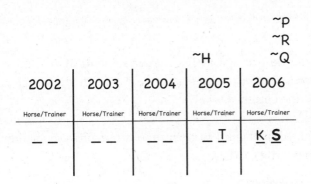

Deduction 6: Now that you know that S trains the horse born in 2006, you can make just one more deduction. Notice that the placement of two out of the five trainers has been ascertained. The remaining three trainers (P, Q, and R) are assigned to the horses born in 2002, 2003, and 2004 (not necessarily in that order). Clue 3 necessitates that trainers Q and R be assigned to horses born in consecutive years, so you can deduce that neither H nor P can be assigned to the year 2003. How? If the HP block were placed in 2003, Q and R would be assigned to years 2002 and 2004 (not necessarily in that order)—nonconsecutive years.

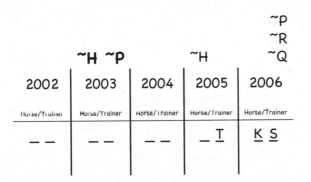

STEP 5 Tackle the questions.

The order in which you answer the questions is important. Remember the optimal sequence: 1. catch-a-clue; 2. restricted; 3. unrestricted; 4. modifiers. For this particular game, that translates to the following order: 2, 3, 5, 1, 4, and then 6.

Answer Key

Answers

Question 2

This restricted, "could-be-true-EXCEPT" question is identical to a "must-be-false" question. Therefore, four answers can be true at least once. These are the wrong answers. One answer is never true. This is the correct answer.

> If the horses trained by R and T were born in consecutive years, then any of the following could be true EXCEPT:
>
> (A) Filly was born in 2004.
> (B) Gem was born in 2005.
> (C) Hawk was born in 2004.
> (D) Jazz was born in 2003.
> (E) Jazz was born in 2004.

Begin by placing the additional restriction into the diagram. Since T is assigned to train the horse born in 2005, and you have deduced that S must be assigned to train the horse born in 2006, R must be assigned to train the horse born in 2004.

	~H ~P		~H	~P ~R ~Q
2002	2003	2004	2005	2006
Horse/Trainer	Horse/Trainer	Horse/Trainer	Horse/Trainer	Horse/Trainer
_ _	_ _	_ **R**	_ T	K S

Pivot to the most restricted components: HP. Prior deductions ban HP from 2003, 2005, and 2006. With the placement of R in the trainer slot in 2004, HP is also banned from that slot. Therefore, HP must be placed in the 2002 slot.

By operation of Clue 2, and also because it's the only one remaining, Q must be placed in the trainer slot in 2003.

	~H ~P		~H	~P ~R ~Q
2002	2003	2004	2005	2006
Horse/Trainer	Horse/Trainer	Horse/Trainer	Horse/Trainer	Horse/Trainer
H P	_ **Q**	_ **R**	_ T	K S

There are no restrictions for horses F, G, and J, so each can be born in 2003, 2004, and 2005 interchangeably.

		~H ~P		~H	~P ~R ~Q
	2002	2003	2004	2005	2006
	Horse/Trainer	Horse/Trainer	Horse/Trainer	Horse/Trainer	Horse/Trainer
	H P	F/G/J Q	F/G/J R	F/G/J T	K S

Answer choices A, B, D, and E can each be true at least once. You are looking for the *exception*. Answer choice C cannot be true.

(C) is the correct answer.

Question 3

This is a restricted, "must-be-false" question. Therefore, four answers can be true at least once. These are the wrong answers. One answer is never true. This is the correct answer.

> If there is exactly one year between the year that Filly was born and the year that Hawk was born, which one of the following must be false?
>
> (A) Qiao was assigned to train Filly.
> (B) Toni was assigned to train Filly.
> (C) Toni was assigned to train Jazz.
> (D) Qiao was assigned to train Jazz.
> (E) Roz was assigned to train Gem.

Since one of the most restricted components (H) is part of the question, you can place the additional restriction $\boxed{F \quad \_\_ \quad H\,P}$ into the diagram in only one of two ways. Either the HP block is placed in slot 2002 and horse F in horse slot 2004 or vice versa.

	~H ~P		~H	~P ~R ~Q	
2002	2003	2004	2005	2006
Horse/Trainer	Horse/Trainer	Horse/Trainer	Horse/Trainer	Horse/Trainer
H P	_ _	F _	_ T	K S
F _	_ _	H P	_ T	K S

The only remaining horse components are G and J. There are no clues or deductions that limit the placement of these components, so both G and J can be placed in horse slots 2003 and 2005 interchangeably.

| | ~H ~P | | ~H | ~P
~R
~Q |
2002	2003	2004	2005	2006
Horse/Trainer	Horse/Trainer	Horse/Trainer	Horse/Trainer	Horse/Trainer
H P	G/J _	F _	J/G T	K S
F _	G/J _	H P	J/G T	K S

The only remaining trainer components are Q and R. Therefore, both Q and R must be placed in trainer slots 2003 and 2004 interchangeably in the top options and in trainer slots 2002 and 2003 interchangeably in the bottom option.

| | ~H ~P | | ~H | ~P
~R
~Q |
2002	2003	2004	2005	2006
Horse/Trainer	Horse/Trainer	Horse/Trainer	Horse/Trainer	Horse/Trainer
H P	G/J Q/R	F R/Q	G/J T	K S
F Q/R	G/J R/Q	H P	G/J T	K S

Answer choices A, C, D, and E can each be true at least once but are not true always. Answer choice B is never true.

(B) is the correct answer.

Question 5

This is a restricted, "must-be-true" question. Therefore, four answers are true sometimes but not always, or they are never true. The correct answer is always true.

If Gem was born in 2002, which one of the following must be true?

(A) Qiao was assigned to train Filly.
(B) Toni was assigned to train Jazz.
(C) Roz was assigned to train Filly.
(D) The horses trained by Paige and Qiao were born in consecutive years.
(E) The horses trained by Paige and Toni were born in consecutive years.

Place the additional restriction into the diagram.

			~H	~P ~R ~Q
	~H ~P		~H	
2002	2003	2004	2005	2006
Horse/Trainer	Horse/Trainer	Horse/Trainer	Horse/Trainer	Horse/Trainer
G _	_ _	_ _	_ T	K S

Pivot to the most restricted components: HP. Prior deductions indicate that HP must be placed in either slot 2002 or 2004. Since G has been placed in slot 2002, the HP block must be placed in slot 2004.

			~H	~P ~R ~Q
	~H ~P		~H	
2002	2003	2004	2005	2006
Horse/Trainer	Horse/Trainer	Horse/Trainer	Horse/Trainer	Horse/Trainer
G _	_ _	H P	_ T	K S

The only remaining horse components are F and J. There are no clues or deductions that limit the placement of these components, so both F and J can be placed in horse slots 2003 and 2005 interchangeably.

			~H	~P ~R ~Q
	~H ~P		~H	
2002	2003	2004	2005	2006
Horse/Trainer	Horse/Trainer	Horse/Trainer	Horse/Trainer	Horse/Trainer
G _	F/J _	H P	J/F T	K S

Likewise, the only remaining trainer components are Q and R, so by operation of Clue 3, both Q and R must be placed in trainer slots 2002 and 2003 interchangeably.

2002	2003	2004	2005	2006
	~H ~P		~H	~P ~R ~Q
Horse/Trainer	Horse/Trainer	Horse/Trainer	Horse/Trainer	Horse/Trainer
G **Q/R**	F/J **R/Q**	H P	J/F T	K S

Answer choices A, B, C, and D can be true at least once but not always. Answer choice E must be true.

(E) is the correct answer.

Question 1

This is an unrestricted, "must-be-true" question. Therefore, four answers are true sometimes but not always, or they are never true. The correct answer is always true.

Which one of the following must be true?

(A) The horse born in 2003 was assigned to trainer Roz.
(B) The horse born in 2006 was assigned to trainer Qiao.
(C) The horse born in 2002 was assigned to trainer Roz.
(D) The horse born in 2006 was assigned to trainer Sam.
(E) The horse born in 2004 was assigned to trainer Sam.

You can answer this question by simply reviewing the deductions. Deduction 5 alerts you to the fact that Sam must be assigned to train the horse born in 2006.

(D) is the correct answer.

Question 4

This is an unrestricted, complete, and accurate list question. Wrong answers omit components that meet the criteria. The absence of components that meet the criteria from the list renders the list incomplete. Wrong answers will also include components that do not meet the criteria. The inclusion of components that do not meet the criteria in the list renders the list inaccurate. The correct response will list only the components that meet the criteria.

Which one of the following is a complete and accurate list of the horses each of whom could have been born in 2003?

(A) Filly, Jazz
(B) Filly, Gem, Jazz
(C) Gem, Jazz, Kix
(D) Filly, Gem, Jazz, Kix
(E) Filly, Gem, Jazz, Hawk

First, review the diagram history to eliminate answer choices. From the history, you can ascertain from question 2 that F, G, and J can each be born in 2003. Since the list is asking for those horses that can be born in 2003, you can eliminate any answer choices that do not contain F, G, or J. Therefore, eliminate answer choices A and C.

Thanks to Deduction 2 you know that horse K was born in 2006 (not 2003). As such, you can eliminate any answers that include K. This means you can eliminate answer choice D. In Deduction 6 you ascertained that horse H cannot be born in 2003, so rule out any answers that include H. Eliminate answer choice E.

(B) is the correct answer.

Question 6

This unrestricted, "cannot-be-true" question is identical to a "must-be-false" question. Four answers could be true at least once. These are the wrong answers. One answer choice can never be true. This is the correct answer.

> Which one of the following CANNOT be the list of horses born in 2002, 2003, and 2004, respectively?
>
> (A) Hawk, Filly, Gem
> (B) Jazz, Gem, Hawk
> (C) Jazz, Filly, Gem
> (D) Gem, Filly, Hawk
> (E) Filly, Gem, Hawk

You can answer this question by reviewing your previous work and/or by reviewing the deductions. Remember, each of the possibilities you worked out on the restricted questions is in compliance with all of the clues and can be relied upon to also answer the unrestricted questions. Look at all of your prior work.

Let's look at the answer choices that have some prior information attached to them. Hawk, Filly, and Gem can be born in the years 2002, 2003, and 2004, respectively, as shown in the work for question 2. So, answer choice A is not correct. Gem, Filly, and Hawk can be born in the years 2002, 2003, and 2004, respectively, as shown in the work for question 5. Answer choice D is not correct. Filly, Gem, and Hawk can be born in the years 2002, 2003, and 2004, respectively, as shown in the work for question 3. So answer choice E is not correct. The prior work does not show that answer choices B and C can be true; therefore, these cannot be eliminated yet.

The answers are narrowed down to two choices: B or C. Whenever you have only two possibilities left, test just one of them.

You may recall that this question is also answerable by deduction. Deduction 6 ascertained that Hawk must be born in either 2002 or 2004. Therefore, answer choice C, which does not include Hawk in either of those years, cannot be a list of horses born in 2002, 2003, and 2004.

(C) is the correct answer.

Game 3

After practice, exactly eight tennis players—Kim, Lara, Moses, Noah, Pablo, Sam, Teresa, and Vaughn—are transported home on the school bus. The bus will make four consecutive stops—one on each of the following streets—Downey, Fields, Gallo, and Hemp. Exactly two tennis players get off the bus at each stop. The following conditions must be met:

Moses will get off of the bus at the same stop as either Teresa or Vaughn.

Lara gets off of the bus at the Gallo Street stop at some time before the bus stops at Downey Street.

Teresa gets off the bus at some time before Sam.

Vaughn gets off of the bus at neither the first nor the last stop.

Kim and Pablo do not get off of the bus at the same stop.

1. If Sam and Vaughn get off the bus at the second stop, then which one of the following must be true?

   (A) Moses gets off the bus at Fields Street.
   (B) Noah gets off the bus at Downey Street.
   (C) Pablo gets off the bus at Gallo Street.
   (D) Kim gets off the bus at Downey Street.
   (E) Teresa gets off the bus at Hemp Street.

2. Which one of the following is a pair of tennis players that could get off the bus at the same street stop?

   (A) Lara and Moses
   (B) Kim and Pablo
   (C) Teresa and Vaughn
   (D) Sam and Teresa
   (E) Lara and Pablo

3. Which one of the following could be the street and the tennis players that get off the bus at stop 4?

   (A) Gallo Street, Lara and Pablo
   (B) Hemp Street, Moses and Teresa
   (C) Downy Street, Kim and Sam
   (D) Fields Street, Kim and Lara
   (E) Hemp Street, Noah and Vaughn

4. Which one of the following is a list of all and only those tennis players any one of whom could be among the players that get off the bus at the fourth stop?

   (A) Lara, Noah, Pablo, and Sam
   (B) Kim, Moses, Noah, Pablo, and Sam
   (C) Kim, Noah, Pablo, and Sam
   (D) Moses, Noah, Pablo, and Sam
   (E) Kim, Lara, Pablo, Sam, and Teresa

5. If Lara and Teresa get off the bus at the third stop, then which one of the following could be false?

   (A) Moses gets off bus at the second stop.
   (B) Noah gets off the bus at the first stop.
   (C) Pablo gets off the bus at the last stop.
   (D) Moses gets off the bus at some time before Sam.
   (E) Sam gets off the bus at the Downey Street stop.

STEP 1 Visualize and draw the diagram.

What are you being asked to figure out? There are two tasks asked of you: (1) identify the order in which the bus makes its stop at each street, and (2) identify which two tennis players get off at each stop. This is a multi-tier game, and the diagram is as follows:

1	2	3	4
Street/Player/Player	Street/Player/Player	Street/Player/Player	Street/Player/Player
— — —	— — —	— — —	— — —

STEP 2 List the components and ascertain the ratio and/or distribution.

The components are:

> Streets: D, F, G, and H
> Players: K, L, M, N, P, S, T, and V

There are four stops with four streets and eight players. The ratio of the streets is 1:1 because the number of streets is equal to the number of stops. The ratio of players is also 1:1 because there are eight players and eight player slots. However, with two players getting off at each slot, the distribution is not 1:1. It is 2:1—two players for every one stop.

STEP 3 Symbolize the clues.

Remember to symbolize clues in a multi-tier format.

Clue 1 Moses gets off the bus at the same stop as either Teresa or Vaughn.

> | _ MT | or | _ MV |

Clue 2 Lara gets off the bus at the Gallo Street stop at some time before the bus stops at Downey Street.

> | GL _ | ... | D __ |

Clue 3 Teresa gets off the bus at some time before Sam.

> | _ T _ | ... | _ S _ |

Clue 4 Vaughn gets off the bus at neither the first nor the last stop.

> V ≠ 1, 4
> (put into the diagram)

Clue 5 Kim and Pablo do not get off the bus at the same stop.

> ⊘ KP

STEP 4 Make deductions.

Remember to determine what slots ban which components and to focus on commonality.

Deduction 1: Clue 4 is put directly into the diagram.

	~V					~V
1		**2**	**3**		**4**	
Street/Player/Player		Street/Player/Player	Street/Player/Player		Street/Player/Player	
— — —		— — —	— — —		— — —	

Deduction 2: From Clue 2, you can deduce that…

- D cannot be placed in street slot 1 because the bus stops on at least one street (G) before it stops at D.
- G cannot be placed in street slot 4 because the bus stops at least one street (D) after it stops at G. Similarly, L cannot be placed in player slot 4 because L always gets off at G. The diagram is updated as follows:

~D	~V				~G	~L ~V
1		**2**	**3**			**4**
Street/Player/Player		Street/Player/Player	Street/Player/Player			Street/Player/Player
— — —		— — —	— — —			— — —

Deduction 3: From Clue 3, you can deduce that S cannot be placed in player slot 1 because T gets off the bus at an earlier stop than S. Likewise, T cannot be placed in player slot 4 because S gets off the bus at a later stop than T.

~D	~S ~V				~G	~T ~L ~V
1		**2**	**3**			**4**
Street/Player/Player		Street/Player/Player	Street/Player/Player			Street/Player/Player
— — —		— — —	— — —			— — —

Deduction 4: From Clue 1, you can deduce that, since M must get off the bus with either T or V and neither T nor V can be placed in player slot 4, M cannot be placed in player slot 4.

	~S			~M
~D	~V			~T
				~L
			~G	~V
1	**2**	**3**	**4**
Street/Player/Player	Street/Player/Player	Street/Player/Player	Street/Player/Player
— — —	— — —	— — —	— — —

Notice the most restricted slot is player slot 4 with four players banned. The next most restricted is player slot 1 with two players banned.

STEP 5 Tackle the questions.

The order in which you answer the questions is important. Remember the optimal sequence: 1. catch-a-clue; 2. restricted; 3. unrestricted; 4. modifiers. For this particular game, that translates to the following order: 1, 5, 2, 3, and then 4.

Answer Key

1. **B**   2. **E**   3. **C**   4. **C**   5. **C**

Answers

Question 1

This is a restricted, "must-be-true" question. Therefore, four answers are true sometimes but not always, or they are never true. The correct answer is always true.

> If Sam and Vaughn get off the bus at the second stop, then which one of the following must be true?
>
> (A) Moses gets off the bus at Fields Street.
> (B) Noah gets off the bus at Downey Street.
> (C) Pablo gets off the bus at Gallo Street.
> (D) Kim gets off the bus at Downey Street.
> (E) Teresa gets off the bus at Hemp Street.

Begin by placing the additional restriction into the diagram.

```
                                                              ~M
                                                              ~T
         ~S                                                   ~L
~D       ~V                                       ~G          ~V
  1                    2                    3                    4

Street/Player/Player   Street/Player/Player   Street/Player/Player   Street/Player/Player
─────────────────────────────────────────────────────────────────────────────────────
 _   _   _        |   _   S   V        |   _   _   _        |   _   _   _
```

By operation of Clue 3, T must be placed in player slot 1.

```
                                                              ~M
                                                              ~T
         ~S                                                   ~L
~D       ~V                                       ~G          ~V
  1                    2                    3                    4

Street/Player/Player   Street/Player/Player   Street/Player/Player   Street/Player/Player
─────────────────────────────────────────────────────────────────────────────────────
 _   T   _        |   _   S   V        |   _   _   _        |   _   _   _
```

By operation of Clue 1, M must be placed in player slot 1 also, since V gets off the bus with S, V is not available to get off the bus with M. Therefore, M must get off the bus with T.

```
                                                              ~M
                                                              ~T
         ~S                                                   ~L
~D       ~V                                       ~G          ~V
  1                    2                    3                    4

Street/Player/Player   Street/Player/Player   Street/Player/Player   Street/Player/Player
─────────────────────────────────────────────────────────────────────────────────────
 _   T   M        |   _   S   V        |   _   _   _        |   _   _   _
```

By operation of Clue 5, K and P cannot get off the bus at the same stop, K and P must be placed in player slots 3 and 4 interchangeably.

				~M
				~T
	~S			~L
~D	~V		~G	~V
1	**2**	**3**	**4**	
Street/Player/Player	Street/Player/Player	Street/Player/Player	Street/Player/Player	
_ T M	_ S V	_ K/P _	_ P/K _	

Pivot to the most restricted player slot—slot 4. L cannot be placed in player slot 4 (Deduction 2). Therefore, L is relegated to the only available player slot (player slot 3), along with street stop G.

				~M
				~T
	~S			~L
~D	~V		~G	~V
1	**2**	**3**	**4**	
Street/Player/Player	Street/Player/Player	Street/Player/Player	Street/Player/Player	
_ T M	_ S V	G K/P L	_ P/K _	

By operation of Clue 2, D must be placed in street slot 4.

				~M
				~T
	~S			~L
~D	~V		~G	~V
1	**2**	**3**	**4**	
Street/Player/Player	Street/Player/Player	Street/Player/Player	Street/Player/Player	
_ T M	_ S V	G K/P L	D P/K _	

The only remaining player (N) must be placed in the only remaining player slot (slot 4).

	~S								~M ~T ~L	
~D	~V							~G	~V	
1			**2**			**3**			**4**	
Street/Player/Player			Street/Player/Player			Street/Player/Player			Street/Player/Player		
_	T	M	_	S	V	G	K/P	L	D	P/K	**N**

Answer choices A, C, D, and E can each be true at least once but are not true always. Answer choice B is always true.

(B) is the correct answer.

Question 5

In this restricted, "could-be-false" question, four answers are always true. These are the wrong answers. One answer choice can be false at least once. This is the correct answer.

If Lara and Teresa get off the bus at the third stop, then which one of the following could be false?

(A) Moses gets off the bus at the second stop.
(B) Noah gets off the bus at the first stop.
(C) Pablo gets off the bus at the last stop.
(D) Moses gets off the bus at some time before Sam.
(E) Sam gets off the bus at the Downey Street stop.

Begin by placing the additional restriction into the diagram.

	~S								~M ~T ~L	
~D	~V.							~G	~V	
1			**2**			**3**			**4**	
Street/Player/Player			Street/Player/Player			Street/Player/Player			Street/Player/Player		
—	—	—	—	—	—	_	L	T	—	—	—

By operation of Clue 2, G must be placed in street slot 3, and D must be placed in street slot 4.

								~M
								~T
	~S							~L
~D	~V					~G	~V	

1	2	3	4
Street/Player/Player	Street/Player/Player	Street/Player/Player	Street/Player/Player
__ __ __	__ __ __	**G** L T	**D** __ __

By operation of Clue 1, M must get off the bus with V because T, having been designated to get off the bus with L, is no longer available to get off the bus with M.

By operation of Clue 4, V must get off the bus at the second stop along with M.

								~M
								~T
	~S							~L
~D	~V					~G	~V	

1	2	3	4
Street/Player/Player	Street/Player/Player	Street/Player/Player	Street/Player/Player
__ __ __	__ **M** **V**	**G** L T	**D** __ __

By operation of Clue 3, S must be placed in player slot 4, since S must get off the bus after T.

								~M
								~T
	~S							~L
~D	~V					~G	~V	

1	2	3	4
Street/Player/Player	Street/Player/Player	Street/Player/Player	Street/Player/Player
__ __ __	__ **M** **V**	**G** L T	**D** **S** __

By operation of Clue 5, K and P cannot get off the bus at the same stop. Therefore, K and P must be placed in player slots 1 and 4 interchangeably.

	~S									~M
~D	~V							~G		~T
										~L
										~V
1			**2**			**3**			**4**	
Street/Player/Player			Street/Player/Player			Street/Player/Player			Street/Player/Player	
_	K/P	_	_	M	V	G	L	T	D	S	P/K

The only remaining player (N) must be placed in the only remaining player slot (slot 1).

	~S									~M
~D	~V							~G		~T
										~L
										~V
1			**2**			**3**			**4**	
Street/Player/Player			Street/Player/Player			Street/Player/Player			Street/Player/Player	
_	K/P	N	_	M	V	G	L	T	D	S	P/K

Answer choices A, B, D, and E must always be true. Answer choice C could be either true or false.

(C) is the correct answer.

Question 2

This is an unrestricted, "could-be-true" question. Therefore, four answers are never true. These are the wrong answers. The correct answer is true at least once or is always true.

Which one of the following is a pair of tennis players that could get off the bus at the same street stop?

(A) Lara and Moses
(B) Kim and Pablo
(C) Teresa and Vaughn
(D) Sam and Teresa
(E) Lara and Pablo

Since this is an unrestricted question, it might be partly answerable by reviewing your previous work. Remember, each of the worked out unrestricted questions is in compliance with all of the clues and can be relied upon to answer the unrestricted questions. Refer to the diagram history.

			~S									~M
	~D		~V						~G		~T
											~L
											~V
	1			**2**			**3**			**4**	
	Street/Player/Player			Street/Player/Player			Street/Player/Player			Street/Player/Player	
#1	_ T M			_ S V			G K/P L			D P/K N	
#5	_ K/P N			_ M V			G L T			D S P/K	

This game has generated very little diagram history. However, if you review the diagram from question 1, you can ascertain that Lara and Pablo can get off the bus together at stop 3. Answer choice E is the correct answer.

However, let's take a look at why the other four answers are wrong, and how you could have deduced your way to the correct answer.

Answer choice A: Moses must get off the bus with either Teresa or Vaughn according to Clue 1. As such, Moses cannot get off the bus with Lara. This answer choice can be eliminated.

Answer choice B: Clue 5 dictates that Kim and Pablo cannot get off the bus at the same stop. This answer choice can be eliminated.

Answer choice C: Clue 1 says that Moses must get off the bus with either Teresa or Vaughn. As such, Teresa and Vaughn can't get off the bus together because it would force Moses to get off the bus with someone other than Teresa or Vaughn in violation of Clue 1. This answer choice can be eliminated.

Answer choice D: Clue 3 indicates that Teresa gets off the bus before Sam. As such, Teresa and Sam cannot get off the bus together. This answer choice can be eliminated.

(E) is the correct answer.

Question 3

This is an unrestricted, "could-be-true" question. Four answers are never true. These are the wrong answers. One answer could be true at least once. This is the correct answer.
This question is completely answerable by reviewing the prior clues and deductions.

1. **DEDUCTION 1:** Vaughn cannot get off at the fourth stop. Answer choice E is incorrect.
2. **DEDUCTION 2:** Gallo cannot be the fourth street stop. Answer choice A is incorrect.
3. **CLUE 2:** Lara must get off at the Gallo Street stop. Answer choice D is incorrect.
4. **DEDUCTION 3:** Teresa does not get off at the fourth stop. Answer choice B is incorrect.

(C) is the correct answer.

Question 4

This is an unrestricted, complete, and accurate list question. Wrong answers will omit components that meet the criteria and, therefore, must be on the list. The absence of components that meet the criteria from the list renders the list incomplete. Wrong answers will also include components that do not meet the criteria. This inclusion of components that don't meet the list criteria renders the list inaccurate. The correct answer will list only components that meet the criteria.

> Which one of the following is a list of all and only those tennis players any one
> of whom could be among the players that get off the bus at the fourth stop?

(A) Lara, Noah, Pablo, and Sam
(B) Kim, Moses, Noah, Pablo, and Sam
(C) Kim, Noah, Pablo, and Sam
(D) Moses, Noah, Pablo, and Sam
(E) Kim, Lara, Pablo, Sam, and Teresa

Answering unrestricted questions involves a review of the deductions and the diagram history.

1. Deduction 2 indicates that Lara cannot get off the bus at the fourth stop. Eliminate answer choice A.
2. Deduction 3 indicates that Teresa cannot get off the bus at the fourth stop. Eliminate answer choice E.
3. Deduction 4 indicates that Moses cannot get off the bus at the fourth stop. Eliminate answer choice B.
4. Review of the diagram history for both questions 1 and 5 indicates that Kim can get off the bus at the fourth stop and, thus, must be on the list. Eliminate answer choice D.

(C) is the correct answer.

HYBRID GAMES

Let's now look at something called hybrid games. Remember, this whole chapter is about games that are made up of sequencing and grouping combinations. As you practiced the multi-tier games, you realized that they were basically sequencing games with a grouping twist. Hybrid games are the inverse of multi-tier games; they're basically grouping games with a sequencing twist. In traditional grouping games, you are asked to determine which components are placed into which group, or perhaps which components are placed into which group(s) and which components are left outside the group (i.e., in/out grouping games). For example:

> From among eight runners—F, G, H, J, K, L, M, and N—exactly five will be chosen
> to run in the upcoming track meet. The selection of runners must meet the
> following conditions:

What are you being asked to figure out? You need to determine which five of the eight runners are selected to run in the track meet. The diagram is as follows:

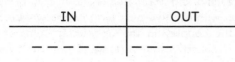

Note that hybrid games not only involve the placement of components into group(s), but they also involve *ordering* those components within the group(s). So if a sequential task were added to the above in/out grouping game, it would transform into a hybrid game. It could look like this:

> From among eight runners—F, G, H, J, K, L, M, and N—exactly five will be chosen to run in the upcoming track meet. *Each of the five runners selected will run in exactly one of five races—the first, second, third, fourth, or fifth*. The selection of runners must meet the following conditions:

The highlighted sentence is the only difference between the two scenarios, and it is that sentence that transforms a simple in/out grouping game into a hybrid game. Now, the answers to the question, "What am I being asked to figure out?" are (1) to select which five runners will participate in the *group* of runners that run in the track meet and (2) to determine the *order* of the races. Notice the sequencing twist referred to earlier. The additional ordering task—that is, the order of the races—also needs to be represented in the diagram.

1	2	3	4	5	OUT
—	—	—	—	—	— — —

Thanks to the complex nature of the hybrid game, you will be confronted with a crossbreed of clues and questions. Often you'll have some clues and questions that center solely on the grouping aspect, center solely on the sequencing aspect, or combine those characteristics.

In Step 4 (making deductions) conditional statements are crucial, just as they are in any other grouping game. Remember to always work out the contrapositive. The ability to quickly link conditional statements will enable you to answer the questions more efficiently. Also, as with sequencing games, some of the deductions will focus on where and how the components and slots are restricted; others will deal with finding the most restricted slots/components and the commonality of the symbols.

Finally, as usual, tackle the questions in the prescribed order.

Game 1

During the Olympic Trials, each of eight athletes—F, G, H, J, K, L, M, and N—will take exactly one long jump. The athletes with the five best long jumps will be selected for the Olympic Team and will represent the country in the upcoming Summer Olympics. The athletes selected for the team will be ranked from first (longest jump) to fifth (shortest jump) and the following conditions must apply:

Either J or K is ranked first.

If G is not selected, then L is selected.

If F is selected, then K is not selected.

If H is selected, then K and N are selected, H ranking higher than K but lower than N.

M cannot be selected unless J is ranked third.

1. Which of the following could be the five athletes selected for the team, listed in order of rank from first to last?

    (A) K, G, J, M, N
    (B) K, M, J, H, L
    (C) J, N, F, L, K
    (D) J, M, G, L, K
    (E) N, H, K, J, L

2. If H ranks third, then which one of the following must be true?

    (A) G is ranked fourth.
    (B) L is ranked fifth.
    (C) K is ranked fourth.
    (D) K is ranked fifth.
    (E) N is ranked second.

3. Which one of the following athletes must be selected for the team?

    (A) M
    (B) K
    (C) J
    (D) G
    (E) L

4. If N is not selected for the team, then each of the following could be true EXCEPT:

    (A) J is ranked higher than L.
    (B) M is ranked higher than G.
    (C) G is ranked higher than J.
    (D) M is ranked higher than K.
    (E) L is ranked higher than M.

5. Which one of the following is a complete and accurate list of the athletes any one of which CANNOT be ranked fifth?

    (A) J, H, M
    (B) K, J, M
    (C) H, M
    (D) J, H
    (E) H

6. Each of the following could be true EXCEPT:

    (A) M is ranked fourth.
    (B) L is ranked second.
    (C) H is ranked second.
    (D) G is ranked fifth.
    (E) N is ranked second.

STEP 1 Visualize and draw the diagram.

What are you being asked to figure out? The game asks you to ascertain which students are selected for the Olympic long jump team, and to rank the selected athletes from longest to shortest jump. Since some students will be left out of the long jump team, the diagram must include in- and out-columns. Furthermore, ranking the team members necessitates that the in-column contain ordering. The diagram is as follows:

1	2	3	4	5	OUT
_	_	_	_	_	_ _ _

STEP 2 List the components and ascertain the ratio and distribution.

The components are F, G, H, J, K, L, M, and N. There are exactly five athletes chosen from a total group of eight students. The ratio is fixed.

STEP 3 Symbolize the clues.

Remember to always write down the contrapositive as well.

Clue 1 Either J or K is ranked first. $\sim J_1 \rightarrow K_1; \sim K_1 \rightarrow J_1$
(Put in diagram)

J/K

1	2	3	4	5	OUT
_	_	_	_	_	_ _ _

Clue 2 If G is not selected, then L is selected. $\sim G \rightarrow L; \sim L \rightarrow G$

Clue 3 If F is selected, then K is not selected. $F \rightarrow \sim K; K \rightarrow \sim F$

Clue 4 If H is selected, then K and N are selected, $H \rightarrow K; \sim K \rightarrow \sim H$
H ranking higher than K but lower than N. $H \rightarrow N; \sim N \rightarrow \sim H$
(Note that the clue has been decoupled.) $H \rightarrow N...H...K$

Clue 5 M cannot be selected unless J is ranked third. $M \rightarrow J_3; \sim J_3 \rightarrow \sim M$

STEP 4 Make deductions.

Remember that linking the conditional statements is crucial.

Link: Clue 5 and Clue 1 are linked. $(M \rightarrow J_3)$ and $(\sim J_1 \rightarrow K_1)$

Deduction 1: $M \rightarrow K_1$

Explanation: If J is third, then it is not first. If J is not first, then K is first.

Link: Clue 3, Clue 1, and Clue 5 are linked. $(F \rightarrow \sim K)$, $(\sim K_1 \rightarrow J_1)$, and $\sim J_3 \rightarrow \sim M$

Deduction 2: $F \rightarrow J_1 \rightarrow \sim M$ and $M \rightarrow J_3 \rightarrow K_1$

Explanation: If F is selected, then K is not selected. If K is not selected, then J must be ranked first (either J or K is first). If J is ranked first (not third), then M is not selected.

Clue 4 (H → N...H...K)

Deduction 3:

1. $H \rightarrow \sim K_1$; $K_1 \rightarrow \sim H$
2. $H \rightarrow \sim K_2$; $K_2 \rightarrow \sim H$
3. $H \rightarrow \sim N_4$; $N_4 \rightarrow \sim H$
4. $H \rightarrow \sim N_5$; $N_5 \rightarrow \sim H$

STEP 5 Tackle the questions.

The order in which you answer the questions is important. Remember the optimal sequence: 1. catch-a-clue; 2. restricted; 3. unrestricted; 4. modifiers. For this particular game, that translates to the following order: 1, 2, 4, 3, 5 and then 6.

Answer Key

1. **A**   2. **E**   3. **C**   4. **D**   5. **E**   6. **C**

Answers

Question 1

This is a catch-a-clue question. Here are the answer choices again:

(A) K, G, J, M, N
(B) K, M, J, H, L
(C) J, N, F, L, K
(D) J, M, G, L, K
(E) N, H, K, J, L

The first clue (*Either J or K is ranked first*) eliminates answer choice E. The second clue (*If G is not selected, then L is selected*) is not violated by any of the answer choices. *The third clue (If F is selected, then K is not selected*) eliminates answer choice C. The fourth clue (*If H is selected, then K and N are selected, H ranking higher than K but lower than N*) eliminates answer choice B. The fifth clue (*M cannot be selected unless J is ranked third*) eliminates answer choice D.

(A) is the correct answer.

Remember that correct answers to the catch-a-clue should be placed into the diagram for future reference.

J/K

1	2	3	4	5	OUT
K	G	J	M	N	F H L

Question 2

This is a restricted, "must-be-true" question. Therefore, four answers are true sometimes but not always, or they are never true. These are the wrong answers. The correct answer is always true.

If H ranks third, then which one of the following must be true?

(A) G is ranked fourth.
(B) L is ranked fifth.
(C) K is ranked fourth.
(D) K is ranked fifth.
(E) N is ranked second.

Place the additional restriction into the diagram.

J/K

1	2	3	4	5	OUT
–	–	H	–	–	– – –

Look at the rule symbols and prior deductions for guidance. By operation of the contrapositive of Clue 5, M is forced into the out-column.

J/K

1	2	3	4	5	OUT
–	–	H	–	–	M _ _

By operation of Clue 4, K must be placed in either slot 4 or 5 and, thus, cannot be first. There-fore, by operation of the contrapositive of Clue 1, J is first.

J/K

1	2	3	4	5	OUT
J	—	H	K	K	M _ _

Also, since K is either fourth or fifth, by operation of the contrapositive of Clue 3, F is forced into the out-column.

J/K

1	2	3	4	5	OUT
J	—	H	K	K	M F _

Again by operation of Clue 4, N must be ranked higher than H. The only slot available for N is slot 2.

J/K

1	2	3	4	5	OUT
J	N	H	K	K	M F _

Is there a clue that governs the obligations of the remaining components, G and L? Clue 2 does. Specifically, it forbids G and L from occupying slots in the out-column simultaneously. This is a moot point because there's no longer space for them to both be placed in the out-column; therefore, one of the pair will be placed in the in-column and the other in the out-column.

J/K

1	2	3	4	5	OUT
J	N	H	K/G/L	K/G/L	M F G/L

Answer choices A, B, C, and D could be true, but they do not have to always be true.

(E) is the correct answer.

Question 4

This is a restricted, "could-be-true-EXCEPT" question. Therefore, four answers could be true at least once. These are the wrong answers. One answer is never true. This is the correct answer.

If N is not selected for the team, then each of the following could be true EXCEPT:

(A) J is ranked higher than L.
(B) M is ranked higher than G.
(C) G is ranked higher than J.
(D) M is ranked higher than K.
(E) L is ranked higher than M.

This question places N in the out-column.

J/K

1	2	3	4	5	OUT
–	–	–	–	–	<u>N</u> _ _

By operation of Clue 4, H is forced into the out-column.

J/K

1	2	3	4	5	OUT
–	–	–	–	–	<u>N</u> **H** _

By operation of Clue 3, F and K cannot both be placed in the in-column simultaneously. In theory, both F and K could be placed in the out-column simultaneously; however, there is only one slot available in there. Therefore, one athlete in the pair must be placed in the in-column and the other in the out-column.

Does it matter which athlete in the pair is placed where? In other words, are F and K interchangeable? Here is where Deduction 2 ($F \rightarrow J_1 \rightarrow \sim M$) helps tremendously. If you were to place F in the in-column and K in the last slot in the out-column, it would force M into the out-column, but there isn't an available slot there for M. Therefore, K must be placed in the in-column and F in the out-column. The result is that all of the out-slots are filled, thereby forcing the remaining components (G, J, L, and M) into the in-column.

With the inclusion of M in the in-column, you now pivot to Deduction 1 (M → J$_3$ → K$_1$). As such, K must be ranked first.

J/K

1	2	3	4	5	OUT
K̲	–	J̲	–	–	N̲ H̲ F̲

The remaining components (G, L, M) are each interchangeable in the second, fourth, and fifth slots.

J/K

1	2	3	4	5	OUT
K̲	G/L/M	J̲	G/L/M	G/L/M	N̲ H̲ F̲

Answer choices A, B, C, and E could be true, but answer choice D is never true.

(D) is the correct answer.

Question 3

This is an unrestricted, "must-be-true" question. Therefore, four answers are true sometimes but not always, or they are never true. These are the wrong answers. The correct answer is always true.

   Which one of the following athletes must be selected for the team?

(A) M
(B) K
(C) J
(D) G
(E) L

Here's a simpler translation of the question: Which one of the following athletes must always be placed in the in-column and, thus, can never be placed in the out-column? Your deductions offer little help here, so look to your previous work for guidance. If you ever see any of the athletes (M, H, J, G, L) occupying a slot in the out-column, you can deduce that the placement of the athlete on the team is not required and, therefore, rule out the corresponding answer choice.

J/K

	1	2	3	4	5	OUT
1	K	G	J	M	N	F H L
2	J	N	H	K/G/L	K/G/L	M F G/L
4	K	G/L/M	J	G/L/M	G/L/M	N H F

Consider the diagram history above. You can see that M, G, and L can each be placed in the out-column. Therefore, you can eliminate answer choices A, D, and E, leaving just two choices remaining. Remember, whenever you have narrowed the answers down to just two, you only need to try one of them. Let's try answer choice C (athlete J). Can J ever be placed in the out-column?

J/K

1	2	3	4	5	OUT
–	–	–	–	–	J _ _

By operation of Clue 1, K is first. Also by operation of Clue 5, M is forced into the out column. Lastly, by operation of Clue 3, F is forced into the out-column.

J/K

1	2	3	4	5	OUT
K	–	–	–	–	J M F

Pivot to any rules or deductions governing the remaining components: H, G, L, and N. Clue 4 requires that both H and N be ranked higher than K when H is placed in the in-column. Given that K is first, this is impossible. Therefore, the placement of J in the out-column will violate the clues; J must always be placed in the in-column.

(C) is the correct answer.

Question 5

This is an unrestricted, complete, and accurate list question. Wrong answers will omit components that meet the criteria and, therefore, must be on the list. The absence of components that meet the criteria from the list renders the list incomplete. Wrong answers will also include components that do not meet the criteria. The inclusion of components that do not meet the criteria in the list renders the list inaccurate. The correct response will list only the components that meet the criteria.

Which one of the following is a complete and accurate list of the athletes any one of which CANNOT be ranked fifth?

(A) J, H, M

(B) K, J, M

(C) H, M

(D) J, H

(E) H

As you attempt to eliminate answer choices, the first step is to review the diagram history. From the answer to question 2 in the diagram history, you can see that K, G, and L can each be ranked fifth. Since you're asked for those components that *cannot* be ranked fifth, eliminate any answer choices that contain K, G, or L. Therefore, answer choice B is eliminated. From question 4 in the diagram history, you can ascertain that M can also be ranked fifth: eliminate answer choices A and C. Just two possible answers are left: J, H, or H. Athlete H is included in both the remaining lists, so you can deduce that H belongs on the list of athletes that cannot be ranked fifth. The difference between the two remaining answers is the inclusion of J in one of them, so really the only question you need to answer is whether J can be ranked fifth. Let's test it:

J/K

1	2	3	4	5	OUT
–	–	–	–	J̲	– – –

By operation of Clue 1, K is ranked first and by operation of Clue 3, F is forced into the out-column. Also, with the placement of J as fifth and by operation of Clue 5, M is forced into the out-column.

J/K

1	2	3	4	5	OUT
K̲	–	–	–	J̲	F̲ M̲

Pivot to Deduction 3. H is forced into the out-column.

J/K

1	2	3	4	5	OUT
K̲	–	–	–	J̲	F̲ M̲ H̲

The remaining components (G, L, N) are interchangeable in the second, third, and fourth slots.

J/K					
1	2	3	4	5	OUT
<u>K</u>	G/L/N	G/L/N	G/L/N	<u>J</u>	<u>F</u> <u>M</u> <u>H</u>

It's now clear: J can indeed be ranked fifth. Eliminate answer choice D.

(E) is the correct answer.

Question 6

This unrestricted, "could-be-true-EXCEPT" question is identical to a "must-be-false" question. Four answers could be true at least once. These are the wrong answers. One answer choice can never be true. This is the correct answer.

Each of the following could be true EXCEPT:

(A) M is ranked fourth.
(B) L is ranked second.
(C) H is ranked second.
(D) G is ranked fifth.
(E) N is ranked second.

Since this is an unrestricted question, it might be answerable, in part, by reviewing your previous work. Remember, each of the possibilities you worked out on the restricted questions is in compliance with all the clues, and they can be relied upon to answer the unrestricted questions too. Refer to the diagram history.

J/K						
	1	2	3	4	5	OUT
1	<u>K</u>	<u>G</u>	<u>J</u>	<u>M</u>	<u>N</u>	<u>F</u> <u>H</u> <u>L</u>
2	<u>J</u>	<u>N</u>	<u>H</u>	K/G/L	K/G/L	<u>M</u> <u>F</u> G/L
4	<u>K</u>	G/L/M	<u>J</u>	G/L/M	G/L/M	<u>N</u> <u>H</u> <u>F</u>

Answer choice A (*M is ranked fourth*) can be true as shown in your work for questions 1 and 4. This is not the correct answer. Answer choice B (*L is ranked second*) can be true as shown in your work for question 2. This is not the correct answer. Answer choice D (*G is ranked fifth*) can be true as shown in your work for questions 4 and 5. This is not the correct answer. Answer choice E (*N is ranked second*) can be true as was shown in the work for question 2.

(C) is the correct answer.

Game 2

In a single morning, a local bakery will bake exactly one batch each of six types of bread—Oatmeal, Pumpernickel, Rye, Sourdough, Tortilla, and Wheat. Each batch of bread will be baked in exactly one of three time slots—6, 7, or 8—in one of two ovens—Oven 1 or Oven 2. For each oven, exactly one batch of bread is baked in each time slot. The following conditions must apply:

Oatmeal and Rye are not baked in the same oven as Wheat.

Sourdough is baked immediately after Pumpernickel, though not necessarily in the same oven.

The Tortilla is baked at 7.

1. Which one of the following could be a complete and accurate list of the breads baked in Oven 1 from 6 to 8?

   (A) Pumpernickel, Sourdough, Tortilla
   (B) Oatmeal, Pumpernickel, Wheat
   (C) Sourdough, Tortilla, Pumpernickel
   (D) Pumpernickel, Tortilla, Sourdough
   (E) Rye, Pumpernickel, Oatmeal

2. If Pumpernickel is baked in Oven 1 at 7, then which of the following must be true?

   (A) Wheat is baked at 6.
   (B) Rye is baked at 6.
   (C) Wheat is baked at 8.
   (D) Oatmeal is baked 8.
   (E) Rye is baked at 8.

3. If Rye and Sourdough are baked in the same oven, then each of the following could be true EXCEPT:

   (A) Oatmeal is baked immediately before Sourdough.
   (B) Sourdough is baked immediately before Wheat.
   (C) Tortilla is baked immediately before Oatmeal.
   (D) Rye is baked immediately before Wheat.
   (E) Sourdough is baked immediately before the Rye.

4. Which one of the following is a complete and accurate list of the breads any one of which could be baked at 6 in Oven 2?

   (A) Oatmeal, Pumpernickel, Rye
   (B) Pumpernickel, Rye, Sourdough
   (C) Pumpernickel, Rye, Sourdough, Wheat
   (D) Oatmeal, Pumpernickel, Rye, Wheat
   (E) Oatmeal, Pumpernickel, Rye, Tortilla, Wheat

5. If Wheat is baked immediately after the Sourdough, then which one of the following could be true?

   (A) Pumpernickel is baked at 7.
   (B) Sourdough is baked at 8.
   (C) Rye is baked at 6.
   (D) Pumpernickel is baked immediately before Oatmeal.
   (E) Rye is baked immediately before Oatmeal.

Visualize and draw the diagram.

What are you being asked to figure out? The game is asking you to ascertain which breads are baked in which ovens and at which times. The breads assigned to each oven are baked in sequential order from 6 to 8, so you have the assignment of breads to a group (in this case an oven). Additionally, the batches of bread are assigned time slots one after another and, thus, require that the oven group contain ordering. The diagram is as follows:

OVEN 1			OVEN 2		
6	7	8	6	7	8
—	—	—	—	—	—

STEP 2 List the components and ascertain the ratio and/or distribution.

Our components are O, P, R, S, T, and W. There are exactly six types of bread, and each type of bread will be assigned once to one of six time slots. The ratio is one-to-one. Three types of bread will be baked in Oven 1, and three types will be baked in Oven 2. The distribution is fixed.

STEP 3 Symbolize the clues.

Remember to always write down the contrapositive as well.

Clue 1	Oatmeal and Rye are not baked in the same oven as Wheat.	$O \rightarrow \sim W;\ W \rightarrow \sim O$ $R \rightarrow \sim W;\ W \rightarrow \sim R$
Clue 2	Sourdough is baked immediately after Pumpernickel but not necessarily in the same oven.	PS (may be in different ovens)
Clue 3	The Tortilla is baked at 7.	T = 7 (oven 1 or 2)

STEP 4 Make deductions.

Deduction 1: R and O are baked in the same oven.

Explanation: Neither O nor R is baked in the same oven as W. There are only two ovens, and each type of bread is baked in one oven or the other. Therefore, O and R are baked in the other oven that W is not and, thus, are always baked together.

Deduction 2: From Clue 2, you can deduce that S is not baked at 6 in both ovens, and P is not baked at 8 in either oven. Update the diagram as follows:

OVEN 1			OVEN 2		
~S		~P	~S		~P
6	7	8	6	7	8
—	—	—	—	—	—

Deduction 3: From Clue 3, you can deduce that T cannot be baked at 6 or 8 in either oven. Remember, you are looking for things that *cannot* be.

OVEN 1			OVEN 2		
~T	~T		~T		~T
~S	~P		~S		~P
6	7	8	6	7	8
—	—	—	—	—	—

(STEP 5) Tackle the questions:

The order in which you answer the questions is important. Remember the optimal sequence: 1. catch-a-clue; 2. restricted; 3. unrestricted; 4. modifiers. For this particular game, that translates to the following order: 1, 2, 3, 5, and then 4.

Answer Key

1. **E**   2. **A**   3. **D**   4. **D**   5. **C**

Answers

Question 1

This is a catch-a-clue question. Remember you need only catch a rule, look for the answer choice that violates that rule, and then eliminate it. Note that when you're working with just two groups, the violation of the rule can be in the group that's not shown.

> Which one of the following could be a complete and accurate list of the breads baked in Oven 1 from 6 to 8?
>
> (A) Pumpernickel, Sourdough, Tortilla
> (B) Oatmeal, Pumpernickel, Wheat
> (C) Sourdough, Tortilla, Pumpernickel
> (D) Pumpernickel, Tortilla, Sourdough
> (E) Rye, Pumpernickel, Oatmeal

The first clue (*Oatmeal and Rye are not baked in the same oven as Wheat*) eliminates answer choices B and D. Answer choice D is eliminated because the remaining breads to be baked in Oven 2 (Oatmeal, Rye, and Wheat) are in violation of Clue 1. The second clue (*Sourdough is baked immediately after Pumpernickel, though not necessarily in the same oven*) eliminates answer choice C. The third clue (*The Tortilla is baked at 7*) eliminates answer choice A.

(E) is the correct answer.

Question 2

This is a restricted, "must-be-true" question. Therefore, four answers are true sometimes but not always, or they are never true. These are the wrong answers. The correct answer is always true.

If Pumpernickel is baked in Oven 1 at 7, then which of the following must be true?

(A) Wheat is baked at 6.
(B) Rye is baked at 6.
(C) Wheat is baked at 8.
(D) Oatmeal is baked 8.
(E) Rye is baked at 8.

Place the additional restriction into the diagram.

	OVEN 1			OVEN 2	
~T		~T	~T		~T
~S		~P	~S		~P
6	7	8	6	7	8
—	—	—	—	—	—

Pivot to the most restricted component: T. Since T is likewise baked at 7, T is assigned to the 7 time slot in Oven 2.

	OVEN 1			OVEN 2	
~T		~T	~T		~T
~S		~P	~S		~P
6	7	8	6	7	8
—	P	—	—	T	—

By operation of Deduction 1, components O and R are baked in the same oven. Therefore, O and R are baked in time slots 6 and 8 interchangeably in Oven 1, or alternatively baked in time slots 6 and 8 in Oven 2. There are now two options:

	OVEN 1			OVEN 2	
~T		~T	~T		~T
~S		~P	~S		~P
6	7	8	6	7	8
O/R	P	O/R	—	T	—
—	P	—	O/R	T	O/R

By operation of Clue 2, because P is baked at 7, S must be baked at 8. Therefore, S must be placed into the only available slot 8 two options.

	OVEN 1			OVEN 2	
~T		~T	~T		~T
~S		~P	~S		~P
6	7	8	6	7	8
O/R	P	O/R	_	T	S
_	P	S	O/R	T	O/R

The last remaining component (W) is placed in the only remaining slot.

	OVEN 1			OVEN 2	
~T		~T	~T		~T
~S		~P	~S		~P
6	7	8	6	7	8
O/R	P	O/R	**W**	T	S
W	P	S	O/R	T	O/R

Answer choices B, D, and E could be true, but they do not always have to be true. Answer choice C is never true. Answer choice A is always true.

(A) is the correct answer.

Question 3

This is a restricted, "could-be-true-EXCEPT" question. Therefore, four answers could be true at least once. These are the wrong answers. One answer is never true. This is the correct answer.

> If Rye and Sourdough are baked in the same oven, then each of the following could be true EXCEPT:
>
> (A) Oatmeal is baked immediately before Sourdough.
> (B) Sourdough is baked immediately before Wheat.
> (C) Tortilla is baked immediately before Oatmeal.
> (D) Rye is baked immediately before Wheat.
> (E) Sourdough is baked immediately before the Rye.

By operation of Deduction 1 (*R and O are baked in the same oven*) you can deduce that with the additional restriction that R and S are baked in the same oven, one oven will bake R, O, and S. Therefore, the other oven will bake the remaining three components (P, T, W).

By operation of Clue 3, T will occupy time slot 7 in the other oven.

Components P and W remain. By operation of Deduction 2, P cannot occupy time slot 8 on either oven, so P must occupy time slot 6 and the remaining component (W) must occupy time slot 8. Therefore, the other oven will bake P, T, and W, respectively.

By operation of Clue 2, you can deduce that S occupies time slot 7. Therefore, O and R will occupy slots 6 and 8 interchangeably. Our two options are:

OVEN 1			OVEN 2		
~T	~T		~T	~T	
~S	~P		~S	~P	
6	7	8	6	7	8
O/R	S	O/R	P	T	W
P	T	W	O/R	S	O/R

Answer choices A, C, and E could be true. Answer choice B (*Sourdough is baked immediately before Wheat*) must be true because sourdough is baked in time slot 7, and Wheat is baked in time slot 8, albeit in two different ovens. Answer choice D is never true.

(D) is the correct answer.

Question 5

This is a restricted, "could-be-true" question. Therefore, four answers are never true. These are the wrong answers. The correct answer is true at least once or is always true.

If Wheat is baked immediately after the Sourdough, then which one of the following could be true?

(A) Pumpernickel is baked at 7.
(B) Sourdough is baked at 8.
(C) Rye is baked at 6.
(D) Pumpernickel is baked immediately before Oatmeal.
(E) Rye is baked immediately before Oatmeal.

Clue 2 says that P is baked immediately before S. With the inclusion of the additional restriction that W is baked immediately after S, you can deduce that P is baked in time slot 6, S is baked in time slot 7, and W is baked in time slot 8 (not necessarily in the same oven).

By operation of Clue 3, T occupies the other time slot 7. Therefore, the remaining components (R and O) must occupy time slots 6 and 8 interchangeably.

So far it has been deduced that:

P = time slot 6
S = time slot 7
W = time slot 8
T = time slot 7
O and R = time slot 6 or 8

Answer choices A, B, D, and E are never true. Answer choice C can be true at least once.

(C) is the correct answer.

Question 4

This is an unrestricted, complete, and accurate list question. Wrong answers will omit components that meet the criteria and, therefore, must be on the list. The absence of components that meet the criteria from the list renders the list incomplete. Wrong answers will also include components that do not meet the criteria. The inclusion of components that do not meet the criteria in the list renders the list inaccurate. The correct answer will list only the components that meet the criteria.

Which one of the following is a complete and accurate list of the breads any one of which could be baked at 6 in Oven 2?

(A) Oatmeal, Pumpernickel, Rye
(B) Pumpernickel, Rye, Sourdough
(C) Pumpernickel, Rye, Sourdough, Wheat
(D) Oatmeal, Pumpernickel, Rye, Wheat
(E) Oatmeal, Pumpernickel, Rye, Tortilla, Wheat

This question is answerable by reviewing the prior deductions or by consulting the diagram history. Remember that the primary reason for delaying answering unrestricted questions until after completing restricted questions is to allow you to eliminate answer choices or sometimes answer the question outright by simply referring to the diagram history. Consider the diagram history below:

		OVEN 1			OVEN 2	
	~T		~T	~T		~T
	~S		~P	~S		~P
	6	7	8	6	7	8
2A	O/R	P	O/R	W	T	S
2B	W	P	S	O/R	T	O/R
3A	O/R	P	O/R	P	T	W
3B	P	T	W	O/R	P	O/R

The workouts of question 2B show that it's possible for Wheat to occupy time slot 6 in Oven 2. Therefore, you can eliminate any answers that don't include Wheat (choices A and B). Likewise, from the workouts of questions 2A and 3B, you know that Oatmeal can occupy time slot 6 in Oven 2—so any answers that don't include Oatmeal can be ruled out. Therefore, eliminate answer choice C. From Deduction 2, you know that it's not possible for Tortilla to occupy time slot 6 in either oven. Eliminate any answers that include Tortilla (answer choice E).

(D) is the correct answer.

Atypical Games

8

In this chapter you will learn about atypical logic games—that is, games that appear less frequently on the LSAT, compared to say, grouping games or sequence games. Although these games are a minority type, you still want to be prepared for them! They are organized for you into two subgroups: pattern games and mapping games.

PATTERN GAMES

Pattern games are rare on the LSAT, but be prepared just in case. Test writers like throwing curveballs into the games section every now and then! Pattern games are just extensions of two tasks you already know well: putting things in order one after the other and/or putting things into groups. Alternatively, sometimes both these tasks are combined in one pattern game. Consider the following sequential game scenario:

> At a diabetes awareness seminar, exactly six endocrinologists—Fong, Gaston, Hermes, Jackson, Kemp, and Lopez—will be scheduled to lecture on the effects of high fructose corn syrup. The professors will lecture one at a time, consecutively, with no professor lecturing more than once. The order in which the endocrinologists lecture will be in accordance with the following conditions:
>
> Hermes lectures either immediately before or immediately after Lopez.
> Fong does not lecture third.
> Jackson lectures at some time after Lopez.

Ask yourself: "What am I being asked to figure out?" Here, you are being asked to determine the endocrinologists' schedule, that is, the order in which they will lecture. Each doctor lectures just once with just one set of circumstances. The diagram is as follows:

1	2	3	4	5	6
—	—	—	—	—	—

Now consider a more complex scenario in which each endocrinologist lectures at not just one seminar, but rather at three consecutive seminars. Next, layer on additional conditions whereby the order in which they lecture in certain seminars determines (sometimes only partially) the order in which they lecture in subsequent seminars. Now you have a pattern game. Let's start with the above simple sequence game and transform it into a pattern game:

At a diabetes awareness *convention*, each of exactly six endocrinologists—
Fong, Gaston, Hermes, Jackson, Kemp, and Lopez—*will be scheduled to lecture
once at each of three seminars—seminars 1, 2, and 3—*on the effects of high
fructose corn syrup. At each seminar, the professors will lecture one at a time,
consecutively, with no professor lecturing more than once. The order in which
the endocrinologists lecture *at each seminar* will be in accordance with the
following conditions:

Hermes lectures either immediately before or immediately after Lopez.
Fong does not lecture third *at seminar 2*.
Jackson *always* lectures at some time after Lopez.
No endocrinologist can lecture first at more than one seminar.
*Any endocrinologist that lectures last at one of the seminars must lecture
first at the next seminar.*

Update the diagram to reflect the three successive seminars, instead of just one seminar.

1	2	3	4	5	6	
—	—	—	—	—	—	Seminar 1
—	—	—	—	—	—	Seminar 2
—	—	—	—	—	—	Seminar 3

Because the placement of one component in one set of circumstances often determines that
component's subsequent placement, it is sometimes useful to use arrows in the diagram. For
example, the last clue in the setup above (*Any endocrinologist that lectures last at one of the
seminars must lecture first at the next seminar*) could be reflected directly in the diagram as
follows:

1	2	3	4	5	6	
—	—	—	—	—	—	Seminar 1
—	—	—	—	—	—	Seminar 2
—	—	—	—	—	—	Seminar 3

Some students will find this tool useful, whereas others may find that it makes the diagram
too cluttered. Use it at your own discretion.

Once your diagram is complete, you are ready to tackle the questions. As usual, approach
them in the following order: catch-a-clue, restricted, unrestricted, modifiers.

Game 1

Exactly five of eight parents will speak about the dangers of texting while driving at each of three successive rallies—rallies 1, 2, and 3. Four of the parents—Jean, Karen, Linda, and Mona—are mothers and four—Patrick, Quincy, Richard, and Steve—are fathers. At each rally, the five speakers will speak one at a time, consecutively, with no parent speaking more than once. Mothers will speak first, second, and third only. Fathers will speak fourth and fifth only. The following conditions must apply:

The mother that speaks first at any given rally does not speak at the following rally.

The mother that speaks third at any given rally will speak first in the following rally.

Each father must speak at least once in any two successive rallies.

If Linda and Karen both speak at the same rally, then Linda speaks before Karen.

Richard never speaks last.

1. Which one of the following could be an acceptable selection of parents for rallies 1, 2, and 3, in the order, from first to last, in which the parents speak?

   (A) Rally 1: Linda, Mona, Karen, Quincy, Sam
   Rally 2: Karen, Jean, Mona, Patrick, Richard
   Rally 3: Mona, Linda, Jean, Sam, Quincy

   (B) Rally 1: Mona, Linda, Jean, Richard, Patrick
   Rally 2: Jean, Linda, Karen, Sam, Quincy
   Rally 3: Karen, Mona, Linda, Richard, Patrick

   (C) Rally 1: Linda, Karen, Mona, Quincy, Patrick
   Rally 2: Mona, Karen, Jean, Richard, Sam
   Rally 3: Jean, Linda, Karen, Patrick, Quincy

   (D) Rally 1: Mona, Jean, Karen, Quincy, Richard
   Rally 2: Karen, Mona, Jean, Sam, Patrick
   Rally 3: Jean, Linda, Mona, Quincy, Richard

   (E) Rally 1: Linda, Karen, Jean, Patrick, Quincy
   Rally 2: Karen, Jean, Linda, Richard, Sam
   Rally 3: Linda, Jean, Mona, Quincy, Patrick

2. Which one of the following CANNOT be true?

   (A) Steve speaks at neither rally 1 nor rally 3.
   (B) Linda speaks at rally 1 and rally 2.
   (C) Quincy speaks at rally 1 and rally 2.
   (D) Mona speaks at rally 1, rally 2, and rally 3.
   (E) Sam speaks neither fourth nor fifth at rally 2.

3. If Karen speaks third at rally 1, then each of the following could be true EXCEPT:

   (A) Linda speaks second at rally 1.
   (B) Mona speaks first at rally 1.
   (C) Jean speaks third at rally 2.
   (D) Jean speaks second at rally 2.
   (E) Mona speaks third at rally 2.

4. If Linda speaks first in rally 2, then which one of the following must be true?

   (A) Karen speaks first at rally 1.
   (B) Mona speaks first at rally 1.
   (C) Neither Jean nor Karen speaks first at rally 1.
   (D) Neither Linda nor Karen speaks first at rally 1.
   (E) Mona speaks second at rally 1.

Continued on next page ⏩

5. Which one of the following must be true of rally 1?

(A) If Karen speaks third, then Linda cannot speak second.
(B) If Steve speaks fifth, then Richard must speak fourth.
(C) If Linda speaks second, then Karen speaks third.
(D) If Quincy speaks fourth, then Steve speaks fifth.
(E) If Mona speaks third, then Linda speaks first.

6. If neither Richard nor Mona speak at rally 1, then which one of the following could be true?

(A) Steve speaks fourth at rally 2.
(B) Jean speaks first at rally 1.
(C) Linda speaks second at rally 1.
(D) Karen speaks first at rally 1.
(E) Mona speaks second at rally 2.

Visualize and draw the diagram.

What are you being asked to figure out? The game asks you to ascertain (1) which five of eight parents are selected to speak at a rally; (2) the order in which they are to speak; (3) for each of which three successive rallies. Since some parents will not speak at every rally, the diagram must include an in- and an out-column. However, the requirement to ascertain the order of speakers necessitates that the in-column contain ordering. So far the diagram is as follows:

1	2	3	4	5	OUT
_	_	_	_	_	_ _ _

If the game involved just one rally, the diagram would be complete. However, this game involves three successive rallies, so the diagram must be repeated two times. The diagram is updated as follows:

1	2	3	4	5	OUT	
_	_	_	_	_	_ _ _	Rally 1
_	_	_	_	_	_ _ _	Rally 2
_	_	_	_	_	_ _ _	Rally 3

This game also limits the first three speakers to mothers and the last two speakers to fathers, so those restrictions must be addressed by labeling the slots. Revise the diagram again:

1 Mom	2 Mom	3 Mom	4 Dad	5 Dad	OUT	
_	_	_	_	_	_ _ _	Rally 1
_	_	_	_	_	_ _ _	Rally 2
_	_	_	_	_	_ _ _	Rally 3

STEP 2 List the components and ascertain the ratio.

The components are: mothers: J, K, L ,M; and fathers: P, Q, R, S. There are exactly five parents selected from a total of eight parents, so the distribution is fixed. In addition, three of four mothers will be selected and, therefore, exactly one mother is always in the out-column. Likewise, two of four fathers will be selected and, therefore, exactly two fathers are always placed in the out-column.

Symbolize the clues.

Clue 1	The mother that speaks first at any given rally does not speak at the following rally.	$\text{Slot } 1_{\text{rally 1}} = \text{OUT}_{\text{rally 2}}$ $\text{Slot } 1_{\text{rally 2}} = \text{OUT}_{\text{rally3}}$
Clue 2	The mother that speaks third at any given rally will speak first in the following rally.	$\text{Slot } 3_{\text{rally 1}} = \text{Slot } 1_{\text{rally 2}}$ $\text{Slot } 3_{\text{rally 2}} = \text{Slot } 1_{\text{rally 3}}$
Clue 3	Each father must speak at least once in any two successive rallies.	$\text{Slots 4 and } 5_{\text{rally 1}} = \text{OUT}_{\text{rally 2}}$ $\text{Slots 4 and } 5_{\text{rally 2}} = \text{OUT}_{\text{rally 3}}$ (see Deduction 1 explanation below)
Clue 4	If Linda and Karen both speak at the same rally, then Linda speaks before Karen.	$\text{L and K} \rightarrow \text{L...K}$
Clue 5	Richard never speaks last.	$R \neq 5$

Make deductions.

Remember that linking the conditional statements is crucial.

Deduction 1: From Step 2, it was ascertained that two of the four fathers are selected to speak at each rally. Since Clue 3 requires each father to speak at least once in each of two successive rallies, you can deduce that any two fathers that speak at a rally do not speak at the one immediately following. And vice versa is also true—the two fathers that do not speak at a given rally must speak at the one immediately following. In other words, fathers never speak in successive rallies.

Deduction 2: From Clue 4, you can deduce that if K speaks first, then L does not speak. Likewise, if L speaks third, then K does not speak at that rally.

Tackle the questions.

The order in which you answer the questions is important. Remember the optimal sequence: 1. catch-a-clue; 2. restricted; 3. unrestricted; 4. modifiers. For this particular game, that translates to the following order 1, 3, 4, 6, 2, and then 5.

Answer Key

Answers

Question 1

This is a catch-a-clue question.

> Which one of the following could be an acceptable selection of parents for rallies 1, 2, and 3, in the order, from first to last, in which the parents speak?
>
> (A) Rally 1: Linda, Mona, Karen, Quincy, Sam
>   Rally 2: Karen, Jean, Mona, Patrick, Richard
>   Rally 3: Mona, Linda, Jean, Sam, Quincy
> (B) Rally 1: Mona, Linda, Jean, Richard, Patrick
>   Rally 2: Jean, Linda, Karen, Sam, Quincy
>   Rally 3: Karen, Mona, Linda, Richard, Patrick
> (C) Rally 1: Linda, Karen, Mona, Quincy, Patrick
>   Rally 2: Mona, Karen, Jean, Richard, Sam
>   Rally 3: Jean, Linda, Karen, Patrick, Quincy
> (D) Rally 1: Mona, Jean, Karen, Quincy, Richard
>   Rally 2: Karen, Mona, Jean, Sam, Patrick
>   Rally 3: Jean, Linda, Mona, Quincy, Richard
> (E) Rally 1: Linda, Karen, Jean, Patrick, Quincy
>   Rally 2: Karen, Jean, Linda, Richard, Sam
>   Rally 3: Linda, Jean, Mona, Quincy, Patrick

The first clue (*The mother that speaks first at any given rally does not speak at the following rally*) eliminates answer choice D. The second clue (*The mother that speaks third at any given rally will speak first in the following rally*) eliminates answer choice E. The third clue (*Each father must speak at least once in any two successive rallies*) is not violated by any of the answer choices. The fourth clue (*If Linda and Karen both speak at the same rally, then Linda speaks before Karen*) eliminates answer choice B. The fifth clue (*Richard never speaks last*) eliminates answer choice A.

(C) is the correct answer.

Remember that correct answers to a catch-a-clue should be placed into the diagram for future reference.

1 Mom	2 Mom	3 Mom	4 Dad	5 Dad	OUT	
L	K	M	Q	P	J R S	Rally 1
M	K	J	R	S	L P Q	Rally 2
J	L	K	P	Q	M R S	Rally 3

Question 3

This is a restricted, "could-be-true-EXCEPT" question. Therefore, four answers could be true at least once. These are the wrong answers. One answer is never true. This is the correct answer.

> If Karen speaks third at rally 1, then each of the following could be true EXCEPT:
>
> (A) Linda speaks second at rally 1.
> (B) Mona speaks first at rally 1.
> (C) Jean speaks third at rally 2.
> (D) Jean speaks second at rally 2.
> (E) Mona speaks third at rally 2.

Place the additional restriction into the diagram.

1 Mom	2 Mom	3 Mom	4 Dad	5 Dad	OUT	
–	–	K	–	–	– – –	Rally 1
–	–	–	–	–	– – –	Rally 2
–	–	–	–	–	– – –	Rally 3

Look at the rule symbols and prior deductions for guidance. By operation of Clue 2, K must speak first in rally 2.

1 Mom	2 Mom	3 Mom	4 Dad	5 Dad	OUT	
–	–	K	–	–	– – –	Rally 1
K	–	–	–	–	– – –	Rally 2
–	–	–	–	–	– – –	Rally 3

By operation of Deduction 2, L is forced into the out-column. Therefore, J and M speak second and third interchangeably in rally 2.

1 Mom	2 Mom	3 Mom	4 Dad	5 Dad	OUT	
–	–	K	–	–	– – –	Rally 1
K	J/M	M/J	–	–	L _ _	Rally 2
–	–	–	–	–	– – –	Rally 3

Choices B, C, D, and E could be true, but they do not have to always be true.

(A) is the correct answer.

Question 4

This is an unrestricted, "must-be-true" question. Therefore, four answers are true sometimes but not always, or they are never true. These are the wrong choices. The correct answer is always true.

> If Linda speaks first in rally 2, then which one of the following must be true?

> (A) Karen speaks first at rally 1.
> (B) Mona speaks first at rally 1.
> (C) Neither Jean nor Karen speaks first at rally 1.
> (D) Neither Linda nor Karen speaks first at rally 1.
> (E) Mona speaks second at rally 1.

This question places L first in rally 2.

1 Mom	2 Mom	3 Mom	4 Dad	5 Dad	OUT	
—	—	—	—	—	– – –	Rally 1
L	—	—	—	—	– – –	Rally 2
—	—	—	—	—	– – –	Rally 3

By operation of Clue 2, L was the third speaker at rally 1.

1 Mom	2 Mom	3 Mom	4 Dad	5 Dad	OUT	
—	—	**L**	—	—	– – –	Rally 1
L	—	—	—	—	– – –	Rally 2
—	—	—	—	—	– – –	Rally 3

By operation of Deduction 2, K is forced into the out-column in rally 1. Therefore, J and M speak first and second interchangeably in rally 1.

1 Mom	2 Mom	3 Mom	4 Dad	5 Dad	OUT	
J/M	M/J	L	—	—	– – –	Rally 1
L	—	—	—	—	– – –	Rally 2
—	—	—	—	—	– – –	Rally 3

Stop! You have enough information to answer the question. Remember that it's a good idea to periodically check your answers choices—especially after major deductions.

Answer choice A is false. Answer choices B, C, and E could be true, but answer choice D is always true.

(D) is the correct answer.

Question 6

This is an unrestricted, "could-be-true" question. Therefore, four answers are never true. These are the wrong answers. The correct answer is true sometimes or is always true.

If neither Richard nor Mona speak at rally 1, then which one of the following could be true?

(A) Steve speaks fourth at rally 2.
(B) Jean speaks first at rally 1.
(C) Linda speaks second at rally 1.
(D) Karen speaks first at rally 1.
(E) Mona speaks second at rally 2.

This question places R and M in the out-column.

1 Mom	2 Mom	3 Mom	4 Dad	5 Dad	OUT	
–	–	–	–	–	R M _	Rally 1
–	–	–	–	–	– – –	Rally 2
–	–	–	–	–	– – –	Rally 3

Since R is placed in the out-column at rally 1, by operation of Deduction 1, R must speak at rally 2. By operation of Clue 5, R cannot speak fifth, so R must speak fourth at rally 2. Answer choice A can be eliminated.

1 Mom	2 Mom	3 Mom	4 Dad	5 Dad	OUT	
–	–	–	–	–	R M _	Rally 1
–	–	–	R	–	– – –	Rally 2
–	–	–	–	–	– – –	Rally 3

Since M is placed in the out-column, J, K, and L must each speak at rally 1. By operation of Clue 4, L must be placed in either slot 1 (Option 1) or slot 2 (Option 2) in rally 1.

Option 1

1 Mom	2 Mom	3 Mom	4 Dad	5 Dad	OUT	
L	–	–	–	–	R M _	Rally 1
–	–	–	R	–	– – –	Rally 2
–	–	–	–	–	– – –	Rally 3

Option 2

1 Mom	2 Mom	3 Mom	4 Dad	5 Dad	OUT	
_	**L**	_	_	_	R M _	Rally 1
_	_	_	R	_	_ _ _	Rally 2
_	_	_	_	_	_ _ _	Rally 3

Work out Option 1 first. With M in the out-column and L placed in slot 1 at rally 1, J and K must be placed in slots 2 and 3 interchangeably.

Option 1

1 Mom	2 Mom	3 Mom	4 Dad	5 Dad	OUT	
L	**J/K**	**K/J**	_	_	R M _	Rally 1
_	_	_	R	_	_ _ _	Rally 2
_	_	_	_	_	_ _ _	Rally 3

By operation of Clue 1, L must be placed in the out-column in rally 2. Accordingly, M must speak at rally 2.

Option 1

1 Mom	2 Mom	3 Mom	4 Dad	5 Dad	OUT	
L	J/K	K/J	_	_	R M _	Rally 1
_	_	_	R	_	**L** _ _	Rally 2
_	_	_	_	_	_ _ _	Rally 3

By operation of Clue 2, either J or K must speak first at Rally 2, and M will speak either second or third.

Option 1

1 Mom	2 Mom	3 Mom	4 Dad	5 Dad	OUT	
L	J/K	K/J	_	_	R M _	Rally 1
J/K	(M)	(M)	R	_	L _ _	Rally 2
_	_	_	_	_	_ _ _	Rally 3

Stop! Again, you have enough information to answer the question. M can speak second at rally 2.

(E) is the correct answer.

Even though you've arrived at a correct answer, some of the answer choices may still seem possible and their implausibility might become apparent only by working out Option 2. So let's work this one out too.

Option 2

1 Mom	2 Mom	3 Mom	4 Dad	5 Dad	OUT	
_	L	_	_	_	R M _	Rally 1
_	_	_	R	_	_ _ _	Rally 2
_	_	_	_	_	_ _ _	Rally 3

By operation of Clue 4, K must be placed in slot 3 at rally 1. Also, J (the only remaining Mom component) must be placed in slot 1 at rally 1.

Option 2

1 Mom	2 Mom	3 Mom	4 Dad	5 Dad	OUT	
J	L	K	_	_	R M _	Rally 1
_	_	_	R	_	_ _ _	Rally 2
_	_	_	_	_	_ _ _	Rally 3

By operation of Clue 1, J must be placed in the out-column at rally 2.

Option 2

1 Mom	2 Mom	3 Mom	4 Dad	5 Dad	OUT	
J	L	K	_	_	R M _	Rally 1
_	_	_	R	_	**J** _ _	Rally 2
_	_	_	_	_	_ _ _	Rally 3

By operation of Clue 2, K must be placed in slot 1 at rally 1.

Option 2

1 Mom	2 Mom	3 Mom	4 Dad	5 Dad	OUT	
J	L	K	_	_	R M _	Rally 1
K	_	_	R	_	J _ _	Rally 2
_	_	_	_	_	_ _ _	Rally 3

By operation of Deduction 2, if K is placed in slot 1, L must be placed in the out-column. Therefore, L must be out, and you know this is not possible as you already have one mother (J) out.

Answer choices B, C, and D cannot be true.

Question 2

This unrestricted, "cannot-be-true" question is identical to a "must-be-false" question. Four answers can be true at least once. These are the wrong answers. One answer choice can never be true. This is the correct answer.

Which one of the following CANNOT be true?

(A) Steve speaks at neither rally 1 nor rally 3.
(B) Linda speaks at rally 1 and rally 2.
(C) Quincy speaks at rally 1 and rally 2.
(D) Mona speaks at rally 1, rally 2, and rally 3.
(E) Sam speaks neither fourth nor fifth at rally 2.

This question is completely answerable by reviewing Deduction 1 (*Fathers cannot speak in successive rallies*). Quincy cannot speak at rally 1 and rally 2.

(C) is the correct answer

Imagine you did not have access to Deduction 1. How could you have solved this question? The first step with all unrestricted questions is to review the diagram history. From the diagram history in question 1, you can ascertain that answer choice A (*Steve speaks at neither rally 1 nor rally 3*) can be true, so you can eliminate it. Likewise, you can ascertain that answer choice E (*Patrick speaks neither fourth nor fifth at rally 2*) can be true. Eliminate answer choice E.

1 Mom	2 Mom	3 Mom	4 Dad	5 Dad	OUT	
L	K	M	Q	P	J R S	Rally 1
M	K	J	R	S	L P Q	Rally 2
J	L	K	P	Q	M R S	Rally 3

Consider the diagram from question 4. You can ascertain that answer choice B (*Linda speaks at rally 1 and rally 2*) can be true, so eliminate answer choice B. Now you have narrowed down the answer choices to just C and D. You would then test just one of them.

1 Mom	2 Mom	3 Mom	4 Dad	5 Dad	OUT	
J/M	M/J	L	_	_	_ _ _	Rally 1
L	_	_	_	_	_ _ _	Rally 2
_	_	_	_	_	_ _ _	Rally 3

Question 5

This is an unrestricted, "must-be-true" question. Therefore, four answers are true sometimes but not always, or they are never true. These are the wrong answers. The correct answer is always true.

Which one of the following must be true of rally 1?

(A) If Karen speaks third, then Linda cannot speak second.
(B) If Steve speaks fifth, then Richard must speak fourth.
(C) If Linda speaks second, then Karen speaks third.
(D) If Quincy speaks fourth, then Steve speaks fifth.
(E) If Mona speaks third, then Linda speaks first.

Since this is an unrestricted question, it might be answerable, in part, by reviewing your previous work. Remember, each of the possibilities you worked out on the restricted questions is in compliance with all of the clues and can be relied upon to answer the unrestricted questions. Indeed, from the work for question 1, it's clear that Q speaks fourth, but S does not speak fifth, therefore answer choice D can be ruled out.

Since the diagram history is scant, it's not possible to eliminate any other answer choices. However, don't forget the work you did that didn't work out—specifically, look at Option 2 in question 6. Here it is again:

Option 2

1 Mom	2 Mom	3 Mom	4 Dad	5 Dad	OUT	
J	L	K	_	_	R M _	Rally 1
K	_	_	R	_	J _ _	Rally 2
_	_	_	_	_	_ _ _	Rally 3

Here K is in slot 3 and L is in slot 2, which is precisely the content of answer choice A. You might recall:

1. By operation of Clue 1, the first Mom speaker, in this case, J must be placed in the out-column at rally 2.
2. By operation of Clue 2, K must be placed in slot 1 at rally 1.
3. By operation of Deduction 2, if K is placed in slot 1, L must be placed in the out-column. This means that L must be out: impossible! If K is placed in slot 3, L cannot be placed in slot 2.

(A) is the correct answer.

MAPPING GAMES

Mapping games, like pattern games, are also uncommon on the LSAT. Mapping games are those in which the typical linear diagram is inappropriate and will not help you at all in solving the game. They often involve language that one would associate with giving directions, for example:

- north, south, east , and west
- directly above, directly below, directly across
- adjacent, next to, beside

Often, a sample diagram is provided for you in a mapping game. This diagram is accurate, and you should always mimic it when solving the game. Even when a diagram is not provided, enough information will be embedded in the setup so that you are able to construct a solid diagram of your own. Follow the provided directions verbatim!

Mapping diagrams are most often geometrical—typically they involve a circle, square, or rectangle. Because the information changes from question to question, you will likely need to recreate a new diagram for each question in order to avoid confusion. Let's try one.

Game 1

Eight university athletes—F, G, H, J, K, L, M, N, and P—are seated at the same table at an awards dinner. Each athlete will sit in one of eight chairs that are arranged around a rectangular table as follows:

```
1  2  3  4
5  6  7  8
```

Three of the athletes—F, G, and H—are on the baseball team; three—J, K, and L—are on the football team; and two—N and P—are on the soccer team. No athlete is a member of more than one team. The following conditions must be met:

No athlete sits directly across from another athlete belonging to the same team.

No athlete sits directly adjacent to another athlete belonging to the same team.

K sits in seat 2.

F sits in seat 8.

1. Which one of the following could be an accurate list of the athletes seated in seats 1, 2, 3, and 4, respectively?

    (A) N, K, P, L
    (B) G, J, H, P
    (C) G, K, P, F
    (D) N, K, P, G
    (E) H, K, G, P

2. If seat 7 is not occupied by a member of the football team, then each of the following could be true EXCEPT:

    (A) J sits adjacent to H.
    (B) G sits adjacent to K.
    (C) L sits adjacent to G.
    (D) F sits directly across from L.
    (E) H sits directly across from L.

3. If G sits in seat 5, then which one of the following must be true?

    (A) N sits in seat 1.
    (B) H sits in seat 3.
    (C) J sits in seat 4.
    (D) L sits in seat 7.
    (E) P sits in seat 6.

4. Which one of the following CANNOT be true?

    (A) N sits adjacent to both G and H.
    (B) P sits adjacent to both H and L.
    (C) H sits adjacent to both K and J.
    (D) L sits adjacent to both F and P.
    (E) K sits adjacent to both H and N.

5. Which one of the following could be true?

    (A) N and P sit in seats 4 and 7, respectively.
    (B) N and P sit in seats 1 and 3, respectively
    (C) N and P sit in seats 5 and 7, respectively.
    (D) N and P sit in seats 4 and 5, respectively.
    (E) N and P sit in seats 3 and 5, respectively.

STEP 1 Visualize and draw the diagram.

What are you being asked to figure out? The game is asking you to assign seating to the athletes at a rectangular table. The diagram has been provided, and you should be certain to use it.

1	2	3	4
5	6	7	8

STEP 2 List the components and ascertain the ratio.

The components are Baseball (F, G, H), Football (J, K, L), and Soccer (N, P). There are exactly eight seats for eight athletes, so the ratio is 1:1.

STEP 3 Symbolize the clues.

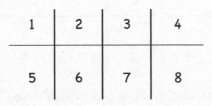

Clue 1 No athlete sits directly across from another athlete belonging to the same team.

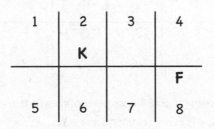

Clue 2 No athlete sits directly adjacent to another athlete belonging to the same team.

Clue 3 K sits in seat 2.   K = 2
(Put in diagram.)

Clue 4 F sits in seat 8.   F = 8
(Put in diagram.)

STEP 4 Make deductions.

First off, put Clues 3 and 4 into your diagram.

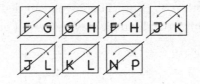

Deduction 1: From Clue 1, you can deduce that since K is a football player, neither of the remaining two football players (J and L) can sit directly across from K in seat 6.

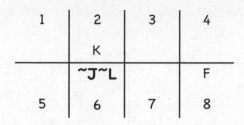

Deduction 2: Similarly from Clue 1, you can deduce that since F is a baseball player, neither of the remaining two baseball players (G and H) can sit directly across from F in seat 4.

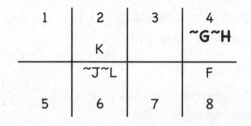

Deduction 3: From Clue 2, you can deduce that since K is a football player, neither of the remaining two football players (J and L) can sit adjacent to K in either seat 1 or seat 3.

1	2	3	4
~J~L	K	~J~L	~G~H
	~J~L		F
5	6	7	8

Deduction 4: As in Clue 2, you can deduce that since F is a baseball player, neither of the remaining two baseball players (G and H) can sit adjacent to F in seat 7.

1	2	3	4
~J~L	K	~J~L	~G~H
	~J~L	~G~H	F
5	6	7	8

Note that J and L are the most restricted components, with three restrictions each. The next most restricted are G and H, with two restrictions each.

STEP 5 Tackle the questions.

The order in which you answer the questions is important. Remember the optimal sequence: 1. catch-a-clue; 2. restricted; 3. unrestricted; 4. modifiers. For this particular game, that translates to the following order 1, 2, 3, 4, and then 5.

Answer Key

Answers

Question 1

This is a catch-a-clue question. Remember you need only catch a rule, look for the answer choice that violates that rule, and then eliminate it.

> Which one of the following could be an accurate list of the athletes seated in seats 1, 2, 3, and 4, respectively?
>
> (A) N, K, P, L
> (B) G, J, H, P
> (C) G, K, P, F
> (D) N, K, P, G
> (E) H, K, G, P

The first clue (*No athlete sits directly across from another athlete belonging to the same team*) eliminates answer choice D because G is sitting in seat 4, which is directly across from fellow baseball teammate F. The second clue (*No athlete sits directly adjacent to another athlete belonging to the same team*) eliminates answer choice A because F, G, and H are all relegated to three out of the four seats 5, 6, 7, and 8. Therefore, at least two must be adjacent to each other. The third clue (*K sits in seat 2*) eliminates answer choice B. The fourth clue (*F sits in seat 8*) eliminates answer choice C.

(E) is the correct answer.

Remember that correct answers to a catch-a-clue question should be placed into the diagram for future reference.

1 ~J~L **H**	2 ~J~L K	3 ~J~L **G**	4 ~G~H **P**
	~J~L	~G~H	F
5	6	7	8

Question 2

This is a restricted, "could-be-true-EXCEPT" question. Therefore, four answers could be true at least once. These are the wrong answers. One answer is never true. This is the correct answer.

> If seat 7 is not occupied by a member of the football team, then each of the following could be true EXCEPT:
>
> (A) J sits adjacent to H.
> (B) G sits adjacent to K.
> (C) L sits adjacent to G.
> (D) F sits directly across from L.
> (E) H sits directly across from L.

With this additional restriction, neither J nor L can be seated in seat 7. By operation of Deduction 4, neither G nor H can be seated at seat 7, so seat 7 must be occupied by one of the soccer players (either N or P).

1	2	3	4
~J~L		~J~L	~G~H
	K		
	~J~L	~G~H	F
		N/P	
5	6	7	8

Pivot to the most restricted components: J and L. By operation of Deductions 1 and 3, neither J nor L can occupy seats 1, 3, or 6, so the only remaining seats available to J and L are seats 4 and 5. J and L must occupy seats 4 and 5 interchangeably.

1	2	3	4
~J~L		~J~L	~G~H
	K		J/L
L/J	~J~L	~G~H	F
		N/P	
5	6	7	8

Since one of the soccer players (N or P) occupies seat 7, Clues 1 and 2 ban the other soccer player from occupying either the seat directly across from seat 7 (seat 3) and the seat adjacent to seat 7 (seat 6). Consequently, the only remaining seat available for the other soccer player is seat 1. Therefore, either N or P occupies seat 1.

1	2	3	4
~J~L		~J~L	~G~H
	K		J/L
P/N			
L/J	~J~L	~G~H	F
		N/P	
5	6	7	8

Finally, the only remaining components (G and H) will occupy the only remaining seats—seats 3 and 6 interchangeably.

1	2	3	4
~J~L		~J~L	~G~H
P/N	K	**G/H**	J/L
L/J	~J~L	~G~H	F
	H/G	N/P	
5	6	7	8

Answer choices A, B, C, and D could be true, but they do not always have to be true. Answer choice E is never true.

(E) is the correct answer.

Question 3

This is a restricted, "must-be-true" question. Therefore, four answers are true sometimes but not always, or they are never true. The correct answer is always true.

> If G sits in seat 5, then which one of the following must be true?
>
> (A) N sits in seat 1.
> (B) H sits in seat 3.
> (C) J sits in seat 4.
> (D) L sits in seat 7.
> (E) P sits in seat 6.

Place the additional restriction into the diagram.

1	2	3	4
~J~L		~J~L	~G~H
	K		
G	~J~L	~G~H	F
5	6	7	8

Pivot to the most restricted components: J and L. By operation of Deductions 1 and 3, J and L are banned from seats 1, 3, and 7. Consequently, the only remaining seats available for J and L are seats 4 and 6, so J and L must be placed in seats 4 and 7 interchangeably.

1	2	3	4
~J~L		~J~L	~G~H
	K		**J/L**
G	~J~L	~G~H	F
		L/J	
5	6	7	8

Clue 1 dictates that H (the only remaining baseball player) cannot be seated directly across from G (another baseball payer) in seat 1. Similarly, by operation of Clue 2, H cannot be seated adjacent to G in seat 6. The only remaining seat available for H is seat 3.

1 ~J~L	2	3 ~J~L	4 ~G~H
	K	**H**	J/L
G	~J~L	~G~H	F
		L/J	
5	6	7	8

The only two remaining components (N and P) must be placed in the only two remaining seats: 1 and 6.

1 ~J~L	2	3 ~J~L	4 ~G~H
N/P	K	H	J/L
G	~J~L	~G~H	F
	P/N	L/J	
5	6	7	8

Answer choices A, C, D, and E could be true, but answer choice D is always true.

(D) is the correct answer.

Question 4

This unrestricted, "cannot-be-true" question is identical to a "must-be-false" question. Four answers could be true at least once. These are the wrong answers. One answer choice can never be true. This is the correct answer.

Which one of the following CANNOT be true?

(A) N sits adjacent to both G and H.
(B) P sits adjacent to both H and L.
(C) H sits adjacent to both K and J.
(D) L sits adjacent to both F and P.
(E) K sits adjacent to both H and N.

Consider the diagram history. From your work in question 3, you can ascertain that answer choices C, D, and E are possible, so eliminate them. This leaves you with just two answer choices.

1	2	3	4
~J~L		~J~L	~G~H
N/P	K	H	J/L
G	~J~L	~G~H	F
	P/N	L/J	
5	6	7	8

Remember that whenever you have narrowed the answers down to just two, you should test only one of them. Try answer choice A (*N sits adjacent to both G and H*). Here is a fresh diagram with the deductions so far:

1	2	3	4
~J~L		~J~L	~G~H
	K		
	~J~L	~G~H	F
5	6	7	8

For N to sit adjacent to both G and H, you need three adjacent seats to accommodate the trio. The only three adjacent seats available are seats 5, 6, and 7. Also, for N to sit adjacent to both G and H, N must sit in the middle with H on one side and G on the other side. This means that N would be placed in seat 6, with G and H forced into seats 5 and 7 interchangeably. However, by operation of Deduction 4, neither G nor H can be in seat 7, so that scenario is not possible. N cannot sit adjacent to both G and H.

(A) is the correct answer.

Question 5

In this unrestricted, "could-be-true" question, four answers are never true. These are the wrong choices. One answer is true at least once. This is the correct choice.

Which one of the following could be true?

(A) N and P sit in seats 4 and 7, respectively.
(B) N and P sit in seats 1 and 3, respectively
(C) N and P sit in seats 5 and 7, respectively.
(D) N and P sit in seats 4 and 5, respectively.
(E) N and P sit in seats 3 and 5, respectively.

Remember that since this is an unrestricted question, it might be partially answerable by reviewing your previous work. Unfortunately, here the diagram history doesn't reveal any of the answer choices as possible. Nevertheless, you do have your deductions and should turn to those for guidance. Here they are again in the diagram below. Consider each answer choice:

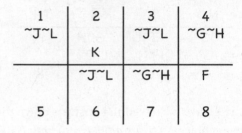

Answer choice A: N and P cannot occupy seats 4 and 7, respectively. If N and P were to occupy seats 4 and 7, respectively, then by operation of Deductions 1 and 3 (*neither J nor L can occupy seats 1, 3, and 6*) there remains just one seat (5) for both J and L.

Answer choice B: N and P cannot occupy seats 1 and 3, respectively. If N and P were to occupy seats 1 and 3, respectively, then by operation of Deductions 2 and 4 (*neither G nor H can occupy seats 4 or 7*) G and H could only occupy seats 5 and 6. These seats are adjacent to each other, and since G and H are both baseball players, this violates Clue 2.

Answer choice C: N and P cannot occupy seats 5 and 7, respectively. If N and P were to occupy seats 5 and 7, respectively, then by operation of Deductions 1 and 3 (*neither J nor L can occupy seats 1, 3, and 6*) there remains just one seat (4) for both J and L.

Answer choice D: N and P cannot occupy seats 4 and 5, respectively. If N and P were to occupy seats 4 and 5, respectively, then by operation of Deductions 1 and 3 (*neither J nor L can occupy seats 1, 3, and 6*) there remains just one seat (7) for both J and L.

(E) is the correct answer.

Drill Exercises

9

DRILL EXERCISE 1

Clue	Conditional	Contrapositive
G cannot be chosen unless B is chosen		
F is chosen if, and only if, P is chosen		
If S is selected, then T is also selected		
A is chosen only if C is chosen		
Every child is learning to read		
If either W or V is selected, then the other must also be selected		
F and G cannot both be selected		
D will be selected only if H is selected		
R cannot be chosen unless P is chosen		
All of the students are buying tickets		
None of girls like sports		
No boy likes to go to the museum		
K is assigned to class 1 if L is assigned to class 1		
T cannot be selected unless R is selected		

Clue	Conditional	Contrapositive
A plays on day 2 if, but only if, B plays on day 2		
If Q is assigned, R is not assigned		
F is not chosen unless either Q or R is chosen		
If W is assigned, then B is assigned to team 1		
Neither R nor S can be on the same team as T		
G is chosen unless F is chosen		

DRILL EXERCISE 2

Clue	Conditional	Contrapositive
R cannot be chosen unless S is selected		
Sam is chosen if, and only if, Ty is chosen		
If F is selected, then H is also selected		
Artie is chosen only if Bobby is chosen		
If William is selected, then Pete must also be selected		
H and R cannot both be selected		
D will be selected only if H is selected		
Dan will be selected if Jean is selected		
R cannot be chosen unless P is chosen		
All of the balls are red		
No student likes homework		
Each and every boy likes to go to the playground		

Clue	Conditional	Contrapositive
A is assigned to group 1 if, and only if, L is assigned to the group		
C cannot teach unless F teaches		
H plays on day 2 if G plays on day 2		
If Q is not assigned, R is not assigned		
A is not chosen unless B is chosen		
L is assigned unless B is assigned to class 1		
Neither F nor G can be on the same team as H		
If G is not chosen, F is chosen		

Drill Exercise 1: Solutions

Clue	Conditional	Contrapositive
G cannot be chosen unless B is chosen	G → B	~B → ~G
F is chosen if, and only if, P is chosen	F ↔ P	~F ↔ ~P
If S is selected, then T is also selected	S → T	~T → ~S
A is chosen only if C is chosen	A → C	~C → ~A
Every child is learning to read	child → learning to read	~learning to read → ~child
If either W or V is selected, then the other must also be selected	W ↔ V	~W ↔ ~V
F and G cannot both be selected	F → ~G	G → ~F
D will be selected only if H is selected	D → H	~H → ~D

Clue	Conditional	Contrapositive
R cannot be chosen unless P is chosen	$R \rightarrow P$	$\sim P \rightarrow \sim R$
All of the students are buying tickets	student $\rightarrow$ buying tickets	$\sim$buying tickets $\rightarrow$ $\sim$students
None of girls like sports	girl $\rightarrow$ $\sim$like sports	like sports $\rightarrow$ $\sim$girl
No boy likes to go to the museum	boy $\rightarrow$ $\sim$like museum	like museum $\rightarrow$ $\sim$boy
K is assigned to class 1 if L is assigned to class 1	$L_1 \rightarrow K_1$	$\sim K_1 \rightarrow \sim L_1$
T cannot be selected unless R is added	$T \rightarrow R$	$\sim R \rightarrow \sim T$
A plays on day 2 if, but only if, B plays on day 2	$A_2 \leftrightarrow B_2$	$\sim A_2 \leftrightarrow \sim B_2$
If Q is assigned, R is not assigned	$Q \rightarrow \sim R$	$R \rightarrow \sim Q$
F is not chosen unless either Q or R is chosen	$F \rightarrow Q$ and/or R	$\sim Q$ and $\sim R \rightarrow \sim F$
If W is assigned then B is assigned to team 1	$W \rightarrow B_1$	$\sim B_1 \rightarrow \sim W$
Neither R nor S can be on the same team as T	$R \rightarrow \sim T$; $S \rightarrow \sim T$	$T \rightarrow \sim R$; $T \rightarrow \sim S$
G is chosen unless F is chosen	$\sim F \rightarrow G$	$\sim G \rightarrow F$

Drill Exercise 2: Solutions

Clue	Conditional	Contrapositive
R cannot be chosen unless S is chosen	$R \rightarrow S$	$\sim S \rightarrow \sim R$
Sam is chosen if, and only if, Ty is chosen	$S \leftrightarrow T$	$\sim S \leftrightarrow \sim T$
If F is selected, then H is also selected	$F \rightarrow H$	$\sim H \rightarrow \sim F$
Artie is chosen only if Bobby is chosen	$A \rightarrow B$	$\sim B \rightarrow \sim A$

Clue	Conditional	Contrapositive
If William is selected, then Pete must also be selected	$W \rightarrow P$	$\sim P \rightarrow \sim W$
H and R cannot both be selected	$H \rightarrow \sim R$	$R \rightarrow \sim H$
D will be selected only if H is selected	$D \rightarrow H$	$\sim H \rightarrow \sim D$
Dan will be selected if Jean is selected	$J \rightarrow D$	$\sim D \rightarrow \sim J$
R cannot be chosen unless P is chosen	$R \rightarrow P$	$\sim P \rightarrow \sim R$
All of the balls are red	ball $\rightarrow$ red	$\sim$red $\rightarrow \sim$ball
No student likes homework	student $\rightarrow \sim$like homework	like homework $\rightarrow \sim$student
Each and every boy likes to go to the playground	boy $\rightarrow$ likes to go to playground	$\sim$likes to go to playground $\rightarrow \sim$boy
A is assigned to group 1 if, and only if, L is assigned to group 1	$A_1 \leftrightarrow L_1$	$\sim A_1 \leftrightarrow \sim L_1$
C cannot teach unless F teaches	$C \rightarrow F$	$\sim F \rightarrow \sim C$
H plays on day 2 if G plays on day 2	$G_2 \rightarrow H_2$	$\sim H_2 \rightarrow \sim G_2$
If Q is not assigned, R is not assigned	$\sim Q \rightarrow \sim R$	$R \rightarrow Q$
A is not chosen unless B is chosen	$A \rightarrow B$	$\sim B \rightarrow \sim A$
L is assigned unless B is assigned to class 1	$\sim L \rightarrow B_1$	$\sim B_1 \rightarrow L$
Neither F nor G can be on the same team as H	$F \rightarrow \sim H$ $G \rightarrow \sim H$	$H \rightarrow \sim F$ $H \rightarrow \sim G$
If G is not chosen, F is chosen	$\sim G \rightarrow F$	$\sim F \rightarrow G$

Practice Games with Explanations

10

Congratulations! You've made it through the really challenging part of this book. You've become familiar with all the concepts that form the basis of LSAT logic game structure. Now that you're smarter, you need to work on getting faster—speed counts on the LSAT! That's what this chapter is all about.

The twenty-five practice games in this chapter test all the concepts you learned in the first half of the book. Once you've gained a thorough understanding of the types of games represented on the exam, practice will enable you to quickly identify them and graphically represent the information presented in each.

The steps contained in the prior explanatory sections of the guide are also represented here in the practice drills. The only major difference is the way the diagrams are drawn. In previous chapters, each new piece of information was shown in a separate chart; eventually these charts collectively formed a comprehensive chart containing all necessary information. In these practice games, however, more data will be depicted in fewer charts. The subscripts in the charts denote the individual step that a particular piece of data references.

Game 1

Four sisters—Corinth, Darsi, Francine, and Gail—are meeting for lunch at the Mesopotamia Delicatessen. Each of the sisters will purchase exactly one of four types of sandwiches—Roast Beef, Salami, Turkey, and Veggie. The sisters will purchase their sandwiches one at a time, and no two sisters will purchase the same type of sandwich. The following conditions must be met:

Gail purchases her sandwich immediately before Darsi.

Francine purchases either the Roast Beef sandwich or the Veggie sandwich.

Darsi does not purchase the Salami sandwich.

The Turkey sandwich is purchased second.

1. Which one of the following could be an accurate list of the sisters in the order in which they purchase their sandwiches, matched with the type of sandwich purchased?

    (A) Gail: Veggie; Darsi: Turkey; Francine: Roast Beef; Corinth: Salami

    (B) Gail: Roast Beef; Darsi: Turkey; Francine: Salami; Corinth: Veggie

    (C) Corinth: Turkey; Gail: Salami; Darsi: Roast Beef; Francine: Veggie

    (D) Francine: Veggie; Darsi: Turkey; Gail: Salami; Corinth: Roast Beef

    (E) Francine: Roast Beef; Corinth: Turkey; Darsi: Salami; Gail: Veggie

2. If Francine purchases her sandwich at some time before Gail, then each of the following could be true EXCEPT:

    (A) Corinth purchases the Roast Beef sandwich.

    (B) Corinth purchases the Turkey sandwich.

    (C) Corinth purchases the Salami sandwich.

    (D) Darsi purchases the Roast Beef sandwich.

    (E) Darsi purchases the Veggie sandwich.

3. If Gail purchases the Roast Beef sandwich, then which one of the following must be true?

    (A) Corinth purchases her sandwich third.

    (B) Corinth purchases her sandwich fourth.

    (C) Darsi purchases her sandwich second.

    (D) Darsi purchases her sandwich fourth.

    (E) Francine purchases her sandwich third.

4. If Corinth purchases her sandwich first, then each of the following could be true EXCEPT:

   (A) Darsi purchases the Roast Beef sandwich.
   (B) Gail purchases the Roast Beef sandwich.
   (C) Francine purchases the Roast Beef sandwich.
   (D) Darsi purchases the Veggie sandwich.
   (E) Gail purchases the Turkey Sandwich.

5. If Darsi purchases her sandwich fourth, then which one of the following must be false?

   (A) Gail purchases the Roast Beef sandwich.
   (B) Corinth purchases the Turkey sandwich.
   (C) Darsi purchases the Veggie sandwich.
   (D) Darsi purchases the Roast Beef sandwich.
   (E) Francine purchases the Veggie sandwich.

STEP 1 Visualize and draw the diagram.

1	2	3	4
Sister/Sandwich	Sister/Sandwich	Sister/Sandwich	Sister/Sandwich
_ _	_ _	_ _	_ _

STEP 2 List the components and ascertain the ratio and/or distribution.

Components:
   Sisters: C, D, F, G
   Sandwiches: R, S, T, V

Distribution: 1-to-1 ratio

STEP 3 Symbolize the clues.

Clue 1

G _	D _

Clue 2

F R/V

Clue 3

D̸ S

Clue 4   T = 2 (Place into the diagram.)

STEP 4 Make deductions.

Deduction 1: From Clue 1, you can deduce that G is banned from sister slot 4, and D is banned from sister slot 1.

Deduction 2: From Clues 2 and 4, you can deduce that F is banned from sister slot 2.

Explanation: Since T is the second sandwich purchased, and F can only purchase either sandwiches R or V, F cannot be second.

~D	~F		~G
1	2	3	4
Sister/Sandwich	Sister/Sandwich	Sister/Sandwich	Sister/Sandwich
_ _	_ T	_ _	_ _

STEP 5 **Tackle the questions.**

Question order: 1, 2, 3, 4, and then 5.

Answer Key

1. **A**   2. **A**   3. **C**   4. **B**   5. **A**

Answers

Question 1 (catch-a-clue)

- Clue 1 eliminates answer choices D and E.
- Clue 2 eliminates answer choice B.
- Clue 3 eliminates answer choice E which has already been eliminated.
- Clue 4 eliminates answer choice C.

(A) is the correct answer.

Question 2 (restricted, "could-be-true-EXCEPT")

1. Create a new symbol that illustrates the additional restriction:

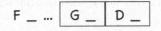

2. Since both G and D purchase their sandwiches after F, F is now banned from sister slots 3 and 4. By operation of Deduction 2 (F ≠ 2), F must be placed in sister slot 1.
3. By operation of Clue 1, G and D are placed in either sister slots 2 and 3, respectively (Option 1) or sister slots 3 and 4, respectively (Option 2).
4. Work out Option 1 first. The last remaining sister (C) must be placed in the only remaining sister slot (4).
5. By operation of Clue 2, S cannot be matched with F and is, therefore, banned from sandwich slot 1. By operation of Clue 3, S cannot be matched with D and is also banned from sandwich slot 3. Therefore, the only remaining position for S is sandwich slot 4.
6. The remaining two sandwiches (R and V) must be placed in slots 1 and 3 interchangeably.
7. Now work out Option 2. The last remaining sister (C) must be placed in the only remaining sister slot (2).
8. By operation of Clue 2, S cannot be matched with F and is, therefore, banned from sandwich slot 1. By operation of Clue 3, S cannot be matched with D and is also banned from sandwich slot 4. Therefore, the only remaining sandwich slot for S is slot 3.
9. The remaining two sandwiches (R and V) must be placed in sandwich slots 1 and 4 interchangeably.

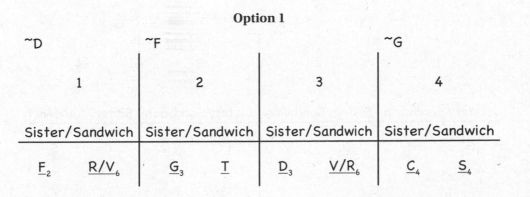

Option 2

$\sim D$	$\sim F$		$\sim G$
1	2	3	4
Sister/Sandwich	Sister/Sandwich	Sister/Sandwich	Sister/Sandwich
$\underline{F}_2$ $\underline{R/V}_9$	$\underline{C}_7$ $\underline{T}$	$\underline{G}_3$ $\underline{S}_8$	$\underline{D}_3$ $\underline{V/R}_9$

Answer choices B, C, D, and E can be true.

(A) is the correct answer.

Question 3 (restricted, "must-be-true")

1. Create a new symbol that illustrates the additional restriction

$$\boxed{G \ R} \quad \boxed{D \ \_}$$

2. Now that G and R are matched, and by operation of Clue 4, G is banned from sister slot 2. By operation of Deduction 1, G is banned from sister slot 4. As such, $\boxed{GR}$ must be placed in either 1 (Option 1) or 3 (Option 2).
3. Work out Option 1 first. By operation of Clue 1, D is placed in sister slot 2.
4. Since R has been matched with G, by operation of Clue 2, F must be matched with V and, thereafter, C is matched with S.
5. The FV and CS matches can be placed in either 3 or 4 interchangeably.
6. Now work out Option 2. By operation of Clue 1, D is placed in sister slot 4.
7. By operation of Deduction 2, F cannot be placed in sister slot 2 and accordingly must be placed in the only other available location—sister slot 1.
8. The only remaining sister (C) must be placed in sister slot 2.
9. By operation of Clue 2, F must be matched with V and placed into sister slot 1.
10. The only remaining sandwich (S) must be matched with D into sandwich slot 4. This is a violation of Clue 3, so option 2 is not valid. Cross it out.

Option 1

$\sim D$	$\sim F$		$\sim G$
1	2	3	4
Sister/Sandwich	Sister/Sandwich	Sister/Sandwich	Sister/Sandwich
$\underline{G}_2$ $\underline{R}_2$	$\underline{D}_3$ $\underline{T}$	$\underline{F}$ $\underline{V}_4$	$\underline{C}$ $\underline{S}_4$
		$\underline{C}$ $\underline{S}_4$	$\underline{F}$ $\underline{V}_4$

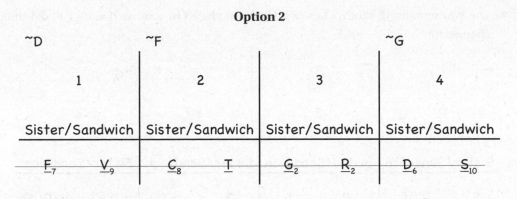

Option 2

	~D	~F			~G	
	1	2	3		4	
	Sister/Sandwich	Sister/Sandwich	Sister/Sandwich		Sister/Sandwich	
	$\underline{F}_7$ $\underline{V}_9$	$\underline{C}_8$ $\underline{T}$	$\underline{G}_2$ $\underline{R}_2$		$\underline{D}_6$ $\underline{S}_{10}$	

(C) is the correct answer.

Question 4 (restricted, "could-be-true-EXCEPT")

1. Place C in sister slot 1.
2. By operation of Clue 1, G and D must be placed in sister slots 2 and 3, respectively, or in sister slots 3 and 4, respectively. However, the placement of G and D in sister slots 3 and 4, respectively, would force the placement of F in sister slot 2 in violation of Deduction 2. Accordingly, G and D can only be placed in sister slots 2 and 3, respectively.
3. The only remaining sister (F) must be placed in sister slot 4.
4. By operation of Clue 3, S cannot be placed in sandwich slot 3. By operation of Clue 2, S cannot be placed in sandwich slot 4; therefore, S must be placed in sandwich slot 1.
5. The two remaining sandwiches (R and V) are placed in sandwich slots 3 and 4 interchangeably.

~D	~F		~G
1	2	3	4
Sister/Sandwich	Sister/Sandwich	Sister/Sandwich	Sister/Sandwich
$\underline{C}_1$ $\underline{S}_4$	$\underline{G}_2$ $\underline{T}$	$\underline{D}_2$ $\underline{R/V}_5$	$\underline{F}_3$ $\underline{V/R}_5$

(B) is the correct answer.

Question 5 (restricted, "must-be-false")

1. Place D in sister slot 4.
2. By operation of Clue 1, G must be placed in sister slot 3.
3. By operation of Deduction 2, F must be place in sister slot 1.
4. The remaining sister (C) must be placed in sister slot 2.
5. By operation of Clue 3, sandwich S cannot be placed in slot 4. By operation of Clue 2, sandwich S cannot be placed in sandwich slot 1. Therefore, S must be placed in sandwich slot 3.

6. The two remaining sandwiches (R and V) are placed in sandwich slots 1 and 4 interchangeably.

~D		~F				~G	
1		2		3		4	
Sister/Sandwich		Sister/Sandwich		Sister/Sandwich		Sister/Sandwich	
F_3	R/V_6	C_4	T	G_2	S_5	D_1	V/R_6

(A) is the correct answer.

Game 2

Exactly six of eight volunteers—K, L, M, N, P, R, S, and T—will be assigned to two three-person clean-up crews—Crew 1 and Crew 2. No volunteer is assigned to more than one crew. The crews' composition must conform to the following conditions:

Neither P nor R nor N is assigned to the same crew as K.

If S is assigned to Crew 1, then K is assigned to Crew 2.

If assigned to a crew, M is assigned to Crew 2.

M is not assigned to the same crew as R.

L is not assigned to the same crew as T.

1. Which one of the following could be an accurate list of the volunteers on the two crews?
   - (A) Crew 1: L, M, N
     Crew 2: K, S, T
   - (B) Crew 1: L, P, S
     Crew 2: K, R, T
   - (C) Crew 1: L, R, S
     Crew 2: M, P, T
   - (D) Crew 1: L, N, T
     Crew 2: M, R, S
   - (E) Crew 1: R, P, S
     Crew 2: K, L, M

2. Which one of the following is a pair of volunteers who CANNOT be two of three volunteers assigned to Crew 1?
   - (A) P and N
   - (B) K and L
   - (C) L and N
   - (D) R and S
   - (E) S and T

3. If S is assigned to Crew 1, which one of the following is a pair of volunteers who could be assigned to Crew 2 together?
   - (A) M and P
   - (B) L and R
   - (C) M and T
   - (D) M and N
   - (E) N and T

4. If P is assigned to Crew 1 and R is assigned to Crew 2, then each of the following must be true EXCEPT:
   - (A) N is assigned to Crew 1.
   - (B) S is assigned to Crew 2.
   - (C) T is assigned to Crew 2.
   - (D) K is not assigned to any crew.
   - (E) M is not assigned to any crew.

5. If neither N nor T is assigned to any crew, then which one of the following must be false?
   - (A) L and K are assigned to the same crew.
   - (B) P and S are assigned to the same crew.
   - (C) M and P are assigned to the same crew.
   - (D) R and S are assigned to the same crew.
   - (E) L and M are assigned to the same crew.

6. Each of following could be true EXCEPT:
   - (A) S is assigned to Crew 2, and K is not assigned to any crew.
   - (B) M is assigned to Crew 2, and R is not assigned to any crew.
   - (C) K and S are both assigned to Crew 2.
   - (D) P is assigned to Crew 1, and N is assigned to Crew 2.
   - (E) S is assigned to Crew 1, and N is assigned to Crew 2.

STEP 1 Visualize and draw the diagram.

Crew 1	Crew 2	Out
_ _ _	_ _ _	_ _

STEP 2 List the components and ascertain the ratio and/or distribution.

Components: K, L, M, N, P, R, S

Distribution: Fixed

STEP 3 Symbolize the clues.

Clue 1   P → ~K; K → ~P
R → ~K; K → ~R
N → ~K, K → ~N

Clue 2 S_1 → K_2; ~K_2 → ~S_1

Clue 3   M → M_2

Clue 4   M → ~R; R → ~M

Clue 5   L → ~T; T → ~L

STEP 4 Make deductions.

First link Clue 2 and the contrapositives of Clue 1:

$$S_1 → K_2 \text{ and } K → ~P; K → ~R \text{ and } K → ~N$$

Deduction 1: S_1 → ~P_2 and ~R_2 → ~N_2

Deduction 2: From Clue 3, deduce that M cannot be assigned to Crew 1.

~M

Crew 1	Crew 2	Out
_ _ _	_ _ _	_ _

STEP 5 **Tackle the questions.**

Question order: 1, 3, 4, 5, 2, and then 6.

Answer Key

1. **E**   2. **B**   3. **C**   4. **C**   5. **C**   6. **E**

Answers

Question 1 (catch-a-clue)

- Clue 1 eliminates answer choice B.
- Clue 2 eliminates answer choice C.
- Clue 3 eliminates answer choice A.
- Clue 4 eliminates answer choice D.

(E) is the correct answer.

Question 3 (restricted, "could-be-true")

1. Place S in Crew 1.
2. By operation of Clue 2, K must be placed in Crew 2.
3. By operation of Deduction 1, N, R, and P are banned from Crew 2. You can therefore rule out options that include N, R, or P. Eliminate answer choices A, B, D, and E.

(C) is the correct answer.

Question 4 (restricted, "must-be-true-EXCEPT")

1. Place P onto Crew 1, and place R in Crew 2.
2. By operation of Clue 1, K must be placed in the out-column.
3. By operation of Deduction 2 and Clue 5, M must be placed in the out-column.
4. By operation of the contrapositive of Clue 2, S is banned from Crew 1 and must therefore be placed on Crew 2.
5. By operation of Clue 5, L and T are placed on Crews 1 and 2 interchangeably.
6. N—the only remaining volunteer—is assigned to the only remaining crew slot on Crew 1.

~M

Crew 1	Crew 2	OUT
P_1 L/T_5 N_6	R_1 S_4 T/L_5	K_2 M_3

(C) is the correct answer.

Question 5 (restricted, "must-be-false")

1. Place N and T in the out-column.
2. With the out-column filled and by operation of Deduction 2, M must be placed on Crew 2.
3. By operation of Clue 4, R must be placed on Crew 1.

4. By operation of Clue 1, K must be placed on Crew 2.

5. By further operation of Clue 1, P must be placed on Crew 1.

6. The only remaining volunteers (L and S) are assigned to the remaining two slots (one on Crew 1 and the other on Crew 2) interchangeably.

~M

Crew 1	Crew 2	OUT
R_3 P_5 L/S_6	M_2 K_4 S/L_6	N_1 T_1

(C) is the correct answer.

Question 2 (unrestricted, "cannot-be-true")

This question is answerable in part by reviewing prior workouts. Answer choices A and C are each shown on Crew 1 in your work for question 4, so eliminate them. Answer choice D is shown as possible in the answer to question 1, so eliminate it too.

Try answer choice B:

1. Place K and L on Crew 1.

2. By operation of Deduction 1, N, P, and R are banned from Crew 1.

3. By operation of the contrapositive of Clue 2, S is banned from Crew 1.

4. By operation of Deduction 2, M is banned from Crew 1.

5. By operation of Clue 5, T is banned from Crew 1.

6. There are no remaining volunteers that could occupy the last slot on Crew 1.

(B) is the correct answer.

Question 6 (unrestricted, "could-be-true-EXCEPT")

This question is completely answerable by reviewing your deductions, specifically Deduction 1 which shows that answer choice E cannot be true.

(E) is the correct answer.

Game 3

During a single week, from Monday through Friday, a geometry professor will hold exactly five tutoring sessions, one session per day. Each session will include either one or two students. Exactly eight students—H, J, K, L, M, N, O, and P—attend these tutoring sessions, and each student must be included in exactly one session. The following conditions must be met:

K and N together constitute one session.

Wednesday's session includes exactly one student.

J's session and P's session are held on consecutive days.

M's session is held at some time before H's session, but after N's session.

P's session includes exactly one student.

1. Which one of the following could be an accurate matching of students to the sessions in which they were tutored?

    (A) Monday: K, L; Tuesday: M, N; Wednesday: H; Thursday: J, O; Friday: P
    (B) Monday: J, Tuesday: P, Wednesday: K, N; Thursday: M, O; Friday: H, L
    (C) Monday: K, N; Tuesday: M; Wednesday: P; Thursday: J, L; Friday: H, O
    (D) Monday: K, N; Tuesday: M, L; Wednesday: P; Thursday: H, O; Friday: J
    (E) Monday: K, N; Tuesday: M; Wednesday: H; Thursday: O, P; Friday: J

2. Which one of the following students could be included in Monday's session?

    (A) H
    (B) J
    (C) L
    (D) M
    (E) P

3. If Monday's session includes exactly one student, then which one of the following could be true?

    (A) J's session is held on Friday.
    (B) H's session is held on Thursday.
    (C) L's session is held on Monday.
    (D) K's session is held on Monday.
    (E) P's session is held on Thursday.

4. If P's session is held on Tuesday, then which one of the following must be true?

    (A) H's session is held on Friday.
    (B) L's session is held on Thursday.
    (C) O's session is held on Friday.
    (D) J's session is held on Monday.
    (E) L's session is held on Friday.

5. If H's session is held on Wednesday, then each of the following could be true EXCEPT:

    (A) Tuesday's session includes exactly one student.
    (B) Friday's session includes exactly one student.
    (C) L's session is held on Tuesday.
    (D) O's session is held on Friday.
    (E) P's session is held on Thursday.

STEP 1 Visualize and draw the diagram.

Mon	Tues	Wed	Thur	Fri

STEP 2 List the components and ascertain the ratio and/or distribution.

Components: H, J, K, L, M, N, O, P

Ratio: 5 days and 8 students. Each day includes either 1 or 2 students; therefore, 3 days will include 2 students and 2 days will include 1 student.

STEP 3 Symbolize the clues.

Clue 1 | KN |

Clue 2 Place directly into the diagram.

Mon	Tues	Wed	Thur	Fri
		–		

Clue 3 | J | P | or | P | J |

Clue 4 N ... M ... H

Clue 5 | P |

STEP 4 Make deductions

First link Clue 1 | KN | and Clue 4, N...M...H.

Deduction 1: KN...M...H

a) Neither K nor N can be assigned to either Thursday or Friday.
b) H cannot be assigned to either Monday or Tuesday.
c) M cannot be assigned to either Monday or Friday.

Deduction 2: From Clues 1 and 2, you can also deduce that neither K nor N can be assigned to Wednesday.

				~K
~M		~K	~K	~N
~H	~H	~N	~N	~M
Mon	Tues	Wed	Thur	Fri
		—		

STEP 5 **Tackle the questions.**

Question order: 1, 3, 4, 5, and then 2.

Answer Key

1. **C**   2. **C**   3. **C**   4. **A**   5. **A**

Answers

Question 1 (catch-a-clue)

- Clue 1 eliminates answer choice A.
- Clue 2 eliminates answer choice B.
- Clue 3 eliminates answer choice D.
- Clue 4 eliminates answer choice A, which has already been eliminated.
- Clue 5 eliminates answer choice E.

(C) is the correct answer.

Question 3 (restricted, "could-be-true")

1. Pivot to your most restricted components: K and N. If Monday's session includes just one student, K and N must be assigned to Tuesday.
2. By operation of Clue 3, neither J nor P can be assigned to Monday. The one student assigned to Monday must be either L or O.
3. By operation of the ratio deduction (3 two-student sessions and 2 one-student sessions) and Clue 5, P must be assigned to Wednesday (the other one-student session).
4. By operation of Clue 3, J must be assigned to Thursday.
5. By operation of Clue 4, M must be assigned to Thursday, and H must be assigned to Friday.
6. The remaining component—either L or O (whichever one is not assigned to Monday)—must be assigned to Friday.

				~K
~M		~K	~K	~N
~H	~H	~N	~N	~M
Mon	Tues	Wed	Thur	Fri
$\tilde{J}_2$ $\tilde{P}_2$ L/O$_2$	K$_1$ N$_1$	$\underline{P}_3$	J$_4$ M$_5$	H$_5$ O/L$_6$

(C) is the correct answer.

Question 4 (restricted, "must-be-true")

1. Place P in Tuesday.
1. By operation of Deductions 1a) and 2, K and N must be placed in Monday.
3. By operation of Clue 3, J must be placed in Wednesday.
4. By operation of Clue 4, M must be placed in Thursday and H in Friday, respectively.
5. By operation of Clue 5, P is the only student assigned to Tuesday. By operation of Clue 2, J is the only student assigned to Wednesday. Accordingly, the remaining components (L and O) must be assigned to Thursday and Friday interchangeably.

				~K
~M		~K	~K	~N
~H	~H	~N	~N	~M
Mon	Tues	Wed	Thur	Fri
K$_2$ N$_2$	P$_1$	J$_3$	M$_4$ L/O$_5$	H$_4$ O/L$_5$

(A) is the correct answer.

Question 5 (restricted, "must-be-false")

1. Place H in Wednesday.
2. By operation of Deduction 1, K and N must be placed in Monday and M in Tuesday.
3. By operation of Clue 3, either J is placed in Thursday and P in Friday (Option 1), or P is placed in Thursday and J is placed in Friday (Option 2).

4. Work out Option 1 first. By operation of Clue 5, P is the only student assigned to Friday. By operation of Clue 2, H is the only student assigned to Wednesday. Accordingly, the remaining components (L and O) must be assigned to Tuesday and Thursday interchangeably.

5. Now work out Option 2. Again, by operation of Clue 5, P is the only student assigned to Thursday. By operation of Clue 2, H is the only student assigned to Wednesday. Accordingly, the remaining components (L and O) must be assigned to Tuesday and Friday interchangeably.

Option 1

				~K
~M		~K	~K	~N
~H	~H	~N	~N	~M
Mon	Tues	Wed	Thur	Fri
K_2 N_2	M_2 L/O_4	H_1	J_3 O/L_4	P_3

Option 2

				~K
~M		~K	~K	~N
~H	~H	~N	~N	~M
Mon	Tues	Wed	Thur	Fri
K_2 N_2	M_2 L/O_5	H_1	P_3	J_3 O/L_5

(A) is the correct answer.

Question 2 (unrestricted, "could-be-true")

This question is completely answerable by reviewing prior workouts. L could be tutored on Monday is shown in your work for question 3.

(C) is the correct answer.

Game 4

A total of nine executives: three vice-presidents—D, F, and G—and six managers—H, J, K, L, M, and N—attend a corporate retreat. Upon arrival, the executives are assigned to three breakout sessions—Personnel, Sales, and Technology—of three executives each. No executive is assigned to more than one breakout session. The following conditions must be met:

There must be exactly one vice-president assigned to each session.

Neither D nor J is assigned to the same session as M.

If L is assigned to the Technology session, then J is assigned to the Technology session.

F is assigned to either the Personnel or the Sales session.

If G is assigned to the Technology session, then M is assigned to the Sales session.

K and N are assigned to the same session.

1. Which one of the following could be an accurate list of the executives assigned to the sessions?

   (A) Personnel: F, J, M
       Sales: G, H, L
       Technology: D, K, N
   (B) Personnel: G, L, M
       Sales: F, J, K
       Technology: D, H, N
   (C) Personnel: F, L, M
       Sales: G, H, J
       Technology: D, K, N
   (D) Personnel: D, K, N
       Sales: F, J, L
       Technology: G, H, M
   (E) Personnel: G, H, M
       Sales: D, K, N
       Technology: F, L, J

2. Which one of the following executives CANNOT be assigned to the Technology session?

   (A) N
   (B) L
   (C) G
   (D) M
   (E) J

3. If J is assigned to the Sales session, which one of the following must be true?

   (A) L is assigned to the Sales session.
   (B) H is assigned to the Personnel session.
   (C) K is assigned to the Personnel session.
   (D) N is assigned to the Technology session.
   (E) F is assigned to the Sales session.

4. If H and J are both assigned to the Personnel session, then each of the following must be true EXCEPT:

   (A) L is assigned to the Sales session.
   (B) F is assigned to the Sales session.
   (C) N is assigned to the Technology session.
   (D) K is assigned to Technology session.
   (E) M is assigned to Sales session.

5. If G is assigned to the Technology session, then which one of the following must be false?

   (A) F and K are assigned to the same session.
   (B) L and M are assigned to the same session.
   (C) D and N are assigned to the same session.
   (D) L and G are assigned to the same session.
   (E) H and M are assigned to the same session.

6. Which one of the following is a complete and accurate list of vice-presidents any one of whom could be the vice-president assigned to the Sales session?

   (A) F
   (B) D, G
   (C) D, F
   (D) F, G
   (E) D, F, G

STEP 1 Visualize and draw the diagram.

Personnel	Sales	Technology
— — —	— — —	— — —

STEP 2 List the components and ascertain the ratio and/or distribution.

Components: Vice-Presidents: D, F, G; Managers: H, J, K, L, M, N

Ratio: one-to-one

Distribution: fixed

STEP 3 Symbolize the clues.

Clue 1   Place directly into the diagram.

Personnel	Sales	Technology
VP	VP	VP
— — —	— — —	— — —

Clue 2 $D \rightarrow {\sim}M;\ M \rightarrow {\sim}D$
              $J \rightarrow {\sim}M;\ M \rightarrow {\sim}J$

Clue 3 $L_{Tech} \rightarrow J_{Tech};\ {\sim}J_{Tech} \rightarrow {\sim}L_{Tech}$

Clue 4 F = Personnel or Sales

Clue 5 $G_{Tech} \rightarrow M_{Sales};\ {\sim}M_{Sales} \rightarrow {\sim}G_{Tech}$

Clue 6 $K \leftrightarrow N;\ {\sim}K \leftrightarrow {\sim}N$

STEP 4 Make deductions.

Deduction 1: From Clue 4, you know that F cannot be placed in Technology.

$${\sim}F$$

Personnel	Sales	Technology
VP	VP	VP
— — —	— — —	— — —

STEP 5 **Tackle the questions.**

Question order: 1, 3, 4, 5, 2, and then 6

Answer Key

1. **C**   2. **D**   3. **C**   4. **B**   5. **A**   6. **D**

Answers

Question 1 (catch-a-clue)

- Clue 1 doesn't eliminate any answer choices.
- Clue 2 eliminates answer choice A.
- Clue 3 doesn't eliminate any answer choices.
- Clue 4 eliminates answer choice E.
- Clue 5 eliminates answer choice D.
- Clue 6 eliminates answer choice B.

(C) is the correct answer.

Question 3 (restricted, "must-be-true")

1. Place J in the Sales group.
2. By operation of Clue 2, M cannot be placed in the Sales group.
3. By operation of the contrapositive of Clue 5, G cannot be placed in the Technology group.
4. With G banned from the Technology group and by operation of Deduction 1, D must be the VP placed in the Technology group.
5. By operation of Clue 2, M is now also banned from the Technology group and, as such, must be placed in the Personnel group.
6. By operation of Clue 6, K and N must be placed in the same group. Accordingly, K and N must be placed in the Technology group.
7. The remaining VP components (F and G) can be placed in the Personnel and Sales groups interchangeably.
8. The remaining manager components (H and L) can be placed in the Personnel and Sales groups interchangeably.

		$\sim$F	
Personnel	Sales		Technology
VP	VP		VP
		$\sim M_2$	$\sim G_3$ $\sim M_5$
F/G_7 M_5 H/L_8	G/F_7 J_1 L/H_8		D_4 K_6 N_6

(D) is the correct answer.

Question 4 (restricted, "must-be-true-EXCEPT")

1. Place H and J in the Personnel group.
2. By operation of the contrapositive of Clue 3, L cannot be placed in the Technology group and must, therefore, be placed in the Sales group.
3. By operation of Clue 6, K and N must be placed in the Technology group.
4. The remaining manager component (M) must be placed in the last manager slot available in the Sales group.
5. By operation of Clue 2, D cannot be placed in the Sales group.

		$\sim$F
Personnel	Sales	Technology
VP	VP	VP
	$\sim D_5$	$\sim G_3$ $\sim M_5$
__ H_1 J_1	__ L_2 M_4	__ K_3 N_3

(B) is the correct answer.

Question 5 (restricted, "must-be-false")

1. Place G in the Technology group.
2. By operation of Clue 5, M must be placed in the Sales group.
3. By operation of Clue 2, D cannot place VP in the Sales group and must, therefore, be placed in the only remaining VP slot in the Personnel group.
4. The remaining VP component (F) must, therefore, be placed in the Sales group.
5. By operation of Clue 2, J cannot be placed in the Sales group.
6. By operation of Clue 6, neither K nor N can be placed in the Sales group.
7. The only available manager components for the Sales group are H and L.

		$\sim$F
Personnel	Sales	Technology
VP	VP	VP
D_3 __ __	$\sim K_6$ $\sim N_6$ $\sim J_5$ F_4 M_2 H/L_7	G_1 __ __

(A) is the correct answer.

Question 2 (unrestricted, "cannot-be-true")

- This question is answerable, in part, by reviewing your prior workouts.
- Based on the solution to question 3, N can be placed in the Technology group. Eliminate answer choice A.
- Based on the solution to question 5, G can be placed in the Technology group. Eliminate answer choice C.
- Even though you did not complete the solution to question 5, you may be able to see that both L and J can be placed in the Technology group.
- M cannot be placed in the Technology group because:

  a) if M is placed in the Technology group, then VP component D cannot be placed in Technology. By operation of Clue 4, F can never be placed in the Technology group, thereby necessitating that VP component G must be placed there instead.

  b) by operation of Clue 5, G and M cannot both be placed in the Technology group.

(D) is the correct answer.

Question 6 (unrestricted, "could-be-true")

- This question is answerable, in part, by reviewing your prior workouts.
- Based on the solution to question 3, F and G can be placed in the Sales group. Eliminate answer choices A, B, and C.
- You must try placing D in the Sales group.

  - Place D in the Sales group.
  - By operation of Clue 2, M cannot be placed in the Sales group.
  - By operation of the contrapositive of Clue 5, G cannot be the VP of the Technology group.
  - By operation of Clue 4, F cannot be placed in the Technology group, leaving no available VP for the Technology group. This does not work. VP component D cannot be placed in the Sales group.

(D) is the correct answer.

Game 5

Exactly six children—Matthew, Noel, Paul, Sara, Tye, and Vicky—will ride at least one of the following four attractions—Bumper Cars, Carousel, Ferris Wheel, and Roller Coaster (and no other rides) at the Fun Blast Amusement Park. No children ride any of the rides more than once. The following conditions must apply:

Noel and Tye ride the Carousel.

Matthew and Noel ride the Ferris Wheel.

If any child rides the Bumper Cars, then that child does not also ride the Ferris Wheel.

Sara rides exactly three rides.

Vicky rides more rides than Matthew, but less than Sara.

Tye does not ride any ride that Vicky rides.

1. If exactly three children ride the Bumper Cars, then which one of the following CANNOT be true?

    (A) Both Paul and Vicky ride the Ferris Wheel.
    (B) Both Sara and Tye ride the Bumper Cars.
    (C) Both Noel and Vicky ride the Ferris Wheel.
    (D) Both Matthew and Tye ride the Ferris Wheel.
    (E) Both Noel and Paul ride the Carousel.

2. Which one of the following must be true?

    (A) Sara rides the Ferris Wheel.
    (B) Vicky rides the Roller Coaster.
    (C) Vicky rides the Bumper Cars.
    (D) Paul rides the Roller Coaster.
    (E) Tye rides the Ferris Wheel.

3. If any child that rides the Roller Coaster also rides the Bumper Cars, which one of the following could be true?

    (A) Tye rides the Roller Coaster.
    (B) Sara rides the Ferris Wheel.
    (C) Noel rides the Roller Coaster.
    (D) Vicky rides the Ferris Wheel.
    (E) Tye rides the Ferris Wheel.

4. Each of the following could be true EXCEPT:

    (A) Tye rides more attractions than Matthew.
    (B) Paul rides more attractions than Noel.
    (C) Vicky rides more attractions than Tye.
    (D) Exactly five of the children ride the Roller Coaster.
    (E) Exactly three of the children ride the Carousel.

5. Which one of the following could be true?

    (A) Paul rides exactly four attractions.
    (B) Noel rides exactly four attractions.
    (C) Vicky rides exactly three attractions.
    (D) Noel rides exactly three attractions.
    (E) Matthew rides exactly two attractions.

Visualize and draw the diagram.

Matthew	Noel	Paul	Sara	Tye	Vicky

STEP 2 List the components and ascertain the ratio and/or distribution.

Components: B, C, F, R

Ratio: not one-to-one

Distribution: Unknown Distribution

STEP 3 Symbolize the clues.

Clue 1 Place directly into the diagram.

Clue 2 Place directly into the diagram.

Clue 3 $B \rightarrow \sim F; F \rightarrow \sim B$

Clue 4 Place directly into the diagram.

Clue 5 $S > V > M$

Clue 6 Place directly into the diagram.   Tye ≠ Vicky

Matthew	Noel	Paul	Sara	Tye	Vicky
F_2	$C_1 F_2$		$_4$	C_1	

STEP 4 Make deductions.

Deduction 1: By operation of Clue 3, neither Matthew nor Noel will ride B.

Deduction 2: From Clue 4, you can deduce that Sara must ride C and R and either B or F. How? Sara must ride three out of four attractions. By operation of Clue 3, Sara cannot ride both B and F. Therefore, Sara must ride either B *or* F with C *and* R

Deduction 3: From Clue 5, you can deduce that Vicky must ride exactly two attractions. How? By operation of Clue 2, you can deduce that Matthew must ride at least one attraction. By operation of Clue 4, you know that Sara must ride exactly three attractions. Therefore, if Vicky rides more attractions than Matthew but less than Sara, Vicky must ride two attractions.

Deduction 4: Now Matthew can only ride F and no other attractions. Hence, Matthew cannot ride either R nor C.

Deduction 5: By operation of Clue 6, you can deduce that Vicky cannot ride C nor can Tye ride R.

Deduction 6: Additionally, Vicky must ride R with either B or F. How do you know? Vicky must ride exactly two attractions. Neither of Vicky's attractions can be C. By operation of Clue 3, Vicky cannot ride both B and F; therefore, she must ride R with either B or F.

~R					
~B ~C	~B			~R	~C
Matthew	Noel	Paul	Sara	Tye	Vicky
F	C F		C R B/F	C	R F/B

STEP 5 **Tackle the questions.**

Question order: 1, 3, 2, 4, and then 5.

Answer Key

1. **A**   2. **B**   3. **E**   4. **D**   5. **D**

Answers

Question 1 (restricted, "cannot-be-true")

1. By operation of Deduction 1, neither Matthew nor Noel rides B. By operation of Clue 6, Tye and Vicky cannot ride the same attractions. Therefore, the three children that ride B must be Paul and Sara, and either Tye or Vicky.
2. By operation of Clue 3, Paul cannot now ride F.

~R					
~B ~C	~B			~R	~C
Matthew	Noel	Paul	Sara	Tye	Vicky
		$\sim F_2$			
F	C F	B_1	C R B_1	C	R B/F

(A) is the correct answer.

Question 3 (restricted, "could-be-true")

- The additional restriction is R → B; ~B → ~R.
- By operation of Deductions 2 and 6, Sara and Vicky ride R. Therefore, both Sara and Vicky ride B and not F. Eliminate answer choices B and D.
- By operation of Deduction 1, Noel does not ride B, and, accordingly, Noel does not ride R. Eliminate answer choice C.
- Answer choice A can never be true by operation of Deduction 5.

(E) is the correct answer.

Question 2 (unrestricted, "must-be-true")

- This question is completely answerable by reviewing the deductions.
- Answer choices A, C, D, and E can each be true but are not always true.

(B) is the correct answer.

Question 4 (unrestricted, "could-be-true-EXCEPT")

- This question is completely answerable by reviewing the deductions.
- Answer choice A can be true. By operation of Deduction 4, Matthew rides one attraction. In addition to C, Tye could also ride either B or F (whichever of those two attractions that is not ridden by Vicky) bringing the number of attractions ridden by Tye to two.
- Answer choice B can be true. Paul can ride three attractions (C, R, B/F) and Noel can ride just two attractions (C and F).
- Answer choice C can be true. By operation of Deduction 3, Vicky rides two attractions. Tye can just ride one attraction (C).
- Answer choice E can be true. Only Noel, Sara, and Tye could just ride C and no others.
- Answer choice D cannot be true. By operation of Deduction 5, Tye cannot ride R. By operation of Deduction 4, Matthew cannot ride R. Therefore, the maximum number of children that can ride R is four.

(D) is the correct answer.

Question 5 (unrestricted, "could-be-true")

- This question is completely answerable by reviewing the deductions.
- By operation of Clue 3, no child can ride all four attractions. Eliminate answer choices A and B.
- By operation of Deduction 3, Vicky rides exactly two attractions, not three. Eliminate answer choice C.
- By operation of Deduction 4, Matthew rides exactly one attraction, not two. Eliminate answer choice E.
- In addition to C and F, Noel could also ride R.

(D) is the correct answer.

Game 6

On a particular day, exactly six of eight sales agents—Flynn, Gopal, Hiba, Inez, Jeremy, Kiara, Lev, and Ming—will be scheduled to work one of three shifts—Morning, Afternoon, and Evening—at the department store. Exactly two sales agents will be scheduled to work each shift, and no sales agent is scheduled to work more than one shift that day. The schedule for the day must conform to the following conditions:

The Morning shift is the only shift for which Ming can be scheduled.

If both Gopal and Kiara are scheduled to work, then Gopal must work an earlier shift than Kiara.

Neither Jeremy nor Lev nor Ming can be scheduled to work the same shift as Kiara.

If Hiba is scheduled to work the Morning shift, then Lev must be scheduled to work the Morning shift.

If Gopal is not scheduled to work that day, then Inez is scheduled for the Afternoon shift.

---

1. Which one of the following is an acceptable work schedule for the sales agents?

   (A) Morning: Flynn, Kiara
       Afternoon: Jeremy, Lev
       Evening: Hiba, Inez
   (B) Morning: Gopal, Ming
       Afternoon: Hiba, Inez
       Evening: Kiara, Flynn
   (C) Morning: Gopal, Flynn
       Afternoon: Hiba, Kiara
       Evening: Inez, Ming
   (D) Morning: Gopal, Ming
       Afternoon: Jeremy, Kiara
       Evening: Hiba, Lev
   (E) Morning: Flynn, Hiba
       Afternoon: Gopal, Lev
       Evening: Inez, Kiara

2. Which one of the following is a pair of sales agents who CANNOT be scheduled to work the Morning shift?

   (A) Flynn and Ming
   (B) Inez and Kiara
   (C) Kiara and Flynn
   (D) Gopal and Inez
   (E) Jeremy and Ming

3. If Kiara is scheduled to work the Morning shift, then which one of the following must be false?

   (A) Jeremy and Hiba are both scheduled to work the Evening shift.
   (B) Hiba and Inez are both scheduled to work the Afternoon shift.
   (C) Hiba and Lev are both scheduled to work the Evening shift.
   (D) Inez and Hiba are both scheduled to work the Evening shift.
   (E) Jeremy and Inez are both scheduled to work the Afternoon shift.

4. If neither Gopal nor Lev is scheduled to work any shift, then which one of the following must be false?

   (A) Flynn and Ming are scheduled to work the Morning shift.
   (B) Hiba and Jeremy are scheduled to work the Evening shift.
   (C) Flynn and Jeremy are scheduled work to the Evening shift.
   (D) Inez and Jeremy are scheduled to work the Afternoon shift.
   (E) Flynn and Kiara are scheduled to work the Evening shift.

5. If Hiba and Kiara are scheduled to work the Morning and Afternoon shifts, respectively, then each of the following must be true EXCEPT:

(A) Lev is scheduled to work the Morning shift.
(B) Flynn is scheduled to work the Evening shift.
(C) Inez is scheduled to work the Evening shift.
(D) M is not scheduled to work any shift.
(E) G is not scheduled to work any shift.

6. Each of following must be false EXCEPT:

(A) Neither Gopal nor Inez is scheduled to work any shift.
(B) Lev and Kiara are both scheduled to work the Evening shift.
(C) Hiba and Ming are both scheduled to work the Morning shift.
(D) Gopal and Kiara are both scheduled to work the Afternoon shift.
(E) Neither Inez nor Kiara are scheduled to work any shift.

STEP 1 Visualize and draw the diagram.

Morning	Afternoon	Evening	OUT
_ _	_ _	_ _	_ _

STEP 2 List the components and ascertain the ratio and/or distribution.

Components: F, G, H, I, J, K, L, M

Distribution: fixed

STEP 3 Symbolize the clues.

Clue 1   M ≠ afternoon and evening

Clue 2   G and K → G...K; K...G → G and K

Clue 3   a) J → ~K; K → ~J
              b) L → ~K; K → ~L
              c) M → ~K; K → ~M

Clue 4 H_{Morn} → L_{Morn}; $\sim L_{Morn}$ → $\sim H_{Morn}$

Clue 5 $\sim G$ → I_{After}; $\sim I_{After}$ → G

STEP 4 Make deductions.

Deduction 1: Place Clue 1 into the chart.

Morning	~M Afternoon	~M Evening	OUT
_ _	_ _	_ _	_ _

STEP 5 Tackle the questions.

Question order: 1, 3, 4, 5, 2, and then 6.

Answer Key

1. **B**   2. **B**   3. **D**   4. **C**   5. **C**   6. **E**

Answers

Question 1 (catch-a-clue)

- Clue 1 eliminates answer choice C.
- Clue 2 doesn't eliminate any answer choices.
- Clue 3 eliminates answer choice D.

- Clue 4 eliminates answer choice E.
- Clue 5 eliminates answer choice A.

(B) is the correct answer.

Question 3 (restricted, "must-be-false")

1. Place K in the Morning group.
2. By operation of Clue 2, G must be placed in the out-column.
3. By operation of Clue 5, I must be placed in the Afternoon group.
4. By operation of Clue 3c), M cannot be placed in the Morning group and, therefore, by operation of Clue 1 must be placed in the out-column.
5. By operation of Clues 3a) and 3b), neither J nor L can be placed in the Morning group.
6. By operation of Clue 4, H cannot be placed in the Morning group.
7. The only remaining component available for the Morning group (F) must, therefore, be placed in the Morning group.
8. The remaining components (L, H, J) can be placed interchangeably in the three remaining slots in the Afternoon and Evening groups.

| | $\sim$M | $\sim$M | |
Morning	Afternoon	Evening	OUT
$\sim$J$_5$ $\sim$L$_5$ $\sim$H$_6$			
$\underline{K}_1$ $\underline{F}_7$	$\underline{I}_3$ $\underline{L/H/J}_8$	$\underline{L/H/J}_8$ $\underline{L/H/J}_8$	$\underline{G}_2$ $\underline{M}_4$

(D) is the correct answer.

Question 4 (restricted, "must-be-false")

1. Place both G and L in the out-column.
2. By operation of Clue 1, M must be placed in the Morning group.
3. By operation of Clue 5, I must be placed in the Afternoon group.
4. By operation of Clue 4, H cannot be placed in the Morning group.
5. By operation of Clue 3, K cannot be placed in the Morning group.
6. The only two available components remaining for the Morning group are F and J.

| | $\sim$M | $\sim$M | |
Morning	Afternoon	Evening	OUT
$\sim$H$_4$ $\sim$K$_5$			
$\underline{M}_2$ $\underline{F/J}_6$	$\underline{I}_3$ —	— —	$\underline{G}_1$ $\underline{L}_1$

(C) is the correct answer.

Question 5 (restricted, "must-be-true-EXCEPT")

1. Place H in the Morning group and K in the Afternoon group.
2. By operation of Clue 4, L must be placed in the Morning group.
3. By operation of Clue 2, G must be placed in the out-column.
4. By operation of Clue 5, I must be placed in the Afternoon group.
5. By operation of Clue 1, M must be placed in the out-column.
6. The only two remaining components (F and J) must, therefore, be placed in the Evening group.

Morning	Afternoon	Evening	OUT
H_1 L_2	K_1 I_4	F_6 J_6	G_3 M_5

(C) is the correct answer.

Question 2 (unrestricted, "cannot-be-true")

- This question is answerable, in part, by reviewing in the prior workouts.
- The solution to question 3 shows that it is possible to have K and F in the Morning group, so eliminate answer choice C.
- Likewise, the solution to question 4 shows that it is possible to have F and M, as well as J and M, in the Morning group, so eliminate answer choices A and E.
- Try answer choice B:
  - Place K and I in the Morning group.
  - By operation of Clue 2, G must be placed in the out-column.
  - By operation of Clue 6, I must be placed in the Afternoon group. However, this is not possible because I has already been placed in the Morning group. This does not work.

(B) is the correct answer.

Question 6 (unrestricted, "must-be-false-EXCEPT")

- This question is completely answerable by reviewing our clues.
- Answer choice A violates Clue 5.
- Answer choice B violates Clue 3.
- Answer choice C violates Clue 4.
- Answer choice D violates Clue 2.

(E) is the correct answer.

Game 7

Seven children—Claudia, Damon, Fatima, Guillermo, Horatio, Jesse, and Kendra—are members of the Child Actors Society. Each child will be assigned to act in exactly one of two movies: Longshot or Millennium. At least three children will be assigned to each movie. Assignment must conform to the following conditions:

Fatima and Claudia are assigned to different movies.

Damon must be assigned to the same movie as either Guillermo or Jesse, but not both.

Kendra is assigned to Longshot, if Horatio is assigned to Longshot.

1. Which one of the following could be a complete and accurate list of the children assigned to Longshot?

   (A) Fatima, Horatio, Jesse
   (B) Claudia, Guillermo, Jesse
   (C) Horatio, Guillermo, Kendra
   (D) Fatima, Horatio, Kendra
   (E) Claudia, Damon, Guillermo

2. Which one of the following pairs of children CANNOT be among those assigned to Millennium?

   (A) Horatio and Kendra
   (B) Guillermo and Jesse
   (C) Claudia and Kendra
   (D) Fatima and Horatio
   (E) Damon and Fatima

3. If Horatio is assigned to Longshot, which one of the following CANNOT be true?

   (A) Damon is assigned to Millennium.
   (B) Damon is assigned to Longshot.
   (C) Fatima is assigned to Longshot.
   (D) Claudia is assigned to Longshot.
   (E) Jesse is assigned to Millennium.

4. If Claudia and Damon are assigned to Longshot, then each of the following could be true EXCEPT:

   (A) Horatio is assigned to Longshot.
   (B) Guillermo is assigned to Millennium.
   (C) Kendra is assigned to Longshot.
   (D) Kendra is assigned to Millennium.
   (E) Jesse is assigned to Longshot.

5. If Fatima and Kendra are assigned to Millennium, then which one of the following must be false?

   (A) Damon and Jesse are assigned to the same movie.
   (B) Horatio and Guillermo are assigned to the same movie.
   (C) Claudia and Jesse are assigned to the same movie.
   (D) Damon and Horatio are assigned to the same movie.
   (E) Horatio and Jesse are assigned to the same movie.

STEP 1 Visualize and draw the diagram.

Longshot	Millennium
_ _ _ ...	_ _ _ ...

STEP 2 List the components and ascertain the ratio and/or distribution.

Components: C, D, F, G, H, J, K

Distribution: Min: 3; Max: 4

STEP 3 Symbolize the clues.

Clue 1 $F \rightarrow \sim C$; $C \rightarrow \sim F$

Clue 2 $D \rightarrow G$ or J; $D \rightarrow \sim(G$ and $J)$

Clue 3 $H_L \rightarrow K_L$; $K_M \rightarrow H_M$

STEP 4 Make deductions.

Deduction 1: From Clue 2, you can deduce that G and J are not in the same group. You know this because D must be accompanied by either G or J but not both.

STEP 5 **Tackle the questions.**

Question order: 1, 3, 4, 5, and then 2.

Answer Key

1. **E**   2. **B**   3. **B**   4. **A**   5. **D**

Answers

Question 1 (catch-a-clue)

- Clue 1 eliminates answer choice C.
- Clue 2 eliminates answer choices B and D.
- Clue 3 eliminates answer choice A.

(E) is the correct answer.

Question 3 (restricted, "cannot-be-true")

1. Place H in the Longshot group.
2. By operation of Clue 3, K must be placed in the Longshot group.
3. By operation of Clue 1, F and C are placed in the Longshot and the Millennium groups interchangeably.

4. By operation of Clue 2, D must be accompanied by either G or J. Longshot no longer has the requisite number of slots to accommodate D and either G or J. Accordingly, D must be placed in the Millennium group with either D or J.

Longshot	Millennium
H_1 K_2 F/C_3 G/J_4	F/C_3 D_4 J/G_4

(B) is the correct answer.

Question 4 (restricted, "could-be-true-EXCEPT")

1. Place C and D in the Longshot group.
2. By operation of Clue 1, F must be placed in the Millennium group.
3. By operation of Clue 2, G and J must be placed in the Longshot and the Millennium groups interchangeably.
4. By operation of Clue 3, if H is placed in the Longshot group, K must also be placed in the Longshot group. The Longshot group no longer has the requisite number of slots to accommodate H and K. Therefore, H must be placed in the Millennium group.
5. The remaining component (K) can be placed in either the Longshot or the Millennium Groups.

Longshot	Millennium
C_1 D_1 G/J_3 $(K)_5$	F_2 J/G_3 H_4 $(K)_5$

(A) is the correct answer.

Question 5 (restricted, "must-be-false")

1. Place F and K in the Millennium group.
2. By operation of Clue 1, C must be placed in the Longshot group.
3. By operation of the contrapositive of Clue 3, H must be placed in the Millennium group.
4. With just one possible slot available in the Millennium group and by operation of Clue 2, D must be placed in the Longshot group.
5. Furthermore, by operation of Clue 2, G and J must be placed in the Longshot and Millennium groups interchangeably.

Longshot	Millennium
C_2 D_4 G/J_5	F_1 K_1 H_3 J/G_5

(D) is the correct answer.

Question 2 (unrestricted, "cannot-be-true")

This question is completely answerable by the deduction. G and J cannot be in the same group.

(B) is the correct answer.

Game 8

In order to finish basic training, exactly eight Marine recruits—Miguel, Nigel, Oleg, Percy, Quincy, Roland, Sasha, and Tovah—will finish the obstacle course. Each marine recruit will finish the obstacle course one at a time, consecutively, in conformity with the following constraints:

Nigel and Tovah finish earlier than Quincy.
Roland and Sasha finish earlier than Oleg.
Miguel and Percy finish later than Sasha.
Quincy finishes earlier than Oleg.

1. Which one of the following could be the order in which the Marine recruits finish the obstacle course, from earliest to latest?

   (A) Tovah, Sasha, Quincy, Nigel, Roland, Oleg, Percy, Miguel
   (B) Sasha, Roland, Nigel, Tovah, Oleg, Quincy, Miguel, Percy
   (C) Roland, Nigel, Tovah, Sasha, Quincy, Oleg, Miguel, Percy
   (D) Nigel, Roland, Tovah, Quincy, Percy, Sasha, Miguel, Oleg
   (E) Sasha, Tovah, Nigel, Quincy, Percy, Oleg, Roland, Miguel

2. Which one of the following CANNOT be the Marine recruit that finishes sixth?

   (A) Sasha
   (B) Tovah
   (C) Quincy
   (D) Miguel
   (E) Roland

3. If Miguel finishes after Percy, but before Quincy, then which one of the following must be true?

   (A) Nigel finishes third.
   (B) Roland finishes third.
   (C) Tovah finishes first.
   (D) Sasha finishes second
   (E) Oleg finishes eighth.

4. If Oleg finishes sixth, then each of the following could be true EXCEPT:

   (A) Sasha finishes first.
   (B) Percy finishes fifth.
   (C) Nigel finishes second.
   (D) Miguel finishes eighth.
   (E) Roland finishes fourth.

5. If Quincy finishes third, then which one of the following CANNOT be true?

   (A) Both Sasha and Tovah finish earlier than Nigel.
   (B) Both Roland and Sasha finish earlier than Percy.
   (C) Both Miguel and Percy finish earlier than Roland.
   (D) Both Oleg and Percy finish earlier than Miguel.
   (E) Both Tovah and Miguel finish earlier than Roland.

6. Which one of the following must be true?

   (A) Roland finishes earlier than Quincy.
   (B) Tovah finishes earlier than Nigel.
   (C) Quincy finishes earlier than Miguel.
   (D) Nigel finishes earlier than Oleg.
   (E) Oleg finishes earlier than Percy.

STEP 1 Symbolize the clues.

| Clue 1 | N...Q |
| | T...Q |

| Clue 2 | R...O |
| | S...O |

| Clue 3 | S...M |
| | S...P |

| Clue 4 | Q...O |

STEP 2 Connect the individual chains to create the longest chain.

T...Q...O

STEP 3 Attach each of the remaining clues to the baseline.

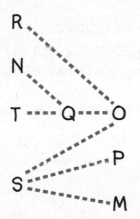

STEP 4 Tackle the questions.

Answer Key

1. **C**   2. **A**   3. **E**   4. **B**   5. **A**   6. **D**

Answers

Question 1 (catch-a-clue)

- Clue 1 eliminates answer choice A.
- Clue 2 eliminates answer choice E.
- Clue 3 eliminates answer choice D.
- Clue 4 eliminates answer choice B.

(C) is the correct answer.

Question 2 (unrestricted, "cannot-be-true")

- S has a minimum of three components (O, M, and P) after it and, as such, cannot be sixth.
- T has a minimum of two components (O and Q) after it. T can be sixth.
- Q has a minimum of one component (O) after it. Q can be sixth.
- M can finish anytime except first.
- R can finish anytime except eighth.

(A) is the correct answer.

Question 3 (restricted, "must-be-true")

- The first/last rule (pay attention to those components that can be first and those that can be last) indicates that there are only three components (O, M, and P) that can be eighth/last.
- The question's additional restriction eliminates the possibility of M and P finishing eighth. This leaves O as the only component that can be eighth.

(E) is the correct answer.

Question 4 (restricted, "could-be-true-EXCEPT")

- O has a minimum of five components (N, Q, R, S, and T) that must finish earlier than O.
- Since the additional restriction places O sixth, only those five components finish earlier than O.
- The two remaining components (P and M) must, therefore, finish after O. As such, P cannot be fifth.

(B) is the correct answer.

Question 5 (restricted, "cannot-be-true")

- Q has a minimum of two components (N and T) that must finish earlier than Q.
- Since the additional restriction places Q third, only those two components finish earlier than Q.
- N and T finish either first or second interchangeably.
- Therefore, S cannot finish before N.

(A) is the correct answer.

Question 6 (unrestricted, "must-be-true")

The zigzag rule (*you can only ascertain the relative position of two components when you can connect them without switching directions*) shows that N finishes earlier than Q, and Q finishes earlier than O.

(D) is the correct answer.

Game 9

In a single day, a housekeeper will perform exactly seven household chores—cooking, dusting, grocery shopping, laundry, mopping, sweeping, and vacuuming. Each chore will be performed consecutively, one at a time, in conformity with the following constraints:

Dusting is performed immediately before mopping.

If mopping is the seventh chore performed, then cooking is performed immediately after sweeping.

Vacuuming is performed either second or fourth.

Laundry is performed at some time before grocery shopping and at some time after sweeping.

1. Which one of the following could be the order, from first to last, in which the chores are performed?

   (A) sweeping, cooking, vacuuming, dusting, mopping, laundry, grocery shopping
   (B) cooking, mopping, dusting, vacuuming, sweeping, laundry, grocery shopping
   (C) sweeping, vacuuming, laundry, cooking, dusting, mopping, grocery shopping
   (D) sweeping, vacuuming, grocery shopping, laundry, dusting, mopping, cooking
   (E) cooking, laundry, sweeping, vacuuming, grocery shopping, dusting, mopping

2. Which one of the following chores CANNOT be performed fourth?

   (A) Vacuuming
   (B) Sweeping
   (C) Grocery shopping
   (D) Mopping
   (E) Dusting

3. If dusting is the sixth chore performed, then each of the following must be true EXCEPT:

   (A) Grocery shopping is the fifth chore performed.
   (B) Mopping is the seventh chore performed.
   (C) Vacuuming is the fourth chore performed.
   (D) Laundry is the third chore performed.
   (E) Cooking is the first chore performed.

4. If grocery shopping is the fourth chore performed, which one of the following must be false?

   (A) Mopping is the sixth chore performed.
   (B) Laundry is the third chore performed.
   (C) Sweeping is the first chore performed.
   (D) Cooking is the fifth chore performed.
   (E) Vacuuming is the second chore performed.

5. Which one of the following pairs of chores CANNOT be performed third and fifth, respectively?

   (A) cooking and sweeping
   (B) laundry and grocery shopping
   (C) sweeping and cooking
   (D) dusting and grocery shopping
   (E) mopping and cooking

Visualize and draw the diagram.

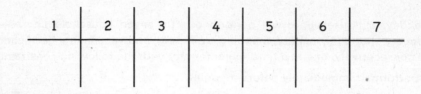

List the components and ascertain the ratio and/or distribution.

Components: C, D, G, L, M, S, V

Ratio: one-to-one

STEP 3 Symbolize the clues.

Clue 1 $\boxed{\text{DM}}$

Clue 2 $M_7 \rightarrow \boxed{\text{SC}}$; $\boxed{\text{S̶C̶}} \rightarrow {}^\sim M_7$

Clue 3   V = 2 or 4

Clue 4   S ... L ... G

STEP 4 Make deductions.

Deduction 1: Clue 1 makes it clear that...

a) D cannot be performed in 7.
b) M cannot be performed in 1.

Deduction 2: From Clue 3, you deduce that V cannot be performed in 1, 3, 5, 6, or 7.

Deduction 3: Clue 4 makes it clear that...

a) S cannot be performed in 6 or 7.
b) L cannot be performed in 1 or 7.
c) G cannot be performed in 1 or 2.

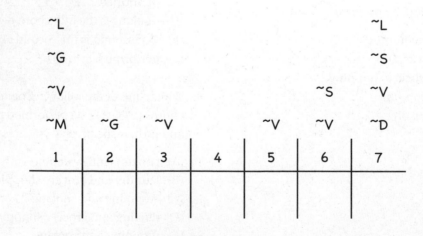

Question order: 1, 3, 4, 2, and then 5.

Answer Key

1. **C**   2. **B**   3. **E**   4. **D**   5. **D**

Answers

Question 1 (catch-a-clue)

- Clue 1 eliminates answer choice B.
- Clue 2 eliminates answer choice E.
- Clue 3 eliminates answer choice A.
- Clue 4 eliminates answer choice D.

(C) is the correct answer.

Question 3 (restricted, "must-be-true-EXCEPT")

1. Place D in slot 6.
2. By operation of Clue 1, M must be placed into slot 7.
3. By operation of Clue 2, S must be placed immediately before C, so C cannot be placed in slot 1.
4. Pivot to the most restricted slot—slot 1. The only available component for slot 1 is S. Place S in slot 1.
5. Again, by operation of Clue 2, C must be placed in slot 2.
6. By operation of Clue 3, V must be placed in slot 4.
7. By operation of Clue 4, L and G must be placed in slots 3 and 5, respectively.

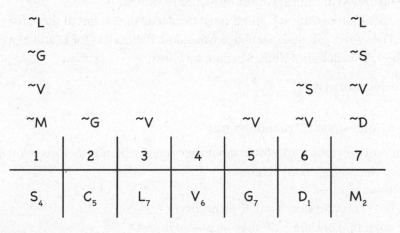

(E) is the correct answer.

Question 4 (restricted, "must-be-false")

1. Place G in slot 4.
2. By operation of Clue 3, V must be placed in slot 2.
3. By operation of Clue 4, S and L must be placed in slots 1 and 3, respectively.

4. By operation of Clue 1, D and M must be placed in either slots 5 and 6, respectively, or slots 6 and 7, respectively.

5. By operation of the contrapositive of Clue 2, D and M cannot be placed in slots 6 and 7, respectively. Therefore, D and M must be placed in slots 5 and 6, respectively.

6. The only remaining component (C) must be placed in the only remaining slot (7).

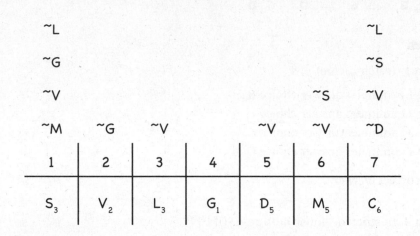

(D) is the correct answer.

Question 2 (unrestricted, "cannot-be-true")

- This question is answerable, in part, by reviewing the prior workouts.

- A review of the workouts to questions to 3 and 4 shows that both V and G can be performed fourth, so eliminate answer choices A and C.

- Try answer choice B:
  - Place S in slot 4.
  - By operation of Clue 3, V must be placed in slot 2.
  - By operation of Clue 4, L and G must be placed in two out of the three slots (5, 6, or 7). Therefore, you no longer have two side-by-side slots for D and M as required by Clue 1. This does not work. S cannot be fourth.

(B) is the correct answer.

Question 5 (unrestricted, "cannot-be-true")

- A review of previous work eliminates answer choice B only. (See question 3.) You must try each remaining answer choice.

- Try answer choice D.
  - Place D and G in slots 3 and 5, respectively.
  - By operation of Clue 1, M must be placed in slot 4.
  - By operation of Clue 3, V must be placed in slot 2.
  - By operation of Clue 4, S and L must be performed earlier than G. However, you have only one (slot 1), not two, available slots before G. This does not work.

(D) is the correct answer.

Game 10

At a tennis tournament, exactly six amateurs—Alex, Boyd, Catisha, Dennis, Edgar, and Foster—will play in at least one of four consecutive matches. Exactly two amateurs will play in each match in accordance with the following conditions:

Boyd does not play against Edgar in any of the matches.

Foster will play in the first and second matches only.

The winner of the second match must play in the third match.

1. Which one of the following could be an accurate list of the amateurs who play in each of the four matches?

   (A) First match: Edgar, Foster; second match: Dennis, Foster; third match: Alex, Dennis; fourth match: Boyd, Catisha

   (B) First match: Alex, Foster; second match: Dennis, Foster; third match: Catisha, Dennis; fourth match: Boyd, Edgar

   (C) First match: Dennis, Edgar; second match: Catisha, Foster; third match: Alex, Catisha; fourth match: Boyd, Foster

   (D) First match: Alex, Foster; second match: Boyd, Foster; third match: Catisha, Dennis; fourth match: Dennis, Edgar

   (E) First match: Edgar, Foster; second match: Catisha, Foster; third match: Alex, Boyd; fourth match: Catisha, Dennis

2. Which one of the following could be true?

   (A) Alex plays in the first and third matches.

   (B) Foster plays the same opponent in both the first and the second matches.

   (C) Catisha wins the second match.

   (D) Edgar plays in the second match, and Boyd plays in the third match.

   (E) Foster wins the second match.

3. If Alex plays in the first match and Boyd plays in the second match, then which one of the following must be false?

   (A) Catisha plays Edgar in the fourth match.

   (B) Boyd plays Catisha in the third match.

   (C) Catisha plays Dennis in the fourth match.

   (D) Dennis plays Edgar in the fourth match.

   (E) Boyd plays Dennis in the third match.

4. If Alex and Catisha play in the fourth match, then which one of the following must be true?

   (A) Dennis plays in the third match.

   (B) Dennis plays in the second match.

   (C) Edgar plays in the first match.

   (D) Edgar plays in the second match.

   (E) Boyd plays in the third match.

5. If Catisha and Dennis play in the third match, then each of the following could be true EXCEPT:

   (A) Boyd plays in the fourth match.

   (B) Edgar plays in the first match.

   (C) Alex plays in the fourth match.

   (D) Dennis plays in the second match.

   (E) Alex plays in the first match.

STEP 1 Visualize and draw the diagram.

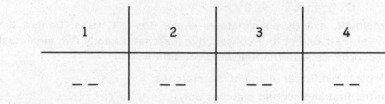

STEP 2 List the components and ascertain the ratio and/or distribution.

Components: A, B, C, D, E, F

Distribution:

- Each component must be placed at least once.
- There arc six components and eight slots.
- One component (F) occupies exactly two slots.
- Therefore, one more component (besides F) must occupy exactly two slots.

STEP 3 Symbolize the clues.

Clue 1 B → ~E; E → ~B

Clue 2 F ≠ 1 and 2 (F is banned from Matches 2 and 3)

Clue 3 Place directly into diagram.

~F   ~F

1	2	3	4
F _	F _	_ _	_ _

STEP 4 Make deductions.

Deduction 1: From Clue 3, you can deduce that…

a) F cannot win Match 2, as F cannot be placed in Match 3.

b) The component that faces F in Match 2 wins and is the other component that occupies two slots

STEP 5 **Tackle the questions.**

Question order: 1, 3, 4, 5, and then 2.

Answer Key

Answers

Question 1 (catch a cluc)

- Clue 1 eliminates answer choice B.
- Clue 2 eliminates answer choice C.
- Clue 3 eliminates answer choices D and E.

(A) is the correct answer.

Question 3 (restricted, "must-be-false")

1. Place A in Match 1 and B in Match 2.
2. By operation of Deduction 1, B must be placed in Match 3.
3. By operation of Clue 1, E cannot be placed in Match 3 and must, therefore, be placed in Match 4.
4. The remaining components (C and D) must be placed in Matches 3 and 4 interchangeably.

		$\sim$F	$\sim$F
1	2	3	4
$\underline{F}$ $\underline{A}_1$	$\underline{F}$ $\underline{B}_1$	$\underline{B}_2$ $\underline{C/D}_4$	$\underline{E}_3$ $\underline{D/C}_4$

(C) is the correct answer.

Question 4 (restricted, "must-be-true")

1. Place A and C in Match 4.
2. By operation of deduction 1(b), neither A or C can be placed in Match 3. The remaining components (B, D, E) must occupy the remaining slots in Matches 1 and 2, as well as, both slots in Match 3. By operation of Clue 1, B and E cannot face each other in Match 3. Therefore, D must occupy one of the slots in Match 3 with either B or E.

		$\sim$F	$\sim$F
1	2	3	4
F __	F __	$\underline{D}_2$ $\underline{B/E}_2$	$\underline{A}_1$ $\underline{C}_1$

(A) is the correct answer.

Question 5 (restricted, "could-be-true-EXCEPT")

1. Place C and D in Match 3.
2. By operation of Deduction 1, either C or D must be placed in the remaining slot in Match 2.
3. By operation of Clue 1, B and E must be placed in Matches 1 and 4 interchangeably.
4. The remaining component (A) must be placed in the only available slot in Match 4.

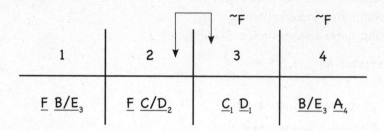

(E) is the correct answer.

Question 2 (unrestricted, "could-be-true")

- This question is completely answerable by reviewing Deduction 1.
- Also, a review of your work in question 3 shows that Catisha could be the winner of the second match.

(C) is the correct answer.

Game 11

Sharon visits the cafeteria salad bar for lunch. She will select at least six, but no more than seven items from among the nine items—beets, carrots, eggs, feta, mushrooms, nuts, radishes, peppers, and tomatoes—available at the salad bar. The selection of items must meet the following conditions:

If either mushrooms or tomatoes are selected, then the other must also be selected.

If beets are selected, then feta is not selected.

If nuts are not selected, then tomatoes are selected.

If radishes are selected, then eggs are selected.

If eggs are selected, then beets are selected.

1. Which one of the following could be a complete and accurate list of the items selected for the salad?

   (A) Beets, Eggs, Feta, Mushrooms, Radishes, Tomatoes
   (B) Beets, Eggs, Mushrooms, Nuts, Peppers, Radishes
   (C) Beets, Carrots, Mushrooms, Peppers, Radishes, Nuts, Tomatoes
   (D) Carrots, Eggs, Feta, Mushrooms, Peppers, Radishes, Tomatoes
   (E) Beets, Carrots, Eggs, Nuts, Peppers, Radishes

2. Which one of the following CANNOT be true?

   (A) Neither Beets nor Mushrooms are selected.
   (B) Neither Eggs nor Feta are selected.
   (C) Neither Mushrooms nor Tomatoes are selected.
   (D) Both Nuts and Tomatoes are selected.
   (E) Neither Radishes nor Eggs are selected.

3. If Eggs are not selected, which one of the following must be true?

   (A) Feta is selected.
   (B) Carrots are selected.
   (C) Beets are not selected.
   (D) Peppers are not selected.
   (E) Nuts are not selected.

4. If Nuts are not selected, then each of the following could be true EXCEPT:

   (A) Radishes are not selected.
   (B) Carrots are selected.
   (C) Peppers are selected.
   (D) Beets are not selected.
   (E) Mushrooms are selected.

5. If Eggs and Mushrooms are selected, then which one of the following must be false?

   (A) Radishes are not selected.
   (B) Nuts are selected.
   (C) Neither Carrots nor Peppers are selected.
   (D) Neither Radishes nor Beets are selected.
   (E) Neither Peppers nor Radishes are selected.

6. Which one of the following is a pair of items of which Sharon must select at least one?

   (A) Beets, Feta
   (B) Nuts, Peppers
   (C) Eggs, Feta
   (D) Peppers, Radishes
   (E) Carrots, Peppers

STEP 1 Visualize and draw the diagram.

IN | OUT

_ _ _ _ _ ... | _ _ ...

STEP 2 List the components and ascertain the ratio and/or distribution.

Components: B, C, E, F, M, N, R, P, T

Distribution: Min—6; Max—7

STEP 3 Symbolize the clues.

Clue 1   M ↔ T; ~M ↔ ~T

Clue 2   B → ~F; F → ~B

Clue 3   ~N → T; ~T → N

Clue 4   R → E; ~E → ~R

Clue 5   E → B; ~B → ~E

STEP 4 Make deductions.

First link Clue 3 and Clue 1: ~N → T and T → M

Deduction 1: ~N → M

Next, link the contrapositive of Clue 4 and Clue 5: ~B → ~E and ~E → ~R.

Deduction 2: ~B → ~E → ~R (If B is out, then the out-column is filled.)

Finally, link the contrapositive of Clue 2, Clue 4, and Clue 5:

F → ~B; ~B → ~E and ~E → ~R; F → ~R

STEP 5 **Tackle the questions.**

Question order: 1, 3, 4, 5, 2, and then 6.

Answer Key

Answers

Question 1 (catch-a-clue)

- Clue 1 eliminates answer choice B.
- Clue 2 eliminates answer choice A.
- Clue 3 does not eliminate any answer choices.
- Clue 4 eliminates answer choice C.
- Clue 5 eliminates answer choice D.

(E) is the correct answer.

Question 3 (restricted, "must-be-true")

1. Place E in the out-column.
2. By operation of Clue 4, R must be placed in the out-column.
3. By operation of Clue 2, B and F cannot both be in the in-column together. At least one of the pair must be placed in the out-column. Only one possible slot remains open. Therefore, that slot must be occupied by either B or F with the other placed in the in-column.
4. The out-column has been filled. Each remaining component (C, M, N, T, P) must be placed in the in-column.

IN	OUT
B/F$_3$ C$_4$ M$_4$ N$_4$ T$_4$ P$_4$	E$_1$ R$_2$ F/B$_3$

(B) is the correct answer.

Question 4 (restricted, "could-be-true-EXCEPT")

1. Place N in the out-column.
2. By operation of Clue 3, T must be placed in the in-column.
3. By operation of Clue 1, M must be placed in the in-column.
4. By operation of Deduction 2, B must be placed in the in-column.
5. By operation of Clue 2, F must be placed in the out-column.

IN	OUT
T$_2$ M$_3$ B$_4$ _ _ ...	N$_1$ F$_5$ ...

(D) is the correct answer.

Question 5 (restricted, "must-be-false")

1. Place E and M in the in-column.
2. By operation of Clue 1, T must be placed in the in-column.
3. By operation of Clue 5, B must be placed in the in-column.
4. By operation of Clue 2, F must be placed in the out-column.
5. At least two of the remaining components (C, N, P, R) must be placed in the in-column.

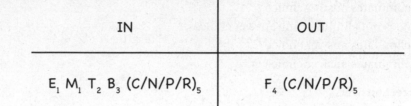

IN	OUT
E_1 M_1 T_2 B_3 $(C/N/P/R)_5$	F_4 $(C/N/P/R)_5$

(D) is the correct answer.

Question 2 (unrestricted, "cannot-be-true")

- This question is answerable, in part, by reviewing prior workouts.
- From the workout of question 3, you can see that answer choices B, D, and E can be eliminated.
- The workout of question 1 shows that answer choice C can be true, so C can be eliminated.
- Answer choice A cannot be true. If B and M are both placed in the out-column, then by operation of Clue 2, F is placed in the out-column. By operation of the contrapositive of Clue 1, T is placed in the out-column, bringing the total components in the out-column to four.

The correct answer choice is (A).

Question 6 (unrestricted, "must-be-true")

- This question is answerable by reviewing your deductions.
- By operation of Deduction 2, if B is placed in the out-column, then E and R are placed in the out-column as well.
- The out-column is filled, and there is no available slot for component F.

(A) is the correct answer.

Game 12

At a community voter registration drive, exactly eight local residents—G, J, K, L, M, N, P, and S—will register to vote for the first time. Three will register as Democrats, three will register as Republicans, and two will register as Independents. No resident can register for more than one political party. The following conditions must be met:

If M registers as a Republican, then K registers as an Independent.

If G registers as a Democrat, then L registers as a Democrat.

Either J or K, but not both, register as an Independent.

K does not register for the same party as P; nor does N register for the same party as S; nor does L register for the same party as M.

1. Which one of the following could be an accurate matching of residents to the political party in which they were registered?

(A) Democrat: K, G, L
   Republican: M, N, P
   Independent: J, S
(B) Democrat: G, L, S
   Republican: J, M, P
   Independent: K, N
(C) Democrat: G, M, P
   Republican: K, L, N
   Independent: J, S
(D) Democrat: J, N, P
   Republican: G, L, M
   Independent: K, S
(E) Democrat: G, L, N
   Republican: J, M, S
   Independent: K, P

2. Which one of the following is a pair of residents that CANNOT register as Democrats?

(A) J and L
(B) K and S
(C) M and N
(D) G and K
(E) L and P

3. If P registers as an Independent, then each of the following must be true EXCEPT:

(A) L registers as a Republican.
(B) N registers as a Democrat.
(C) M registers as a Democrat.
(D) G registers as a Republican.
(E) J registers as an Independent.

4. If G and J both register as Democrats, then which one of the following must be false?

(A) P registers as a Republican.
(B) M registers as an Independent.
(C) S registers as a Republican.
(D) N registers as an Independent.
(E) S registers as an Independent.

5. If J and L both register as Independents, then each of the following could be true EXCEPT:

(A) Both K and S register as Republicans.
(B) Both G and S register as Republicans.
(C) Neither M nor S registers as Democrats.
(D) Neither K nor N registers as Democrats.
(E) Neither G nor L registers as Democrats.

STEP 1 Visualize and draw the diagram.

Democrat	Republican	Independent
– – –	– – –	– –

STEP 2 List the components and ascertain the ratio and/or distribution.

Components: G, J, K, L, M, N, P, S

Distribution: fixed

STEP 3 Symbolize the clues.

Clue 1 $M_{Rep} \rightarrow K_{Ind}$; $\sim K_{Ind} \rightarrow \sim M_{Rep}$

Clue 2 $G_{Dem} \rightarrow L_{Dem}$; $\sim L_{Dem} \rightarrow \sim G_{Dem}$

Clue 3   a) $\sim K_{Ind} \rightarrow J_{Ind}$; $\sim J_{Ind} \rightarrow K_{Ind}$
b) $K_{Ind} \rightarrow \sim J_{Ind}$; $J_{Ind} \rightarrow \sim K_{Ind}$

Clue 4   a) $K \rightarrow \sim P$; $P \rightarrow \sim K$
b) $N \rightarrow \sim S$; $S \rightarrow \sim N$
c) $L \rightarrow \sim M$; $M \rightarrow \sim L$

STEP 4 Make deductions.

First link Clue 1 and Clue 3b): $M_{Rep} \rightarrow K_{Ind}$ and $K_{Ind} \rightarrow \sim J_{Ind}$

Deduction 1: $M_{Rep} \rightarrow \sim J_{Ind}$

STEP 5 **Tackle the questions.**

Question order: 1, 3, 4, 5, and then 2.

Answer Key

1. **B**   2. **D**   3. **B**   4. **B**   5. **C**

Answers

Question 1 (catch-a-clue)

- Clue 1 eliminates answer choice A.
- Clue 2 eliminates answer choice C.
- Clue 3 does not eliminate any answer choices.
- Clue 4 eliminates answer choices D and E.

(B) is the correct answer.

Question 3 (restricted, "must-be-true-EXCEPT")

1. Place P in the Independent group.
2. By operation of Clue 4a), K cannot be placed in the Independent group. By operation of Clue 3a), J must be placed in the Independent group.
3. By operation of contrapositive of Clue 1, M cannot be placed in the Republican group. As such, M must be placed in the Democrat group.
4. By operation of Clue 4c), L cannot be placed in the Democrat group and must, therefore, be placed in the Republican group.
5. By operation of the contrapositive to Clue 2, G cannot be placed in the Democrat group and must, therefore, be placed in the Republican group.
6. By operation of Clue 4b), N and S must be placed in the Democrat and Republican groups interchangeably.
7. The remaining component (K) must be placed in the only available slot in the Democrat group.

Democrat	Republican	Independent
M_3 N/S_6 K_7	L_4 G_5 S/N_6	P_1 J_2

(B) is the correct answer.

Question 4 (restricted, "must-be-false")

1. Place G and J in the Democrat group.
2. By operation of Clue 2, L must be placed in the Democrat group.
3. By operation of the contrapositive of Clue 3a), K must be placed in the Independent group.
4. By operation of Clue 4a), P must be placed in the Republican group.
5. By operation of Clue 4b), N and S must be placed in the Republican and Independent groups interchangeably.
6. The remaining component (M) must be placed in the only available slot in the Republican group.

Democrat	Republican	Independent
G_1 J_1 L_2	P_4 N/S_5 M_6	K_3 S/N_5

(B) is the correct answer.

Question 5 (restricted, "could-be-true-EXCEPT")

1. Place J and L in the Independent group.
2. By operation of the contrapositive of Clue 2, G cannot be placed in the Democrat group. Therefore, G must be placed in the Republican group.
3. By operation of the contrapositive of Clue 1, M cannot be placed in the Republican group and must, therefore, be placed in the Democrat group.
4. By operation of Clue 4a), K and P must be placed in the Democrat and Republican groups interchangeably.
5. By operation of Clue 4b), N and S must be placed in the Democrat and Republican groups interchangeably.

Democrat	Republican	Independent
M_3 K/P_4 N/S_5	G_2 P/K_4 S/N_5	J_1 L_1

(C) is the correct answer.

Question 2 (unrestricted, "cannot-be-true")

- This question is answerable, in part, by reviewing the workouts to prior questions.
- Based on the solution to question 3, each of the pairs listed in answer choices B and C can register as Democrats.
- Based on the solution to question 4, the pair listed in answer choice A can register as Democrats.
- Answer choices D and E remain. Try answer choice D:

  1. Place G and K in the Democrat group.
  2. By operation of Clue 2, L must be placed in the Democrat group.
  3. By operation of Clue 3a), J must be placed in the Independent group.
  4. By operation of the contrapositive of Clue 1, M cannot be placed in the Republican group and must, therefore, be placed in the Independent group.
  5. The remaining components (N, S, P) must be placed in the Republican group, which violates Clue 4b). This does not work.

Democrat	Republican	Independent
G_1 K_1 L_2	N_5 S_5 P_5	J_3 M_4

(D) is the correct answer.

Game 13

Exactly seven job applicants—Cece, Dawn, Felipe, Grace, Jerry, King, and Lina—will be interviewed by a restaurant owner for a new manager's position. Each interview will be conducted one at a time, consecutively, and no two applicants are interviewed more than once. The following conditions must apply:

If Dawn is not interviewed third, she is interviewed fourth.

Lina is interviewed at some time before Jerry.

Cece is interviewed immediately before Jerry or immediately after King.

Felipe is interviewed after either King or Grace, but not after both.

1. Which one of the following could be the order in which the interviews are conducted, from first to last?

   (A) Lina, Cece, Jerry, Grace, Dawn, Felipe, King
   (B) Felipe, Lina, Grace, Dawn, Cece, Jerry, King
   (C) Grace, Jerry, Dawn, Lina, Felipe, King, Cece
   (D) Lina, King, Dawn, Felipe, Cece, Grace, Jerry
   (E) King, Lina, Dawn, Cece, Jerry, Felipe, Grace

2. How many job applicants are there any of which could be interviewed first?

   (A) Three
   (B) Four
   (C) Five
   (D) Six
   (E) Seven

3. If Cece is interviewed third, then which one of the following must be true?

   (A) Jerry is interviewed fifth.
   (B) Felipe is interviewed sixth.
   (C) Lina is interviewed first.
   (D) Jerry is interviewed seventh.
   (E) Grace is interviewed sixth.

4. If King is interviewed immediately before Lina and immediately after Dawn, then each of the following must be true EXCEPT:

   (A) Felipe is interviewed second.
   (B) Cece is interviewed sixth.
   (C) Grace is interviewed second.
   (D) Lina is interviewed fifth.
   (E) Jerry is interviewed seventh.

5. If Jerry is interviewed before Cece, then which one of the following CANNOT be true?

   (A) Felipe is interviewed immediately before Grace.
   (B) Lina is interviewed immediately before King.
   (C) Felipe is interviewed immediately before Lina.
   (D) Dawn is interviewed immediately before Grace.
   (E) Grace is interviewed immediately before Dawn.

6. The order in which the interviews are conducted is completely determined if which one of the following is true?

   (A) Felipe is interviewed sixth.
   (B) Cece is interviewed third.
   (C) Grace is interviewed seventh.
   (D) Lina is interviewed first.
   (E) King is interviewed third.

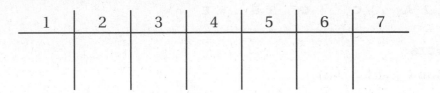

STEP 1 Visualize and draw the diagram.

1	2	3	4	5	6	7

STEP 2 List the components and ascertain the ratio and/or distribution.

Components: C, D, F, G, J, K, L

Ratio: one-to-one

STEP 3 Symbolize the clues.

Clue 1 $\sim D_3 \rightarrow D_4$ (Translation: D = 3 or 4)
              $\sim D_4 \rightarrow \sim D_3$

Clue 2   L ... J

Clue 3 $\boxed{CJ}$ or $\boxed{KC}$

Clue 4   K ... F ... G or G ... F ... K

STEP 4 Make deductions.

Deduction 1: From Clue 1, D = 3 or 4. D cannot be interviewed first, second, fifth, sixth, or seventh.

Deduction 2: From Clue 2, L cannot be interviewed seventh, and J cannot be interviewed first.

Deduction 3: From Clue 4, F cannot be interviewed either first or seventh.

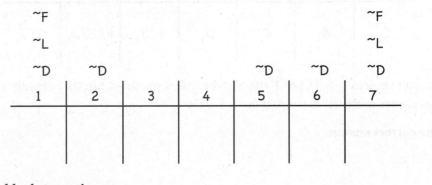

STEP 5 **Tackle the questions.**

Question order: 1, 3, 4, 5, 2, and then 6.

Answer Key

1. **E**   2. **A**   3. **C**   4. **C**   5. **B**   6. **E**

Answers

Question 1 (catch-a-clue)

- Clue 1 eliminates answer choice A.
- Clue 2 eliminates answer choice C.
- Clue 3 eliminates answer choice D.
- Clue 4 eliminates answer choice B.

(E) is the correct answer.

Question 3 (restricted, "must-be-true")

1. Place C in interview slot 3.
2. By operation of Deduction 1, D must be assigned to interview slot 4.
3. By operation of Clue 3, K must be assigned to interview slot 2.
4. By operation of Clue 4, G cannot be assigned to interview slot 1 because F must be sandwiched between G and K. Deductions 1, 2, and 3 ban D, F, and J from interview slot 1. Therefore, L is the only component available for assignment to interview slot 1, so L is assigned to interview slot 1.
5. The remaining components are F, G, and J. By operation of Clue 4, F must be interviewed before G. Therefore, F can be interviewed either fifth or sixth, and G can be interviewed either sixth or seventh. There are no additional restrictions on J, and, accordingly, J can be assigned to the fifth, sixth, or seventh interview slot.

~F						~F
~J						~L
~D	~D			~D	~D	~D
1	2	3	4	5	6	7
L_4	K_3	C_1	D_2	F/J_5	$F/G/J_5$	G/J_5

- Answer choices A, B, D, and E can each be true sometimes, but they are not always true. L is always assigned as the first interview slot.

(C) is the correct answer.

Question 4 (restricted, "must-be-true-EXCEPT")

1. Create a new symbol to illustrate the additional restriction: DKL

2. Link DKL and Clue 2 DKL ... J

3. By operation of Clue 3, C must be interviewed immediately before J. DKL ... CJ

4. By operation of Deduction 1, D must be assigned to interview slot 3. You know this because K, L, C, and J are interviewed after D. D cannot be slotted for the fourth interview.

5. Accordingly, K, L, C, and J must be assigned to the fourth, fifth, sixth, and seventh interview slots, respectively.

6. By operation of Clue 4, G and F must be assigned to interview slots 1 and 2, respectively. This is because F must be sandwiched between G and K.

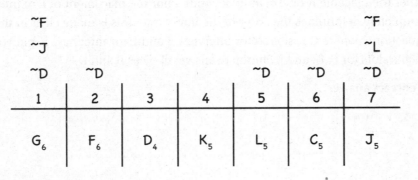

(C) is the correct answer.

Question 5 (restricted, "cannot-be-true")

- Create a new symbol to illustrate the additional restriction: J... C.

- With the additional restriction and by operation of Clue 3, CJ is no longer possible. As such, KC is required.

- Link J ... C and KC to arrive at J ... KC.

- Link Clue 2: L ... J... KC.

- L cannot be interviewed immediately before K.

(B) is the correct answer.

Question 2 (unrestricted, "must-be-true")

- This is answerable in part by Deductions 1, 2, and 3 and by reviewing the question history.

- Deductions 1, 2, and 3 ban D, F, and J from interview slot 1.

- Review of the catch-a-clue question and questions 3 and 4 indicate that G, K, and L can each be slotted for interview slot 1.

- The only remaining component (C) has neither been included nor excluded from the pool of components that can be slotted for interview slot 1. You must try C in interview slot 1.

- Place C in interview slot 1.

- By operation of Clue 3, J must be placed in interview slot 2.
- This violates Clue 2. C cannot be placed in interview slot 1. Therefore, there are only three components that can be slotted for interview slot 1.

(A) is the correct answer.

Question 6 (modifier)

- The question is completely answerable by reviewing prior history.
- Neither the placement of F in interview slot 6 nor the placement of G in interview slot 7 completely determines the order of the interviews, since questions 1 and 3 both have F slotted for interview 6 and G slotted for interview 7, but with two different acceptable orders. Eliminate answer choices A and C.
- Neither the placement of C in interview slot 3 nor the placement of L in interview slot 1 completely determines the order of the interview—this is made clear in the workout to question 3 where C is slotted for interview 3 and L for interview 1, but with several possible slots for F, G, and J. Eliminate answer choices B and D.

(E) is the correct answer.

Game 14

Each of eight pre-med students—D, F, G, H, K, L, M, and N—is registered for at least one of the following three courses: Biology, Chemistry, and Physics. Biology and Chemistry will gain three pre-med students each, and Physics will gain four pre-med students. The following conditions must apply:

At least one of the pre-med students will register for all three courses.

D is not registered for the same course as either F or G.

H is not registered for the same course as either K or L.

If F is registered for the Chemistry course, then M is not registered for the Physics course.

1. Which one of the following is an acceptable assignment of pre-med students to the courses?

   (A) Biology: H, M, N
       Chemistry: F, L, N
       Physics: D, G, K, N
   (B) Biology: D, K, M
       Chemistry: F, G, M
       Physics: H, L, M, N
   (C) Biology: F, K, M
       Chemistry: D, H, M
       Physics: G, L, M, N
   (D) Biology: G, H, N
       Chemistry: F, K, N
       Physics: D, L, M, N
   (E) Biology: F, M, N
       Chemistry: G, H, M
       Physics: D, K, L, N

2. Which one of the following must be false?

   (A) D and H are registered for the same course.
   (B) K and M are registered for the same course.
   (C) H and N are registered for the same course.
   (D) F and G are never registered for the same course.
   (E) M and N are never registered for the same course.

3. If neither K nor N is registered for Chemistry, then each of the following could be true EXCEPT:

   (A) D and H are both registered for Chemistry.
   (B) F and M are both registered for Chemistry.
   (C) L and N are both registered for Biology.
   (D) M and N are both registered for Biology.
   (E) H and M are both registered for Physics.

4. If G and L are both registered for Biology, then which one of the following must be true?

   (A) D is registered for Chemistry.
   (B) N is registered for Biology.
   (C) H is registered for Chemistry.
   (D) K is registered for Physics.
   (E) M is registered for Biology.

Continued on next page ▐▶

5. If D and H are both registered for Physics, then which one of the following must be true?

(A) M is registered for Chemistry.
(B) K is registered for Physics.
(C) L is registered for Chemistry.
(D) G is registered for Biology.
(E) F is registered for Biology.

6. Which one of the following could be true?

(A) H is registered for all three courses.
(B) K and L are both registered for Biology.
(C) F is registered for Chemistry and N is not registered for Biology.
(D) M is registered for exactly two courses.
(E) Neither M nor N is registered for Chemistry.

Visualize and draw the diagram.

Biology	Chemistry	Physics
– – –	– – –	– – – –

STEP 2 List the components and ascertain the ratio and/or distribution.

Components: D, F, G, H, K, L, M, N

Distribution deduction:

- There are eight students and ten slots. Each student is registering for at least one course, thereby establishing two extra slots.
- From Clue 1, it can be deduced that the two extra slots must both be given to the same student so that at least one student registers for all three courses. There is only one student who takes all three courses. The remaining seven students are registered for just one course each.

STEP 3 Symbolize the clues.

Clue 1 See distribution deduction above.

Clue 2 $D \rightarrow \sim F$; $F \rightarrow \sim D$
$D \rightarrow \sim G$; $G \rightarrow \sim D$

Clue 3 $H \rightarrow \sim K$; $K \rightarrow \sim H$
$H \rightarrow \sim L$; $L \rightarrow \sim H$

Clue 4 $F_{chem} \rightarrow \sim M_{physics}$; $M_{physics} \rightarrow \sim F_{chem}$

STEP 4 Make deductions.

Deduction 1: The distribution deduction outlined in Step 2 shows that that there is just one pre-med student who is registered for all three courses.

Deduction 2: From Clues 2, 3, and 4, you can deduce that the pre-med student who registers for all three courses must be either M or N. How? The pre-med student who registers for all three courses will be registered for the same course as each of the remaining seven pre-med students. Therefore, neither D, F, G, H, K, nor L can be the student who registers for all three courses because each has at least one student with whom they cannot be concurrently registered.

STEP 5 **Tackle the questions.**

Question order: 1, 3, 4, 5, 2, and then 6.

Answer Key

Answers

Question 1 (catch-a-clue)

- Clue 1 eliminates answer choice E.
- Clue 2 eliminates answer choice A.
- Clue 3 eliminates answer choice B.
- Clue 4 eliminates answer choice D and answer choice B which has already been eliminated.

(C) is the correct answer.

Question 3 (restricted, "could-be-true-EXCEPT")

1. The exclusion of N from the Chemistry group triggers Deduction 1.
2. By operation of Deduction 1, M must be added to all three groups.
3. By operation of the contrapositive of Clue 4, F is excluded from the chemistry group.

Stop! You have enough information to answer the question.

Biology	Chemistry	Physics
M_2 _ _	M_2 _ ~F_3	M_2 _ _ _

(B) is the correct answer.

Question 4 (restricted, "must-be-true")

1. Place G and L in the Biology group.
2. By operation of Deduction 1, M is placed in the remaining Biology slot as well as the Chemistry and Physics groups (Option 1), or N is placed in the remaining Biology slot, as well as the Chemistry and Physics groups (Option 2).
3. Look at both options simultaneously. By operation of Clue 3, H and K cannot be registered for the same course. Therefore, each is placed in the Chemistry and Physics groups interchangeably.
4. Work out Option 1 first. By operation of the contrapositive of Clue 4, F is excluded from the Chemistry group and must, therefore, be placed in the Physics group.
5. By operation of Clue 2, D must be placed in the Chemistry group.
6. The remaining component (N) is placed in the remaining slot in the Physics group.
7. Now work out Option 2. The remaining components are D, F, and M. By operation of Clue 2, D and F must be split between the Chemistry group and the Physics group (although not interchangeably as you will see in a moment), forcing M in the Physics group.

8. By operation of the contrapositive of Clue 4, F is excluded from the Chemistry group and must, therefore, be placed in the Physics group, forcing D in the Chemistry group.

Option 1

Biology	Chemistry	Physics
$G_1\ L_1\ M_2$	$M_2\ H/K_3\ D_5$	$M_2\ K/H_3\ F_4\ N_6$

Option 2

Biology	Chemistry	Physics
$G_2\ L_1\ N_2$	$N_2\ H/K_3\ D_8$	$N_2\ K/H_3\ M_7\ F_8$

D is placed in the Chemistry group in both options.

(A) is the correct answer.

Question 5 (restricted, "must-be-true")

1. Place D and H in the Physics group.
2. By operation of Clue 2, F and G are excluded from the Physics group. By operation of Clue 3, K and L are excluded from the Physics group. Only two components remain (M and N), and both must be placed in the Physics group.
3. By operation of the contrapositive of Clue 4, F is excluded from the Chemistry group and must, therefore, be placed in the Biology group.

Biology	Chemistry	Physics
F_3 _ _	_ _ _	$D_1\ H_1\ M_2\ N_2$

(E) is the correct answer.

Question 2 (unrestricted, "must-be-false")

- The question is completely answerable by the distribution deduction. M and N must be registered for a course together.
- Additionally, the workout to question 4 illustrates that A, B, C, and D can each be true.

(E) is the correct answer.

Question 6 (unrestricted, "could-be-true")

- The distribution deduction causes answer choices A, D, and E to be eliminated.
- By operation of Clue 4, if F is registered for Chemistry, then M is not registered for Physics. Therefore, M is not the pre-med student who registers for all three courses. N must be the pre-med student who registers for all three courses, including Biology. Eliminate answer choice C.

(B) is the correct answer.

Game 15

Seven professional golfers—Choi, Deng, Farrell, Gallo, Harris, Jorge, and Kumar—will play a round of golf at a charity golf tournament. Each of the golfers will be assigned to exactly one of the following three tee times—9 A.M., 10 A.M., and 11 A.M. The assignment of golfers must conform to the following conditions:

At least two golfers are assigned to each tee time.
Deng is assigned to the same tee time as either Jorge or Kumar, but not both.
Farrell is assigned an earlier tee time than Harris.
Choi's tee time is not later than Deng's tee time.
Gallo is assigned an earlier tee time than Kumar.

1. Which one of the following is an acceptable assignment of golfers to the tee times?

    (A) 9 A.M.: Farrell, Gallo
        10 A.M.: Deng, Jorge, Kumar
        11 A.M.: Choi, Harris
    (B) 9 A.M.: Choi, Deng, Jorge
        10 A.M.: Gallo, Harris
        11 A.M.: Farrell, Kumar
    (C) 9 A.M.: Choi, Farrell, Gallo
        10 A.M.: Deng, Jorge
        11 A.M.: Harris, Kumar
    (D) 9 A.M.: Choi, Farrell
        10 A.M.: Harris, Kumar
        11 A.M.: Deng, Gallo, Jorge
    (E) 9 A.M.: Gallo, Farrell, Jorge
        10 A.M.: Choi, Kumar
        11 A.M.: Deng, Harris

2. Which one of the following is a pair of golfers who could be the only two golfers assigned a 9 A.M. tee time?

    (A) Deng and Kumar
    (B) Jorge and Kumar
    (C) Choi and Harris
    (D) Deng and Gallo
    (E) Choi and Gallo

3. If Choi is assigned an 11 A.M. tee time, then which one of the following is a complete and accurate list of golfers any one of whom could be assigned to the 10 A.M. tee time?

    (A) Gallo, Harris, Jorge
    (B) Farrell, Gallo, Harris, Jorge, Kumar
    (C) Gallo, Harris, Jorge, Kumar
    (D) Gallo, Harris, Kumar
    (E) Farrell, Jorge, Kumar

4. If Choi and Farrell are the only two golfers assigned to the 10 A.M. tee time, then each of the following must be true EXCEPT:

    (A) Jorge is assigned to the 9 A.M. tee time.
    (B) Deng is assigned to the 11 A.M. tee time.
    (C) Gallo is assigned to the 9 A.M. tee time.
    (D) Harris is assigned to the 11 A.M. tee time.
    (E) Kumar is assigned to the 9 A.M. tee time.

Continued on next page ▮▶

5. Which one of the following must be true?

(A) Choi is assigned to an earlier tee time than Deng.
(B) Farrell is assigned to an earlier tee time than Kumar.
(C) Either Jorge or Kumar is assigned to the 11 A.M. tee time.
(D) Either Farrell or Gallo is assigned to the 9 A.M. tee time.
(E) Either Choi or Deng is assigned to the 10 A.M. tee time.

6. There is only one acceptable assignment of golfers to tee times if which one of the following assignments is made?

(A) Choi is assigned to the 11 A.M. tee time.
(B) Deng is assigned to the 9 A.M. tee time.
(C) Gallo is assigned to the 9 A.M. tee time.
(D) Kumar is assigned to the 11 A.M. tee time.
(E) Harris is assigned to the 10 A.M. tee time.

Visualize and draw the diagram.

9:00 A.M.	10:00 A.M.	11:00 A.M.
_ _	_ _	_ _ ......

STEP 2 List the components and ascertain the ratio and/or distribution.

Components: C, D, F, G, H, J, K

Distribution: By operation of Clue 1, one tee time will be assigned three golfers. The remaining two tee times will be assigned two golfers.

STEP 3 Symbolize the clues.

Clue 1 See distribution deduction in Step 2.

Clue 2 D → J or K; ~J and ~K → ~D

Clue 3 F ... H

Clue 4 ~~D ... C~~

Clue 5 G ... K

STEP 4 Make deductions.

Deduction 1: From Clue 3, you can deduce that H is not assigned to the 9:00 A.M. tee time, and F is not assigned to the 11:00 A.M. tee time.

Deduction 2: From Clue 4, you can deduce that C must be assigned either to the same tee time or to an earlier tee time than D. Alternate symbol: CD or C...D

Deduction 3: From Clue 5, you can deduce that K is not assigned to the 9:00 A.M. tee time, and G is not assigned to the 11:00 A.M. tee time.

~H		~F
~K		~G
9:00 A.M.	10:00 A.M.	11:00 A.M.
_ _ ...	_ _ ...	_ _ ...

STEP 5 Tackle the questions.

Question order: 1, 3, 4, 2, 5, and then 6.

Answer Key

1. **C**   2. **E**   3. **C**   4. **E**   5. **C**   6. **B**

Answers

Question 1 (catch-a-clue)

- Clue 1 does not eliminate any answer choices.
- Clue 2 eliminates answer choices A and E.
- Clue 3 eliminates answer choice B.
- Clue 4 eliminates answer choice A which has already been eliminated.
- Clue 5 eliminates answer choice D.

(C) is the correct answer.

Question 3 (restricted, "could-be-true")

1. Place C in the 11:00 A.M. tee time.
2. By operation of Deduction 2, D must be assigned to the 11:00 A.M. tee time.
3. With the assignment of D to the 11:00 A.M. tee time, Clue 2 is triggered. Either J or K must be assigned to the 11:00 A.M. tee time. Create two options: Option 1 with J assigned to the 11:00 A.M. tee time, and Option 2 with K assigned to it.
4. Solve Option 1. By operation of Clue 3, F and H must be assigned to the 9:00 A.M. and 10:00 A.M. tee times, respectively.
5. By operation of Clue 5, G and K must be assigned to the 9:00 A.M. and 10:00 A.M. tee times, respectively.
6. Solve Option 2. By operation of Clue 3, F and H must be assigned to the 9:00 A.M. and 10:00 A.M. tee times, respectively.
7. There are no additional restrictions on the remaining components, G and J. Therefore, they are placed in the 9:00 A.M. and 10:00 A.M. tee times interchangeably.

Option 1

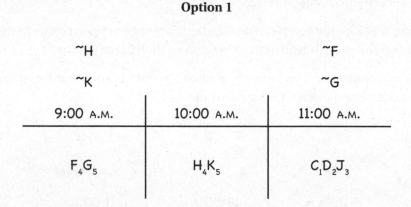

Option 2

~H		~F
~K		~G
9:00 A.M.	10:00 A.M.	11:00 A.M.
F_6 G/J_7	H_6 J/G_7	$C_1D_2K_3$

- In Option 1, H and K can be assigned to the 10:00 A.M. tee time. In Option 2, G, H, and J can be assigned to the 10:00 A.M. tee time. Therefore, the complete and accurate list would be G, H, J, and K.

(C) is the correct answer.

Question 4 (restricted, "must-be-true-EXCEPT")

1. Place C and F in the 10:00 A.M. tee time.
2. By operation of Clue 3, H must be assigned to the 11:00 A.M. tee time.
3. By operation of Deduction 2, D must be assigned to the 11:00 A.M. tee time. Why? Even though CD would ordinarily allow for D to be assigned to the 10:00 A.M. tee time, this question restricts the number of 10:00 A.M. golfers to just two.
4. By operation of Deduction 3, K must be assigned to the 11:00 A.M. tee time.
5. The remaining components (G and J) must both be assigned to the 9:00 A.M. tee time to satisfy the minimum two-golfer requirement in Clue 1.

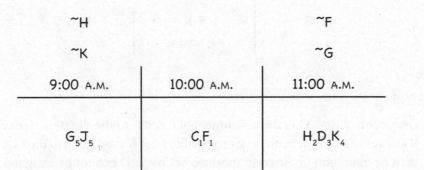

~H		~F
~K		~G
9:00 A.M.	10:00 A.M.	11:00 A.M.
G_5J_5	C_1F_1	$H_2D_3K_4$

(E) is the correct answer.

Question 2 (unrestricted, "could-be-true")

- This question is answerable by Deduction 3 and Clue 2.
- Deduction 3 bans the assignment of H and K from the 9:00 A.M. tee time, so answer choices A, B, and C can be eliminated.
- Clue 2 mandates the assignment of either K or J with D, so answer choice D can be eliminated.

(E) is the correct answer.

Question 5 (unrestricted, "must-be-true")

- You may be able to make an additional deduction to answer this question outright. If not, by reviewing the prior deductions and workouts, two answer choices can eliminated.
- Both Deduction 3 and the workout to question 3 indicate that C and D can both be assigned to the same tee time. Answer choice A is eliminated.
- Similarly, the workout to question 3 indicates an acceptable assignment of golfers that does not include the assignment of either C or D to the 10:00 A.M. tee time. Answer choice E is eliminated.
- Moving forward, you must try the remaining answer choices.
- Answer choice B is not required. Consider:

~H		~F
~K		~G
9:00 A.M.	10:00 A.M.	11:00 A.M.
C G	F K	D H J

- Answer choice C must be true because…

  - Deductions 1 and 3 bar the assignment of F and G to the 11:00 A.M. tee time.
  - If answer choice C were not true and neither J nor K is assigned to the 11 A.M. tee time, then by operation of the contrapositive of Clue 2, D cannot be assigned. Therefore, D nor J nor K is assigned to the 11:00 A.M. tee time.
  - The only remaining components available for assignment to the 11:00 A.M. tee time are F and H.
  - By operation of Deduction 1, F cannot be assigned to the 11:00 A.M. tee time. Furthermore, by operation of Clue 3, F and H cannot be assigned to the same tee time.
  - The exclusion of both K and J from the 11:00 A.M. tee time will not yield an acceptable assignment of golfers, so one of the pair must go to the 11:00 A.M. tee time.

- Answer choice D is not required. Consider:

9:00 A.M.	10:00 A.M.	11:00 A.M.
~H		~F
~K		~G
C D J	F G	H K

(C) is the correct answer.

Question 6 (modifier)

- The question is asking which additional restriction has the effect of rendering just one acceptable assignment of golfers.
- This question is entirely answerable by reviewing your prior workouts.
- The workout to question 3 (Options 1 and 2) indicates two (not one) acceptable assignments of golfers when C is assigned to the 11:00 A.M. tee time. Eliminate answer choice A.
- Similarly, the workout to question 3 (Option 2) indicates two (not one) acceptable assignments of golfers when H is assigned to the 10:00 A.M. tee time. Eliminate answer choice E.
- A review of the workouts to questions 1, 3, and 4 indicates three (not one) acceptable assignments of golfers when G is assigned to the 9:00 A.M. tee time. Eliminate answer choice C.
- Similarly, a review of the workouts for questions 1, 3 (Option 2), and 4 indicates three (not one) acceptable assignments of golfers when K is assigned to the 11:00 A.M. tee time. Eliminate answer choice D.
- The assignment of D to the 9 A.M. tee time yields only one acceptable assignment of golfers. Here's how:

  - By operation of Clue 2, J or K must be assigned with D to a tee time.
  - By operation of Deduction 3, K is not assigned to the 9:00 A.M. tee time. Therefore, J is assigned to the 9:00 A.M. tee time.
  - By operation of Deduction 2, C must be assigned to the same tee time as D or earlier. Since an earlier time is not possible, C must be assigned to the 9:00 A.M. tee time.
  - By operation of Deduction 2, F and H must be assigned to the 10:00 A.M. and 11:00 A.M. tee times, respectively.
  - By operation of Deductions 4, G and K must be assigned to the 10:00 A.M. and 11:00 A.M. tee times, respectively.

(B) is the correct answer.

Game 16

Exactly seven staff members—Liu, Mancini, North, Padilla, Ross, Stein, and Tate—will visit their supervisor at home while she convaleses after minor surgery. No staff member visits at the same time as any other staff member, nor does any staff member visit more than once. The order in which the staff members visit is consistent with the following conditions:

Stein visits after Liu but before Padilla.

North and Ross both visit after Stein.

Either Padilla visits after Mancini and before Tate, or Padilla visits after Tate and before Mancini.

1. Which one of the following could be the order, from first to last, in which the staff members visit?

   (A) Tate, Liu, Stein, Ross, Padilla, Mancini, North
   (B) Mancini, Padilla, Stein, Liu, Ross, North, Tate
   (C) Liu, Ross, Stein, North, Mancini, Padilla, Tate
   (D) Stein, Mancini, Padilla, Liu, Tate, Ross, North
   (E) Mancini, Liu, Stein, Tate, Padilla, North, Ross

2. Which one of the following CANNOT be the staff member that visits fourth?

   (A) Mancini
   (B) North
   (C) Stein
   (D) Padilla
   (E) Tate

3. If Tate visits first, then exactly how many staff members are there any one of which could visit second?

   (A) One
   (B) Two
   (C) Three
   (D) Four
   (E) Five

4. If Mancini visits third, then which one of the following must be true?

   (A) Padilla visits fourth.
   (B) Ross visits seventh.
   (C) Tate visits fifth.
   (D) North visits sixth.
   (E) Liu visits first.

5. Each of the following could be false EXCEPT:

   (A) At least one staff member visits before Liu.
   (B) At least two staff members visit before Stein.
   (C) At least three staff members visit before Ross.
   (D) At least three staff members visit before Padilla.
   (E) At least five staff members visit before Mancini.

6. Which one of the following pairs of staff members CANNOT visit third and fourth, respectively?

   (A) Mancini and Padilla
   (B) Stein and Ross
   (C) North and Tate
   (D) Ross and North
   (E) Stein and Mancini

STEP 1 Symbolize the clues.

    Clue 1   L ... S ... P

    Clue 2   S ... N

                   S ... R

    Clue 3   M ... P ... T (Option 1) or T ... P ... M (Option 2)

STEP 2 Connect the individual chains to create the largest chain (two options).

             L ... S ... P ... T (Option 1) or L ... S ... P ... M (Option 2)

STEP 3 Attach each of the remaining rules to the baseline.

           Option 1   **Option 2**

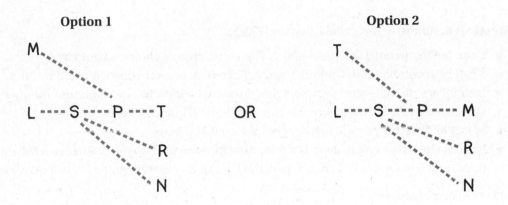

STEP 4 **Tackle the questions.**

Answer Key

1. **A**   2. **C**   3. **A**   4. **E**   5. **D**   6. **E**

Answers

Question 1 (catch-a-clue)

- Clue 1 eliminates answer choices B and D.
- Clue 2 eliminates answer choice C.
- Clue 3 eliminates answer choice E.

The correct answer is (A).

Question 2 (unrestricted, "cannot-be-true")

- In both Options 1 and 2, there are a minimum of four staff members who visit after S.
- In Option 1, those four staff members are N, P, R, and T; in Option 2, those four staff members are M, N, P, and R.
- Accordingly, the latest that S can visit is third.

(C) is the correct answer.

Question 3 (restricted, "could-be-true")

- T cannot visit first in Option 1. Accordingly, refer only to Option 2 to answer this question.
- In Option 2, only L can be second if T is first.

(A) is the correct answer.

Question 4 (restricted, "must-be-true")

- M cannot be third in Option 2. Accordingly, refer only to Option 1 to answer this question.
- If M is third, then the only two staff members that can visit before M are L and S.
- L and S must visit first and second, respectively.

(E) is the correct answer.

Question 5 (unrestricted, "could-be-false-EXCEPT")

- L can be first in both Options 1 and 2. Therefore, answer choice A could be false.
- S can be second in both Options 1 and 2. Therefore, answer choice B could be false.
- L and S are the only staff members that must visit before R. The minimum number of staff members that visit before R is two, not three. Eliminate answer choice C.
- M can be first in Option 1. Answer choice E could be false.
- In both Options 1 and 2, there is a minimum of three staff members that visit before P (L, M, and S in Option 1; and L, S, and T in Option 2). Answer choice D must be true.

(D) is the correct answer.

Question 6 (unrestricted, "cannot-be-true")

- S and M cannot visit third and fourth, respectively, in Option 1, because in order for S to visit third, M must visit before S.
- S and M cannot visit third and fourth, respectively, in Option 2 because P must visit in between S and M.

(E) is the correct answer.

Game 17

Four women—Camille, Demi, Eleni, and Fola—and four men—Hector, Jacque, Kadeem, and Lance—are giving a ballroom dance exhibition. Four dances—Paso Doble, Quickstep, Rumba, and Salsa—are performed one at a time, consecutively. Each dance will be performed by a couple consisting of exactly one woman and one man. Each person dances in exactly one dance. The following conditions apply:

Fola partners with either Jacque or Kadeem.

Camille does not partner with Hector.

Kadeem performs at some time after Demi, who performs the Paso Doble.

The Quickstep is performed second.

Camille does not perform fourth.

1. Which one of the following could be the dancers included in each performance?

   (A) First performance: Fola, Kadeem
   Second performance: Camille, Jacque
   Third performance: Demi, Hector
   Fourth performance: Eleni, Lance

   (B) First performance: Fola, Jacque
   Second performance: Demi, Lance
   Third performance: Eleni, Hector
   Fourth performance: Camille, Kadeem

   (C) First performance: Camille, Lance
   Second performance: Eleni, Jacque
   Third performance: Demi, Hector
   Fourth performance: Fola, Kadeem

   (D) First performance: Camille, Kadeem
   Second performance: Eleni, Jacque
   Third performance: Demi, Hector
   Fourth performance: Fola, Lance

   (E) First performance: Eleni, Lance
   Second performance: Camille, Hector
   Third performance: Demi, Kadeem
   Fourth performance: Fola, Jacque

2. Which one of the following could be the pair of dancers for the first dance, matched with the ballroom dance?

   (A) Demi; Lance; Salsa
   (B) Eleni; Hector; Rumba
   (C) Eleni; Lance; Quickstep
   (D) Camille; Hector; Salsa
   (E) Fola; Kadeem; Rumba

3. If Fola performs the first dance, then which one of the following could be false?

   (A) Lance performs the second dance.
   (B) Hector performs the third dance.
   (C) Eleni partners with Kadeem.
   (D) Camille performs the Quickstep.
   (E) Jacque performs the Salsa.

4. Which one of the following must be true?

   (A) If Demi partners with Hector, Fola must partner with Kadeem.
   (B) If Fola partners with Kadeem, Camille must partner with Jacque.
   (C) If Eleni partners with Jacque, Camille must partner with Lance.
   (D) If Camille partners with Lance, Eleni must partner with Jacque.
   (E) If Camille partners with Jacque, Demi must partner with Lance.

Continued on next page ⏺⏺▶

5. If Camille performs the first dance and Jacque performs the second dance, then each of the following could be true EXCEPT:

(A) Fola partners with Kadeem.
(B) Lance performs the Rumba.
(C) Eleni performs the Salsa.
(D) Hector performs the Rumba.
(E) Fola performs the Salsa.

6. Which one of the following must be true?

(A) The Paso Doble and the Quickstep are performed consecutively.
(B) The Rumba and the Salsa are performed consecutively.
(C) The Paso Doble and the Salsa are performed consecutively.
(D) Demi partners with either Hector or Lance.
(E) Camille partners with either Kadeem or Lance.

Visualize and draw the diagram.

1	2	3	4
Women/Men/Dance	Women/Men/Dance	Women/Men/Dance	Women/Men/Dance

_ _ _ | _ _ _ | _ _ _ | _ _ _

STEP 2 List the components and ascertain the ratio and/or distribution.

Components:

Women: C D E F
Men: H J K L
Dances: P Q R S

Ratio: one-to-one

STEP 3 Symbolize the clues.

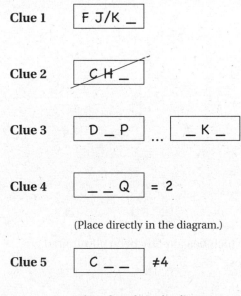

Clue 1   F J/K _

Clue 2   C H _   (crossed out)

Clue 3   D _ P ... _ K _

Clue 4   _ _ Q   = 2

(Place directly in the diagram.)

Clue 5   C _ _   ≠4

(Place directly in the diagram.)

STEP 4 Make deductions.

Deduction 1: From Clue 3, you can deduce:

   a) D cannot be placed in Women slot 4.
   b) P cannot be placed in Dance slot 4.
   c) K cannot be placed in Men slot 1.

Deduction 2: If you link Clues 3 and 4, you will deduce that D cannot be placed in Women slot 2.

~K	~D		~C ~D	~P
1	2	3	4
Women/Men/Dance	Women/Men/Dance	Women/Men/Dance	Women/Men/Dance
_ _ _	_ _ Q	_ _ _	_ _ _

STEP 5 Tackle the questions.

Question order: 1, 3, 5, 2, 4, and then 6.

Answer Key

1. **C**   2. **B**   3. **E**   4. **C**   5. **D**   6. **A**

Answers

Question 1 (catch-a-clue)

- Clue 1 eliminates answer choice D.
- Clue 2 eliminates answer choice E.
- Clue 3 eliminates answer choices A and D, which has already been eliminated.
- Clue 4 does not eliminate any answer choices.
- Clue 5 eliminates answer choice B.

(C) is the correct answer.

Question 3 (restricted, "could-be-false")

1. Place F in the Women slot 1.
2. By operation of Clue 2, F must be partnered with either J or K. By operation of Deduction 1c), K cannot be placed in the Men slot 1. Therefore, J must be placed in the Men slot 1.
3. By operation of Deductions 1a) and 2, D cannot be placed in either Women slot 2 or Women slot 4. Accordingly, D must be placed in Women slot 3 and P in Dance slot 3.
4. By operation of Clue 3, K must be placed in Men slot 4.
5. By operation of Clue 5, C cannot be placed in Women slot 4, and, as such, E must be placed in Women slot 4.
6. The remaining woman (C) must be placed in the final Women slot 2.
7. By operation of Clue 2, H cannot be placed in Men slot 2 and, as such, H must be placed in Men slot 3.
8. The remaining man (L) must be placed in the final Men slot 2.
9. The remaining Dance components (R and S) must be placed in the remaining Dance slots 1 and 4 interchangeably.

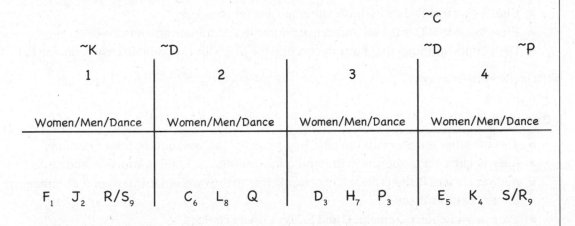

(E) is the correct answer.

Question 5 (restricted, "could-be-true-EXCEPT")

1. Place C in the Women slot 1 and J in the Men slot 2.
2. By operation of Deductions 1a) and 2, D cannot be placed in either Women slot 2 or Women slot 4. Therefore, D must be placed in Women slot 3 and P in Dance slot 3.
3. By operation of Clue 3, K must be placed in Men slot 4.
4. By operation of Clue 2, H cannot be placed in Men slot 1 and, as such, H must be placed in Men slot 3.
5. The remaining men component (L) must be placed in the final Men slot 1.
6. The remaining women components (E, F) must be placed in the remaining Women slots 2 and 4 interchangeably.
7. The remaining dance components (R, S) must be placed in the remaining Dance slots 1 and 4 interchangeably.

~C

~K   ~D   ~D   ~P

1	2	3	4
Women/Men/Dance	Women/Men/Dance	Women/Men/Dance	Women/Men/Dance
C_1 L_5 R/S_7	E/F_6 J_1 Q	D_2 H_4 P_2	F/E_6 K_3 S/R_7

(D) is the correct answer.

Question 2 (unrestricted, "could-be-true")

- This question is completely answerable by reviewing the clues and deductions.
- Clue 2 says that C cannot partner with H. Eliminate answer choice D.
- Clue 3 says that D dances the P. Eliminate answer choice A.
- Clue 4 says that Q is the second dance performed. Eliminate answer choice C.
- Deduction 1c) shows that K cannot occupy the Men slot 1. Eliminate answer choice E.

(B) is the correct answer.

Question 4 (unrestricted, "must-be-true")

- This question is answerable, in part, by a review of the workouts to prior questions.
- Answer choice A is not true in the workout to question 3. Eliminate answer choice A.
- Answer choices B and D are not necessarily true in the workout to question 5. Eliminate answer choices B and D.
- Two answer choices remain (C and E). Try answer choice C.

  - If E partners with J, then by operation of Clue 1, F must partner with K.
  - Women C and D and Men H and L remain.
  - By operation of Clue 2, C cannot partner with H and, thus, must partner with L. This must be true.

(C) is the correct answer.

Question 6 (unrestricted, "must-be-true")

- This question is answerable by reviewing the clues and deductions.
- From Deduction 1a), it can be deduced that P cannot be performed in Dance slot 4.
- From Clue 4, Q is performed second.
- P must be performed either in Dance slots 1 or 3. In either event, P will be performed consecutively with Q.

(A) is the correct answer.

Game 18

A five-person commission will be formed to study the effects of global warming on individual crops. The commission will be selected from among three farmers—G, H, and J; three horticulturists—K, L, and M; and three climatologists—S, T, and V. The selection of the commission must conform to following conditions:

The commission must include at least one farmer, at least one horticulturist, and at least one climatologist.

G and S cannot both be selected.

K and M cannot both be selected.

V cannot be selected unless G is selected.

If L is selected, both S and J are selected.

1. Which one of the following is an acceptable selection of commission members?

   (A) G, H, K, S, V
   (B) H, J, M, S, V
   (C) H, K, M, S, T
   (D) G, K, J, T, V
   (E) G, J, L, M, V

2. Which one of the following pairs of people CANNOT both be selected?

   (A) L and V
   (B) H and J
   (C) K and T
   (D) L and H
   (E) S and T

3. If exactly two horticulturists are selected, each of the following could be true EXCEPT:

   (A) Both H and T are selected.
   (B) Both K and S are selected.
   (C) T is not selected.
   (D) Exactly one farmer is selected.
   (E) Exactly two climatologists are selected.

4. If neither T nor V is selected, which one of the following is a pair of people that must be selected?

   (A) H and K
   (B) L and M
   (C) G and J
   (D) J and S
   (E) H and M

5. Which one of the following could be true?

   (A) All three horticulturists are selected.
   (B) All three climatologists are selected.
   (C) All three farmers are selected.
   (D) V and S are both selected.
   (E) G and L and both selected.

STEP 1 Visualize and draw the diagram.

IN	OUT
_ _ _ _ _	_ _ _ _

STEP 2 List the components and ascertain the ratio and/or distribution.

Components:

Farmers: G, H, J
Horticulturists: K, L, M
Climatologists: S, T, V

Distribution: Fixed

STEP 3 Symbolize the clues.

Clue 1   Farmers—1+
                 Horticulturists—1+
                 Climatologists—1+

Clue 2   G → ~S; S → ~G

Clue 3   K → ~M; M → ~K

Clue 4   V → G; ~G → ~V

Clue 5   L → S; ~S → ~L
                 L → J; ~J → ~L

STEP 4 Make deductions.

First link Clue 2 and the contrapositive of Clue 5: G → ~S and ~S → ~L
Deduction 1: G → ~L

Next, link Clue 4 and Clue 2: V → G and G → ~S
Deduction 2: V → ~S

Finally, link Clue 5 with the contrapositive of Clue 2 and the contrapositive of Clue 4:
L → S, S → ~G, and ~G → ~V
Deduction 3: L → ~G; L → ~V

STEP 5 **Tackle the questions.**

Question order: 1, 3, 4, 2, and then 5.

Answer Key

1. **D**   2. **A**   3. **A**   4. **D**   5. **C**

Answers

Question 1 (catch-a-clue)

- Clue 1 does not eliminate any answer choices.
- Clue 2 eliminates answer choice A.
- Clue 3 eliminates answer choice C.
- Clue 4 eliminates answer choice B.
- Clue 5 eliminates answer choice E.

(D) is the correct answer.

Question 3 (restricted, "could-be-true-EXCEPT")

1. The horticulturists are K, L, and M. By operation of Clue 3, you cannot select both K and M, so you must select either K or M and L.
2. By operation of Clue 5, S and J must be selected.
3. By operation of the contrapositive of Clue 2, G cannot be selected.
4. By operation of the contrapositive of Clue 4, V cannot be selected.
5. There are no additional restrictions on the remaining components, H and T; therefore, one of the pair is selected.

IN	OUT
K/M_1 L_1 S_2 J_2 H/T_5	M/K_1 G_3 V_4 T/H_5

- Answer choices B, C, D, and E can each be true. Answer choice A is never true.

(A) is the correct answer.

Question 4 (restricted, "must-be-true")

1. Place T and V (both climatologists) in the out-column.
2. By operation of Clue 1, at least one climatologist must be selected. Therefore, you must select S. Place S in the in-column.
3. By operation of the contrapositive to Clue 2, G cannot be selected. Place G in the out-column.
4. By operation of Clue 3, at least one of the pair (K and M) cannot be selected. There is only one slot remaining in the out-column. Accordingly, K or M must occupy the last available out-slot, with the other placed in the in-column.
5. The remaining components (H, J, and L) must be placed in the only available slots in the in-column.

	IN	OUT
	S_2 K/M_4 H_5 J_5 L_5	T_1 V_1 G_3 M/K_4

- Answer choices A, B, and E could be true but are not necessarily true. Answer choice C is false because G is not selected.

(D) is the correct answer.

Question 2 (unrestricted, "cannot-be-true")

- This question is answerable by Deduction 3.
- Based on the solution to question 3, each of the pairs listed in answer choices B, C, D, and E are possible answers.

(A) is the correct answer.

Question 5 (unrestricted, "could-be-true")

- This question is answerable in part by reviewing the deductions, and in part by reviewing the clues.
  - By operation of Clue 3, you cannot select all of these horticulturists. Eliminate answer choice A.
  - By operation of Deduction 2, you cannot select both S and V. Therefore, you cannot select all three climatologists. Eliminate answer choice B.
  - By operation of Deduction 2, V and S cannot be selected simultaneously. Eliminate answer choice D.
  - By operation of Deduction 1, G and L cannot be selected simultaneously. Eliminate answer choice E.

(C) is the correct answer.

Game 19

During the international food street festival, exactly seven food trucks—Falafel truck, Hot dog truck, Korean BBQ truck, Masala truck, Pasta truck, Sushi truck, and Taco truck—will be assigned to seven parking spaces arranged in a straight line and numbered consecutively 1 through 7. No food truck is assigned to the same parking space. The food trucks are assigned to the parking spaces in accordance with the following restrictions:

The Sushi truck must be assigned to a higher numbered parking space than the Masala truck.

The Korean BBQ truck must be assigned to the parking space numbered one higher than the Masala truck.

If the Hot dog truck is assigned to parking space 3, then the Falafel truck is assigned to parking space 4.

If the Taco truck is not assigned to parking space 2, it is assigned to parking space 3.

1. Which one of the following lists an acceptable assignment of food trucks to parking spaces 1 through 7, respectively?

   (A) Falafel, Taco, Masala, Korean BBQ, Sushi, Hot dog, Pasta
   (B) Hot dog, Sushi, Taco, Masala, Korean BBQ, Pasta, Falafcl
   (C) Falafel, Taco, Hot dog, Masala, Korean BBQ, Sushi, Pasta
   (D) Pasta, Taco, Masala, Falafel, Korean BBQ, Sushi, Hot dog
   (E) Masala, Korean BBQ, Pasta, Taco, Falafel, Sushi, Hot dog

2. Which one of the following can be true?

   (A) The Korean BBQ truck is assigned to parking space 7.
   (B) The Masala truck is assigned to parking space 6.
   (C) The Hot dog truck is assigned to parking space 6.
   (D) The Sushi truck is assigned to parking space 3.
   (E) The Taco truck is assigned to parking space 4.

3. If the Hot dog truck is assigned to parking space 3, then each of the following must be true EXCEPT:

   (A) The Masala truck is assigned to parking space 5.
   (B) The Pasta truck is assigned to parking space 6.
   (C) The Sushi truck is assigned to parking space 7.
   (D) The Korean BBQ truck is assigned to parking space 6.
   (E) The Taco truck is assigned to parking space 2.

4. If the Sushi truck is assigned to parking space 4, which one of the following must be false?

   (A) The Taco truck is assigned to a lower numbered parking space than the Falafel truck.

   (B) The Falafel truck is assigned to a higher numbered parking space than the Hot dog truck.

   (C) The Pasta truck is assigned to a higher numbered parking space than the Falafel truck.

   (D) The Hot dog truck is assigned to a higher numbered parking space than the Taco truck.

   (E) The Korean BBQ truck is assigned to a lower numbered parking space than the Pasta truck.

5. Each of the following food trucks could be assigned to parking space 2 EXCEPT:

   (A) Korean BBQ truck
   (B) Masala truck
   (C) Taco truck
   (D) Falafel truck
   (E) Pasta truck

STEP 1 Visualize and draw the diagram.

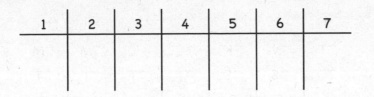

STEP 2 List the components and ascertain the ratio and/or distribution.

Components: F, H, K, M, P, S, T

Ratio: 1-to-1

Distribution: fixed

STEP 3 Symbolize the clues.

Clue 1   M ... S

Clue 2 $\boxed{\text{MK}}$

Clue 3 $H_3 \rightarrow F_4$; $\sim F_4 \rightarrow \sim H_3$

Clue 4 $\sim T_2 \rightarrow T_3$
             $\sim T_3 \rightarrow T_2$ (Translation: T = 2 or 3)

STEP 4 Make deductions.

Deduction 1: First link Clue 1 and Clue 2: MK...S

     a) M cannot be assigned parking spaces 6 and 7.
     b) K cannot be assigned parking spaces 1 and 7.
     c) S cannot be assigned parking spaces 1 and 2.

Deduction 2: T = 2 or 3; therefore, T is not assigned to parking spaces 1, 4, 5, 6, or 7.

Deduction 3: Next, link Clue 2 and Clue 4.

     a) M cannot be assigned to parking space 2 and K cannot be assigned to parking space 3. Why not? Because if M is assigned to parking space 2, then K must be assigned to parking space 3, thereby rendering no acceptable parking space for T.

b) Similarly, K cannot be assigned to parking space 3.

~K						~K
~T	~M	~K			~M	~M
~S	~S	~S	~T	~T	~T	~T
1	2	3	4	5	6	7

STEP 5 Tackle the questions.

Question order: 1, 3, 4, 2, and then 5.

Answer Key

1. **A**   2. **C**   3. **B**   4. **D**   5. **B**

Answers

Question 1 (catch-a-clue)

- Clue 1 eliminates answer choice B.
- Clue 2 eliminates answer choice D.
- Clue 3 eliminates answer choice C.
- Clue 4 eliminates answer choice E.

(A) is the correct answer.

Question 3 (restricted, "must-be-true-EXCEPT")

1. Place H in parking space 3.
2. By operation of Clue 3, F is assigned to parking space 4.
3. By operation of Clue 4, and with H in parking space 3, T must be assigned to parking space 2.
4. By operation of Clue 2, two adjacent parking spaces are needed. Therefore, M cannot be assigned to parking space 1. The only available parking space for M is 5, and for K is parking space 6.
5. Pivot to Deduction 1: S is assigned to parking space 7.
6. The only remaining component (P) is assigned to the only remaining parking space: 1.

1	2	3	4	5	6	7
P_6	T_3	H_1	F_2	M_4	K_4	S_5

(B) is the correct answer.

Question 4 (restricted, "must-be-false")

- Place S in parking space 4.
- By operation of Deduction 1, M and K must be assigned to consecutive parking spaces that are lower in number to S. By operation of Deduction 3, M and K cannot be assigned to parking spaces 2 and 3, respectively. Therefore, M and K must be assigned to parking spaces 1 and 2, respectively.
- By operation of Clue 4, and with K assigned to parking space 2, T must be assigned to parking space 3.
- There are no additional deductions or clues to restrict the remaining components F, H, and P, so they are assigned to parking spaces 5, 6, and 7 interchangeably.

1	2	3	4	5	6	7
M_2	K_2	T_3	S_1	$F/H/P_4$	$F/H/P_4$	$F/H/P_4$

- Answer choices A and E are always true. Answer choices B and C could be false but are not always false. Answer choice D is always false. Answer choice D is the correct answer.

(D) is the correct answer.

Question 2 (unrestricted, "can-be-true")

- This question is answerable by Deductions 1, 2, and 3 or by reviewing prior history.
- See the solution to Question 4 in which the Hot Dog truck can be assigned to parking space 6.

(C) is the correct answer.

Question 5 (unrestricted, "could-be-true-EXCEPT")

- This question is answerable by Deduction 3a). The Masala truck cannot be assigned to parking slot 2.
- However, if you had not made that previous deduction, you could also use prior history. Your history indicates that both the Korean BBQ truck and the Taco truck can be assigned to parking space 2, thereby eliminating answer choices A and C. Therefore, you would need to try each answer choice.

(B) is the correct answer.

Game 20

Exactly eight exercise trainers—Felix, Grace, Jean, Kelly, Liam, Miranda, Nathan, and Paul—will be hired by exactly one of three newly opened gyms—Biceps, Curls, and Deltoids. Each gym must hire at least one trainer. The following is known:

Exactly three times as many trainers are hired by Curls as are hired by Biceps.

Jean and Miranda are hired by the same gym.

Kelly and Nathan are not hired by the same gym.

Felix is hired by Deltoids.

If Jean is not hired by Deltoids, then Grace is hired by Biceps.

1. If Miranda is hired by Curls, then which one of the following must be true?

   (A) Nathan is hired by Deltoids.
   (B) Paul is hired by Curls.
   (C) Liam is hired by Deltoids.
   (D) Kelly is hired by Curls.
   (E) Nathan is hired by Curls.

2. Which one of the following could be true?

   (A) Liam and Paul are both hired by Biceps.
   (B) Felix, Grace, and Liam are all hired by the same gym.
   (C) Miranda is the only trainer hired by Biceps.
   (D) Exactly three trainers are hired by Deltoids.
   (E) Grace and Liam are both hired by Curls.

3. If Grace is hired by Deltoids, then exactly how many trainers are there any one of which could be hired by Curls?

   (A) Two
   (B) Three
   (C) Four
   (D) Five
   (E) Six

4. Which one of the following could be a complete and accurate list of the trainers who are hired by Deltoids?

   (A) Felix, Kelly, Liam, Paul
   (B) Felix, Kelly, Liam, Nathan
   (C) Jean, Liam, Miranda, Paul
   (D) Felix, Liam, Jean, Paul
   (E) Felix, Liam, Nathan

5. If Liam is hired by Biceps, then which one of the following could be false?

   (A) Paul is hired by Curls.
   (B) Miranda is hired by Deltoids.
   (C) Jean and Paul are not hired by the same gym.
   (D) Kelly and Paul are not hired by the same gym.
   (E) Grace and Jean are not hired by the same gym.

6. Which one of the following pairs of trainers CANNOT be hired by Curls?

   (A) Grace and Miranda
   (B) Kelly and Liam
   (C) Miranda and Nathan
   (D) Liam and Nathan
   (E) Kelly and Paul

STEP 1 Visualize and draw the diagram.

Biceps	Curls	Deltoids

STEP 2 List the components and ascertain the ratio and/or distribution.

Components: F, G, J, K, L, M, N, P

Distribution Deduction: Biceps, Curls, and Deltoids hire one, three, and four trainers, respectively.

Explanation: Each gym must hire at least one trainer, and Curls hires three times the number of trainers as Biceps. Should Biceps hire two trainers, Curls would need to hire six (2×3) trainers, bringing the total trainers hired to eight. In such a case, no trainer is hired by Deltoids. Accordingly, Biceps must hire one trainer, Curls three trainers, and Deltoids four trainers (distribution deduction). Update the diagram.

Biceps	Curls	Deltoids
—	— — —	— — — —

STEP 3 Symbolize the clues.

Clue 1   See updated diagram.

Clue 2 $J \leftrightarrow M$; $\sim J \leftrightarrow \sim M$

Clue 3 $K \rightarrow \sim N$; $N \rightarrow \sim K$

Clue 4   Place directly in the diagram.

Clue 5 $\sim J_{Delt} \rightarrow G_{Biceps}$; $\sim G_{Biceps} \rightarrow J_{Delt}$

Biceps	Curls	Deltoids
—	— — —	F — — —

STEP 4 Make deductions.

Deduction 1: Link Clue 5 and Clue 2: $\sim G_{Biceps} \rightarrow J_{Delt} \rightarrow M_{Delt}$

STEP 5 Tackle the questions.

Question order: 1, 3, 5, 2, 4, and then 6.

Answer Key

1. **C**   2. **E**   3. **C**   4. **A**   5. **D**   6. **A**

Answers

Question 1 (restricted, "must-be-true")

1. Place M in the Curls group
2. By operation of Clue 2, J must be placed in the Curls group.
3. By operation of Clue 5, G must be placed in the Biceps group.
4. By operation of Clue 3, K and N must be placed in the Curls and Deltoids groups interchangeably.
5. The remaining components (L and P) must be placed in the Deltoids group.

Biceps	Curls	Deltoids
G_3	M_1 J_2 K/N_4	F N/K_4 L_5 P_5

(C) is the correct answer.

Question 3 (restricted, "could-be-true")

1. Place G in the Deltoids group.
2. By operation of the contrapositive of Clue 5, J must be placed in the Deltoids group.
3. By operation of Clue 2, M must be placed in the Deltoids group.
4. By operation of Clue 3, K and N must be placed in the Biceps and Curls groups interchangeably.
5. The remaining components (L and P) must be placed in the only available slots in the Curls group.

Biceps	Curls	Deltoids
K/N_4	N/K_3 L_5 P_5	F G_1 J_2 M_3

6. K, L, N, and P can each be placed in the Curls group.

(C) is the correct answer.

Question 5 (unrestricted, "could-be-false")

1. Place L in the Biceps group.
2. By operation of the contrapositive of Clue 5, J must be placed in the Deltoids group.
3. By operation of Clue 2, M must be placed in the Deltoids group.
4. By operation of Clue 3, K and N must be placed in the Curls and Deltoids groups interchangeably.
5. G and P—the remaining components must be placed in the only remaining slots in the Curls group.

Biceps	Curls	Deltoids
L_1	K/N_4 G_5 P_5	F J_2 M_3 N/K_4

(D) is the correct answer.

Question 2 (unrestricted, "could-be-true")

- This question is completely answerable by reviewing the clues and deductions.

 - Answer choice A violates the distribution deduction.
 - Answer choice B: F, G, and L must be placed in the Deltoids group (Clue 4). However, by operation of Deduction 1, with G not in the Biceps group, J and M must be placed in the Deltoids group. This brings the total number of components in Deltoids to five, in violation of the distribution deduction.
 - Answer choice C violates Clue 2.
 - Answer choice D violates the distribution deduction.

(E) is the correct answer.

Question 4 (unrestricted, "could-be-true")

- This question is completely answerable by reviewing the clues and deductions.
- Answer choice B violates Clue 3.
- Answer choice C violates Clue 4.
- Answer choice D violates Clue 2.
- Answer choice E violates the distribution deduction.

(A) is the correct answer.

Question 6 (unrestricted, "cannot-be-true")

- This question is completely answerable by reviewing the deductions.

 - If G is in the Curls group (the equivalent of not being placed in the Biceps group), then both J and M must be placed in Deltoids.
 - Therefore, G and M cannot be together in the Curls group.

(A) is the correct answer.

Game 21

A Hollywood producer is casting for an upcoming new sitcom scheduled to go into production next spring. The producer will cast at least one actor from the following seven actors: Coco, Damien, Fela, Glory, Kai, Lance, and Meyer. The casting of the sitcom must be consistent with the following conditions:

If Kai is cast, then so is Fela.

If Glory is cast, then neither Coco nor Meyer is cast.

If Damien is not cast, then Coco is cast.

If Lance is not cast, then Meyer is cast.

If Fela is cast, then Lance is not cast.

1. Which one of the following is an acceptable casting of actors for the sitcom?

   (A) Fela, Kai, Meyer
   (B) Damien, Glory, Kai, Lance
   (C) Damien, Glory, Lance
   (D) Coco, Fela, Kai
   (E) Damien, Glory, Fela, Meyer

2. Which one of the following pairs of people CANNOT both be cast?

   (A) Coco and Damien
   (B) Glory and Lance
   (C) Damien and Glory
   (D) Lance and Meyer
   (E) Fela and Glory

3. If Glory is cast, which one of the following actors could also be cast?

   (A) Kai
   (B) Damien
   (C) Fela
   (D) Coco
   (E) Meyer

4. If Kai is cast, then each of the following could be true EXCEPT:

   (A) Meyer is cast.
   (B) Coco is not cast.
   (C) Exactly three of the actors are cast.
   (D) Exactly four of the actors are cast.
   (E) Exactly five of the actors are cast.

5. If neither Fela nor Lance is cast, then which of the following must be false?

   (A) Damien is cast.
   (B) Coco is cast.
   (C) Coco and Meyer are the only actors cast.
   (D) Neither Coco nor Glory is cast.
   (E) Neither Damien nor Meyer is cast.

6. Which one of the following is the maximum number of actors that can be cast in the sitcom?

   (A) Three
   (B) Four
   (C) Five
   (D) Six
   (E) Seven

Visualize and draw the diagram.

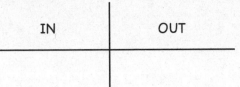

IN	OUT

STEP 2 List the components and ascertain the ratio and/or distribution.

Components: C, D, F, G, K, L, M

Distribution: unknown distribution

STEP 3 Symbolize the clues.

Clue 1   K → F; ~F → ~K

Clue 2a   G → ~C; C → ~G

Clue 2b   G → ~M; M → ~G

Clue 3   ~D → C; ~C → D

Clue 4   ~L → M; ~M → L

Clue 5   F → ~L; L → ~F

STEP 4 Make deductions.

First link Clue 1 and Clue 5: K → F and F → ~L
Deduction 1: K → ~L; L → ~K

Link Clue 2a and the contrapositive of Clue 3: G → ~C and ~C → D
Deduction 2: G → D; ~D → ~G

Link Clue 2b and the contrapositive of Clue 4: G → ~M and ~M → L
Deduction 3: G → L; ~L → ~G

Link Clue 5 and Clue 4: F → ~L and ~L → M
Deduction 4: F → M.

Finally, link the contrapositive of Clue 2b with this deduction: F → M and M → ~G
Deduction 5: F → ~G

STEP 5 **Tackle the questions.**

Question order: 1, 3, 4, 5, 2, and then 6.

Answer Key

Answers

Question 1 (catch-a-clue)

- Clue 1 eliminates answer choice B.
- Clue 2 eliminates answer choice E.
- Clue 3 eliminates answer choice A.
- Clue 4 eliminates answer choice D.

(C) is the correct answer.

Question 3 (restricted, "could-be-true")

- This question is completely answerable by Deduction 1 ($G \rightarrow D$).
- Without the help of the deduction, this question can be answered as follows:

1. Place G in the in-column.
2. By operation of Clue 2, C and M must be placed in the out-column.
3. With M placed in the out-column, the contrapositive of Clue 4 is triggered, and L must be placed in the in-column.
4. With C placed in the out-column, the contrapositive of Clue 3 is triggered, and D must be placed in the in-column.
5. With L placed in the in-column, the contrapositive of Clue 5 is triggered, and F must be placed in the out-column.
6. With F placed in the out-column, the contrapositive of Clue 1 is triggered, and K must be placed in the out-column.

IN	OUT
G_1 L_3 D_4	C_2 M_2 F_5 K_6

(B) is the correct answer.

Question 4 (restricted, "could-be-true-EXCEPT")

1. Place K in the in-column.
2. By operation of Clue 1, F must also be placed in the in-column.
3. With F placed in the in-column, Clue 5 is triggered, and L must be place in the out-column.
4. With L placed in the out-column, Clue 4 is triggered, and M must be placed in the in-column.
5. With M placed in the in-column, the contrapositive of Clue 2 is triggered, and G is placed in the out-column.
6. The remaining components (C and D) are governed by Clue 3. By operation of Clue 3, C and D cannot both be out together. Either one or both of the pair must be placed in the

in-column. Accordingly, you need a minimum of four components in the in-column. Answer choice C cannot be true.

IN	OUT
K_1 F_2 M_4 C and/or D_6	L_3 G_5

(C) is the correct answer.

Question 5 (restricted, "must-be-false")

1. Place F and L in the out-column. Note: Clue 5 only requires that F and L cannot both be placed in the in-column. F and L can be placed in the out-column together.
2. By operation of the contrapositive of Clue 1, K must be placed in the out-column.
3. By operation of Clue 4, M must be placed in the in-column.
4. By operation of the contrapositive of Clue 2b, G must be placed in the out-column.
5. The remaining components (C and D) are governed by Clue 3. Either one or both of the pair must be placed in the in-column.

IN	OUT
M_3 C and/or D_5	F_1 L_1 K_2 G_4

(E) is the correct answer.

Question 2 (unrestricted, "cannot-be-true")

This question is completely answerable by Deduction 4 (F → ~G).

(E) is the correct answer.

Question 6 (unrestricted, "must-be-true")

- The question is answerable by review of the clues and prior workouts.
- The workout to question 4 shows as many as five components in the in-column. Eliminate answer choices A and B.
- From Clue 5, you know that both F and L cannot be in the in-column together. At least one of the pair must be placed in the out-column. The maximum is, therefore, not seven. Eliminate answer choice E.
- From Clue 2, you ascertain that both G and C cannot be in the in-column together, nor can G and M be in the in-column together. Therefore, placing G in the in-column would force an additional two components into the out-column. However, to reach your maximum number of components, you should place one component (G) in the out-column, thus allowing the placement of both C and M in the in-column. With G placed in the out-column, the maximum is five.

(C) is the correct answer.

Game 22

From among seven children—F, G, H, J, K, L, and M—Primetime School will select at least one child for admission to its elite pre-school. The selection of children must meet the following conditions:

If G is selected, then neither J nor M is selected.
F and H cannot both be selected.
If K is not selected, then F is selected.
If H is not selected, then J is not selected.

1. Which one of the following could be a complete and accurate list of the children selected for admission?

   (A) F, G, L, M
   (B) F, G, K, L
   (C) F, G, H, L
   (D) H, J, M
   (E) F, J, K, L

2. Each of the following is a pair of children that could be selected together EXCEPT:

   (A) F and K
   (B) F and J
   (C) J and M
   (D) H and K
   (E) G and L

3. If J is selected, then which one of the following could be false?

   (A) F is not selected.
   (B) G is not selected.
   (C) K is selected.
   (D) H is selected.
   (E) M is not selected.

4. If neither F nor H is selected, then which one of the following must be true?

   (A) G is not selected.
   (B) M is not selected.
   (C) K is not selected.
   (D) At most three children are selected.
   (E) At least three children are selected.

5. If both G and K are selected, then which one of the following must be true?

   (A) F is not selected.
   (B) L is selected.
   (C) At least two other children are selected.
   (D) At most two other children are selected.
   (E) Neither H nor F is selected.

6. Which one of the following must be false?

   (A) H is selected, and K is not selected.
   (B) F is not selected, and H is selected.
   (C) H is selected, and J is not selected.
   (D) Both F and K are selected.
   (E) Neither G nor J is selected.

STEP 1 Visualize and draw the diagram.

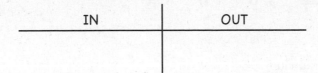

STEP 2 List the components and ascertain the ratio and/or distribution.

Components: F, G, H, J, K, L, M

Distribution: unknown distribution

STEP 3 Symbolize the clues.

Clue 1   a) G → ~J; J → ~G
             b) G → ~M; M → ~G

Clue 2   F → ~H; H → ~F

Clue 3   ~K → F; ~F → K

Clue 4   ~H → ~J; J → H

STEP 5 Make deductions.

Link the contrapositives of Clue 4, Clue 2, and Clue 3:
J → H; H → ~F; ~F → K

Deduction 1: J → H → ~F → K

STEP 5 **Tackle the questions.**

Question order: 1, 3, 4, 5, 2, and then 6.

Answer Key

1. **B**   2. **B**   3. **E**   4. **D**   5. **D**   6. **A**

Answers

Question 1 (catch-a-clue)

- Clue 1 eliminates answer choice A.
- Clue 2 eliminates answer choice C.
- Clue 3 eliminates answer choice D.
- Clue 4 eliminates answer choice E.

(B) is the correct answer.

Question 3 (restricted, "could-be-false")

1. Place J in the in-column.
2. By operation of the contrapositive of Clue 4, H must be placed in the in-column.
3. By operation of the contrapositive of Clue 2, F must be placed in the out-column.
4. By operation of the contrapositive of Clue 3, K must be placed in the in-column.
5. By operation of the contrapositive of Clue 1a), G must be placed in the out-column.

IN	OUT
J_1 H_2 K_4	F_3 G_5

(E) is the correct answer.

Question 4 (restricted, "must-be-true")

1. Place F and H in the out-column.
2. By operation of the contrapositive of Clue 3, K must be placed in the in-column.
3. By operation of Clue 4, J must be placed in the out-column.
4. G, M, and L are the remaining components. By operation of Clue 1b), G and M cannot both be together in the in-column. At least one or both must be placed in the out-column.

IN	OUT
K_2	F_1 H_1 J_3 G &/or M_4

(D) is the correct answer.

Question 5 (unrestricted, "must-be-true")

1. Place G and K in the in-column.
2. By operation of Clues 1a) and 1b), both J and M must be placed in the out-column.
3. H, F, and L are the remaining components. By operation of Clue 2, H and F cannot both be together in the in-column. At least one or both must be placed in the out-column.

IN	OUT
G_1 K_1	J_2 M_2 H &/or F_3

(D) is the correct answer.

Question 2 (unrestricted, "could-be-true-EXCEPT")

■ This question is completely answerable by Deduction 1, $J \rightarrow H \rightarrow \sim F \rightarrow K$.
■ F and J cannot both be in together.

(B) is the correct answer.

Question 6 (unrestricted, "must-be-false")

■ This question is completely answerable by the deduction: $J \rightarrow H \rightarrow \sim F \rightarrow K$.
■ If H is selected, K must be selected.
■ Answer choice A is false.

(A) is the correct answer.

Game 23

As a requirement for Honors English, Johanny must read exactly eight books—F, G, H, J, K, L, M, and N—during her summer vacation. Johanny does not read any two books at the same time nor does she read any book more than once. The order in which the books are read are in accordance with the following conditions:

G is read earlier than N, but later than J.

G is read earlier than L, but later than M.

Both H and K are read earlier than F.

1. Which one of the following could be the order in which the books are read, from first to last?

    (A) J, K, M, II, G, L, F, N
    (B) K, J, M, F, G, N, H, L
    (C) H, J, K, F, G, M, L, N
    (D) J, M, H, K, F, N, G, L
    (E) M, H, K, J, L, G, N, F

2. Which one of the following CANNOT be true?

    (A) J is read second.
    (B) M is read sixth.
    (C) L is read fifth.
    (D) F is read fourth.
    (E) N is read seventh.

3. If there are exactly two books read later than F, but earlier than G, then each of the following could be true EXCEPT:

    (A) M is read fifth.
    (B) H is read second.
    (C) J is read fourth.
    (D) L is read sixth.
    (E) N is read seventh.

4. If N is read earlier than H, then which one of the following must be true?

    (A) M is read earlier than K.
    (B) L is read earlier than F.
    (C) K is read earlier than L.
    (D) G is read earlier than K.
    (E) J is read earlier than F.

5. If L is read fourth, then which one of the following could be the books read fifth, sixth, and seventh, respectively?

    (A) H, F, N
    (B) N, H, F
    (C) G, H, K
    (D) H, N, K
    (E) H, G, N

6. How many books are there any of which could be read second?

    (A) One
    (B) Two
    (C) Three
    (D) Four
    (E) Five

STEP 1 Symbolize the clues.

Clue 1   J ---- G ---- N

Clue 2   M ---- G ---- L

Clue 3   H ---- F
                            K

STEP 2 Connect the individual chains to create the longest possible chain.

J ---- G ---- N

STEP 3 Attach each of the remaining rules to the baseline.

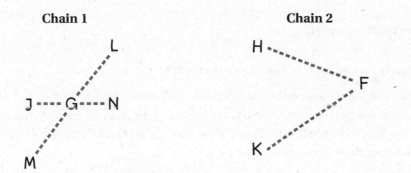

Chain 1

Chain 2

- There is no commonality of components between the two chains, and, thus, they cannot be connected to one another.
- The questions will pertain to the individual chains or provide an additional restriction that will connect the two chains.
- Remember the two rules that allow you to efficiently answer the questions.

STEP 4 **Tackle the questions.**

Answer Key

1. **A**   2. **D**   3. **B**   4. **E**   5. **D**   6. **D**

Answers

Question 1 (catch-a-clue)

- Clue 1 eliminates answer choice D.
- Clue 2 eliminates answer choices C and E.
- Clue 3 eliminates answer choice B.

(A) is the correct answer.

Question 2 (unrestricted, "cannot-be-true-EXCEPT")

According to Chain 1, G, L, and N must all be read later than M. As such, M cannot be read sixth.

(B) is the correct answer.

Question 3 (restricted, "could-be-true-EXCEPT")

- First you need to ascertain which books can be read later than F, but earlier than G. Since F is a part of Chain 1 and G is a part of Chain 2, combine the chains.
- According to Chain 2, both H and K are read earlier than F and, as such, neither can be read later than F but earlier than G.
- According to Chain 1, both L and N are read later than G and, as such, neither can be read later than F but earlier than G.
- The remaining books (J and M) are the only books that can be read later than F, but earlier than G.

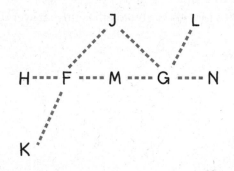

- According to the "new" chain, L cannot be sixth. Why? H, K, F, J, M, and G (six books total) must all be read earlier than L.

(D) is the correct answer.

Question 4 (restricted, "must-be-true")

- Since N is a part of Chain 1 and H is a part of Chain 2, you need to combine the chains. Add N...H to connect the chains.

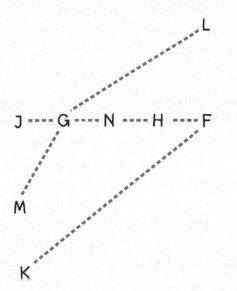

- According to the zigzag rule, answer choices A, B, C, and D can be true, not must be true.
- According to the "new" chain, J must be read earlier than F.

(E) is the correct answer.

Question 5 (restricted, "could-be-true")

- According to Chain 1, J, G, and M must be read earlier than L. If L is read fourth, J, G, and M are the only books read earlier than L. Therefore, G cannot be among those books read fifth, sixth, and seventh. Eliminate answer choices C and E.
- Both answer choices A and B would force K later than F, which would be in violation of Clue 3. Eliminate answer choice A and B.

(D) is the correct answer.

Question 6 (unrestricted, "could-be-true")

- According to Chain 1, neither G nor L nor N can be read second.
- According to Chain 2, F cannot be read second. Therefore, four books are eliminated. The remaining four books can each be read second.

(D) is the correct answer.

Game 24

Six attorneys—four partners: Kraus, Lai, Mendez, and Nelson; and two associates: Ortiz and Porter—are each sitting in one of exactly six chairs, evenly spaced, around a circular conference table. The following conditions must be met:

Kraus sits immediately next to either Mendez or Nelson, but not both.

The two associates do not sit next to each other.

Kraus does not sit next to Porter.

1. Which one of the following could be the order in which the six attorneys are seated, counting clockwise around the conference table?

   (A) Mendez, Kraus, Porter, Lai, Ortiz, Nelson
   (B) Ortiz, Nelson, Kraus, Mendez: Porter, Lai
   (C) Porter, Nelson, Kraus, Lai, Mendez, Ortiz
   (D) Lai, Mendez, Kraus, Porter, Ortiz, Nelson
   (E) Nelson, Porter, Lai, Ortiz, Kraus, Mendez

2. Which one of the following must be false?

   (A) Nelson sits immediately next to Lai and Porter.
   (B) Lai sits immediately next to Mendez and Nelson.
   (C) Ortiz sits immediately next to Kraus and Mendez.
   (D) Mendez sits immediately next to Kraus and Porter.
   (E) Lai sits immediately next to Krause and Porter.

3. If Kraus sits immediately next to Lai, then which one of the following is a pair of attorneys that CANNOT sit immediately next to each other?

   (A) Lai and Porter
   (B) Nelson and Porter
   (C) Mendez and Ortiz
   (D) Lai and Mendez
   (E) Mendez and Porter

4. If Ortiz sits immediately next to Mendez and Nelson, then which one of the following must be false?

   (A) Nelson sits immediately next to Porter.
   (B) Lai sits immediately next to Nelson.
   (C) Kraus sits immediately next to Mendez.
   (D) Mendez sits immediately next to Porter.
   (E) Lai sits immediately next to Porter.

5. If exactly two attorneys sit between Ortiz and Porter, then each of the following could be true EXCEPT:

   (A) Mendez sits immediately next to Porter.
   (B) Kraus sits immediately next to Ortiz.
   (C) Nelson sits immediately next to Porter.
   (D) Lai sits immediately next to Ortiz.
   (E) Lai sits immediately next to Kraus.

6. Which one of the following CANNOT be the order in which three of the attorneys are seated, with no one else seated between them, counting clockwise around the conference table?

   (A) Mendez, Lai, Nelson
   (B) Porter, Lai, Kraus
   (C) Kraus, Nelson, Porter
   (D) Porter, Mendez, Ortiz
   (E) Ortiz, Nelson, Kraus

Visualize and draw the diagram

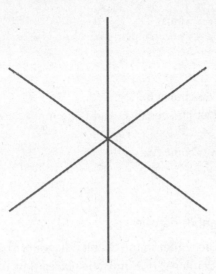

STEP 2 List the components and ascertain the ratio and/or distribution.

Components: Partners: K, L, M, N

Associates: O, P

Ratio: one-to-one

STEP 3 Symbolize the clues.

Clue 1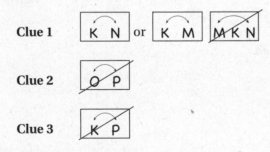

Clue 2

Clue 3

STEP 4 **Make deductions.**

There are no deductions.

STEP 5 **Tackle the questions.**

Question order: 1, 3, 4, 5, 2, and then 6.

Answer Key

1. **E**   2. **B**   3. **D**   4. **B**   5. **E**   6. **A**

Answers

Question 1 (catch-a-clue)

- Clue 1 eliminates answer choice B.
- Clue 2 eliminates answer choices C (O and P are on the end, so they are next to each other) and D.
- Clue 3 eliminates answer choice A.

(E) is the correct answer.

Question 3 (restricted, "cannot-be-true")

1. Place K and L next to each other in the circular diagram.
2. By operation of Clue 1, either M or N must be placed next to K.
3. There are three adjacent slots and three remaining components: O, P, and either M or N.
4. By operation of Clue 2, O and P must be split (interchangeably) by M or N.

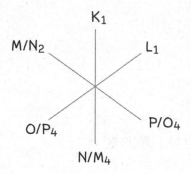

(D) is the correct answer.

Question 4 (restricted, "must-be-false")

- Place O in between M and N in the circular diagram.
- By operation of Clue 1, K must be placed adjacent to M (Option 1) or adjacent to N (Option 2).
- Work out Option 1 first. By operation of Clue 3, P cannot be placed next to K, so it must be placed next to N. The remaining component (L) must be placed in the remaining slot between P and K.
- Work out Option 2. By operation of Clue 3, P cannot be placed next to K, so it must be placed next to M. The remaining component (L) must be placed in the remaining slot between P and K.

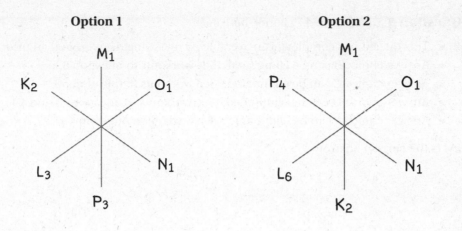

Option 1   Option 2

(B) is the correct answer.

Question 5 (restricted, "could-be-true-EXCEPT")

1. Place O __ __ P in the circular diagram.
2. All that remains are two sets of two adjacent slots. By operation of Clue 1, one of those sets of adjacent slots must be occupied by K with either M or N. By operation of Clue 3, K cannot sit next to P and, therefore, must sit next to O.
3. The opposite set of adjacent slots must be occupied by L with either M or N interchangeably.

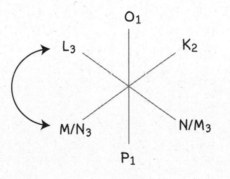

(E) is the correct answer.

Question 2 (unrestricted, "must-be-false")

- This question is completely answerable by reviewing the workouts to prior questions.
- Answer choices A and C can be eliminated. (See workout to question 5.)
- Answer choice D can be eliminated. (See workouts to questions 3 and 5.)
- Answer choice E can be eliminated. (See workouts to questions 3 and 4.)

(B) is the correct answer.

Question 6 (unrestricted, "cannot-be-true")

- This question is completely answerable by reviewing the workouts to prior questions.
- Answer choice B can be eliminated. (See workouts to question 3.)
- Answer choice C can be eliminated. (See workouts to question 5.)
- Answer choice D can be eliminated. (See workouts to questions 3 and 4.)
- Answer choice E can be eliminated. (See workout to question 4.)

(A) is the correct answer.

Game 25

During a single weekend, Joshua will visit exactly seven universities—K, L, M, N, P, Q, and R—from which he had been offered admission this fall. No two universities are visited at the same time, and no university is visited more than once. The following conditions must apply:

N is visited before P.
K is visited before N, but after R.
Q is visited before M, but after R.
L is visited before K.
Q is visited before N.

1. Which one of the following could be true?

   (A) P is the fourth university visited.
   (B) K is the second university visited.
   (C) Q is the third university visited.
   (D) N is the fourth university visited.
   (E) R is the third university visited.

2. If K is the third university visited, then which one of the following must be false?

   (A) R is the first university visited.
   (B) L is the second university visited.
   (C) N is the fourth university visited.
   (D) M is the sixth university visited.
   (E) P is the seventh university visited.

3. How many universities are there any one of which could be the fourth university visited?

   (A) One
   (B) Two
   (C) Three
   (D) Four
   (E) Five

4. If P is the sixth university visited, then which one of the following must be false?

   (A) M is visited before N.
   (B) R is visited before L.
   (C) K is visited before Q.
   (D) Q is visited before L.
   (E) P is visited before M.

5. If there are exactly two universities visited after R and before N, then which one of the following must be true?

   (A) L is the first university visited.
   (B) K is the third university visited.
   (C) Q is the fourth university visited.
   (D) M is the seventh university visited.
   (E) P is the sixth university visited.

STEP 1 Symbolize the clues.

Clue 1   N ... P

Clue 2   R ... K ... N

Clue 3   R ... Q ... M

Clue 4   L ... K

Clue 5   Q ... N

STEP 2 Connect the individual chains to create the longest possible chain.

R ... K ... N ... P

STEP 3 Attach each of the remaining rules to the baseline.

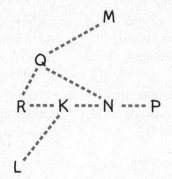

STEP 4 Tackle the questions.

Answer Key

1. **C**   2. **C**   3. **D**   4. **E**   5. **A**

Answers

Question 1 (restricted, "could-be-true")

- P cannot be fourth, since L, R, Q, K, and N must all be visited before P. Eliminate answer choice A.
- K cannot be second, since R and L must be visited before K. Eliminate answer choice B.
- N cannot be fourth, since R, L, K, and Q must all be visited before N. Eliminate answer choice D.
- R cannot be third, since all of the universities except L must be visited after R. Eliminate answer choice E.

(C) is the correct answer.

Question 2 (restricted, "must-be-false")

- If K is third, R and L are the first and second universities visited interchangeably. Eliminate answer choices A and B.
- If K is third, Q must be the fourth and N the fifth universities visited.

(C) is the correct answer.

Question 3 (unrestricted, "could-be-true")

L, K, Q, and M can all be fourth.

(D) is the correct answer.

Question 4 (restricted, "must-be-false")

- The first/last rule focuses on the fact that only M and P can be the last universities visited.
- If P is the sixth university, M must be the last university.
- All universities are visited before M.

(E) is the correct answer.

Question 5 (restricted, "must-be-true")

- Q and K must be visited after R and before N.
- Without any additional restrictions, L could be visited after R and before N.
- However, with the additional restriction posed by the fact that *"there are exactly two universities visited after R and before N,"* L must be visited before R.
- L must be visited first.

(A) is the correct answer.